The Business of Fitness

Understanding the Financial Side of Owning a Fitness Business

Thomas Plummer

www.healthylearning.com

ISBN: 978-1-58518-853-6
Library of Congress Control Number: 2003102384

Book layout and diagrams: Jennifer Bokelmann
Cover design: Kerry Hartjen

Healthy Learning
P.O. Box 1828
Monterey, CA 93942
www.healthylearning.com

DEDICATION

This book is dedicated to all my clients, friends, and students. By instilling their faith and trust in me, they allowed me to help them grow in their businesses and to grow personally, which has resulted in an unusual but very fulfilling life. To all those who have let me share some part of their life and business, I thank you.

ACKNOWLEDGMENTS

No one ever runs alone.

I have had an amazing run in the fitness industry for over 25 years and it just gets better every day. But as the line above says, no one ever runs alone. I have been extremely blessed with people around me who have always supported what I wanted to do with my life no matter where it led, or if indeed it would even work enough to pay the bills. I'd like to say thank you to a few friends and family who have made this particular effort possible.

My mother and father, Delores and Joe Richeson, still hang my articles on the refrigerator and stack my books on the coffee table. At various times over the years they've let me stay at home, loaned me money, washed my clothes, picked me up at far too many airports, and have never asked for a thing in return. Thank you.

My partner Lloyd Collins reinvented our company and has grown it to the point that we are in front of over 4,000 people a year, just in seminars. His faith and enthusiasm have given me many more years to look forward to in this business at a time when I thought it might be better to move on to other things. Thank you.

There have also been a slew of industry people who have helped me during the last several years of my career. These people have opened doors that have greatly enhanced my career and my opportunities in the business. Thank you to Norm Cates, John McCarthy; Will, Norm, and Crystal Dabish; Mike Uretz; Jim Bottin and Paul Schaller; the Plummer Company team including Lori Miller, Terry Van Der Mark, Dennis Holcum, Victoria Pegler, and Shannon Haik; and all of our alliance partners and their representatives who have supported our efforts.

And a special note to my family-support team: thank you with all my love to Susan, Jill, CJ, and my typing and filing assistant Honey.

PREFACE

This book is a compilation of 26 years in the fitness business and reflects my system and how I feel a club should be run. To get the most out of this book, you need to read it very carefully and look for the hidden surprises. There are many tidbits of information, formulas, and the use of numbers that I've stuck in places you may not think they belong, but where I felt they best fit at the time.

Also be aware that these are my working numbers and formulas that I've created during my years as a consultant. What this means is that you're not likely to find much of this information anywhere else and that this book will probably start many an interesting conversation with your accountant.

And by the nature of being a writer, it was impossible not to intertwine some of the material from my first book, *Making Money in the Fitness Business*, which is currently published by Healthy Learning. This is especially true in the section on building a receivable base. I took the core material from the first book and expanded it to give more numbers support and background in this attempt. You'll also find a few key *Plummerisms*, as our staff likes to call them, which have made it into this book from the first.

This book was not designed to read like a novel, where you start at the front and work your way through a story. Gym and fitness facility owners, as are all small-business owners, are notoriously short of time and working through a long drawn out text just to find a few ideas that might help their business wouldn't be appealing. That's why I wrote this book in a format where each chapter can stand alone. Key points are discussed in several different chapters of the book because the assumption was, as a reader, you might read one chapter and then come back to the book weeks later and begin another one.

I think you'll find there are plenty of fresh ideas and concepts to keep you busy growing your business and making more money in the fitness industry. I also hope that this book can in some way keep the passion and enthusiasm you had for the business when you first started alive and thriving. The world of small business can be a tough and lonely place, but perhaps this book can help you realize the dreams that set you on the path to opening a fitness business.

NOTE TO THE READER

Use the material in this book at your own risk. Much of what is written here is based on my own opinions and assumptions and is provided for you to use as an information resource.

In all cases, and especially valuing a business, you are always advised to seek the advice of qualified business professionals that support your business locally such as accountants, attorneys, and other business professionals that may know your business on a more intimate level.

Neither the author, publisher, nor any party related to the information and development of this book assumes any responsibility or liability for the consequences, whether good or bad, of your application of this material.

CONTENTS

The Foundational Numbers That Build a Business

The numbers that affect a fitness business can be classified into several distinct areas, each with its own unique formulas and ratios. What these numbers mean and how they affect the business change depending on the age and maturity of the business itself. The four distinct analysis areas for a fitness business are:

- The *foundational numbers* or numbers that allow an owner to build the business properly from the inception. These could also be called the conceptual numbers because many of these need to be considered and worked through before the business is actually opened. An example is the impact of the rent factor.

- A fitness business owner should gain an understanding of the *foundational numbers and concepts* that drive a business. Examples in this area of the business are a receivable-base analysis and understanding how to develop and control the yield from a member payment.

- Building a successful fitness business based on the numbers also includes the *operational numbers*. These are the numbers that affect the day-to-day operations of the business, such as sales analysis, basic budgeting and budget controls, and developing an effective pricing system.

- The last area needing review is the *conceptual projection of the business*. This area of review is geared toward business plans, projections, and the valuation process of a business, which are all neglected areas by a business owner.

The first section of this book is about the foundational numbers and the effect they have on your business. Every owner should read this section first because it is the most important section for those who are just getting started in the business.

- **Chapter 1: The Power of the Rent Factor**
- **Chapter 2: The Levels of Maturity for a Fitness Business**
- **Chapter 3: Building a Future on Renewals and Member Retention**
- **Chapter 4: You Have to Have Cash Flow to Survive**

1

The Power of the
Rent Factor

The most important thing you should get from this chapter is:

You can't be everything to everyone in the fitness business.

Definitions and concepts you will need to know:

- *Target market:* 85% to 90% of your membership will come from within a 12-minute drive time to and from your club during primetime.
- *BOE:* This is the *base operating expense*, or what it costs a club owner to pay all of the bills including debt service each month. The owner's salary is in this number if he is in on-site and taking an equivalent manager's pay.
- The right lease or *lease factor* is a determining factor in the future success of a fitness business.
- Your *target market* should determine the size and scope of your club.
- *Capture rate:* The percentage of the market that might join a gym.
- *Target market:* 80% of your club will be composed of a defined target market usually spread over two generations. For example, your market might be 24- to 40-years old or 30- to 50-years old. This means that 80% of your club will probably be from that demographic.
- Clubs can be overbuilt for the market.
- Poor visibility, a poor location, and lack of accessibility can kill a business.

Getting the Business Right
Before You Open

One of the worst mistakes a new owner can make is to set the business up for failure before he even does his first day of business. This mistake is one that can't be negated by even the best sales effort and is usually fatal to the business over the first few years of the business's life.

This classic mistake is getting yourself into the wrong lease, with the wrong options, and with the accompanying payment that is also wrong for that stage of the business's growth. Buying a building will be discussed Chapter 16, but since the majority of owners begin their careers by renting, the discussion should start here first.

The rent factor drives the business plan for that business.

The rent factor drives the business plan for that business. An out of whack rent payment will negatively affect the business, its cash flow, and its chance of survival; done realistically, and the business has moved a long way toward gaining a chance to survive.

The first thing you should consider about your new business is the size. How much space do you really need to operate a profitable fitness business? Most fitness businesses are conceived one piece of equipment and one program at a time during that hour before you fall asleep each night when you're dreaming about your new business. The longer it takes to get the financing together, the more nights you spend dreaming, and the bigger the gym gets. New owners try to build the perfect gym when they open and most of the time it ends up too big or overbuilt for the market and tries to appeal to too big of an audience.

The size of the business should match the demographic area, the niche being filled by that club, and the capital the owner has to invest. Existing owners often let their egos run wild with their second business and attempt to make a statement instead of trying to build a profitable business. A competitor built a bigger club down the street but our new club will kick his ass despite the fact that it may be too big for the market, the available money, and the owner's skill level of management.

The business should try and capitalize on a niche that is not being filled in the area instead of building a bigger, better gym than the competitors. Money is made by either filling a void in the market or by doing the job better than the other guy. Building an ego business based on the biggest square footage seldom makes a viable business opportunity. Actually, bigger facilities often work against a gym owner because most consumers don't associate the biggest facility with a quality member-service delivery system.

A few basics to consider when looking for space are:

• How far is the consumer willing to drive to be a member of a gym?

The number one point considered by a potential member when looking for a gym is convenience to their home. A club can count on 85 to 90 percent of their members coming from a 12-minute drive time to and from their gym. Drive time is defined as Monday night at 6:00 p.m. How far can you drive from the business at this time? In most metro markets this is normally about three to five miles. In rural markets this could be as far as 15 miles. In Los Angeles, 15 minutes may be the exact same spot. When looking for a location, start with this key basic. The members just don't travel as far as you hope they will and the limits of your marketplace are clearly defined by the drive time a member is willing to commit to as part of their daily routine. The 12-minute ring is also why a market can hold so many clubs due to the fact the primary market area is usually smaller than most people realize.

The members just don't travel as far as you hope.

- The defined level sizes of the market are:

√ *Level-one markets:* These markets are defined as having populations of 250,000 plus and are usually considered the major metro markets. A lot of territorial dispute for these markets occurs between the major players who are generally the only ones who will take on the giant rent factors that go with these areas. An example is Manhattan where the monthly rents for a decent space might be $24 to $48 per square foot or more.

√ *Level-two markets:* These markets are defined as being 100,000 to 250,000 in population and represent some of the hottest growth in the industry. These could be defined as either single markets such as Redding, California, or as suburban markets such as Lakewood, Colorado. The chains have finally discovered these markets but these are still excellent areas for the independent operators.

√ *Level-three markets:* These markets are defined as having populations of 50,000 to 100,000 and may represent the last great club markets in America. These are the areas overlooked by the chains because they fail to meet their normal stamp and the licensed players usually demand physical plants too large for these markets. This is where all the growth should occur during the next decade or two because of the workable rent factors and prime demographics. A prime example of this type of market would be Santa Fe, New Mexico, a beautiful, upscale area underserved by the club business.

√ *Level-four markets:* These markets are usually overlooked completely and have been relegated to the mom-and-pop arena. These markets are defined as 50,000 or less and are mostly small-town America. These are, however, great places for the gym businesses because the rents reflect the area and the fitness businesses in these markets pull a higher percentage of the market per capita than the larger areas. Examples here would be Los Osos, California, or Souderton, Pennsylvania.

- Demographic size and population targets

The first term to understand when looking at a potential market is *capture rate*. Capture rate is defined as the percentage of the market that might join a gym. Pay attention to three factors that affect this. First of all, how far is the consumer willing to travel to come to a gym? The second factor is whether the gym is filling a niche or is going heads up against a competitor across the street. The third factor is what kind of level or market is the club being placed in?

The basic rule is 3.5 percent of the defined market, which in this case is the 12-minute drive time. This may sound high, but keep in mind that in the more densely populated markets, the drive-time restrictions shrink the perceived area of draw. In other words, you may live in a town of 200,000 people but only draw from a ring of three miles, which might include only a 50,000 population. In this example, 50,000 times 3.5 percent equals a potential membership of 1,750 members, which would be the desired number of members at this club's maturity at the 25th month.

Smaller markets, meaning level three or four, enjoy a much higher capture rate and can often attract as high as nine percent of the drive time. In these markets, the clubs fill much more of a social role for the community than in the larger areas.

Keep in mind that this is a simple formula based on the entire market. Obviously your club wouldn't draw from the extremes in your demographic market in any great numbers. For example, it's unlikely that you would attract too many 96-year-old guys into a typical licensed gym. The 3.5 number is simply an overall guideline and is simpler to use than breaking down your market into smaller demographic niches. And more importantly, it works well for determining your potential market.

The niche being filled by your club

As repeatedly mentioned in *Making Money in the Fitness Business*, my first book, you can't be everything to everyone when it comes to the fitness consumer. The trend is away from one-size-fits-all businesses and toward building a business that targets a specific niche, or target population. Target population is defined as the core 80 percent of the members in a gym. This group should be from a clearly defined age and demographic population.

> The trend is away from one-size-fits-all businesses and toward building a business that targets a specific niche, or target population.

Before you build your first or next club, you should have an exact idea of the true target market. Once this is established, then every decision after that point should be matched to that defined niche and target market. Remember, you cannot build a single facility that will properly service and retain a vastly differentiated membership. For example, variables such as programming, staff uniforms, colors in the club, and even the music you play would vary greatly depending upon the age of the target market you attract in your club.

You're better off picking one target market and then building the entire club around that market. This will increase longevity and retention by developing a specialist image in the market. Defining and narrowing your market will also allow you to build a target-specific, intimate service-delivery system, thereby allowing for a better positioning statement in your marketing. It's easier for a club to attract new members when the potential members understand what specific populations the club services. The following are examples of target populations and their matching appropriate sizes:

√ *The 18- to 22-year-old population:* A gym could be built around this group, but unless this was an exceptional college town without a campus facility, what owner would want to have a business centered on this group? Too young, not enough money, and excessive wear and tear on a facility are characteristics of this group. Yes, exceptions apply to this stereotype, but do you really want to invest hundreds of thousands of dollars on that one guy who is 18 and does have money?

√ *The 22- to 35-year-old serious bodybuilding gym:* This is still a viable option for some owners and in a few defined locations. The old trend was to build these big and open, but the consumer is moving away from the big-box concept and toward smaller and more intimate physical plants that cater to their specific needs. This style of gym was reminiscent of the old-style license gyms, but even those groups have moved away from this part of their history. If you still want one of these, and this style of gym can still be viable, consider 5,000 to 8,000 square feet in a dense metro area such as a level-one or level-two market. This type of facility serves as an alternative to the more sterile box-style clubs and caters to the serious workout person.

√ *The 22- to 40-year-old population:* This population provides the core of an exceptional business. Think of the best nightclub you've ever seen without the alcohol. Bright colors, a serious sound system, and great entertainment systems, or in other words, a high-energy rock-and-roll club. This type of club can be the social source in the community for this population but is narrowly defined for this age group. These clubs could be built in as small of a space as 7,500 square feet, but no more than 20,000 square feet. This club would do quite well in a level- two market.

√ *The 30- to 50-year-old population:* This type of club should match the increased boomer market during the coming years. The industry analysts were right about the boomers affecting the fitness business, but they were wrong on the timing: approximately 10 years in fact. It was predicted that by the year 2000 about 50% of a typical club's membership would be 40-years old or older. For most clubs this didn't happen because the projection was off by about 10 years or so.

Using the year 2000 as the base year, those boomers already over 50 will not affect the market in large numbers. They didn't grow up with fitness and probably won't acquire the habit later in life. Those boomers who are under 50 in the year 2000 are going to positively affect the markets because many of them did have more fitness opportunities as a child and were exposed to other social factors such as the running craze in the 1970s. This type of specialized adult club will appeal to this group. The adult alternative, or upscale adult fitness club, as this type of club is called, would be anywhere from 5,000 square feet to no more than 12,000. These clubs should have a very high degree of finish, great amenities and support

Yes, exceptions apply to this stereotype, but do you really want to invest hundreds of thousands of dollars on that one guy who is 18 and does have money?

services, and be designed to appeal to the top 30% to 40% of the demographic market.

√ *The 28- to 48-year-old women's only market:* These clubs are back, currently defensible, and appeal to a very affluent segment of the population. These clubs are designed as elite women's facilities, not mainstream clubs. The difference is in the offerings and the price structures. An elite club would be centered on top-end profit centers such as a day spa as opposed to the old-style mainstream women's facilities, which were nothing more than women's only membership mills with one little room and an open aerobics floor in the middle. This club would normally be 5,000 to 8,000 square feet, but in specific markets that have density and affluence in great enough numbers, this type of club could be bigger in the 10,000 to 14,000-square-foot range.

You may find numerous other possibilities for size and potential niches that could be filled. The following are a few of the more common types including size and potential market:

√ *The 35- to 55-year-old hospital-based wellness-center population:* If this type of facility ever had to become financially accountable, the nature of this type of business would change greatly and in a very short period of time. The old-style hospital-based business generally appeals to a much older population who is generally seeking wellness. White walls, poor entertainment offerings, sterile environments, and even the wellness name itself combine to produce a very limiting business plan.

The more progressive hospital-based facilities are improving on the concept by building smaller, more mass-appeal clubs that can actually pay their own way in the business world. These new-style offerings are about 15,000 to 25,000 square feet, tie themselves to their medical partner by the word affiliated or associated with, and usually embrace the mainstream more readily by supplying current offerings and programming.

√ *The 25- to 50-year-old family center:* These are very regional in nature with the largest density of this type of club found in the southern part of the country. These are the only true family clubs offering mixed family programming and all the support services that go along with this type of concept, such as family pools, outdoor kid playgrounds, and volleyball courts. This somewhat breaks the rule of offering something for everyone, but the core in these clubs is the family membership.

These clubs are very susceptible to competition that takes away their 22- to 40-year-old crowd seeking to avoid children, wading pools, and hundreds of old-timers who still think blue and black chain-driven equipment is all the rage. These clubs are usually measured in acreage instead of square footage and might be 60,000 square feet or more under roof situated on 5 to 10 acres. This type of facility can work in the right market because they become the social center of the community,

The more progressive hospital-based facilities are improving on the concept by building smaller, more mass-appeal clubs that can actually pay their own way in the business world.

something that very few owners really understand or capitalize in as part of their image with the public.

√ *The mixed-use recreation-center concept:* The community center is a common type of facility usually started by the community itself and seldom by individual investors. This type of overstuffed facility will suffer in the future because they are too large and the cost of operation will eventually work against them in their mission to offer just about anything the local residents might want. These clubs are very susceptible to lean-and-mean competitors who can cream different segments of their membership away from them. For example, a recreation center might lose the top 10% to 20% of its membership to a sleek, upscale adult-alternative club that opens across the street from it.

Finding the Proper Site for Your New Business

The next factor to discuss is actually finding a site. Do you look at freestanding buildings or mall sites? Rent or purchase the building? Warehouse/industrial park space at a bargain or should you commit it all to prime retail? These are just a few of the questions that you have to answer before you get your first space or before you expand into another location.

These are also important issues to understand because each one has an effect on the rent factor, which drives the business plan, which determines the chances for success in the business. A number of factors that determine the strength of the location must be considered. The key is not the individual factor but how all the factors total up in relationship to each other.

For example, one site might have great visibility but the mall or town has unusual restrictions on signage, which might cancel out the value of the site. As you review the factors, look at how each one affects the other and that a good site for a new fitness business would be one with the strongest total of all the factors.

Demographics of the Area

Demographics are probably the most talked about factor and yet always the most misunderstood when it comes to finding a home for your business. You don't have to have a set number of residents in an area to open a gym. Manhattan might have hundreds of thousands of people in a small drive-time area while a club in central Pennsylvania might only have 15,000 in the entire county. The key is: does the rent factor make sense and will you pick the size of facility right for that area?

Demographics are probably the most talked about factor and yet always the most misunderstood when it comes to finding a home for your business.

The two well-known components of a demographic study are the *total population* and the *affluence* of those living in the area. Affluence will be discussed separately because this component has many factors that are easily misunderstood.

As mentioned earlier, the first consideration is the number of people in the 12-minute drive time to and from the proposed site. Again, the capture rate or possible number of members a club should expect at maturation is 3.5 percent of the market for a normal level-three market or higher. Level-four markets play by their own rules and allow for a greater penetration rate in the drive-time circle.

The smallest market you should consider would be no less than 15,000 people in your 12-minute drive-time ring. This size of a market could hold a small fitness facility in the 5,000 to 7,500 square foot range if the rent was right and the average household income, which will be discussed later in this chapter, would be at least $30,000 or higher.

The next consideration is the ratio of single-family residences compared to multiple- family homes. Many rookie owners like to be right in the middle of the section of town that has the nicest, biggest homes. The problem with this scenario is the owners of these homes only sell about every seven years. There just isn't enough turnover to support a growing gym business. In other words, if the current homeowner doesn't buy into the gym concept, you might just have to wait another seven years for the next opportunity.

The other problem with just singe-family homes is density. Too few people in too big of a space leave you with not enough members. The solution is to look for a combination of single-family homes and multiple-family complexes, meaning townhouse, condos, and apartments. The preferred ratio is two-thirds of the market multiple family and one-third single family.

The solution is to look for a combination of single-family homes and multiple-family complexes, meaning townhouse, condos, and apartments.

Multiple-family homes turnover residents much more quickly. It's estimated that 33 percent of a multiple-family complex will turnover every year. This turnover, combined with the stability of the single-family residents, provides the best of both worlds for the fitness business owner; a stable and somewhat affluent base combined with an influx of new members on a regular basis.

Population is also an area where you can make your biggest mistake because the natural lay of community may prevent you from capitalizing on the people actually in the market. These natural barriers exist in almost every area but you have to be somewhat of a local to be aware of them.

For example, a 12,000-square-foot club located on a major north/south local artery shows a five-mile ring of almost 100,000 people. The club's actual draw, however, is only about 60,000 because of a natural barrier that the locals won't cross to get to the club. This barrier is simply a large industrial park immediately south of the facility. Residents south of the industrial park, although still within five miles of the club, prefer to drive to other clubs on their side of the park. The park represents a barrier that deters the locals from shopping or attending a club north of their immediate home area.

Other examples of barriers that need to be looked for are railroad tracks, low-rent housing areas, rivers, and communities that touch but have different income averages or images and industrial zones. All of these may decrease the effective market a club can draw from in the 12-minute drive-time target market.

The Affluence in the Area

Too much can be made out of too few people in an area making a lot of money. With a few exceptions, a good and profitable gym can be built in almost any level of average income if the rent matches the space and the gym matches the area. For purposes here, an average household income might start at about $30,000. Keep in mind that a single administrative assistant living alone is a household according to most demographic packages.

You can find research showing that the higher the average household income, the more likely someone is to join a health club. In John McCarthy's book, *IHRSA's Guide to the Health Club Industry for Lenders and Investors*, research is quoted from American Sports Data that those folks in the household income range of $50,000 to $74,900 join a club at the 13.3 per hundred rate, while those people in the over $75,000 category of household income join clubs at the rate of 21 per hundred. It is interesting to note that even those people in the $25,000 to $49,000 range joined at a rate 10 per hundred.

Another very important point to remember is that average income usually matches all the other important factors of the area. Rents, taxes, insurances, wages, and average income all blend together to define an area. Seldom does one of these factors emerge apart from the others, which would force the business owner to have to drastically adjust the business plan in some unusual way.

For example, a town in the Midwest might have an average income of $30,000. Entry-level employees start at $7 to $8 per hour and the owner expects to open her club with a $39 per month average price. After looking for several months for space of about 10,000 square feet, however, she narrows her choice to a spot she likes with a gross rent of $18 per square foot. All the other spaces in this town were in the $9 to $12-per-square-foot range.

This would have to be a very unusual spot for this gym to work. Is it an exceptional location with tremendous walk-in potential? Can she build a smaller, more elite facility and use less space, therefore saving build-out cost and rent? Is this a boutique space in a very elite part of town that would allow her to charge $49 to $59 per month per member? Since the rent factor doesn't match the majority of the spaces she is looking at, she would have to drastically alter her business plan to make this site pay off.

Another factor of affluence and site selection is that the site and finish have to match the average income. San Francisco, for example, has a very high average income; it's over $70,000 per household in many areas of the city. But if you pay $36 per month per square foot in rent and then build a

> With a few exceptions, a good and profitable gym can be built in almost any level of average income if the rent matches the space and the gym matches the area.

typical white-walled, box-style unfinished gym typical in the Midwest or a Southern states that reflects a finish of $20 to $30 per square foot, you won't be competitive in the market place.

On the other hand, if you move to a small town in Iowa, with a much smaller lower average income that might be in the $25,000 to $30,000 range, and overbuild by creating a gym right out of the New York/Connecticut market that are usually finished in the $40 to $50 per foot range or higher, you may have wasted money on build out and equipment that wasn't needed to make money in that market. A good basic rule to follow is that the facility should be built at least one level higher than the market dictates. In other words, build it nicer than your target population would expect and appreciate but that's still appropriate for the area.

Many of the terms once associated with site location, such as blue collar versus white collar, don't really have much bearing anymore. A roofer might make $40,000 a year or more and a manager of a small mall store might make considerably less.

On the lower end of average income, the consideration is how low does the average income in an area have to go before those people who live there actually shop somewhere else besides the community they live. The quality of stores available to the consumer may drop so substantially because of lower average income that the residents choose to shop elsewhere. Very few owners look in these areas but this is an important factor. If the residents of an area don't shop in that area, then they won't buy a membership from a gym there either.

The Visibility of the Site

Visibility means whether the facility can be seen and recognized for what it is. If a site can be seen from major intersections or by the drive-by traffic, then it has visibility. If it is easily recognizable as a fitness facility because of front windows or great signage, then the value of the site and the business it can do is increased.

The debate in this factor is freestanding buildings versus strip-mall sites. Freestanding means the building stands alone. It does not mean that the gym is the only business in the building. For example, you could have a freestanding building in the front parking area of a mall but that building might contain two businesses.

Strip-mall sites mean you share a multi-tenant building with other businesses. In this case you might be one of five different businesses in a strip mall, which simply means one building in either a straight line or perhaps L shape that holds more than one business.

Advantages and disadvantages exist for both types of sites. In a freestanding building, you don't have the advantage of drawing potential

A good basic rule to follow is that the facility should be built at least one level higher than the market dictates.

members from your business neighbors. Although in the club business you might be known as a destination business, or a business the consumer leaves home and intends to end up there, the benefits of having many other businesses around you is that you can also draw their customers to you.

When negotiating a site, it is very important to stress the fitness business as a destination business. In many small strip malls, a thriving fitness business will often feed the other tenants in the plaza because the consumer leaves home to drive to the gym but will then shop at your neighbors because he doesn't have to get in his car again.

An advantage of a freestanding business is that it will usually add to the visibility factor. Freestanding businesses are also often easier to see by a drive-by if they are near the roadway. However, a killer for many freestanding businesses is the lack of parking. A normal facility will need about 13 spaces per thousand square feet during its busiest months of the year, which are normally February and March.

For example, a 10,000 square foot building would need 130 parking spaces during its busy months. The minimum is 10 per thousand, or 100 spaces, which is usually closer to local parking codes from the city and county.

Keep in mind that you will probably have to make a judgment call on parking. The site might only have 95 spaces lined out that actually belong to the business. Plus, it might not have curbs or concrete parking islands.

Always remember that the members will find a way. If no physical restrictions limit parking, the members will often create their own parking spaces in unlikely places. Some sites lend themselves to this and some don't so the judgment call is needed here. What you want to avoid under any circumstances is a member driving around for 15 minutes after work trying to find a parking space before he can workout. If this happens, you can expect member retention to drop rather quickly.

In a large strip-mall location, parking is seldom an issue. In the smaller plazas, however, it could be a very limiting factor. Be sure and consider the hours of your fellow tenants and the effect your parking will have on the entire plaza during your prime time.

Know When the Money Arrives

A typical club will generally do about 65 percent of its total revenue between 4:00 to 9:00 p.m., Monday through Thursday, and Saturday mornings. This might change by up to an hour depending on the local work culture, meaning that prime time may shift to somewhere around 5:00 to 10:00 p.m., but for most facilities, you will make most of your money in a very limited time frame. The realization of prime time affects your location choice because your neighbors in the plaza might be the type of businesses that

A typical club will generally do about 65 percent of its total revenue between 4:00 to 9:00 p.m., Monday through Thursday, and Saturday mornings.

close at 5:00 p.m., such as a doctor's suite, or they might be the type of business that just gets going at 5:00 p.m., such as a pizza restaurant.

The exceptions to this rule are women-only clubs and true corporate clubs. These two hybrids usually have two prime times because of their unusually heavy morning traffic, but again, these are the exceptions and not the rule. Women's clubs, for example, usually have a second prime time in the morning from 8:00 to 11:00 a.m.

In the smaller strip malls, you might become what is known as an *anchor tenant*. This means that you assume the prime location in the plaza, get the lead position on the plaza's sign, and control the key parking areas. Anchor tenants drive the plaza because they bring in very high-traffic counts, sign longer leases, and attract other businesses to the plaza because these businesses want to be next to the anchor.

When negotiating for a new plaza site, use the anchor-tenant strategy based on your daily traffic numbers. Look at the following breakdown of a typical club and the traffic it can generate. Be sure and use these numbers for your own negotiations.

Let's look at a 10,000-square-foot club that expects to have 800 members at the end of its first year, which includes a small presale. To get a working number of members a club has to obtain each month, start with the following formula:

$60,000 BOE divided by one new annual membership per thousand dollars of expense.

In this example, the club has a monthly *base operating expense* (BOE) of $60,000, and its monthly membership price must be at least $39 per member per month for the formula to work. In other words, this club would have to write one new annual membership each month for every $1,000 of BOE.

> **...this club would have to write one new annual membership each month for every $1,000 of BOE.**

This also means the club would have to write a minimum of 60 new annual memberships a month to achieve a 20 percent pre-tax net, which is one of the first financial goals for any new club. This assumes the club understands and operates at least four profit centers in the club all netting 20 percent minimum. Assuming the club has obtained its 800 members, you can then move on to the following formula that determines traffic and usage:

**800 members times 60 percent is the total
of a club's membership it will see each month.
800 x 60% = 480**

This formula means that over a 30-day period, this club can expect to see up to 480 of its members at least once.

**800 members times 25 percent equals a club's
expected workouts on a Monday, the busiest day of the week
for the majority of fitness businesses.**
800 x 25% = 200

This formula means that on a typical Monday, the club will do about 200 workouts, or 200 different individuals, out of the total population of 800 that will stop by to workout. If you live in California, Las Vegas, Manhattan, or Hawaii, these numbers are light because the usage is so much higher there than compared to other areas in the country. A fair adjustment here would be 80 percent for the monthly usage and 40 percent for the typical Monday workouts.

If a club generates 200 member workouts a day, it has a great influence on its neighboring businesses because those 200 members will most likely shop near the club to avoid additional car trips. This can be a strong negotiating point for owners when looking for a site, especially in smaller markets.

Signing Is a Key Factor

The ability to properly sign a location is often a deciding factor for many locations. A site with low visibility that is somewhat hidden from the drive-by traffic can turn out to be a strong location if a distinctive street sign is available.

The problem with signage is that local sign codes vary so dramatically from town to town across the country. You will not find anything remotely resembling a consistent sign code you can count on to guide you.

A hidden problem you most likely will encounter is that the landlord will tell you can put any sign up you want, and will even put this in a lease knowing that the city or county has strong sign codes that will overrule what's in the lease. Before committing to any lease or even building your own building, research the local sign codes. If you have something unique, make sure you have written permission from the governing powers before you sign your lease.

A basic rule of business marketing that most new owners break when they build and even name their first business is: *tell me fast, tell me true, or my friend the hell with you*. This old marketing adage seems like it was specifically written for new owners who spend entirely too much time trying to name their business. Trust me, every cute name available has been taken and the fitness world just doesn't need another *Unique Physique* or *Jim's Gym*. A solid rule to live by when naming your first business is that *cute sucks*. If it's cute or catchy, and your relatives and friends giggle when they first here the name, then you are entirely on the wrong track.

What the little *tell-me-fast* rhyme means is that your name, and eventually your signage, should clearly tell the consumer what it is and where it is in the fewest possible words. For example, if your facility in on 6th Street

A site with low visibility that is somewhat hidden from the drive-by traffic can turn out to be a strong location if a distinctive street sign is available.

Tell me fast, tell me true, or my friend the hell with you.

and you were building a gym concept, then something shockingly simple such as *6th Street Gym* would make an ideal name. Tell the consumer fast what it is and where it is: it's a gym on 6th Street.

If you're using a franchise name such as *World Gym*, the franchise name for one of the largest club chains in the world, you should still add a local identifier to the name that gives the potential consumer a clue. For example, *World Gym of Melbourne* clearly states what it is and where it is, and if the owner adds another business to her portfolio, she simply adds another town name as that identifier.

Many signs are too complicated because the names are too indistinct and the owners feel the need to spend too much time explaining what they actually own with their signs. When it comes to signage, think as few words as possible and keep it as simple as possible. In the previous example, *World Gym of Melbourne*, the town name would not have to go on the sign. Simply *World Gym* would be sufficient. You are assuming of course that the potential member is smart enough to understand what town he is currently living in when they read the sign. If they don't know, they have already failed the first test to become a member; they are just too dumb.

> **When it comes to signage, think as few words as possible and keep it as simple as possible.**

If it is an unusual site with severe sign codes, a simple sign stating *Gym* would work as a clear identifier. If you are a licensed or franchised gym, make sure you have permission from your parent organization to use the one-word identifier on your sign.

Some sign codes restrict the amount of outside signage you can have, but do not restrict the amount of signage you can have inside the club that can still be seen from the outside. Clubs with plenty of window space can often add signs inside the windows that are lit and can be seen from the streets. This would be an excellent way to promote additional parts of the business, such as a sports bar, a juice bar, or a nutrition program.

Signage is one of those things that can make or break a small business, but is often one of those things that are taken for granted. Everyone just assumes that because you own a business, you can put up a sign. But if you are lost in the middle of a strip center and don't have the ability to put up strong signage, your business can suffer accordingly. Again, make sure you understand just what signage is available and what is legal for your business, and don't ever sign anything until you have a clear, legal understanding of what rights you have. Get it in writing if you suspect any hint of controversy that might later sneak in to harm your business.

Density and How It Affects Your Business

How many people will it take to make your gym successful? This might be the most asked question by rookies everywhere. What *density* means to most people is how many people live in your town. This is the wrong interpretation for business purposes.

What density should mean is how many *qualified* potential members live within a 12-minute drive time, measured at the prime driving time of 6:00 p.m., from my club? Qualified means can they afford the discretionary income to commit to some type of membership and are they also in the target population for this type of facility?

Unfortunately, it's easy to fall into the trap of trying to expand your potential market by trying to build one club that will attract every possible consumer in that market. This fails because you simply can't build one facility that will appeal to the entire market, and it ignores the fact that 85 to 90 percent of your gym's members will come from 12 minutes from the club. The bigger the club, the more density it needs to feed it, and the farther away it has to draw from to be successful.

The trend in the coming years will be toward *niching* the club, or building smaller, more target-specific clubs that are easier to defend in the marketplace and less costly to build and maintain. The ideal square footage would be less than 15,000 square feet for most projects. Of course, exceptions to every rule exist, and certain large metro markets might warrant a larger facility, but this is again only an exception. The consumer will demand more service in the future and it's pretty hard to provide legendary, intimate customer service in a monster facility with 4,000 to 5,000 of your closet friends.

As discussed previously, it's going to be likely that 80 percent of the people in your facility will be in some segment of the 22- to 48-year-old population depending on the niche you choose. When you look at density for a facility, you're looking for how many people match your desired target population.

For example, you wouldn't want to build a high-energy rock-and-roll gym in a town of 15,000 if the median age was in the late 40's. However, a women-only or adult-alternative facility might work well in that type of market.

The 12-minute drive-time rule is an important place to start when analyzing a potential location or even an existing club that might be experiencing problems. As a new club you will seldom draw potential members in any significant numbers from a longer drive time other than the 12-minute ring.

Existing clubs might be having trouble because they don't understand the club's true market and the owners spend too much money marketing beyond their actual drawing area. Radio might be an example of spending for coverage beyond your actual draw.

Another problem for an existing club that doesn't understand its market is that its current marketing might not be effective at saturating the 12-minute ring. Your current marketing might only hit certain areas of your draw ring instead of totally saturating your entire market.

The bigger the club, the more density it needs to feed it, and the farther away it has to draw from to be successful.

Don't Forget the Accessibility Factor

A site may have a great sign, nice visibility, tons of nice cars whipping buy on the main road just in front of the club, but the location might still not work because the site is not *accessible*.

Accessibility means how easy is it to get to the location once you've see it. You might have strong visibility from the main road, but if you have to drive several miles to the next exit and then take a frontage road back to the location, this makes your marketing and impulse shopping much more difficult. Driving by at 55 miles per hour and getting a full view of the club is one thing. Pulling off and inquiring about a membership on impulse is a whole different location factor.

The keys to look at are very simple. Can the consumer pull into your lot from several different entrances? Is the club on road that has a center island that prohibits cars on the opposite side of road from pulling in on impulse? Are you in New Jersey, an entire state dedicated to no left turns and tortures its residents with the insidious jug handles, meaning that all turns to the left start with a loop to the right?

Test your potential site during prime time by accessing the location from every conceivable angle. If you get frustrated trying to turn across an intersection and get stuck for a light or two, then your members will experience that same frustration, only compounded by how many days a week they work out.

Members want simplicity in their lives. As club owners, you are supposed to help them achieve that in their experience with your business. A member leaves work, drives to your club, parks close, works out, and then goes home. This concept should be very simple and clean and not complicated by five minutes of frustration trying to cross traffic to pull into your plaza. Of course, disregard this if you are in Los Angeles where all driving is frustrating and getting anywhere is not simple.

One important point to consider, which is a somewhat dated point not found in much of the current site data, is whether the club is on the going-to-work or the coming-home side of the street. In small towns this is irrelevant, but if your club is going to be on a major road this could be a factor.

For example, a club is located on an exit of a major four-lane road leading to a bedroom community about 30 minutes outside of a major-metro market. Everyone in the community works in the major city and drives in each morning to the big city. After work they drive home on the same road. If the owner could pick, the club would be better off on the going-home side of the four-lane because it would be more readily visible and accessible to the majority of the heavy traffic at the right time of day. Some final tips for finding a site for a potential gym are:

> **Members want simplicity in their lives. As club owners, you are supposed to help them achieve that in their experience with your business.**

- If you're looking in an area where you don't live, spend more time than you think looking at a location. What looks good the first or second visit may not hold up after a few weeks of scrutiny.

- *If it ain't in writing, it ain't real* are poorly written words to live by when looking for a location. Signs, promises, parking agreements, and everything else have to be clearly spelled out in writing or it just doesn't exist.

- Don't get too emotional about a site for your new business. Getting emotionally tied to a site can lead to some very bad decisions. You often end up trying to make a club fit rather than regroup and find a better solution. You can always find other locations and if you can't find one in that area, then get over it and move on to the next town.

- Find out if you are wanted before you go too far in your search. Wal-Mart and most of the other major players have an antiquated clause in their leases that prevent health clubs from being in the same plaza as they are. Before you go too far in a mall location that contains a major anchor tenant, be sure you can actually put a fitness business in that location.

- Worrying too much about competitors is also something to be avoided. If you niche your club against competitors rather than trying to out-ego them by going heads- up with an identical business plan, you can open across the street from most any fitness business. For example, a top-end, adult upscale club would work nicely across the street from a big-box chain club. You won't take all of their members, just the top 20 percent or so who appreciate quality and who are willing to pay for it.

If you niche your club against competitors rather than trying to out-ego them by going heads- up with an identical business plan, you can open across the street from most any fitness business.

Building a Club from the Lease Up

An entire book could be written on just leases alone and how they affect a fitness business. The point of this section is to give an owner a working guideline as to what a lease should look like when completed and to avoid some of the more painful trial-and-error learning that can take place with lease negotiations.

The first point when it comes to leases is that everything is negotiable except your name. This means that the slate is relatively clean when you first start looking at a potential space. Nothing is firm and almost anything can be discussed as part of your lease. Landlords like to deal and will usually approach the negotiation with few expectations when it comes to dealing with a fitness business.

The first point when it comes to leases is that everything is negotiable except your name.

After you have analyzed a potential site and have narrowed your choices down to just one, you are ready to start the negotiation process. At this time you have already hooked up with an agent or will soon encounter one. Keep in mind this one hard rule concerning agents: find out who the agent is really working for in the deal. Most of the time the agents are getting paid by the landlord to fill the spot. Even if you find an agent off the street, their commissions usually come from the landlord for filling the space. If this is the case, then the agent may not be working in your best interests.

Assuming that you have representation that actually works for you, the next move is to get an offering sheet from the landlord. This is usually a one page sheet that defines the space, base rent, and a little about the plaza or building. An absolute rule is never ever begin a negotiation without an offering sheet from the property manager or landlord. You should only respond to a sheet that offers beginning numbers.

> An absolute rule is never ever begin a negotiation without an offering sheet from the property manager or landlord.

The Basics of a Lease

The ultimate goal of course is to sign a lease structured to allow your business to grow over a long period of time, and then sell your business to the next person who will have the right to perpetuate the business for a reasonable length of time. When you get the offering sheet, it's helpful to have a working plan of what you want to accomplish with your lease. If you have a plan going in it makes it a lot easier to react to what's happening in front of you at the time. Before you lay out a plan, you need to look at a few key terms that will come up early in any space acquisition:

- *Base rent:* Base rent is the asking price for the space itself and does not include the extra charges you pay, such as your share of the taxes, common area maintenance, and insurance. When you get your first offering sheet from the property manager or landlord, the number usually presented on the sheet is the base rent. They show you this number first because it is smaller than the real total rent you will end up paying for the space. Base rent is a component of *gross rent*, which represents the actual rent you will pay for your space.

- *Triple net:* Triple net is the combination of taxes, insurance, and common area maintenance (CAM). If you are in a strip mall or other type of mall situation, you will pay your pro-rata share of the combination of these charges. If you are a freestanding building, you usually get to pay for all these charges as they apply to your building. A common mistake is to interchange the term CAM with triple net, which can lead to some nasty surprises. CAM is just common area maintenance and does not pertain to taxes and insurance.

    If someone quotes you CAM charges, don't assume the taxes and insurances are included in the fee. Triple net should be paid monthly as part of the rent package. Avoid paying quarterly, or worse yet annual, triple-net charges since this system can wreak havoc on budgeting. Also be sure and ask the property manager or landlord for verification of the triple-net charges. Most property managers and landlords pad the triple-net charges by charging an additional management fee of about 20 percent, which can usually be negotiated out if you ask about it before the lease is signed.

- *Gross rent:* Gross rent is the combination of the base rent of the space and the triple-net charges. This is the actual rent you will pay for the space. Rent can either be defined as monthly or annual depending on the region of the country you are in. For example, to figure an annual rent, use this formula:

(Square footage) x (gross rent) divided by 12 (months)

If you were looking at a 12,000-square-foot building and the negotiated gross rent was $10 per foot, the actual rent paid each month would be $10,000, which is 12,000 square feet times $10, equaling $120,000, and then divided by 12.

Some rents are presented monthly. For example, an offering sheet might list $.90 for the space. Simply take $.90 times 12 (months) and then insert that number in the previous formula. In this example, $.90 times 12 equals $10.80 gross rent, which is used as the gross-rent number in the formula.

This number has changed over time but the current maximum gross rent most fitness businesses could handle would be $14 to $16 per foot on an annual basis. Of course Manhattan, most of California, and Las Vegas are not part of this rule. If you are considering paying more than this for your space, it better be one prime location.

- *Vanilla box:* Vanilla box is another of those classic real estate terms that are defined by whoever is standing in front of you at that minute. Vanilla box normally means that you are getting a shell with one bathroom (meets local codes so the work people can go to the bathroom), a bare concrete floor, cheap lights with an open ceiling, electrical to one box on the wall, and a basic heating and air conditioning unit normally underpowered for our needs in the fitness business. The walls may be dry walled but with tape only or they may be just concrete.

If the site has been rented before as another business, the landlord or property managers usually have to demolish the existing structure and then restore the space to the vanilla box. As of this book's publication, this is usually about $1 to $2 per foot and the landlord should pay for this as part of the deal. The lease would read that the landlord will restore the property to vanilla-box condition, meaning that you are back to a base shell and get to start from scratch.

A word of caution: get a definition of what the vanilla box will contain. One client doing a franchised gym in the Northeast signed a lease based on receiving a vanilla-box shell ready for the tenant improvements. This was new construction and the assumption was that the landlord's definition of a vanilla box was standard. It wasn't. The new gym owner signed a lease based upon raw space that had everything but the heating and air conditioning units, a $40,000 upgrade for the owner. The landlord's interpretation of vanilla box did not include heating and air.

Remember, if it isn't in writing it isn't real. Get a written definition of what's included in the vanilla box.

> **This number has changed over time but the current maximum gross rent most fitness businesses could handle would be $14 to $16 per foot on an annual basis.**

- *Consumer price index:* Consumer price index (CPI) is a government derived number that compares the buying power of money in the base year 1967 compared to how much more money it would take to have the same buying power today. For example, a year's increase for the CPI might be 1.5 percent, meaning that if a landlord wanted to get the same value for her money, she would have to increase your rent by 1.5 percent. In other words, she needs 1.5 percent more of your money to achieve the same value or buying power.

  CPI is important in lease negotiations because it is often the universally accepted number used to determine increase in rent either each year or during the option periods. Everyone usually agrees to use CPI because the government publishes the index each year and it's easy for all parties to access.

- *Build out or tenant improvements:* Build out or tenant improvements (TI) are what it takes to finish the space except for equipment. This includes wall coverings, lighting, floor covering, finished plumbing and locker rooms, and the electrical work. TIs are very much negotiable as to who pays for what when.

  Build-out costs have gone up continuously every year and are currently about $35 to $40 per square foot for a competitive club in most markets, which again does not include equipment. In the 1980s, build out was often under $10 per square foot. In the 1990s, the industry saw an increase to an average of just at $30 per square foot. But in the year 2000, this number jumped to $35 to $40. Owners looking at an upscale adult or woman's only centers could easily spend $40 or more per square foot depending upon the region of the country. Again, these are averages and some regions of the country can get by with less cost per foot, but these numbers will be close to what a quality club will cost to build.

The Lease Itself

The lease itself can be a simple document, easy to read and easy to implement, or it can be the nightmare of all business experiences, depending on the property manager or landlord. Most are what's called *boilerplates*, an old term meaning most of the parts are interchangeable and standardized.

When responding to an offer sheet, start with these basics that form the core for most fitness center commercial leases. Remember, the goal is to secure a space for the best possible rent today and then be able to sell the business later if you desire, and the new owner has the right to perpetuate the business. This right to perpetuate the business adds a great deal of value to your business if you do indeed decide to sell in the future. A basic lease should contain the following components:

- *The initial lease period is for five years.*

This is the starting time period for your negotiations and can be used as a tool to trade for something else later. For example, most landlords usually

> The lease itself can be a simple document, easy to read and easy to implement, or it can be the nightmare of all business experiences, depending on the property manager or landlord.

take your lease to their banks and leverage its value against other projects they might want to do. The building or space you occupy makes the landlord's property worth about 40 percent more filled on the real estate market than it does empty. The landlord may balk at three option periods for example, but you can then counter with increasing your initial period to seven years rather than five. If it's prime space, you may even extend all the way to 10 years, but be careful after that point. Unless you are reasonably sure that area will not decline, don't sign a lease that requires more than a 10-year period of time. That way if the neighborhood goes bad you still have time to escape and relocate your business.

- *Option periods are for five years each and you should normally ask for three five-year options.*

Three five-year option periods are fast becoming obsolete, but they are still options worth pursuing. You want the right to perpetuate your business into the future, either yourself or through a sale to someone else. The economy at the time this book was written was still hot and most landlords were fighting giving you space that far into the future, especially in the major markets such as Southern California and New York. But again, start here and then back off. The deal breaker for most owners when it comes to option periods is not the time, but what they will have to pay for that future time, as discussed in the next point.

- *Option periods are based on CPI and you should usually ask for a cap of three percent.*

What this point tries to achieve is having a known rent into the future. Fitness facilities need a great deal of reinvestment and this usually comes from long-term debt through banks. Without fixed, definable option-period increases, you are stuck with what's called *market value*. Simply put, this means that at the end of your initial period the landlord can increase your rent to whatever the market will bear.

If it's a hot market, or your landlord has other properties or friends in the business to draw comparable current rents from, your rent might go from $9 a foot to $14 overnight. It's hard to build that much of a jump into a fitness business's working business plan. By tying your option-period increases to CPI and capping the increase at three percent, you can adjust your price increases and capitalization accordingly. If the landlord balks at CPI, then try for a fixed increase of 2.5 percent per year during the option periods and if you have to settle for three percent. A fitness business works well with a fixed increase of 2.5 percent per year or 12.5 percent over every five-year option period.

- *Ask for two months free rent, including no triple-net charges, for build-out time.*

It's hard to ask a landlord for five months of free rent. As landlords, they are automatically conditioned to give a traditional three-month period. To break their auto- response habit, you have to bring a different negotiation strategy

A fitness business works well with a fixed increase of 2.5 percent per year or 12.5 percent over every five-year option period.

to the table. Try this strategy that separates your desired free-rent period into two distinct areas:

√   The first is a *two-month period* that allows you to push your build out along prior to the official opening of your club, defined as the time you can actually start doing workouts. Two months is normally not enough time to do a proper build out but it is reasonable to the landlord.

√   The second is that landlords and property managers understand the need to build out from a retail orientation that is a lot less complicated than a typical gym, and they need to be educated to the difference.

•   *Ask for three months free rent, including no triple-net charges, from date of certificate of occupancy (CO), which is issued by the local permit people and states that you can immediately start working people out in the club.*

In addition to the two-month build out period previously discussed, you should also ask the landlord for an additional three-month period from the date of certificate of occupancy, which is the date of the final inspection and the date that you can actually occupy your building for its intended purpose. It's important to get at least three-months free rent up front at the minimum even if the additional two-month period is not accepted. Fitness businesses are very dependent on building a strong receivable base that will be discussed in a later section.

Your new business needs time to get healthy and have a growth phase of its own. Having no rent, or reduced rent, during the first three months to a year allows your new business to get healthy on its own.

Your new business needs time to get healthy and have a growth phase of its own. Having no rent, or reduced rent, during the first three months to a year allows your new business to get healthy on its own. Without this time period, many new owners are forced to get creative early in their first year because they are short of cash. The perfect combination would be five months of no rent, followed by seven months of reduced rent, coupled with two months operating expense in reserve capital. It would be hard to kill a fitness business that started based on these assumptions.

•   *Ask for a build-out allowance from the landlord of at least one third of the build-out costs.*

You should follow some general guidelines when it comes to anticipating your build-out costs. According to Rudy Fabiano, of Fabiano Designs International, the leading fitness-facility architectural firm in the industry, if you base your total build out at $35 per square foot, you can follow these general guidelines as a reference point.

These costs will vary according to the project scope and actual market rate for the construction period and the area you are building in. They are also for interior only but they will give you a working reference point to get started with in your plans (See Figure 1-1). The goal would be to negotiate with the landlord for the big-ticket items. At this point you have three options for your negotiations.

Demolition, general conditions	$1.
General interior building such as walls, doors and the ceiling	$7.
Specialty items	$1.
Misc. metals, railings, staircases, etc.	$1.
Paint including the ceiling	$1.50
Cabinetry including lockers	$2.50
Glass, mirrors and specialty doors	$2.50
Flooring	$3.
Aerobics flooring	$1.
Ceramic tile	$1.50
Electrical	$6.
HVAC	$4.
Plumbing	$3.
Total cost per square foot	**$35.**

Figure 1-1. Construction costs per square foot.

√ *Option one* — You should normally ask the landlord for about $15 per square foot for the build out. If you refer to Figure 1-1, you will see that this gets you HVAC, electrical, and basic plumbing. If you don't have strong financial statements to back up your business plan, the landlord may give you the $15 a foot build out, but you'll have to pay it back over the initial term of your lease with usually modest interest. In other words, you get a $15 a foot break but you have to pay it back. It's sort of like borrowing money from a backer or investor and allows to you to get into the game with less cash.

√ *Option two* — If the landlord is a little happier with your statements and believes that your business might help his center, he might be willing to put up the $15 per square foot and you'll only have to pay back half over the initial term of the lease.

For example, you are looking at a 10,000-square-foot gym. The total build out would be $350,000 based on $35 per square foot. If the landlord puts up $15 per square foot, this would reduce your initial cash need by $150,000. In this scenario, the landlord may only make you pay back half, or $75,000 amortized over the initial lease period.

√ *Option three* — If you have great statements, plenty of cash, and don't need the landlords help, he will usually give you the entire build out and not make you pay any back. That's the way it works in the real world, but this option does free up cash and reduce your monthly operating cost if you have any debt service on the money you are using. *When negotiating, always start with option three and work backwards.*

√ *A possible fourth option* — Sometimes a possible fourth option comes up. If the landlord has been sitting on space for a long period of time, she may want to dump it at somewhat of discount and then use your presence to rent the rest of her center. In that case she may, as landlord, not agree to any build-out allowance. You should then trade an additional free rent against the build-out money. For example, if you ask for $15 per

If the landlord has been sitting on space for a long period of time, she may want to dump it at somewhat of discount and then use your presence to rent the rest of her center.

square foot and she says no, then you should counter with nine more months of free rent (you should have already gotten the first three months free at the minimum) and end up with the first year free. This does happen and is worth considering if you are looking at space that has been vacant for a long period of time.

Ask for exclusions that limit the landlord from accepting competing businesses in the same mall.

• *Ask for exclusions that limit the landlord from accepting competing businesses in the same mall.*

It's always smart to ask the landlord for exclusions in your lease. This means you should ask that other similar businesses that might compete with yours not be allowed in the mall. Of course, if you are a freestanding building this won't matter, but it could be important in a strip-mall situation.

Exclusions are often done as an addendum to the lease and your list of possible exclusions should include: tanning centers, weight-loss clinics, supplement stores, stand-alone juice businesses, day spas if that happens to be part of your club, and you might even try for athletic clothing stores if that is going to be a part of your business plan. *Always include other fitness centers.* A landlord that doesn't have an exclusion clause in your lease may not figure that a women's only club in the same center would hurt your gym. Ask for everything and then back down from that point.

• *Ask for the right to sublet space in your own space to other small businesses such as chiropractors or physical therapists.*

Subletting space in your business can be a great profit center in itself. Chiropractors, physical therapists, massage people, and even small insurance companies like to have a gym address and it's passive income for the club. The problem arises when a landlord gets greedy and wants a percentage of that sublet rent, too. You should negotiate for the right to sublet space in your business as part of your business plan upfront and the landlord will usually stay out of the game.

Ask for the right to assign the lease without a lot of legal hassle in case you sell the business to someone else.

• *Ask for the right to assign the lease without a lot of legal hassle in case you sell the business to someone else.*

You may want to sell your business to someone else someday in the future. You're tired, an offer is just too good, or you just want a change of address and it's time to move on to the next opportunity. In any case, you need to have a strong right of assignment clause in your lease.

Most of the boilerplate leases have a very generic clause about the landlord not withholding the option to assign. You want to go stronger than this by having your attorney draw up a clause that you submit as part of the lease approval. If you find a qualified buyer, you'll want the right to get out without undue landlord interference. Negotiate it up front and it's usually not a problem later when you need it to happen.

- *Ask for an option to buy the property, if applicable, between years two and five.*

Even if you are in a strip mall and every dime you have is going into the new club, you should still always ask. You may make a lot of money quickly, may find a money person, or otherwise get to the point that you could buy the plaza. Think big and always ask for the right to purchase the building in the future. You should usually ask for this right between years two and five, and base the purchase price either on a predetermined price or on the average of three appraisals (you get one, the landlord gets one, and you get a third-party you agree on as the third appraisal). For many owners, their buildings will be a big part of their retirement package. If you get a chance to own you should consider it and try building in the option with every lease you do just in case.

- *Ask for a clear, written addendum stating your signage rights.*

Find out your legal rights for signage and get that in writing as part of your lease. Again, the landlord may agree to something that isn't legal in your community. Carefully research the sign codes in your town and then get the landlord to put in writing what your rights are concerning that space. Too many owners have been badly surprised by not being able to properly sign their new businesses because they didn't understand the local codes.

- *Ask for a written understanding from the landlord of your parking needs.*

It is always good to address the parking needs of your location up front instead of trying to solve the problem later. If you have any doubt whatsoever about parking, get it in writing as part of the lease and get spelled out what spaces your business controls and where you can park. Attach a diagram if you still have any doubt about any usage situations.

- *Ask for a written plan on sound proofing your location if you are in a strip-mall location because your sound may irritate the other tenants. The landlord should participate in properly insulating your space from the others.*

If you are in a multi-level mall situation or an older strip mall with thin walls between the neighbors, address the sound issue in the lease phase. Fitness businesses produce sound at a higher level than many landlords anticipate and this ruins the quiet enjoyment of your neighbors.

Ask for a written plan on sound proofing your location if you are in a strip-mall location because your sound may irritate the other tenants. The landlord should participate in properly insulating your space from the others.

The remedies for this problem are easy during the build-out stage, but much more difficult after the club is open and small-business owners are in your face threatening you because your members' shoes are vibrating the shelves in their stores. The landlord should pay for any additional sound insulation that is needed as part of the package since it affects your business and the ones adjacent to it.

Remember that the lease factor is the most important number in your business plan. If it's wrong, it's hard to sell enough memberships to get you out of trouble.

These 13 basic points form the lease for your new business, but most importantly, if negotiated correctly, give your business a higher chance for success. Remember that the lease factor is the most important number in your business plan. If it's wrong, it's hard to sell enough memberships to get you out of trouble.

Other Negotiation Issues

*   *Using rent averaging*

Rent averaging means you give the landlord what she wants, you just don't give it how she wants it. The fitness business, as previously mentioned, needs every advantage it can get during the first year. Besides trying to aggressively negotiate as much free rent as possible, you may also try rent averaging. For example, the landlord may ask the following rent for the first five years (per square foot):

> Year one -- $10
> Year two -- $10.50
> Year three -- $11
> Year four -- $11.50
> Year five -- $12

The average of these five years is $11 per square foot. To give the business an extra edge during the first year, you may offer something like this:

> Year one -- $8.50
> Year two -- $9.50
> Year three -- $10.50
> Year four -- $11.50
> Year five -- $12.50

The average of these five years would be $10.50, a little under the average the landlord was seeking, but still within the negotiation game. Most importantly for the landlord, he gets what he wants in the last year, a number big enough to have a strong effect on the first option period. And you get what you need during the first two years: reduced rent that allows more of the cash flow to get into the business where it can make a difference.

*   *Personal guarantees*

Landlords want every guarantee known to man. If they could get your mother and the family cow tied up legally they would most likely do it. You might have to compromise, however, to personally guaranteeing a lease for the entire duration you will be in the space. Keep in mind that you will never know exactly what is going to happen. Your club might fail for some reason down the line. You may want to open another facility in a couple of years. You may want to sell your club and to then get cleanly off of the lease.

To do this you have to limit your liability by limiting how long you stay as a personal guarantor of the lease. The easiest thing to try is to offer an addendum from your attorney that states that you will sign personally on the lease for two years. If you pay your rent according to schedule and meet all of your other obligations to the landlord, you will then have the right to resign the lease again in two years corporately. If you are an established businessperson with assets and several businesses, this issue usually doesn't come up, but for many of the new owners this will be an issue. By signing for two personally and then resigning again if you meet your obligations, you have offered a compromise that everyone should buy into up front.

- *Signing before you get the money*

This shouldn't have to be explained, but it is an actual common mistake with new owners who are too emotional about getting into their dream club. Under no circumstances sign anything until you have the actual money, meaning bank loans, investor money, or your own money actually liquidated and in a pile. The order of gym project would look like this:

√ *Dream big and do the research.* What do you want to own, where will it be, how much will it cost to open, do you have the skills to run it successfully, and do you understand how a small business really works? If you don't have the answers to any of these questions, then start here.

√ *Build a small business plan.* You'll find a complete model business plan in Chapter 13 that can be used as a template for your fitness facility. This type of plan is nothing more than a *who is it, what is it, where is it, and how much will it cost* type of simple plan you would show an investor. The key is that this plan should demonstrate an ability to repay and answer the age-old question, "What's in it for me the investor."

√ *Search around the area you want to open in and get a real rent factor.* This actually goes hand-in-hand with the previous point since you will have to have a rent factor to write even a simple business plan. This is also the stage where you should begin your initial discussions with an architect as to the actual costs of the build out and what you will get for the money. This should also be the time to harass your equipment representatives and get an entire gym priced out. This too should go into the previously mentioned business plan.

√ *Get your money together.* Whether it be investor money, parent money, your money, or whatever, get the money in the back before you move on to the next step.

√ *Negotiate on the lease.* At this point you can negotiate in good faith since the money is behind you. If you have experience and really know the money is there without actually having to move it to the bank, you can begin your negotiations earlier and simply add a contingent on the final project-financing addendum.

Under no circumstances sign anything until you have the actual money, meaning bank loans, investor money, or your own money actually liquidated and in a pile.

This entire process could be done in as little as six to nine months. However, you should allow for at least a year to be safe. And don't forget the 20/20 rule that states the project will take at least 20 percent longer than you think and cost 20 percent more than you expected.

But What If I Buy and Simply Have a Mortgage?

If you are buying a building you probably have a different business plan with perhaps stronger assets. For the sake of business planning for the day-to-day operations of your business, the mortgage and the rent factor with triple net are interchangeable. You will find obvious tax advantages beyond the extent of this book when you buy a building, but the monthly payment on the mortgage has the same affect on your business plan that the rent factor does. Later in this book rent and mortgage factors and the effects they have on your business will be detailed. At this point, just interchange them for the sale of discussion.

One rule of thumb you should use as a reference point when you have to choose between buying a building and renting is the fact that if you can buy for the same monthly payment as the anticipated rent, or have a monthly payment that is no more than 30 percent more than the rent payment would be, it's usually safe to buy. If the new mortgage payment is 30 percent or more than your anticipated rent payment, it's usually a good idea to just keep renting and take the extra money you would have paid and invest in it. What you're doing is just keeping more cash flow free each month to help your business get healthy. Of course your accountant should be involved in the final decision since your tax situation may warrant a higher payment, but as a starting reference point this is the place to begin.

A Few Final Tips on Negotiating Your Lease

- *Find an agent that you like and work with him over the long run.* Finding the right space may take longer than you think and you need an agent that will see you through the entire project.

- *Don't get too emotional about a space or a time frame.* A sure way to lose money is to push too hard and force a gym to happen in a space or situation that may not be right for you.

- *Don't take no for an answer.* When it comes to banks, it will take more no answers than yeses to get the job done. It isn't unusual to get turned down by four or five different banks before you get someone willing to work with you. The same applies for finding space. Keep looking even if you can't find anything there today. Tomorrow may be a different story.

- *Budget at lease $35 per foot for your build out.* You can do it for less, but some time during the first year to 18 months you will have to reinvest again to bring the club up to a minimum standard. You're going to spend $35 sooner or later and that's about what it takes to do it right. If you are building from the ground up then budget about $40 to $60

Don't get too emotional about a space or a time frame. A sure way to lose money is to push too hard and force a gym to happen in a space or situation that may not be right for you.

per square foot for the shell depending on the region of the country. Total cost for doing your own building will be around $90 per square foot, which includes the shell and the build out but not the equipment.

A point to consider is that according to Rudy Fabiano, an architect who has built well over 200 different health club and fitness facilities, your industry is still less build out intensive than most other businesses. For example, Rudy cites that restaurants are normally built at $80 per square foot and most of the competitive retail stores come in about $50 to $60 per square foot just for the interior. The $35 number sounds high, but as membership fees continue to increase this number will also rise to match the increased expectations of the clients you'll attract at that higher membership rate.

- *Negotiate for the future of your business from the first day.* The right to perpetuate your business over a long period of time adds a great deal of value to the business. Assume that you may sell the business or pass it along to your kids and negotiate accordingly from the first day.

The Key Points You Should Have Gotten from this Chapter

- The right rent factor can make or break a business plan for a club.

- The most basic of all numbers in the fitness business is this: 85% to 90% of a club's membership comes from within a 12-minute drive time to and from the club.

- You will only attract about 3.5% of your defined market.

- The future of the fitness business will be specialization for your club without trying to be everything to everyone.

- A strong location for a fitness business is a combination of factors including affluence, accessibility, and the ability to sign the property.

- The minimum annual memberships a club has to write each month to survive is one per thousand dollars of expense.

- Build your club from the lease up.

- Don't get emotional about leases and locations; there will always be other options.

Negotiate for the future of your business from the first day. The right to perpetuate your business over a long period of time adds a great deal of value to the business. Assume that you may sell the business or pass it along to your kids and negotiate accordingly from the first day.

2

The Levels of Maturity for a Fitness Business

The most important thing you should get from this chapter is:

Fitness businesses have a set pattern of maturity and an owner must constantly reinvest to stay competitive in the marketplace.

Definitions and concepts you will need to know:

- The best time to open a new club is between August 15th and February 15th.

- *Presale:* Selling memberships prior to the club being open. The traditional extended presale is dated and has been replaced by a shorter and more efficient soft presale lasting about a month.

- A new club should be able to cover its operating expenses in seven to nine months.

- *70% coverage rule:* Your goal is to cover 70% of your BOE (base operating expense) through your net receivable check from the accumulated member payments.

- *25th month:* The most important month in a new generation because this is where the business plan should be validated through income from the receivable base, profit centers, and renewals.

- *Renewals:* Members who have completed a fixed membership with a club and signed again for another fixed term such as one year.

- Member retention and the ability to remain competitive in your market come from reinvestment in your club.

Every Fitness Business Passes Through Defined Stages of Maturity

Before you can really understand the working numbers that form the foundation of a fitness business, it's best to step back and look at how a fitness business grows through its first four to five years of existence. Most fitness businesses pass through the same stages of maturity at approximately the same time periods. These are important phases to be aware of because at each level of maturity certain things should be happening in the business that will indicate whether the business is on its proper track to be successful. The *four levels of maturity* are:

- The club's first year of business.
- The club's second year of business.
- The 25th month after the club opens.
- The 48th month through the beginning of the fifth year.

Each of these stages is a distinct phase the business will pass through and each will have its own implications and effects on your business. Again, by being aware of these phases of maturity you will be able to make better business decisions concerning your club, and you will also be less likely to panic and overreact to what's happening in the business at the present time.

...by being aware of these phases of maturity you will be able to make better business decisions concerning your club, and you will also be less likely to panic and overreact to what's happening in the business at the present time.

The First Year

The first year always surprises new owners, and not just a few experienced ones, because of the way the cash arrives and the receivable base grows. To give your business the best chance of survival you should be very particular about the time of year you plan to open. The best time frame for opening would be around August 15th, but no later than February 15th. By opening in this time frame, you can take advantage of the fall selling season, defined as the increase in potential member traffic after the Labor Day holiday, as well as the normal rush in February and March.

By opening in this time period you should also be able to minimize the cash reserves the new business needs to cover operating losses until the business reaches its breakeven point. Opening earlier in the summer means opening for a nonexistent clientele. You'll have some business but not enough to create any energy or excitement for you or your staff. It's just hard to generate a substantial opening when most of your potential market is locked into their outdoor summer activities and won't begin thinking about joining a fitness facility until fall.

Opening later than February 15th eliminates the chance to develop any type of monthly income from the member payments, called *building a receivable base*, because normal traffic decreases for most clubs in late April and May. Your profit centers over the summer, after a late spring opening, will also suffer because you don't have enough members on a daily basis to generate any type of significant cash flow. Opening anytime between February 15th and the middle of August will force you to add at least a third month of operating reserve to your cash pool that will be spent on base operating expenses before the club reaches its breakeven point.

Trying to Change the Game Through Presales

Presales are part of the history of the fitness industry, but they are definitely not part of the future. The presale dates back to the 1960s and was used to raise enough capital to actually get the club opened. Most owners were terribly undercapitalized in those days and to make up for their lack of cash they attempted to presale their way into the business.

It was not unusual in those early days of the fitness industry for a presale to last for two years. Compared to doing business in today's more sophisticated markets, early presales were somewhat primitive, usually featuring two guys in an old trailer on a vacant lot in a town that had not yet seen its first fitness center. There was always a huge sign on the lot making a bold statement, *Coming Soon! New Fitness Center Phase One.*

If the presale, meaning the two guys in the trailer, sold enough memberships, then they poured the foundation and started on phase two. If you were successful in phase two, you built the walls and the build outs, and if you made it to the last phase you added the equipment and were open.

Not many guys made it to opening. Somebody ran off with somebody's wife or a trip to Las Vegas went bad and you packed up the trailer, found another lot, and started all over again at phase one. This, by the way, is why any member over 30-years old hates presales.

Eventually the attorney generals in most states wised up to this game and the rules were changed to prevent the consumer from being taken. However, you might consider other reasons for a different type of presale.

The goal of a presale was to generate enough member payments so that the club opened with a substantial monthly check from its receivable base, which again is the total of all monthly payments owned the club by the members. Theoretically, this is a sound idea but the system does have some flaws if analyzed carefully.

First of all, a supposed modern presale should only last six months. Simply put, an owner sets up a small office in their new gym space and sells memberships prior to the club opening while the construction is going on around them. A sales guy for a presale is armed with a piece of equipment that will be featured in the club, sketches of what the club will look like when done, and a serious discount off of what the normal prices will be when the club opens.

> **Compared to doing business in today's more sophisticated markets, early presales were somewhat primitive, usually featuring two guys in an old trailer on a vacant lot in a town that had not yet seen its first fitness center.**

This is flawed because the owner is giving up way too much return per member to buy these first few sales. If someone is going to buy a membership six months out, then he is going to want a serious discount. Why would an owner give this potential added income up by discounting so far out? Because they are short of cash and desperately need the money to open? This is usually not the case anymore. In the Plummer Company seminars over the last few years, we have seen more well-funded startups then we have in the preceding 15 years. More money in the economy means more people are getting into the fitness business well capitalized.

If you are not well capitalized, then your chances of success are much lower today than they were 10 years ago because your competitors are well capitalized and will beat you to death with a better business plan.

If you are not well capitalized, then your chances of success are much lower today than they were 10 years ago because your competitors are well capitalized and will beat you to death with a better business plan. The old system of selling your way into the business just doesn't work anymore since so many of today's owners have access to relatively cheap capital through banks, private investors, and the SBA.

So assuming the club has enough money not to give their future away before they even open in membership discounts, start with the first 500 new members a club will get through the doors. Whether you discount starting six months out, or patiently wait and get full price the last 30 days before you open, the first 500 people will be the same. In other words, by restricting your presale to 30 days or less, you will get the same first 500 at full price. Don't forget the 12-minute drive-time rule: *85-90 percent of your members will come from within 12-minutes of your club.* You are going to get these people anyway.

For example, you plan to open the club at $49 per month per member with a membership fee of $89. If you presale six months out you will probably discount down to about $30 per member instead of the $49. You'll have to go this low because no member is going to give you full price that far out. The only way you will get him to join is by giving him a deal, which reduces the return per member.

The scam in the old days was using charter memberships, which was another way of saying you're the first sucker who was talked into paying for an unfinished gym six months out. They had nothing to sell you so instead they'll give you a cool piece of paper stating that you're a charter member if you give them money today.

By waiting and doing a presale of about 30 days prior to opening, those first 500 members could have been signed into the club for the full $49 per month with a somewhat reduced membership fee. The membership fee could have been discounted to $49 and the club could have developed a presale package that might have included a gym bag, water bottle, tee shirt, a prepaid card to the club's juice bar, and other small items that would add value. Instead of discounting, you are giving positive incentives to buy the sale prior to opening; and most importantly, getting the full monthly price per member.

Another Major Flaw

What happens to the presale people if the club doesn't open on time? It is normal operating procedure for a club to open 60 days or more late. What about those people who signed up six months out in a normal presale? They are not happy and they will vent their frustration. Don't forget the 20/20 rule: *In any new project you'll be 20% over budget and it will take 20% longer than you plan.*

Opening a new club is hard enough without trying to start with negative word of mouth in the newspapers and in the local population. By waiting until you are just 30 days out from opening, you can actually show a potential member an almost finished physical plant. And if you're 30 days out, you are probably pretty likely to open on time.

The 90-Member Per Month Customer-Service Rule

Suppose you do an old-style presale and it works. During the six months prior to opening you sign up 500 members. The date is set for your actual opening and during the first two weeks about 400 of the 500 new members show up for their first workouts. How many of these people will need help getting started on their new programs? You'd be safe to plan for all of them, because even if they have gym experience they don't have experience with your new gym.

After years of studying the service issue in clubs, it's safe to say a fitness business can't handle more than 90 new members added to their system each month and still service those members properly. It also gets to the point that it's not economically feasible for a club, especially in labor costs, to try and properly set up more than 90 new members per month.

Back to the previous example, if 400 or so new members appeared during the first week, the club would be out of control. Sure, you would have a pretty large check coming in that first month but your member service word of mouth for the new club would be horrible. Your first month out and the only word on the street is that your club is too crowded and you have no member service because you have too many new members. This is not the word of mouth you just invested 1.5 million dollars in your new club to hear. The basic rule that governs this situation is: *Most members make up their minds to renew their memberships during their first 30 days as a member, not their last 30 days.*

What this means is that your father was right; you only get one chance to make a good first impression. By stuffing the club through your successful presale, you will actually severely hurt yourself 12 months later when those first 500 members are up for renewal.

They may pay for a year because they are honest citizens, but when the time comes to reinvest in the club, they will be seeking other facilities. Put

Your first month out and the only word on the street is that your club is too crowded and you have no member service because you have too many new members.

everything you can into the new members first 30-day experience and you'll reap the rewards later with long-term member retention. Overload the club with an aggressive discounted presale and you'll pay that price later in lost members and bad word of mouth.

The alternative to this is to stagger your marketing by taking your same presale budget and spreading it over the 30 days prior to opening and during the first 90 days of operation. You will still buy the same number of new sales but you'll give yourself a chance to properly service the new members since they will be arriving in a more controlled pattern (See Figure 2-1).

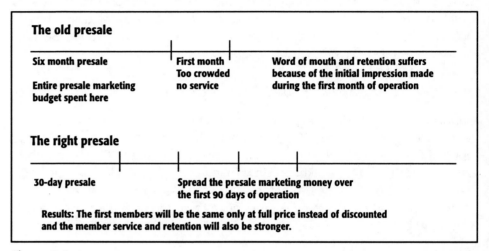

The old presale

Six month presale	First month	Word of mouth and retention suffers
	Too crowded	because of the initial impression made
Entire presale marketing	no service	during the first month of operation
budget spent here		

The right presale

30-day presale   Spread the presale marketing money over
the first 90 days of operation

Results: The first members will be the same only at full price instead of discounted and the member service and retention will also be stronger.

Figure 2-1.

And even if you don't do the same number of new sales you will still make more money because you won't be discounting six months out. By waiting until the last 30 days prior to opening and then loading up the first 90 days you're actually opened, you will get full price for the members who do join and that means you will be getting a higher return per member.

Understanding the First Year of a New Fitness Business

If you get the club opened during the months previously described, your first year should look something like Figure 2-2. This chart is a graphic representation of how the expenses and revenues should flow in the first year.

By waiting until the last 30 days prior to opening and then loading up the first 90 days you're actually opened, you will get full price for the members who do join and that means you will be getting a higher return per member.

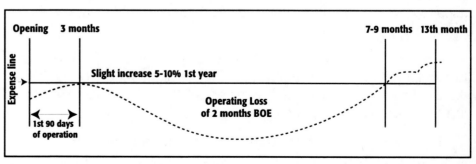

Figure 2-2.

Beginning at the left of the chart is the first 90 days of actual operation. The club's monthly *base operating expense* (BOE) is usually consistent from the day you open. BOE is defined as what it takes each month to pay the club's bills. This includes all salaries, debt service, leases, and general operating costs.

A more common term is called the *breakeven point*, but this is not quite as accurate since this is usually defined as the bills actually paid, not the total bills due. BOE represents the actual cost of running a business on a month-to-month basis.

Most clubs will begin with a almost full staff contingent, profit centers should be in place, loans and the debt structure are already being paid back, and of course the basics such as phones and utilities are on and functioning. The expenses will gradually increase over the first year, usually in the 5 to 10 percent range, as the profit centers become more expensive to operate due to increased sales and your increased traffic forces you to hire another staff person or two.

A side note at this point is don't forget about your *Yellow Page* ad. Find out when you are going to open and make sure you're in the book. A standard rule is go for a quarter-page ad in the main book in black and yellow. Do not ever pay extra for color unless the ad person is a relative you are trying to support in commissions. Many first time owners forget about the ad until they are open and then have to go without for a full year before the book is reprinted.

The one substantial bill you normally won't have your first 90 days of operation is *rent*. It's pretty unusual not to end up with at least 90-days free rent for a new business. Referring to Figure 2-2, you will see that expenses and revenues are pretty close during that time period because the rent has not yet kicked in. You also have the revenue from your new sales, the club's monthly receivable check is starting to grow slowly but steadily, and your first wave of members is starting to support your profit centers.

At the end of the third month you'll notice that the expenses and revenues separate rather dramatically. This is when the rent kicks in. At this stage of the business the club is growing according to plan, but is still running negative cash flow. This is also the stage where most new owners panic and run their first desperation sale.

The shaded area represents operating loss (See Figure 2-2). A new club can expect to lose at least two full months of BOE before the club will reach the point that it is paying its own bills. If you know this is coming and plan for it, you're less likely to start running 2-for-1 sales or some other type of blowout special because the club is running negative cash flow. It is supposed to run negative cash flow for at least a few months; the amount

A new club can expect to lose at least two full months of BOE before the club will reach the point that it is paying its own bills.

will equal about two months BOE. Planning for it and being aware of it will make you less likely to panic and start giving away the club.

At about the seven- to nine-month period, the club should start covering its expenses through monthly cash flow. This is actually an amazing thing to happen in small business. The *Small Business Administration* states in their publications that an owner should have at least three years of operating reserve in place before the business will cover its expenses. With a fitness business, you should be able to start showing a positive cash flow in your first year.

As discussed so far, time of opening and getting a decent lease has a lot to do with when you become profitable. If these two factors are in line with the business plan, the club should be able to cover its expenses somewhere at the seven- to nine-month period.

If you open at a less desirable time, such as in May, add at least one extra month of BOE to your reserve. Looking again at Figure 2-2, that dry period between the end of month three and the targeted seven- to nine-month window will be stretched out by at least another month or two. The extra reserve will ensure that the club can survive and keep the owner from running his first panic sale of the long summer.

Between the targeted breakeven point and the end of the year, the club should slowly build a stronger receivable base, start gaining more daily cash flow from its profit centers, and be able to maintain a consistent expense budget. At the end of the first year, at the 13th month, the club should see a surge in its revenue stream due to the first wave of renewals.

Renewals will be discussed in depth in Chapter 3, but for the sake of discussion at this point, renewals fall into two distinct categories. First of all are the closed-end renewals, which means the club actively goes after the members at the end of their initial time period and attempts to renew them for another set time period, a year for example if that was their first membership period. This system builds a solid, defensible receivable base built upon your entire membership always being under some type of contractual obligation.

The other system is a popular but less-effective renewal method. It's called an *open-ended month-to-month* plan. This is less desirable since it turns your best payers into open-ended accounts at the end of their first year. This is a very difficult plan to defend since your most valuable asset, which is your receivable base, can then walk out the door with little notice and join a new competitor down the street.

Both plans will be discussed in depth in Chapter 3, but at this point just assume that you are using closed-end renewals. By again referring to Figure 2-2, you'll see the revenue surge at the 13th month because your presale and first month memberships are renewing in addition to your normal monthly new memberships.

> At about the seven- to nine-month period, the club should start covering its expenses through monthly cash flow. This is actually an amazing thing to happen in small business.

A point here to consider is that if your renewal percentage is small, defined as less than 40 percent, your members most likely took a vote and decided your business plan sucked. They trusted you for a year and then went away. What did you do to drive them out of the business? Make sure you do everything possible to set the members up correctly during their first 30 days rather than loading up your efforts at just renewing them during their last 30 days.

By analyzing the first year, you should be able to get a feel of how a fitness business grows. Of course you could blow this model apart by being obstinate and making profits from the first day. If your club works out this way, celebrate by getting naked and running through the club with a rose in your teeth. The members will love it and it's guaranteed to get your club into the local paper. Don't plan, however, for a club to carry its expenses from the day you open. It may happen but it's safer to plan for a realistic growth pattern and allow for enough reserves to keep you safe.

For the rest of you who are planning for a short-term negative cash flow, you need to build a business plan that follows this model illustrated in Figure 2-2. It's a key component of your business plan to build a lease that gives the business time to get healthy slowly during the first year. The two factors contributing to this health are an extended time of *free rent up front*, and then rent averaging or *reduced rent* for the rest of the first year.

It's a must to plan on operating losses during the first year. Build at least two month's BOE into your business plan as reserve capital. This reserve allows you to stick with the long-term approach of building a strong receivable base that arrives as ever increasing checks from your third-party financial company.

Once the club reaches the point revenues are covering monthly operating expenses, you then slowly build your reserve back up to the point where you have two months BOE. After that point, you can start reinvesting back into the club and still have a degree of safety into the future.

The Second Year

Several milestones should be reached during the second year of operation. All four of these will be discussed in detail later in the book, but at this point each will be highlighted with some basic coverage.

The Single Most Important Number to Track

If there is one number that conveys the strength and stability of a business, it's the *70% coverage rule*. This rule addresses the relationship between the club's monthly base operating expense (BOE) and the monthly receivable check, which is derived from the club's total outstanding receivable base. The rule states: *a club's BOE = 70% coverage.*

A point here to consider is that if your renewal percentage is small, defined as less than 40 percent, your members most likely took a vote and decided your business plan sucked.

A primary goal of your business is to develop a monthly receivable check that covers at least 70% of your BOE.

For example, *if a club's BOE equals $60,000, the 70% coverage will equal $42,000.* What this comparison means is that a primary goal of your business is to develop a monthly receivable check that covers at least 70% of your BOE. This should happen somewhere after the 13th month of operation and before the 25th month. This is the single most important number to track because it determines the strength of the receivable base, the ability to withstand competitors, the retention rate of your membership, and how dependent you are each month on cash flow.

A club that has 70% coverage is a healthy business that has the bulk of its monthly expenses paid by the members making their monthly payments. In the previous example, the club only needs $18,000 of additional revenue from membership sales and profit centers to breakeven. If a club sold too many cash prepaid memberships each month it will always feel like it is operating as if it just opened. The club with 70% coverage could actually last a number of months with slow membership sales and still stay in business because of its cash flow from its existing members.

Getting a First Look at Your Renewals

As discussed earlier, your first wave of renewals hit during the 13th month. Each month after that you will have members whose memberships expire and who then have the option to renew again for another year.

The national average for renewals has hovered around 20 percent for a number of years. Put another way, if your club has 1,000 members today, 12 months later there would only be 200 left. This is a bad business plan but has been acceptable for a number of years because that was the state of the industry at the time.

A more acceptable goal is *40 percent renewal rate*. About 30 percent of the clubs I've explored over the last 10 years can maintain a renewal rate in this range. It's better than 20 percent but it's still not acceptable for a club trying to play at a higher level.

The goal your club should strive for is 65 percent, which would get you into the top 20 percent of the clubs researched. This is a number you would start looking for during your second year of operation and again, you should starting seeing this number somewhere between months 13 to 25 of your business.

Some clubs claim a higher rate than 65 percent in the national magazines, but it's pretty rare to find a legitimate number in that range. Often the number appears higher because the score-keeping system is different. To check your math you should use the following formula: Total members sold during the same month last year (adjusted for losses) = possible renewals for same month this year.

Possible renewals x desired renewal percentage = target renewals

For example, 100 memberships were sold in May of last year (minus 10% losses associated with annual contracts) would equal 90 possible renewals for May (and overlapped into June) for this year. Ninety possible renewals times 65 percent equals 59 members (rounded up) as a target renewal number. Some clubs purge their possible renewals by eliminating those members who haven't attended the club during the last 90 days. Except for losses, meaning the member defaulted on their contract, you should count everyone to keep the math consistent. Whatever system you use, keep it consistent and try to break out of the national average, which is pathetic compared to real business in the real world.

A problem in the fitness business is that it fosters too much inbreeding. You all share your numbers, attend the same trade shows and conferences, and slowly accept being mediocre as the normal way to do business. Could you imagine a meeting at Federal Express where the company president states, "Congratulations gang, we had another great year at good old Fed X; we only lost 80 percent of the packages the public trusted us with to handle. What a year, we did great!"

You have packages that you are entrusted to handle too, and many of your fellow owners lose 80 percent of them each year. At this point, just shoot for a 65-percent retention rate and start looking for that number to happen during the second year.

The Joys of Cash Flow from Profit Centers

One of the most overlooked sources of income in the fitness business is selling products and services to the members you already have in the system. They're in your club, thirsty, hungry, and needing everything from supplements to tanning, and yet most clubs generate very little of their monthly income from profit centers.

The number you derive from this is called the *usage rate* and it compares the number of member workouts per day to the amount of money spent in the profit centers. While this too will be discussed in depth Chapter 9, you do need to review it here since it is something that you need to look for between the 13th and 25th month of operation.

Profit center income is money received from the members for services or amenities in club on a daily basis. Examples here would be munchie bars, personal training, supplements, headphones, and soft drinks and shakes from the juice bar. Not included would be daily drop-in fees for one-day member workouts, payments made at the club, or other monies someone would pay in regards to their ability to work out in the club. In other words, profit center income is money you make from members you already have in the system.

Assuming that the club has at least four profit centers all netting at least 20 percent each per month (less than 20 percent and it becomes a non-profit profit center -- see childcare for an example), the club should be

> They're in your club, thirsty, hungry, and needing everything from supplements to tanning, and yet most clubs generate very little of their monthly income from profit centers.

generating $5 per day per member workout somewhere after the 13th month and before the 25th month. Use this formula to figure this number:

**$ from profit centers for the day divided by
number of member workouts for the day**

For example, $1,000 comes through the register from profit centers for the day divided by 400 member workouts for the day equals $2.50. In this example, the club is doing $2.50 per day per member workout. Your goal during your second year of business is $5 per day per member workout. This is possible during the first year but most owners find that profit centers are accumulative and that they have to reach a certain saturation point with member usage, total members, and club age before it's possible to reach that magical $5 per day number.

When Should the Profit Arrive?

The final second-year reference point to track is your monthly profitability. Obviously you should be aware of profitability during your first year, and as you can tell from Figure 2-2, the seven- to nine-month point to the end of the year the club should be in a profit mode. It's an amazing thing, however, how few owners actually use their monthly profitability as a goal setting reference point.

Based on financial information from fitness facilities across the nation going back to 1971, only about 15 percent of the clubs in the country actually net 20 percent pretax per month. For example, a small club has a monthly BOE of $50,000. For this club to net 20 percent, it should deposit $60,000 per month. The $10,000 difference reflects 20 percent of $50,000 giving the club a $10,000 pretax net for the month.

This doesn't sound like a huge number, but 85 percent of the clubs in the country don't achieve this on a regular basis. Those clubs may hit a month or two during the prime months such as February or March, but they can't maintain that number for a sustained period of time.

The 20 percent net number becomes more important during the second year since the business should be starting to stabilize. The goal is to record six consecutive months of 20 percent net. That signals a secure business that has reached a certain level of financial maturity.

It is also a sign that it may be time to do a second club. That is one of the most often- asked questions by an owner: *When should I open my second club?* The answer to that question is in the net. Net 20 percent for six consecutive months and that current business is probably stable enough to risk another business venture.

The 25th Month

This is a pivotal level of maturity and may be the single most important month for a new fitness business. The 25th month is where the business

> Your goal during your second year of business is $5 per day per member workout.

plan should have been proven out and renewals are strong. The club should have achieved 70 percent coverage of the BOE by the monthly receivable check, a 65-percent renewal or member retention rate, be generating at least $5 per day per member visit usage rate from the multiple profit centers, and showing a consistent net of 20 percent on a monthly basis.

Your banks or investors may want to see a longer-term financial projection than just 25 months when you first start, but for actual financial planning in the trenches, this is an optimal time period because you've experienced two complete renewal cycles. If you remember, the first renewal cycle, reflected by a surge in the monthly income due to the combination of new sales and renewals going back into the system, was at the 13th month.

The second surge of renewals should hit at the 25th month. This is when your first year people are up for their second renewal period. The comforting thing about renewal memberships is that once a member settles in and completes his second year of membership, you almost have to kill them to get them out of the club. Members who sign for a second year only have a loss rate of about three percent per year. This translates into solid, dependable income going into the third year.

And Every 48 Months

The final stage of maturity for a fitness business is actually one that is repeated as a cycle every 48 months. This is also an important stage to be aware of because if you track fitness businesses closely, you'll find that few actually fail during their first year. Where the major problems arise, and where clubs and owners start to disappear, is somewhere in that 48-month period.

For clubs to stay competitive, the owners have to reinvest. A club may look fresh for a year or two depending on how it was built, the clientele, and the traffic flow, but after that any physical plant starts to deteriorate. For clubs to stay successful, reinvestment is needed, but most owners don't know when or how much to plan for as part of their yearly business plans.

A good rule to use is to tie your reinvestment to your initial startup investment for your build out. Be aware of a strong correlation between the cost of your build out and what you will have to spend over every four-year period to keep the club competitive in the marketplace. For example, the following are typical startup costs for a 10,000 square foot mainstream fitness center that is leased and was started as a standard vanilla box:

- The build out will be $35 per square foot for the interior. This again is without equipment but includes floor covering, wall covering, lighting, mirrors and glass, and the rest of the items discussed earlier in the first chapter (total cost at 10,000 square feet is $350,000).

- Equipment cost for this facility will be $300,000. To figure equipment cost for your facility you should use the following formula:

First 10,000 square feet use $30,000 per 1,000

**For every 1,000 square feet after the
initial 10,000 use $8,000 per thousand**

This formula uses the entire square footage of your building, not just your workout floor. This formula also reflects current trends in cardio, such as running two distinct cardio pods in the club instead of one massive cardio exhibit, which is good for the owner's ego but really bad for the members. Working out in a huge pile with about 90 of your most intimate friends, intimate because the equipment almost touches and you can smell your neighbor, is not a member's idea of a great fitness experience. Using this formula, a 15,000 square foot club would have equipment costs of $340,000. A 20,000-square-foot facility would be $380,000 (total cost at 10,000 square feet is $300,000).

> **Working out in a huge pile with about 90 of your most intimate friends, intimate because the equipment almost touches and you can smell your neighbor, is not a member's idea of a great fitness experience.**

Your reserve capital would be two month's BOE, or figuring the rent at $10,000 would make the total BOE $50,000. As will be explained later in detail, the rent or mortgage factor is about one-fifth of the entire BOE. If you know your rent factor, simply take it times five and that should be your approximate total BOE. In this example, two month's BOE would be $50,000 times two, or $100,000 (total cost at 10,000 square feet is $100,000).

Stuff is the final category. Stuff includes desks, computers, initial inventory, the mandatory extras such as a Cardio Theater system, and just general stuff that we need to get opened. To figure stuff, use the following formula:

First 10,000 square feet use $7,500 per 1,000

**For every 1,000 square feet after the
initial 10,000 use $1,500 per thousand**

This formula also uses the entire square footage of the club and reflects all the basics a club needs to get started including a core base of at least four profit centers. Using this formula, a 15,000 square foot club would have about $82,500 of stuff needed to open. This is based on $75,000 for the first 10,000 square feet, and then an additional $1,500 per 1,000 square feet, or a total of $82,500 (total cost at 10,000 square feet is $75,000).

Initial marketing would also be a separate line item for a startup. Using the 30-day presale model discussed earlier, you should allow at least $10,000 for initial marketing. Marketing from the date of opening is included in the anticipated BOE. Budgeting will be discussed in Chapter 11, but at this point just figure 8% of the total BOE will be your monthly marketing budget.

In the following example, a startup club budgeted $350,000 for build out. *In relationship to the maturity levels a fitness business goes through, the club will have to reinvest this same amount (equal to the build out) over every four-year period to stay competitive.* The total cost for this 10,000 square foot startup would be:

Build out -- $350,000
Equipment -- $300,000
Reserve capital -- $100,000
Stuff -- $75,000
Marketing -- $10,000
Total startup costs -- $835,000

Although the initial investment didn't include equipment, the reinvestment would include all aspects of the club including equipment, redoing walls, adding cardio decks, upgrading juice bars, or adding a new trendy piece of cardio or programming, such as the impact ellipticals and Pilates.

To plan for this reinvestment, you should use two monthly budgeting tools. Both of these will be separately explained under accrual accounts in the budgeting section, but they are also relevant to this section, too.

Repairs and Maintenance as a Planning Tool

Most owners have a deathly fear of spending any money to keep their facilities up to competitive speed, because if you can't lift it or play with it, they don't want it. This is an area where a little thought and extra budgeting will make a big difference in your business. The repair-and-maintenance rule is: *Budget $150 for every 1,000 square feet with a minimum of $1,500.*

You should use this number as part of an accrual system. This means that you write the check each month whether you incur actual expenses or not. For example, say you have a 15,000-square-foot facility. Using this rule, you should budget $2,250 per month for repairs and maintenance. During an actual month you might only spend $800. A more sophisticated owner would move the budgeted $1,450 that wasn't spent to an accrual account, which is a separate savings account the club maintains just for accrual categories in the budget.

You're going to spend this money sooner or later, so you might as well create a forced savings account that allows for the inevitable. If you don't save the unspent budget item, just when you least expect it your air conditioning dies or 30 tiles in your shower area take a high dive to floor. Accrual budgeting forces you save money for reinvestment in the business for the day-to-day necessities of facility maintenance, that left undone, cost you new business, and member retention.

Budgeting for Capital Improvements

The second accrual budget item you should use is for capital improvements such as equipment or structural changes. The line item on the budget is capital improvement and you should use the same repair-and-maintenance rule: *Budget $150 for every 1,000 square feet with a minimum of $1,500.*

This budget item is also used as part of an accrual system. You obviously won't buy equipment every month, but by budgeting for future purchases,

The repair-and-maintenance rule is: *Budget $150 for every 1,000 square feet with a minimum of $1,500.*

you will ultimately reduce your operating debt ratio by saving enough to be able to put enough down a significant amount on future purchases, keeping your debt service manageable. During the months you don't buy anything, move your capital improvement number to the savings account. This will allow you to have a working war chest of money to reinvest and stay current as the need arises.

The True Power of Reinvestment

> **Reinvestment in your facility on a regular, planned basis can be defined to an owner as member retention and it also means making a new sale much easier.**

Reinvestment in your facility on a regular, planned basis can be defined to an owner as member retention and it also means making a new sale much easier. By keeping the club competitive, you also force competitors to reinvest to match your progress.

It's just like the *Cold War* all over again. Sooner or later America just had to outspend the USSR, forcing them to either keep up or get out of the game. The USSR couldn't maintain the pace and folded their hand, and your competitors will do the same if you follow a systematic approach to reinvestment in your club.

Another way to look at reinvestment is to compare it to poker. It's a small, friendly, Thursday night game with your competitors. Your first competitor across town antes $10, your competitor down the street is in for $10, and then it's your turn. You put $10,000 in the pot and it's back to them. By reinvesting in your club you are keeping the stakes in the game high enough to force your competitors to either keep up or get out of the game.

To better understand reinvestment, you should understand a few key points in your club that need to be reviewed on a daily or monthly basis. You should also create and maintain a reinvestment schedule for a four-year period of time. An example of a reinvestment schedule for atypical 10,000-square-foot facility will be reviewed later in this chapter.

Reinvesting in Your Club During Your First Year

Architect Rudy Fabiano's Ten Economical Things that Will Keep Your Business Fresh

- *Paint:* Touch up the paint in the club every month or more as often as needed. The smell of fresh paints makes members think about a nice clean club. Also, change a few highlight walls every year. If an accent wall is blue, and it would work with yellow, then consider changing that wall every year to give the members a sense of change.

- *Drop-ceiling tiles:* Put this on a checklist and look at them every month. At the first sign of a stain, replace the offending tile immediately. Stained tiles give the members a sense of an unclean club. Remember to force yourself to look. Most owners just stop seeing the damage because they stop truly seeing the club. But a prospective member on her first tour sees everything. If all else fails, let your mom take a look at your club. Don't worry, she'll find everything that needs to be fixed including that 20 pounds you need to lose.

- *Wax the floors:* Once a month have a service strip and wax any flooring in the club. Waxed floors are very impressive and dull floors are just that — dull.

- *Move the equipment and vacuum:* Once a month move everything and vacuum. A lot of dirt accumulates on the inside of grounded equipment frames. To properly clean around most of this type of equipment, you need to move it and do it right.

- *Bathrooms:* Seal the tile the first time correctly and cleaning the bathrooms gets a lot easier. Paint often in the bathroom to hide scuffs, dust the top of your lockers, fix all locks, hinges, and hooks, and try to add amenities such as nice stainless coat racks on a regular basis. For the women's locker room, barter with a florist and have large displays of fresh cut flowers in a decorative vase on the vanity that are changed weekly. I tried this in the guy's locker room, but they kept eating them so we had to stop.

- *Equipment:* You have to stock spare parts for your equipment. Broken equipment is an absolute retention killer in any club. When you buy cardio, commit to one line and then stock all of the spare parts necessary to maintain that line. For example, if you buy four different types of treads, you have to have four different repair kits, something no owner on earth will stick with for long. If you buy all your treads from one company, then you only have to stock one repair kit, something more likely to happen in a working club.

- *The front desk:* Members equate clutter with being dirty, and the home of all clutter in a club is the front-desk area. It always starts nice and clean when the club opens, and then the signal is sent that it's time to clutter up the front counter. This opening gambit in the clutter war is usually the American Express application box.

    In the over 25 years of being around fitness facilities, I have never actually seen a real person deliver one of those boxes. It's like it just magically appears on the counter one day. After the seal is broken the flood follows with charity boxes, race forms, notebooks, and piles of paperwork, all combining to give the club a cluttered and messy appearance, especially to potential members on their first visit.

    Remember that most owners and managers spend more time in the club than they do at home, and after a while they stop seeing the club in a business light. It's like home and they nest in it and the clutter begins. Once a month completely clean the counter area down to its most simple and basic form. This is the area of your first impression and it should be a strong as you can make it.

- *The juice bar:* If a juice bar is done correctly, it becomes the social center of the club. This is where everyone meets, socializes, and does business

If all else fails, let your mom take a look at your club. Don't worry, she'll find everything that needs to be fixed including that 20 pounds you need to lose.

If a juice bar is done correctly, it becomes the social center of the club. This is where everyone meets, socializes, and does business within the club. The concept behind a good juice bar, besides it being a profit center in itself, is to stop members for a few minutes entering and leaving the club.

within the club. The concept behind a good juice bar, besides it being a profit center in itself, is to stop members for a few minutes entering and leaving the club. If you can stop them, then you can sell them just about anything. The juice bar allows you to slow the member down long enough to get them to notice the other profit centers in the club. Because you do other business at the bar besides make shakes and deliver food, you often forget that the juice bar is really like a restaurant in the member's minds. They are buying food and expect the delivery system to be as clean as a McDonald's restaurant, nationally known as perhaps the cleanest of all fast-food delivery systems. The juice bar needs to be cleaned thoroughly on a daily basis.

- *Clean the mirrors:* Mirrors are like driving a white car in Chicago in the winter. If you want it to look nice, you need to clean it everyday. Mirrors magnify the slightest spots and smears and have to be constantly maintained to give the club that extra clean image.

- *Take care of the rubber mats:* Dust balls and black rubber mats go together like peanut butter and jelly, and are just about as messy. These need to be cleaned daily especially around and under the treadmills and in the center areas of the support legs on your equipment.

Other Reinvestment Considerations During Your First Year

A common mistake for most new owners is that they try and open a perfect gym their first time out. Every conceivable piece of equipment is in its place, all the programming is there and working perfectly, and the club is on the cover of a major fitness trade publication as club as the year.

Several flaws permeate this perfect-world scenario. First of all, an owner who in her mind builds the prefect fitness business has a difficult time making any changes to that business later as the club matures. For example, an owner might open with a perfect, state-of-the-art 1989 aerobics room because that's where her mind is frozen in time, and then she finds that aerobics is out and an entirely different form of group exercise is in, and the room needs to be redesigned to be effective. Because she is emotionally tied to her prefect club, she might make the change, but probably much later than it needs to be done.

The second flaw in opening a totally completed gym is that the members have nowhere to go that will impress them. They spend money every day and the owner must be taking it home because he sure isn't reinvesting in the business. Members need to see a constant reinvestment in the club or they lose faith. Think of members as a herd of four- year olds. They have a big Christmas and then the next day they want to know where today's packages are.

To keep the members entertained, member retention high, and to keep the competitors anteing up in the business game, you need to reinvest on a set, regular basis in the club. In relationship to fixed equipment, you need to show members the money starting near the end of your first year of business.

Equipment

Never open a club with all of the equipment. Instead, plan for opening the club with about 80 percent of your anticipated equipment needs and then add additional pieces toward the end of the first year. Make sure you get credit with the members when you add new toys. Most owners simply put the equipment on the floor and hope the members get excited.

Compare this to club owner Joseph Bencomo from El Paso, Texas, who bought his members a 13-piece circuit for Christmas. On December 1st, he set the equipment around a 30-foot Christmas tree, put giant red ribbons on each piece, and made a giant Christmas card to the members thanking them for the year and letting them know about his Christmas present to the membership.

When you reinvest with only one piece, get credit for it. Set it in front of the counter for a week, set up an easel with the company's brochure detailing the piece, and then have a trainer assigned to it for a few days when it's moved to the floor.

Programming

The same theory goes for programming, too. Never open with everything in place. Add additional programming throughout the first year as membership increases and the seasons change. Most owners move to posting quarterly schedules that give them the option of adding new offerings as needed, as well as giving them the chance to drop the dogs. Never get stuck with a perpetual schedule from the 1990s that makes it difficult to change any classes or times because of those last three women still doing the last step class in America.

Staff Training and Development

Your business's profit potential will flatten out quickly if you don't reinvest in your staff starting from the day you open. Get an outside, structured-sales trainer into your club just prior to opening and again at about the six-month mark. Staff will have changed and six months of experience will mandate a second major training session.

After the ninth month of operation, begin budgeting for staff training. Your future is a trained staff and you need to budget on a monthly basis for training and development. A consistent staff budget would be:

Budget 3% of your monthly base operating expense.

For example, if your monthly base operating expense (BOE) is $60,000, your staff budget for training and development would be three percent of that number, or $1,800 per month. This is also an accrual-account line item. You won't spend $1,800 every month, but move the money anyway to your accrual savings account.

Never open a club with all of the equipment. Instead, plan for opening the club with about 80 percent of your anticipated equipment needs and then add additional pieces toward the end of the first year.

Staff training usually occurs in large chunks, such as sending your staff to an IHRSA convention or other major trade show, or bringing in a trainer to the club that may cost $3,000 a weekend plus expenses. By saving each month, taking your key people to a show won't seem like such a big hit in your monthly budget.

Your Second Year of Business

If you're doing your monthly work on the club, it still should be somewhat fresh and ready for new business. The second year, however, is when the wear and tear of consistent member traffic begins to show.

The second year is also where you realize that somewhere in your game plan you guessed wrong. You will miss something you need and that the members can't live without whether it is a vital program, space consideration, or profit center you missed. The second year is usually about correcting the mistakes you made in your original business plan. The following is a list of things to look for during your second year that may need revision or correction.

It May Be in the Equipment

You're probably going to be short of equipment by plan and today is the time to correct. If you opened at 80 percent of perfect, adjusted again near the end of the first year, and are achieving your membership numbers, you will still be short. Most of the mistakes are usually in the cardio area, but don't forget your entertainment areas. Things like televisions are cheap visuals and can be added to dead corners in the workout floors, locker rooms, and near the juice bar.

Things like televisions are cheap visuals and can be added to dead corners in the workout floors, locker rooms, and near the juice bar.

It May Be in the Profit Centers

You should have opened with your core profit centers in place. As a review, the core centers would be drink coolers, the Apex weight loss management system, supplements and snack bars, a full blown juice/sports bar configuration, basic clothing built upon tee shirts and shorts, and support items for your group activities and sports enhancement program such as boxing gloves, yoga mats, bike shorts, and workout gloves. For more information on profit centers refer to my first book, *Making Money in the Fitness Business*, which has a dedicated chapter to profit centers and how to get them to work for your club.

During the second year you may need to add another profit center or two to your club. Add profit centers one at a time, master that center, and then move on slowly. If you opened with your core centers, only look to add another center or two during your second year. You are better off doing fewer but doing each center as well as possible.

It May Be in the Locker Rooms

Out of everything in your physical plant, it's the locker rooms that take the biggest beating during the first year of operation. That, coupled with the fact that locker rooms are traditionally underfinished anyway by owners short on money but long on no fear of getting started, makes dealing with your back area a prime consideration in the second year. Small tips that pay off in the back area are:

- Getting real doors on the showers instead of curtains.

- Painting everything in the back area at least once a year.

- Upgrading your benches if needed.

- Placing short partitions between the urinals to add privacy.

- Insetting the sinks as opposed to those that sit on top of the counters is a classy touch.

- Adding more tile work if you were short the first time.

- Cleaning and repairing the lockers, especially hinges, locks, and the hooks inside. Don't forget to paint any stains or scuffs inside the lockers.

- Adding amenities such as cut flowers in the woman's locker area, soaps, and personal service items on the counters, quality (not low rent stuff) hairdryers, and other upscale touches the members may not be expecting.

- Piping in a quiet music background to the locker rooms separate from the main system.

- Installing better quality towel dispensers.

- Conducting major repairs and maintenance in the wet areas including removing stains in the sauna and replacing detail work in the steam room.

- Installing coat racks with stainless hangers.

- Purchasing wastebaskets with tops.

These may seem like small items but combined can turn a mediocre locker room into a quality presentation. Most of these items may not have been on your first-year list but should be mandatory for your second year of business.

> Locker rooms are traditionally underfinished anyway by owners short on money but long on no fear of getting started.

It May Be in the Employees

Employees in today's market are very valuable assets that are difficult to replace once they understand and can make money in your system. During your second year you need to start giving the employees a sense that this is a real job with benefits and training beyond what they could expect on the real market.

If you could not afford it during your first year, you need to add insurance for all full-timers during the second year. A full-time employee is one who works more than 32 hours per week, but your local insurance person may have his own definition of what defines full-time when it comes to providing benefits.

If your club is meeting its revenue projections and is operating with profit, then during the second year consider adding other employee benefits beyond insurance such as a 401(K) plan. You should talk to a financial advisor about the many options here before getting started, but to keep quality staff any length of time you need to add a form of the same basic benefits he would find in the real working world.

Staff education should be a standard part of your second year, especially at the management-team level. Your three percent of BOE is enough to cover a lot of training, but make sure you are directing your staff toward education that is going to advance the club. Management schools, intensive sales training, IHRSA conventions, and training directed at covering the employee's individual weaknesses should be part of all the education for management-team members.

> **Management schools, intensive sales training, IHRSA conventions, and training directed at covering the employee's individual weaknesses should be part of all the education for management-team members.**

Beware of the Trends

Most programming has about a two-year window for a consumer's attention span. A typical member has that *been there, done that, what's next* mindset that severely cramps an owner's long-term planning ability. Just when you master a new program, get the instructors going, and buy the toys that go with it, the members want something else they read about that's new and exciting and that you don't have any idea of what it is, how to get it, or how to teach it.

Don't get married to your programming. Programming is very short-term in nature and has a limited lifespan. Unfortunately, most owners can't get past this point: "Hey, I own 50 steps and you will do steps even if we are the last step program in the free world. I own steps and you will step and I don't care who is kickboxing (or whatever else is the rage today)."

The other side of this issue is that you will have to introduce new programming into your club every year to stay current. Some of the newer programming in the market, such as Pilates and kickboxing, which were still in style at the time of this writing, are relatively expensive to add, but both are extremely desirable to the members.

Your Third and Fourth Years of Business

Nightclubs last about six months and then the theme is dead. Restaurants look dated after just a few years in business. Even your house gets rearranged on a regular basis. Why is it then that most fitness facilities don't change until member retention falters, new sales drop off, and your spouse leaves you for someone with a fresher gym?

> **Why is it then that most fitness facilities don't change until member retention falters, new sales drop off, and your spouse leaves you for someone with a fresher gym?**

Every three or four years you need to reinvent your business from the ground up. Not just remodeling, but also a major reinvention of your business plan, from how you charge and collect your money to the name of the place. You change, your members change, the cultural expectations of what a fitness business should be changes, and your business needs to change as well.

By the third year your business starts to become flat to the consumer especially if nothing major has happened. It's not unusual for a club three years into business to have the equipment sitting in the exact same place the sales people set it up, the exact same colors as the day it opened, and the exact same programming schedule, all very much out of date.

This sameness is a business killer because your members drift away and really don't know the exact reasons as to why. To them it's just not as exciting coming to workout as it was a year or so ago. They can't really put their finger on the exact reason when you call them at home to find out where they went. They will try and come up with something vague, such as no time or working out at home, but the important thing is they are gone and no longer paying you.

What's the real reason they are gone? You bored them to death slowly during every visit to the club. They simply lost the excitement of working out in your club because nothing ever changed, and in fact, it got worse because everything started wearing out and you didn't even notice it.

Major changes need to happen in the third and fourth years to drive member retention and to maintain club profitability. Major changes mean major reinvention starting with the concept of the club. The following are a few questions that need to be answered during this time period that will direct your planning.

Is Your Concept Still Valid?

You built an upscale gym expecting the 22- to 40-year-old market and three years later you own a facility filled with people in their mid-30s and older. In this case your market didn't turn out like you expected and your game plan needs to change.

If you are a licensed gym your name may not be a legitimate choice for the market you actually attract and may limit new sales since your potential population has the wrong connotation about your business. Or, your members have become the types that might embrace a licensed name and program. Your marketing approach is another factor that may be limiting your profits since you may be still targeting the wrong demographic groups in your ad campaign. Part of your new business plan should be to identify and change your concept to match your current club population and then make all the necessary changes that would support the new direction.

Is Your Equipment Still Right for What You Own?

You bought too many stair machines when you opened, but today elliptical drive machines are what the members want and you only have two. You may have too much free-weight stuff and not nearly enough cardio for prime times. Those steel plates are tearing up your equipment and today you have the money for rubber coated. Your prime cardio are treads and they are wearing out quickly. Even your first generation studio cycles are three-years old and are showing their age in repair bills.

Equipment is one of those areas that demand a serious amount of attention during your third and fourth year of business because this is when all of the flaws in your initial plan are highlighted. If you added equipment as advised at the end of your first year, and again during your second, then your third and fourth won't hurt you as badly. If you didn't, you may need to replace a high percentage of your existing equipment as well as add pieces you are missing.

Is Your Name Outdated?

Contrary to popular belief, it is okay to change your name.

Contrary to popular belief, it is okay to change your name. It's not something you do weekly, but it is something you can do if you picked wrong name in the beginning and your name either no longer reflects the population in your gym, or it became dated and gives potential members a negative image of what to expect from your business.

An example would be the name *Athletic Club*. Using athletic club in your name had a solid run for about 8 to 10 years starting in the mid-1980s. Sometime in the early 1990's someone looked around and said, "Wow, this name is no longer groovy and seems so 1980's." And they were right as determined from member surveys. A group of members who were shown a list of names and asked to comment about each name stated that *athletic club* was out of style and sounded rather stuffy to them.

Another name that has had its ups and downs over the years is *gym*. In the early 1980s, the licensed guys had to add something such as *fitness-and-aerobic center* to their licensed name to let the consumer know that the gym they owned wasn't a gym but rather a fitness facility with a gym name. In the year 2000, *gym* is back and is actually a desirable name again because of its use in current popular magazines.

If your name does become dated, then change it but do it with a plan. Run simultaneous names for at least six months and state in the ads that the name has changed but it's still the same great owners and management team. The only thing that has changed is the name to reflect a broader concept and expanded services.

Is Your Design Getting in the Way of Making Money?

This is the one that really hurts. You've opened and had three years of business experience and today you have to admit that a blind monk on hallucinogenics designed your gym. Hey, this is easier than admitting that you designed it yourself and it looks like a blind monk did it. Nothing flows, the workout area is too big, the cardio area is too small, the juice bar/check-in area is not functional, and the locker rooms aren't used because they were never finished correctly in the first place.

If the place isn't functional to you, then it probably isn't functional to your members either. To you it's workable; to them it's an annoyance and they punish you by drifting away to another club that is just as bad, but as members they just haven't had the time to get annoyed there yet. If a club is not working functionally, there could be three distinct issues causing the problem, each with its own cost factor to solve it:

- *The efficiency of design:* You probably didn't really need that 3,000-square-foot aerobics room after all. Nor did that enormous lounge area, designed at the sacrifice of reduced cardio, end up being used as you thought. These are deficiency-of-design flaws, similar to the ones mentioned previously, that annoy members and frustrate your sales efforts to new members.

    Flow-and-space allocation is an art form that can change over time depending on offerings in the club, current membership, competition, and personal taste. When a club has deficiencies in this area, a redesign is necessary. A starting number for redesign of a club, which would include moving rooms, possibly redesigning ceilings, upgrading flooring, and adding new features such as a functional juice bar, would start at approximately $15 to $20 per square foot.

    This number could be smaller if some of the core elements don't need to be changed, such as a decent locker room, or it could be higher if it involves a total demolition of the existing physical plant and you are basically starting all over again.

- *Quality of construction:* You just might not have had as much money as you needed to open and you had to cut something to get into the business. What is usually cut is the quality of construction. Assuming that your club flows and that the space usage is somewhat correct, upgrades to the quality of construction during the third and fourth year can add to your curb appeal and member retention. Examples here would be adding a higher quality of shower, better sinks, distinctive doors rather than cheap hollow core, or making improvements to the lighting and construction of the juice bar area. Doing a retrofit on the quality of the club's construction materials can run anywhere from $2 to $5 per square foot. Much of this will be spent in the back-shop areas, which are areas that the members appreciate much more than an owner trying to scrimp and save a little money.

- *Quality of experience:* The quality of experience is a term used by very few owners. To a young owner, the experience comes from having the most equipment or the biggest workout floor. To a jaded owner who has a large mainstream facility, the quality of experience usually comes from

> You've opened and had three years of business experience and today you have to admit that a blind monk on hallucinogenics designed your gym.

providing the program of the month or bragging rights to who has the most service employees. You can find huge facilities in the southern part of the country, most notably Louisiana, which are measured by acreage. These clubs may have every program and offering available for the member, but the quality of the experience is horrible. To the owners, it's bragging about being the biggest and the best. To the members, it's the quality of the delivery system.

To the owners, it's bragging about being the biggest and the best. To the members, it's the quality of the delivery system.

During your third year and beyond you will have to address the quality of the member's experience in the club. This would include looking at, but not limited to, a complete color and energy change based on new carpet and a new paint scheme, upgrading or adding to your mirrors, taking your ceiling presentation to the next level, possibly adding lights or a complete upgrading of your lighting system (you don't know how dead fluorescent lighting really is), or a complete renovation of your juice bar area.

Don't forget that members get bored rather easily and the club will need a major- impact change delivered through colors and design about every three to four years. If your physical plant is functional in the flow and usage, and your goal is upgrade the experience level of the member, your starting number will be somewhere between $5 and $12 a square foot. As you'll notice, this number is somewhere between the two categories previously listed and reflects a more aggressive plan than just trying to retrofit your construction mistakes.

- *A final note:* According to Rudy, the quality of experience may actually be in the efficiency of design factor. In other words, the club has problems in space allocation and usage that prevents the members from truly enjoying the workout experience. A club done right should convey energy and should be something that a member looks forward to each day of their life. Bad design can prevent that from happening. Of course the worse combination would be inefficiency of design coupled with a faded member experience; the club was designed poorly and is whipped and out of date in its carpets and colors.

Building an Obsolescence Plan into Your Working Business Plan

Your club is going to wear out beginning the day you open. By planning for this eventual redesign early on, you will be better prepared later to make the right changes. It's a simple rule of life: *nothing lasts forever.* This includes your new fitness business.

Every three to four years you need to plan for a complete restructuring of your physical plant. What you have today will not last nor will it be competitive in the future. In the fitness business, the average owner only has about an eight-year life span and he is gone. In other words, you can only make about two major cycles of the business and then you just can't do it again. For review, take a look at the cycles again:

- *The first year:* This is where the foundation is laid, both in the financial foundation through the development of a strong receivable base, and through the groundwork of member retention, which is nothing more than hanging on to the members you already bought once.

- *The 13th month:* This is when the first wave of renewals kick in and the club sees a surge in renewal income. This income is being channeled to future improvements through a budget based on using accruals. The club should already be using a forced savings account for repairs and maintenance and capital improvements.

- *The 25th month:* This is when the second wave of renewals hit and the club stabilizes. Key financial goals should have been hit between the 13th and 25th months, including the 70% rule, renewals of annual memberships at 65%, a daily-usage number of $5 per day per member visit, and a 20% pretax net on the monthly BOE (base operating expense).

- *Years three and four:* Between 36 and 48 months of operation, and every 36- to 48-month period after that, your club will need to be reinvented. Times change and so does programming, colors, cardio equipment, the members, and even you and what you want from your business.

An old truism in the fitness business that has been around for years is:

New sales cover the cost of doing business monthly and keeping the doors open.

Renewals (member retention) cover the cost of reinvestment and future growth.

While this adage doesn't allow for any profit centers, which were not part of business plans when this was probably written, it still holds a great deal of truth. If you want to make money you have to keep the customers you have happy and not direct your sole concentration toward just new sales.

If your members are happy they will stay longer and pay longer, which will lead to increased revenues, ultimately leading to enough money to reinvest in your business about every 48 months or as needed. By following and understanding the stages of maturity, you'll make better long-term decisions in your business and learn to face change with a proactive attitude rather than a reactive reaction when things start to deteriorate in your club's physical plant and in your revenue generating capacity.

If your members are happy they will stay longer and pay longer, which will lead to increased revenues, ultimately leading to enough money to reinvest in your business about every 48 months or as needed.

The Key Points You Should Have Gotten from this Chapter

- A club will pass through four levels of maturity over time.

- Old-style presales cause more problems than they solve and have been replaced with a soft presale that provides for more emphasis on the first 30 days a club is open.

- Members make up their mind to renew the first 30 days of their membership, not the last 30 days, which means you need to load up the first 30 with whatever it takes to get a new member comfortably into the system.

- Most new clubs should be able to cover their expenses somewhere during their seven- to nine-month mark if the club is opened during the right months of the year.

- The club owner's ultimate goal is to cover 70% of the base operating expenses (BOE) with its net receivable check.

- The 25th month is the most important month for any fitness business since this is the month when the business plan is validated and the business becomes secure through the strength of the receivable base and renewals.

- Clubs have to stay competitive through consistent reinvestment during the first year.

- Over every three- to four-year period the club may need to be reinvented from the ground up.

3

Building a Future on Renewals and Member Retention

The most important thing you should get from this chapter is:

The future of your business is already in your club.

Definitions and concepts you will need to know:

- *Closed-ended renewals:* A member who originally joined the club with at least a one-year membership, and who at the end of that membership makes a conscious decision to rejoin the club for another fixed term, usually another year.

- *Open-ended renewal:* A member who originally joined the club with at least a one-year membership, and who at the end of that membership then becomes an open-ended member who the club continues to draft each month until the member discontinues it. These members began at the club on contractual obligations but became open-ended during the 13th month. These are also called auto renewals.

- Your target for member retention is 65%.

- The national average for a mainstream fitness center or gym is 30% to 40% retention.

- The club owner controls the member retention. Members don't leave because they are no longer using the club. Members leave because you don't give them a reason to use the club any longer.

- Members thrive on contact, but postcards, paper newsletters, and phone calls are no longer effective. E-mail and electronic newsletters give you an advantage in staying in contact with members.

The Financial Future of Your Business May Already Be in Your Club

Pick up any trade magazine in the country and you'll always see at least one sales article in it geared toward capturing new members, increasing your marketing, or training your staff for a more effective sales presentation. Very few articles, however, are written with solid information as to how to keep the members you already have purchased through your marketing and sales efforts. Granted, you might see the occasional touchy/feely article referring to some club that has a 120 percent renewal rate because the staff smiles, knows names, and gives out free towels. Often these stories are based more on an owner's delusion than any real facts but hey, when you're a club owner, you have don't have to let reality get in your way.

But if you've been in the business any length of time you realize how difficult it is to hold on to your members in significant numbers for any real length of time. Increasing your revenues from retaining members already in the system takes more than getting your staff to smile and read names off a computer screen; it takes a long-term working customer service plan and a tremendous reinvestment in the club on a yearly basis. The majority of fitness businesses never maximize the potential of their business because they never maximize the vast, untapped income that is available through learning how to increase your renewals.

As an industry, you need to find out why you lose people who trusted you with their fitness future by agreeing to be a member for 12 months. Part of your future in this business is to learn how to capitalize on generating income from repeat business, or reoccurring business, through increasing your renewal rate beyond the industry standard.

What Is a Renewal and What Is the Industry Standard?

Owners use many interpretations of what a *renewal* actually is. You can also call your renewals your *member retention rate*. A renewal is defined as a member who originally joined the club on at least a one-year membership, and who at the end of that membership makes a conscious decision to stay with the club for another fixed period of time.

This type of renewal system is called using *closed-ended renewals*. Obviously in this definition, owners using *open-ended renewals*, defined as members who reach the end of the initial period and then continue to get billed month-to-month without having to make a decision as to whether they wish to continue, would not use the renewal term but instead use member retention. This system is also called an *auto renewal*.

The difference between the two terms is defined by making a conscious decision to continue as a member versus the club making the assumption for the member. With open-ended renewal options, the club is not renewing

The difference between the two terms is defined by making a conscious decision to continue as a member versus the club making the assumption for the member.

a member for a fixed period of time, but rather retaining members beyond the first year *(retention rate)* by simply continuing to bill the members until the member decides otherwise *(no conscious decision to continue)*.

Members who join the club on less than one-year memberships are not usually counted in renewal tracking. By restricting your score counting to only one-year and longer memberships, you obtain consistency and will get better numbers to help improve your business.

The philosophy outlined in Chapter 6 uses a 12-month membership as the centerpiece of your financial foundation because of the lower cost of the sale, a higher collection rate due to lower-loss rates, and the competitive advantage a 12-month contractual obligation gives you in the market against a club using a longer-term membership tool. The reasoning behind this is defined in that chapter when building and growing a receivable base is discussed. All renewal information in this chapter will be based upon the use of a 12-month core membership.

Industry information on member retention and renewals is contradictory at best and downright confusing at its worst. Numbers are thrown around trade-show seminars and magazine articles with little background and no back up. The point is that very few owners actually understand a true renewal rate because they don't have key information to determine realistic numbers nor a consistent truthful national guide to compare against.

Without an understanding of loss rates, it's very difficult to develop a working analysis of open-ended renewals. For example, an owner reported in a national trade magazine in the summer of 2000 that she had an 80 percent retention rate at her club after a member completed an initial one-year membership.

An 80 percent retention rate is virtually impossible in any metro area since the number of people that move or even die would be greater than 20 percent. This owner would at least have 15 percent of her members move more than 25 miles away from the club, which mimics the national move-rate average.

Did she adjust for losses from the original population? Is she editing moves and medical cancellations out first and then comparing renewals to the leftover number? Did she have open-ended renewals and only count the 13th month and then didn't compound the losses after that month? To get a true understanding of renewals and how they affect your business you have to gain a working understanding and answers to these questions.

What Are Real Numbers?

With a closed-end system, again referring to a system where members agree to an additional fixed period of renewal time after completing their initial time period, the national average for retention is 30 to 40 percent for a

> Industry information on member retention and renewals is contradictory at best and downright confusing at its worst. Numbers are thrown around trade-show seminars and magazine articles with little background and no back up.

mainstream fitness center or gym. If a club had a base of 1,000 members, and didn't sign up any new members to change the mix, 12 months from today the club would only have 300 to 400 members left. About 30 percent of the clubs reach a number in the 40- to 50-percent level and only about 15 to 20 percent of the clubs in the country reach a 65-percent renewal rate.

These numbers assume a club that uses 12-month memberships, renews members for 12 months at a time, and adjusts the number of members up for renewal according to known loss rates. For example, a club has 100 members who join in March of 1999. The club uses 12-month contracts and has a known loss rate of 10 percent. In February of 2000, the club would have 90 members up for renewal for another year. Using the previous numbers, the club would renew some percentage of the 90, which has been adjusted for losses, not the original 100 members.

Clubs using open-ended renewals have to track their non-renewals for a year to get a real retention rate because after the initial year membership erosion occurs slowly over a 12-month period of time. Take a look at Figure 3-1 to compare how renewals occur in the two systems.

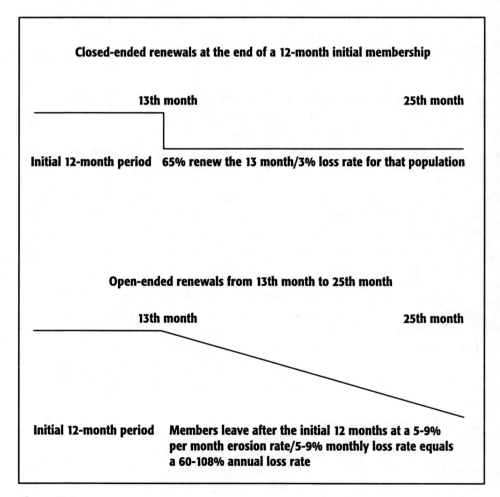

Figure 3-1.

Closed-ended renewals occur at the end of the initial one-year membership. The club actively seeks renewals in this system by going back to the members and asking them to stay another year. The 65 percent demonstrated in Figure 3-1 is the realistic target number for a club to seek for their annual renewals. This takes into account normal loss rates for a 12-month contract including moves and medical as well as members who simply wish to go away at the end of their year.

The magic occurs with a closed-end system after the 13th month. Members who renew for another year only drop out at about *three percent per year*. In other words, you almost have to kill these members to get rid of them after they make the commitment to stay for another fixed time period.

In Figure 3-1, member erosion appears in the open-ended section beginning the 13th month and lasting through the 25th month. From the clubs analyzed, this erosion is in the five- to nine-percent range per month. Compounded annually, this means somewhere between 60 to 108 percent of your memberships on open-ended renewals will disappear during the second year. Remember, these people are no longer on any contractual obligation and can simply stop their drafts or monthly payments and leave at their earliest whim. If a new club opens in the neighborhood and it is a real competitor, everyone with an open-ended membership can simply walk out the door and into the other club.

What does this mean to an owner? At this early stage of reviewing renewal concepts, an owner is better off bucking the national trend toward open-ended renewals and building a financial foundation in the club based upon closed-end fixed-term renewals. Two major reasons to consider for this are:

- The downward line of the open-ended renewal system crosses the stabilized line of the closed-ended at month seven, assuming a five-percent monthly erosion rate in the open-ended renewals. This means that the 35 percent advantage in the open-ended system enjoyed at month 13 over the closed-ended is negated at month seven.

  The final five months of the year run as a negative income stream for the open-ends compared to the steady line of the closed-ended renewals. If the club is running at the high end with nine percent monthly losses from its open-ended renewals, the advantage over closed-ended disappears in only four months. Figure 3-2 overlaps the two systems and demonstrates what happens in the seventh month.

- At the end of the second year is where the most significant difference appears. At this time a club has members going into their third year of membership (second year of renewal). The third year's renewals are based on how many members are left at the end of the second year. Simply put, there will be significantly more members left to renew from the closed-ended system as opposed to the open-ended going into the third year. The number of members left at the end of the second year is

Members who renew for another year only drop out at about three percent per year. In other words, you almost have to kill these members to get rid of them after they make the commitment to stay for another fixed time period.

the key because over time member retention should compound. This is also why clubs that use open-ended memberships do well for a year or two and then go into the scramble mode since the losses for open-ended memberships are the same for opened-ended renewals and both of these systems have losses that compound going into the third year and beyond.

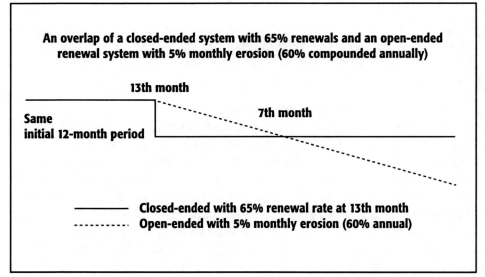

An overlap of a closed-ended system with 65% renewals and an open-ended renewal system with 5% monthly erosion (60% compounded annually)

13th month

Same initial 12-month period

7th month

——— **Closed-ended with 65% renewal rate at 13th month**
------- **Open-ended with 5% monthly erosion (60% annual)**

Figure 3-2.

What Drives Renewals?

The reason renewals are so poor in most clubs is that the club is sales driven. Sales-driven clubs are easy to recognize because of their total dependency on new sales for their revenues. Signs that a club is sales driven are:

- *Sales offices with desks.* When is the last time anyone took you into an office, shut the door, sat you across a desk, and told you good news?

- *The club has less than five percent of its total deposit from profit center income.* If 95 percent of a club's incomes are derived from daily membership sales, including membership dues and only five percent from profit centers, then the club is dependent on a sales-driven environment.

- *Pressure for first-visit sales closes.* 70% of potential members need two or more visits to the club before they can make up their minds, if the monthly membership amount is more than $34 to $39. Too much pressure at the point of sale artificially keeps the monthly membership amount down.

- *The bulk of the money goes into salespeople, not service people.* A good sign you're in a sales-driven club is that when you walk in you see a very young, under-trained person at the front desk, no club representative on the workout floor, and about seven salespeople looking at you like you have $100 bills hanging out of your zipper.

> 70% of potential members need two or more visits to the club before they can make up their minds, if the monthly membership amount is more than $34 to $39. Too much pressure at the point of sale artificially keeps the monthly membership amount down.

The Member Needs More Help During the First 30 Days than You Think

As was said earlier, members often decide about their renewals the first 30 days of their membership, not the last 30. Easily the biggest mistake you'll make with your members is not setting them up properly during the first 30 days of their memberships.

The fitness business has been around about 50 years or so, and when it comes to getting a new member started at a fitness facility, the industry certainly hasn't progressed very far at all. It's hard to believe that after this much experience, too many clubs still have a policy that states the new member only gets two workouts and then she has to go solo or buy her own personal training.

But you know from experience that the hardest person to get and keep in the club is a female about 32- to 34-years old, has a kid or two, and is about 10 to 15 pounds overweight. This woman needs seven to nine workouts with supervision before she can go solo. If you just give her two she is lost, confused, and gone from the typical club. She may struggle for a while and even pay for a trainer but she will quietly hate you for 12 months and it's guaranteed that she will take out her frustration with your club at renewal time.

She did pay to term, however, because she is an honest person who honors her commitments. She agreed to pay and she does, but she isn't happy about it. And then her paying misleads the owner into thinking that everything is all right in the member's little workout world. The owner and staff even have cute little rationalizations that cover her disappearance, such as, "She wasn't really serious about working out and changing her life. She was just wasting our time."

Do you know how hard it was for that woman to walk into a club, admit that her body isn't what it used to be, seek help and then feel like a failure because she didn't catch on after a few workouts? In fact, clubs build failure into the system by telling this woman that to get results she needs to be lifting three days a week. Monday she is fine, Wednesday she hangs on, but Friday is her day to drive for soccer practice and she misses.

Because she was told it had to be three days, preached by a 24-year-old trainer with no kids and who has never been out of shape, she feels like she fails and gives up. The system she came to for help defeated her before she even had a chance. And don't forget that as the owner you would be thrilled to actually get two uninterrupted workouts per week.

Because you live at the gym more than at home, own more workout clothes than real clothes, and are a workout person with years of experience, you think everyone else is too. You are wrong. They are not and they need more help than you would ever realize.

> Easily the biggest mistake you'll make with your members is not setting them up properly during the first 30 days of their memberships.

Get Them into the Zone

The goal is to get them into a comfort zone as early as possible. The problem is that every member coming through the door needs some help and then it becomes a cost of labor issue for the owner. The willingness may be there but not the money, especially if you have those trainers that don't know how or when to wean the new members away from their dependency on their help.

The first step in giving the new member enough help, keeping them in the system longer, and paying longer, is to identify the potential labor needs at the time of sale. Not everyone is going to need the maximum help. In fact, a few of the gym-rat variety won't need any help and resents the fact that you asked.

To help ensure the people that truly need the extra help get it, and those that really don't need as much guidance don't burn up your labor budget, try the menu system shown in Figure 3-3. This menu is given to a potential member during their first tour and again at point of sale. It is then up to the salesperson and the new member to find the right starting place. These are, by the way, all offered at no charge to the member (see Figure 3-3).

In this menu system, the club tailors its startup efforts toward giving the members exactly what he needs to get the most out of the fitness experience. Most importantly, the member gets enough help to get the most out of their first 30 days of fitness.

The Members Want to See Reinvestment

> The members have this strange notion that once they pay you for a while it becomes their club. This is exactly the mentality you want and work toward as an owner.

The members have this strange notion that once they pay you for a while it becomes their club. This is exactly the mentality you want and work toward as an owner. While reinvestment has already been beaten pretty hard earlier in the book, it's worth mentioning again here. As noted, the members assume ownership of the club because they pay and attend everyday. For that kind of attendance and money, they expect to see something happening regularly that reflects the fact you are making their second home a better place to hangout.

Beware that reinvestment doesn't always have to be in equipment. This is a rookie mistake that is repeated over and over again. Some gyms start to look like equipment warehouses, with so much equipment that a member can't even move, much less get a safe workout. These owners equate member service with the amount of equipment or toys that can be stuffed into one room.

Reinvestment to the members means are you keeping the place clean, is the paint fresh, is there enough current equipment to get a good workout, and do you have enough stuff so the member doesn't have to wait for 20 minutes to get on piece of cardio? The key is constant and consistent change in areas the member can recognize and appreciate. It's good to remember that the things that mean the most to the members, such enough toilet paper, doesn't always have that same mental impact on an owner's head.

The New Members Menu for Their First 30 Days

You should give all of your new members exactly the help they need to get started at your club. The following menu will help your training teamwork with new members in your club and find the right starting point for them. Please work with your salespeople on this menu and together you'll find the right place for your new members.

You're a First-Time Experience Person

If you haven't worked out in a club before, or it's been so long that you don't really remember much of your routine, you are a first-time experience person. To help you get started and enjoy your membership, we would like to offer you seven workouts with a trainer, either private or in small groups, depending on your schedule. The goal is to get you on a full-body routine you are comfortable with comprised of various workout equipment and programs in the gym. The choices are somewhat endless and will be structured to what you want from your workouts.

The first-time experience also provides some minimal testing. We will offer you a list of five basic workout-analysis tools and you may pick any three off of the list depending on your personal interest. (Depending on the club and testing available, the list might contain items such as body-fat analysis, basic weighting and measuring, or more advanced if available. Keep in mind the members seldom want to know as much as you think they do. If you're fat do you really want to know how fat?)

You're an Experienced Fitness Person with Recent Club Experience or Other Physical Training Skills

Our experienced program is designed for new members who have recent club experience or compatible training skills and who will need less help to get started. Compared to the first time experience program that centers on a basic full body workout done at a beginning level, the experienced program finds out where the member is in their workouts and then a program is designed over three workouts to meet those individual needs. This program also has a testing component available and the member may pick any three items off of the list.

You Are a True Gym Rat

Working out is already a vital part of your life, you have a routine that works for you, and you simply want to know where you're at on your path to personal fitness. This new member option is testing based and our training staff will run the entire gamut on you, including some advance testing, to determine where you are and where you want to go from here. To find our more about this option make sure you spend a few minutes with a member of our training staff for details.

Figure 3-3.

Remember these words of advice:

*It's not what you want that will make you money,
it's giving the members what they want.*

Too many owners spend too much time building a club for themselves and not enough time and research learning what it's going to take to capture and hold a consistent membership. The members feel that they are supporting the club by their monthly payments and their purchases. All they want for that is a constant flow of reinforcement that some of the money they spend is coming back to them.

The Members Want to be Appreciated for the Money They Spend

"I spend money every month with you. The least you can do is know who I am." This sounds so simple and most owners believe they have this concept mastered, but to a member who has been paying for several years and is not known by the staff, this can be the greatest of all insults. Being appreciated for a person's financial support is the foundation of all customer service. Without this basic premise, nothing else you can do under the member-service banner makes sense to the consumer.

At the heart of this is a problem central to the future of the fitness business: finding and keeping a consistent, mature staff. Your staff has to match the target demographics of your club. If your target membership is 30 to 50-years old, then your entire staff should be as close to that age range as you can get. Likes attract likes and this is true for member/staff relationships, too.

Staffing, in relation to the issue of renewals, is a matter of hiring a mature and stable enough workforce that gives the members a sense of consistency every time they come to workout. A young, poorly trained staff, without communication skills that have been developed through years of interrelating to other people in a variety of job settings, will alienate a membership in a very short period of time.

Members Want Contact

If you really love me, then show me, and boy, do the members ever live by this one. It's like dating the highest maintenance person on the planet; you don't have one, you have hundreds or even thousands running around your club.

Contact for the members has grown beyond the simple postcard, quarterly newsletter, and phone call. All of these were fine techniques when the Beatles were still touring, but the average member has grown beyond these basic technologies. The members need to be in the loop and made to feel they belong to something special, and that as a member they contribute to the club with their money and their presence.

One way to keep members in the know is to develop a total membership e-mail system. Unless your facility services the lowest tech trailer park on the planet, at least 80-90 percent of your members have a personal e-mail address. Even if they don't yet have a personal e-mail, they may have a personal fax you can substitute. Get these numbers and use them. The prime use of e-mail today in clubs is member retention. The following are a few simple ways to use e-mail with your members.

- Your main e-mail tool should be a fitness tip of the week in a one-page format with a small special-of-the-week paragraph at the bottom of the page. The members will start to look forward to these and they keep them thinking about the gym.

- Seasonal success stories are good to work in at the right time of the year, but simply highlighting members who have achieved some type of success in the club will keep everyone motivated and thinking about working out.

- Stop wasting money on old fashion paper newsletters. E-mail it, save the money, and more members will see it anyway. With an e-mail newsletter, you can do a four-pager monthly. Use this to let members know of scheduling changes, coming events, and don't forget to get the sales value out of any money you spend in the gym by informing the members of what you bought, how much it was, and why they are going to love it. Light graphics are good here but don't over do it since not every member will have a strong computer.

- Send a quarterly fitness report. Once a quarter, e-mail your members a fitness report you borrow from a magazine or one of your trainers compiles. It could be on cross training on a bike, a new program the club is offering and what it does for the members, or some fitness profile that informs the member about an aspect of working out. They want to learn and will read anything from the club so use this power to get them information that excites them about maintaining a fitness routine of some type.

If you have an existing club and don't have e-mail addresses on your existing members, you need to go back and get them for a new database. The easiest way to do this is by using a *member profile card*. This is a 10-question survey card the members fill out in hopes of winning something. The following section outlines how to use a profile card and build your first e-mail database.

Step 1 — Write a Profile for Your Club

You can switch or substitute any of the following questions, depending on your club, except the personal e-mail and personal fax. You need both of those to build a workable member database.

- What is your favorite soft drink or sports drink that the club doesn't carry?

- Do you take supplements? If so, where do you buy your supplements?

Stop wasting money on old fashion paper newsletters. E-mail it, save the money, and more members will see it anyway.

- What is your personal e-mail address?
- List three things the club could do better.
- What activity or programming have you tried outside the club that we might offer?
- What is your favorite personal sport when not at the gym?
- What is your personal fax number?
- What piece of equipment should the club add as our next purchase?
- What was the main reason you joined our club?
- Have you been on any type of diet during the last 12 months? If so, did it work for you? Did you lose and keep the weight off that you hoped for?

Step 2 — Set Up a Drawing

It's much easier to get the members to participate and fill out the profiles if they have a chance to win something. Barter for something big you can use to get the member's attention. You'll need at least two high-profile items that should be different, such as a 32″ televisions and a decent mountain bike, at least 30 days from your target date to start gathering the information.

Step 3 — Set a 90-day Gathering Period

Run this member profile over a 90-day period using the bartered prizes. Have the member fill out a profile and put it in a box with all the other members who have also filled one out.

For example, say your target date to start is September 1st. This is a good time since so many members return to the club after drifting away for the summer. During September you might offer the television as the prize. Take October off and then during November give away the mountain bike. By doing it twice over a 90-day period you will get a deeper base and a wider selection of members.

Don't forget to modify your existing membership paperwork immediately so that all new members are giving you their personal e-mail and personal fax number.

Don't forget to modify your existing membership paperwork immediately so that all new members are giving you their personal e-mail and personal fax number. Don't ask for their work e-mail since they may change jobs. They may leave work but they will most likely keep their personal e-mail account. You could add the member profile as part of all new member paperwork, with slight modifications, to help with your marketing and profit center planning.

Your Collection System May Work Against Your Renewals

A common mistake that often goes unnoticed by owners who aren't *numbers* people is to miss the effect their collection system has upon their renewal rate. If your collection effort is lax, then your renewals will suffer and be disappointing in the long run.

Your receivable base is the most important asset your club owns. To protect it and your future you should consider using the strongest third-party collection system you can find, such as ABC Financial Services out of Little Rock, Arkansas.

With a strong third-party system in place you give yourself a much better chance of hitting the target 65 percent renewal goal. With a weak third-party system, or worse yet collecting your own membership payments, you have fewer members left at the end of their initial period due to the ineffectiveness of the collection system.

The following is a comparison of two clubs: one with a high loss rate and low renewals, and another with a low loss rate and high renewals. In this example, *club one* signed up 100 members a year ago. Over the following year, the club's losses, due to a weak third-party collection effort, are running at two percent per month, which compounded annually, is 24 percent.

100 members join the club in one month
-24 percent annual losses
= 76 members left in the system at the end of the year

If the club is at the 20 percent national average for renewals, only 20 percent of the 76 remaining members will renew. We assume 20 percent in this example because if the club is using a weak third-party collection company, it is probably making other financial foundation and customer-service mistakes, too.

76 remaining members up for renewal x 20% renewal average
= 15 members

Those 15 members represent the remaining population base from the initial 100 signed up a year ago. Going into the second year the club only has a core of 15. Next year's renewals will be based on this number, which will be adjusted for at least three percent losses. The three percent is based on what a strong third-party can do and the actual number for this club would probably be higher.

Compare this to club two, which signs up 100 members during the same month period. The club's losses, because of a solid collection system, are only about 10 percent annually. A 10 percent loss rate is the expected annual loss rate for 12-month contracts using a strong, third-party financial-service company.

100 members join the club in one month
-10 percent annual loss rate
= 90 members left in the system at the end of the year

Assuming that this club is doing other things right, such as reinvestment, better staff training, and a better financial foundation, it should renew at the high-end average of 65 percent.

With a strong third-party system in place you give yourself a much better chance of hitting the target 65 percent renewal goal. With a weak third-party system, or worse yet collecting your own membership payments, you have fewer members left at the end of their initial period due to the ineffectiveness of the collection system.

**90 remaining members up for renewal x 65% renewal average
= 58 members**

Those 58 members are this club's core population base left over from the original 100 members. Going into another cycle of renewals this club will have 58 to start with as opposed to *club one's* 15.

If the annual contract for each club was $588, or $49 per month per member, and each club locked in its members at their original price, then *club one* would generate $8,820 in revenue during the first month of renewals and *club two* would generate $34,104.

**Club One --15 members x $588 = $8,820
Club Two -- 58 members x $588 = $34,104**

The difference between these two numbers is $25,284. If *club two* could maintain that pace for a year with all the members that come up for renewal each month, the owner of *club two* would add $303,408 more to her receivable base than her competitor, all derived from having a stronger third-party service company take care of collecting the monthly member payments.

Methods and Tips for Better Renewals

While no one absolute way exists to help you go after your renewals, some methods and tips that will help you become more efficient at the process are as follows. The overall key to hitting a targeted 65 percent renewal rate is to have a set, consistent system in place and not to forget that renewals are a 365-day-a-year project because of their importance to your business plan.

- *Don't use a team approach for renewals*

Renewals represent an extremely important part of your business plan and shouldn't be left to anyone but your single best staff person. Assign your renewal follow-up programs to your strongest staff person in terms of longevity, follow-up skills, communication skills, and sales ability, and make this part of the person's job on an on-going basis.

- *Let your third-party collection company take the first shot*

Your third-party company should have a system of auto renewal, or automatic contract extensions in place that lets them take the first shot. *Auto renewals are nothing more than contract extensions* that the member receives in the mail, signs, mails to either the club or third-party financial company, and obligates them to another 12-month period without ever setting foot in your club.

These normally work well because of the psychology behind them. If you don't sign it and send it back you are admitting to yourself that your fitness program is over and you'll be fat forever. As an additional part of your renewal system with your third-party, you should be able to access what

The overall key to hitting a targeted 65 percent renewal rate is to have a set, consistent system in place and not to forget that renewals are a 365-day-a-year project because of their importance to your business plan.

members are coming up for renewal at least two months prior to their expiration date. Based on this list, you want to approach the renewals using the following system:

√   45 days prior to member's expiration date send an auto renewal from the third-party financial-service company.

√   30 days prior to the expiration date send a second auto renewal.

√   15 days prior to expiration send a third auto renewal.

From the date of expiration to 30 days past have your most experienced person work the members who didn't auto renew through the mailings. Expect at least 50 percent of all members who will renew to do so through the auto renewals.

Send three identical auto renewals because it is a cost effective method to ensure the member at least sees one out of three. Your key staff person then works the list because the member's rate is guaranteed if he renews within 30 days of expiration. If he doesn't renew within that 30-day period, he must then pay another membership fee and rejoin the club at whatever the current rates are.

An often-asked question is should an owner pay commissions on renewals? The answer to this is yes and no. It's *no* to the salespeople and general team since the owner, through reinvestment in the club, contact with the member, adding programs, and keeping the club fresh is actually the one who is earning the renewals.

The *yes* part means that the key person who is chasing the renewals each month should receive a commission since she is protecting one of the club's most valuable assets. The national average for a renewal commission would be about $20 to $25 for each 12-month renewal generated. Keep in mind that at least half of your renewals would be done automatically through your third-party financial company.

• *Don't discount to buy renewals*

The temptation is to wait a week before a member comes up for renewal and then throw a discount at him hoping to buy the deal. This is simply a matter of too little too late. The member already made up his mind if he was going to renew months before a discount would ever figure in.

The real issue here, however, is that the member has faithfully paid for a full year. He is trained and already has the payment amount budgeted into his monthly living expense. *By guaranteeing not to raise his rates, through protecting his monthly dues no matter what your current prices have gone up to during his membership, you are already giving him a deal and still protecting a higher return per member.*

The temptation is to wait a week before a member comes up for renewal and then throw a discount at him hoping to buy the deal.

Discounts are negative images that tell the member your membership is actually worth less than it was last year. By protecting the rate, however, you send the message that you appreciate their loyalty and want to reward it by guaranteeing their rate for another year, as long as they commit again to the club with 30 days of their expiration.

• *You can reward the member if the club is profitable*

On the positive side, you can reward the member at time of renewal if your club is profitable. This added value enhances the membership for the member and confirms she made the right choice in committing for another year. The reward doesn't have to be extravagant but should be something conveying value. For example, a signature gym bag that can't be purchased by the member but only earned through renewing will cost the club under $15, which is very little compared to receiving a full-price 12-month renewal. If you are going to offer a reward, send a special oversized postcard to the member 30-days prior to the member's expiration date listing the gift and the terms: *bring this card in and renew prior to expiration and pick up your gift.*

• *Don't assume the member has cash every year*

Some members have money and prepay for the entire year at one time. Don't assume, however, they will have cash every year. Always give a member a choice to either pay cash again or make monthly payments if that works better for them that year.

For example, a member might have paid $400 for a year's membership several years back and is again up for renewal. Last year he had cash, a job, a home, a wife, and a loyal dog. This year, his ex-wife has cash, a job, a home, a new boyfriend, and a dog who's loyal to the new boyfriend. He kept his job, but all it does is pay her bills.

The guy still wants to belong to the club but just doesn't have any cash left. He thinks, wrongly, that because the club sent a renewal letter citing his $400 renewal rate that the cash option is his only option.

Suppose that the club's current rates are $40 per month, or $480 per year. His renewal could have given him the old option of $400 cash or monthly payments of $40 per month, allowing the club the chance to gracefully bring his rate up to a higher level and still reward his loyalty by guaranteeing his old membership amount.

• *Target the best members*

All members aren't born equal. Some are kind, caring, and supportive of you and your club and others are the lunatic fringe; gross disgusting non-human gym hogs who by day are normal people and who by night in the gym turn into weight droppers, fountain spitters, or gossip pigs. When you work your renewal list, spend your time and energy on those members who really do make a difference in your club and eliminate the lunatic fringe.

All members aren't born equal. Some are kind, caring, and supportive of you and your club and others are the lunatic fringe; gross disgusting non-human gym hogs who by day are normal people and who by night in the gym turn into weight droppers, fountain spitters, or gossip pigs.

The Key Points You Should Have Gotten from this Chapter

- The financial future of your club is your ability to maintain a high level of renewal memberships year after year.

- Out of the two types of current membership renewal options, which are open-ended and closed-ended, the closed-ended option is the most effective over time.

- Open-ended renewals are effective during the first year to two years of a business but then fade quickly after that point.

- Closed-ended renewals show the most power going into the third year of business because the club will have retained the largest amount of members over the longest period of time.

- The factors that drive renewals are controllable by the club owner.

- Renewals are important because of the cumulative income they generate over time.

- The club has to put more effort into the member during the first 30 days. If the member is set up correctly, he will stay longer and pay longer than a member who has the traditional one or two workouts and is then blown off.

- The length of your membership contract and how those contracts are collected greatly affect long-term renewals for a club.

- To drive renewals in the club, the owner should have a year-round program in place to target members approaching their renewal point.

4

You Have to Have Cash Flow to Survive

The most important thing you should get from this chapter is:

Daily cash flow from at least three to four different sources is the lifeblood of a small fitness business.

Definitions and concepts you will need to know:

- *Cash flow:* This is your daily revenue arriving in the club from a variety of different sources, such as new sales cash and profit center income. Cash flow can also be added to the club through debt management that frees money once spent on debt that can then be used as cash flow.

- A typical club has 95% of its revenue from its memberships and only 5% cash flow from other sources. Your goal as an owner is to get at least 40% to 50% of your entire deposit from profit centers.

- The average member should spend $5 per day per member visit that will average into your profit- center income.

- *Short-term debt:* Debt that's less than three years in length characterized by high interest.

- *Long-term debt:* Debt that's five years or longer characterized by a lower interest rate.

- You will always have debt. Your goal is long-term manageable debt.

- *Portals:* You should consider all-inclusive, no membership required, solution-based programming aimed at specific target markets such as golfers.

Generating Cash Beyond Selling Memberships

Most clubs either sell a membership or have no cash. The only cash the club brings in on a daily basis is from membership generated revenue, such as membership fees, paid-in-full memberships, daily drop-in fees, or other income derived from someone paying to do some type of workout. This is cash flow but usually not enough to drive a club into the profitability it wants.

This dependency on this type of cash flow makes the club extremely vulnerable to market conditions and fluctuations in the market due to actions from the competitors. The goal when building a successful club is to break this dependency on sales related cash and to develop a daily cash flow from multiple areas.

What actually does *cash flow* mean? Cash flow can be defined as any revenue coming into the club on a daily basis from any area including someone paying to workout. Cash flow can also be defined as extra cash made available for the operation of the club due to refinancing existing debt or freeing up cash from other sources, such as the manipulation of the club's current debt structure.

The large majority of the clubs analyzed over the last few years usually have about 95 percent of all the club's revenues coming from sales-related revenue, and only about five percent or less from profit centers, portals, or other areas of the club that can generate cash through the register daily without selling a membership or someone paying for a workout. In other words, out of every dollar this club deposits, less than a nickel comes from the members the club already has in the system.

The goal for a club that understands cash flow would be to have at least 40 to 50 percent of every dollar come from members the club already owns. This type of club is hard to hurt in a competitive market since a competitor can do very little to disrupt the club's income stream.

> The goal for a club that understands cash flow would be to have at least 40 to 50 percent of every dollar come from members the club already owns.

As competition increases, the need to develop other areas of revenue becomes more important. Clubs that are totally dependent on sales-related revenue are virtually non-competitive in today's fitness market. A solid club using a strong third-party collection system, annual contracts as its core offering, and understands cash flow and debt structure is as hard to hurt as some of your more thick-headed gym members.

Where Does Cash Flow Come From?

Cash flow comes from four primary sources: *sales related incomes* such as membership fees and paid-in-fulls, *profit centers in the club* that derive income from members already in the system, *all types of debt management*, and *portals*, which are a new concept *offering all-inclusive short-term lifestyle courses*, such as an eight-week golf-conditioning course, for bringing potential members into the club without an actual membership. Sales-related income will be discussed in the next section under pricing systems and receivable-base development, and the other three sources will be discussed in depth later in this chapter.

Profit Centers and Their Financial Contribution to a Club

Once a person has a membership, the club then has the opportunity to make her a repeat customer every single time she is in the club. This repeat business comes from the potential of selling a member something every time she works out, which combined with all the other member traffic a club has during a typical day, adds up to a steady stream of cash flow without selling anybody a membership.

Specific profit centers and their individual effects on the club are discussed in Chapter 12. In this chapter, just the overall effect profit centers have on the club's cash flow are noted.

Worth noting again from Chapter 1 is the amount of traffic a club can generate on a typical day. For example, a moderate sized club has 2,000 members in its active file. Even this number is hard to find in most clubs since some clubs don't edit or simply count every member who has ever existed no matter how many years the club has been opened.

To define a club's membership, only count any member who could walk in the door today and workout without paying additional money. If a person paid cash for an annual membership six months ago and you haven't seen him, he is still an active member since he could walk in the door tomorrow and workout because he does have an open membership.

In this example, the club has 2,000 members who could use the facility if they so desired. They may not be active but they are members. For cash-flow purposes, how many of these members will you see over a typical month and how many will you see in a day?

For a month's traffic:

2,000 members x 60% (the monthly usage number)
= 1,200 members you will see at least once that month

For daily traffic on a typical Monday:

2,000 members x 25% (the heaviest single day traffic number)
= 500 members you will see on a busy Monday

What should 500 members a day through a club mean financially beyond their memberships? Two ways to chart these expectations for cash flow are from multiple profit centers. The first method is the return-per-member workout and the second is to look at a percentage of the total actual deposit for the month.

> Once a person has a membership, the club then has the opportunity to make her a repeat customer every single time she is in the club.

Both of these methods are based on key assumptions, however, starting with the premise that you have at least the minimum number of core profit centers in place and that you have made the move to either eliminate, or reduce, the damage caused by the nonprofit profit centers such as childcare.

There Has to Be at Least Four Core Profit Centers to Reach Your Individual Daily Target

A club should have at least four profit centers that do a minimum of 20 percent net each on a monthly basis with a target net of 35 to 40 percent. If a profit center does less than 20 percent a month net, then it really isn't a profit center and should either be fixed so that it does or eliminated from the club altogether.

The core profit centers again are cooler drinks, a nutritional/educational system, supplementation, the juice/sports bar, basic clothing, and personal training, especially if you are using the newer model explained in Chapter 12. Of course, other profit centers could be created, but these are the basic ones that most clubs can do well.

If you have four core profit centers in place, then you're looking for at a minimum of $5 per day per member visit, called the *usage rate*, from just the members who are already in the club supporting the profit centers. None of this $5 per day comes from any sales- related income such as daily-workout fees or any form of member payment to workout. Using the 500-member example previously mentioned, this club would generate:

**500 members on a Monday x $5 per member
= $2,500 in cash flow without doing a single membership sale**

The club should expect to net at least 40 percent on the $2,500, or around a $1,000. Again, the usage rate is one of those numbers that should arrive as early as the 13th month of operation but no later than the 25th month. As daily traffic increases, the club gets to the point that it has enough saturation to reach the $5 per day number. Clubs that are existing and are past their first year could reach $5 per day soon as their core profit centers are in place and they start their internal promotions to expose these centers to their members on a daily basis.

Your nonprofit profit centers are a factor that can block the true net from your profit centers.

Your nonprofit profit centers are a factor that can block the true net from your profit centers. Take a look at the following example to see how a nonprofit area of the club can affect your actual profit.

The club has a childcare program that is open 50-plus hours per week, is given as part of the membership, and incurs the normal expenses for this type of service including: rent for the space, labor costs, payroll taxes, repair and maintenance on the room, extras such as video tapes, diapers, snacks, and toys, all costing the club about $1,500 per month. This is negative cash flow after adjusting for the member payments from those actually using the program. The national average for childcare usage, by the way, is that less than six percent of a club's membership will use childcare over a 30-day period of time.

The effect of nonprofit profit centers:

The club loses $1,500 per month in its childcare program   -$1,500

The club nets $1,500 from its cooler drinks   +$1,500

The owner runs these two separate areas of the club
for 30 days and nets   - $0
(zero, nada, the big nothing, loser money, you would have
made more working at 7-Eleven, what's the point of the exercise)

It's hard to believe that any owner actually got into business to break even. Can you imagine saying to your banker that we aren't really interested in profit, we just want to give areas in the club for free because we love to keep those members happy. In fact, this example really doesn't break even for the owner because if she figures her time in, figuring out that she didn't make any money, then she really lost money. *In real business in the club industry, if you aren't netting at least 20 percent then don't do it. It's not worth it and anything under 20 percent means you are probably losing money anyway.*

This is where an owner says, "But a lot of members signed up at the club because they saw the childcare room. It's a sales tool and it's worth a loss." No, it's not worth a loss. If you can't quantify it then it's not real. If less than 10 percent of your members use a service or program in the club, then 95 percent of the time you are losing money in that area of your business. If the members really wanted it they would use it and it would be paying for itself.

Childcare is an excellent example of an area of the club that everyone gets emotional over, but no one is willing to look at the numbers and make the hard decision. It's a matter of saying no, if you want childcare you'll have to go somewhere else and become a member. It's okay to say no once in a while keeping in mind that the member is not always right. The way to think of it is like this: *Member service ends where bad business begins.*

If it doesn't net 20 percent on a monthly basis, then don't do it. If you can't get that area to net 20 percent after researching successful programs, learning how to promote profit centers, and giving yourself 90 days to fix it, then get rid of that area because it will affect the areas that do make money.

The other effect of profit centers is on your total cash flow. A club that masters the promotion of the profit centers can expect 40 to 50 percent of its entire total deposit to be derived from the members it already has in the system. This makes a club very difficult for a competitor to hurt since half of its income is internally driven and not dependent on having to do as many new sales each month.

…zero, nada, the big nothing, loser money, you would have made more working at 7-Eleven, what's the point of the exercise…

Reaching this percentage of deposit is accumulative and you most likely won't reach 40 percent until you are well into your second year. You should, however, reach at least the 40-percent mark no later than the 25th month of operation. This number also works for large clubs with over 3,500 members because the sheer amount of daily traffic will still drive your usage rate to $5 per day leading to the 40 percent of the total deposit number.

Cash Flow from Managing Debt

One rule in the fitness business that is seldom ever broken is: *If you're successful, you will always have debt.*

One rule in the fitness business that is seldom ever broken is: *If you're successful, you will always have debt.* The secret is to make sure the debt is controllable, right for the business and its level of maturity, and is part of your business plan.

Two types of debt a fitness business owner will have to deal with in her career are *short-term debt* and *long-term debt*. Short-term debt is defined as debt that is three years or less in length and normally has a higher interest rate than conventional financing. This is the evil debt because too much of it can choke a small business too death during its early levels of maturity.

Short-term debt has many faces but is normally comprised of equipment leases, car payments, credit card debt, interest-only loans, or excessively fast paybacks on investor money. Since the paybacks are aggressive, the interest is usually higher than what is offered through banks on more traditional ways of borrowing money. A simple rule of thumb at the time this was written is anything over 12-percent interest is considered fairly aggressive. The problem with this type of debt is that because of the interest being paid and the length of the payback, the club doesn't have the ability to develop any cash flow and get healthy on its own.

In other words, what could be additional cash flow for the club, allowing for increased operational capital, becomes a high-interest payment. Too many of these high interest payments and the club is overwhelmed by such a large percentage of its BOE (monthly base operating expense) that it drains the club of its potential operating capital.

The second type of debt is simply know as long-term debt and is defined as any debt that is five years or longer. This is usually healthier debt for the business since it is characterized by lower interest rates and a longer payback period. Long-term debt is a good thing, especially if it is manipulated as a tool for investment in the club every 18 months to two years. Once the debt is established as part of the club's BOE, meaning the payment becomes fixed part of the club's monthly operating expense, the owner can then continue to borrow by refinancing the equity in the note every couple of years or so.

Short-Term Debt and Its Effect on Your Business

Short-term debt is a normal part of any club less than three years old, and can be a part of an older club if it is handled correctly. To make sure the short-term debt stays within financially good sense, it must stay within fixed parameters. During the first three years of operations, a club can handle about 10 percent of its BOE in short-term debt. For example:

Your club has a BOE of $60,000
$60,000 x 10% = $6,000

The maximum this club can handle in short-term debt during its first three years is $6,000 per month. In other words, this club could pay a monthly total of short-term debt payments, including equipment leases, car payments, credit card payments, or other short-term debt up to $6,000. Over $6,000, and the club would be in a poor financial situation during its first three years and have a much higher chance of failing than a club that didn't have this debt structure.

The maximum this club can handle in short-term debt during its first three years is $6,000 per month.

The goal is to reduce the club's total short-term debt; again an ideal situation would be no more than 10 percent of the BOE, from this 10-percent maximum to five percent. Figure 4-1 illustrates the reduction short-term debt over a three-year period.

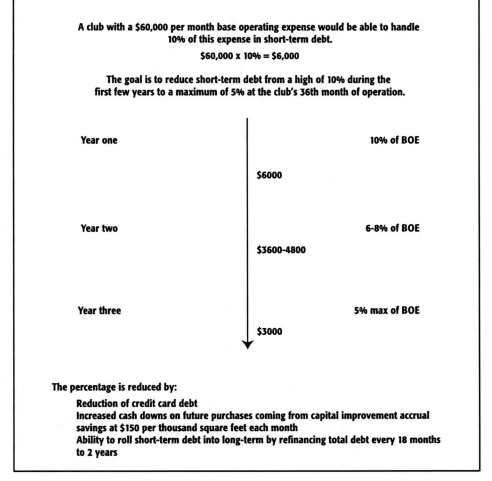

A club with a $60,000 per month base operating expense would be able to handle 10% of this expense in short-term debt.

$60,000 x 10% = $6,000

The goal is to reduce short-term debt from a high of 10% during the first few years to a maximum of 5% at the club's 36th month of operation.

Year one	10% of BOE
$6000	
Year two	6-8% of BOE
$3600-4800	
Year three	5% max of BOE
$3000	

The percentage is reduced by:
Reduction of credit card debt
Increased cash downs on future purchases coming from capital improvement accrual savings at $150 per thousand square feet each month
Ability to roll short-term debt into long-term by refinancing total debt every 18 months to 2 years

Figure 4-1.

In Figure 4-1, the club is experiencing a slow reduction in its short-term debt from its first few years of operation through its third year. The reduction comes from several areas all under the control of the owner.

• Reduction of Credit Card Debt

A club may have to have some credit card debt when it first starts (including airline miles, free stuff, or cash back plans), but for no reason should a club have any credit card debt that isn't paid off completely each month. You may need credit cards to get started because you are undercapitalized, but you shouldn't need any ongoing credit card debt after your second full year of operation.

The temptation is just too great to keep spending and the interest that you will pay will more than cancel any benefits such as air miles you would have received by using the credit card. If you're not going to pay it off completely, then don't use it at all because it will affect your monthly cash flow negatively.

• Using the Capital-Improvement Accrual Account

As mentioned earlier in the book, your club should have an accrual savings account that you use for future purchases in the club and to slowly bring the short-term debt ratio down to its ideal five-percent position. Your club should be budgeting $150 per thousand square feet, with a minimum of $1,000 each month, for future capital- improvement purchases.

In this example, you might pay off a three-year lease at the end of the third year but need to upgrade a few cardio pieces. Originally, you might have only been able to put down 10 percent on the lease. Three years later, due to your cash available in your accrual account, you can then order more equipment but be in a position to put down 30 percent. This would reduce the amount financed, therefore, lowering your monthly payment, leading to a reduction in your short-term debt ratio.

• Going from Short-Term to Long-Term Debt

With the right long-term debt, short-term debt can be eliminated altogether, or at least drastically reduced. For example, you are two years into your business, you're hitting your maturity marks, and the club is doing fine. This is the time you should go back to the bank and look to refinance all your debt into a long-term note through either conventional financing or through tools available from the SBA (the US Small Business Administration, an agency of the federal government — see SBA.gov).

Even though you only have approximately a year on your leases, it may be worth it to include the payouts on those notes into your long-term refinance and pick up the extra cash flow each month. You normally won't save anything on the early payout of the remaining balance on the leases, but you may pick up a significant amount of extra cash flow each month that will offset the payoff.

If you're not going to pay it off completely, then don't use it at all because it will affect your monthly cash flow negatively.

Long-Term Debt Will Also Be Part of Your Business Plan

A club can also handle a certain amount of *long-term debt* as part of its base operating cost. Long-term debt again is defined as debt that is usually between five to seven years in length and includes such things as conventional financing, SBA loans and guarantees, and investor paybacks.

The percentage of BOE a club can handle in long-term debt is 10%. If a club is just getting started it might have 10 percent short-term debt and an additional 10 percent in long-term debt for a total of 20 percent of the BOE in debt service.

As the club matures at around three years, the long-term debt would remain the same but the short-term debt would slowly be reduced to a maximum of five percent for a total debt service of 15 percent.

This cap of 15 percent total debt will always be there for most clubs as part of their monthly overhead since it reflects a constant ability to reinvent the club as needed through continual reinvestment. You will always have debt; it's learning to live with a fixed controllable amount of debt service that will make or break almost any small business.

Refinancing can be defined simply as borrowing the equity you've already paid back to the bank and then moving the original note forward into the future. A simple example would be if you borrowed $200,000 for five years, paid back approximately $70,000 over two years by making your regular payments, and then took another note for $200,000 at that point in time for five years (this would include refinancing the remaining $130,000). You would then have another $70,000 liquid to reinvest in the club and you would also have the same original payment projected another five years into the future.

Take a look at this example more closely. The original loan amount is $200,000 based on a five-year payback and at 10 percent interest. Where would the owner be in two years and how much equity would he have to draw from using this note?

Based on these numbers, the monthly payments would be $4,241.91. After 24 months, the owner would have paid the note down to $131,694. This would allow an equity balance of $68,305 that could be refinanced.

In other words, this owner could go back to the bank at the end of two years, refinance this note for another five years, keep the same payment that she has already made part of her monthly operation expense, and still take approximately $70,000 cash back from the bank to use to reinvest in the club.

This method of financing improvements in the club provides the owner with a consistent method of projecting cash flow since the monthly payment stays the same and is built into the club's monthly operating expense. This system can also be used to reduce short-term debt since leases and other

> This cap of 15 percent total debt will always be there for most clubs as part of their monthly overhead since it reflects a constant ability to reinvent the club as needed through continual reinvestment.

short-term vehicles could be eliminated from the club's budget by being rolled into the long-term debt.

Portals as a Cash Flow Tool

Most clubs have only one entry into their system, and that is by acquiring a membership in some form. In other words, if you want to experience the club you have to purchase some type of membership.

This entry into the club is referred as a *portal*. This term comes from the dot.com companies and is used to describe the multitude of ways a consumer can access that web site. For example, you might be exploring a cooking web page, hit a button that takes you to cook books, and end up at the Amazon.com site. This is an example of one of many thousand entryways, or portals, into the world of Amazon.com.

In the fitness business, most clubs have only one: the basic club membership. Variations of the membership are possible, such as a daily drop-in or short-term membership, but the basic concept is that if you want to work out, you must buy some length of a membership, even if it is only one day at a time.

This System Has Several Major Flaws in It that Limits the Club's Ability to Make Money

First of all, the modern member in the year 2000 and beyond has the patience of a three-year old. The member who wants to get in shape in a few weeks for a special occasion doesn't really connect with buying any type of on-going membership. *In fact, he doesn't want a membership at all but a solution that is self-contained, all-inclusive, and can be purchased as a one-time option.*

The second major flaw is that the club competes with the potential member for a portion of his life. A variety of statistics were published late in 1999 and early in 2000 that cited the increase per week in hours worked by the average white-collar person. One study cited that the average person today is working 57.5 hours per week compared to only 47.5 five years earlier.

This person only has a relatively few hours for their personal pursuits during the week. If this person is a golfer, then the club is asking the member to give up golf in exchange for coming to the gym. Owners don't do this intentionally, but you are asking the potential member to choose between the club and their favorite activity since he only has a few hours of discretionary time a week.

Portals were designed to solve both of these problems. Portals are self-contained, all-inclusive courses that enhance a member's lifestyle rather than compete with it. A portal also provides cash flow and leads to future

> **First of all, the modern member in the year 2000 and beyond has the patience of a three-year old.**

memberships by exposing the member to the club from a viewpoint that he can relate to, rather than viewing it through the concept of making a long-term commitment to an endless fitness program that really doesn't have any ending in sight.

An example of a portal would be an eight-week golf-conditioning program. This would be an all-inclusive, *no-membership-necessary* course designed to enhance a person's golf conditioning and basic skills that is marketed as a separate identity from the club's normal membership pieces.

You might design a separate marketing piece that would be generated at the top 40 percent of the club's demographic population within five miles of the club. The piece might have a headline that states: Does your golf game suck? A little bold perhaps, but many weekend golfers will get a laugh from the headline and instantly identify with the *my-game-sucks* part. The copy might look like this:

Does your golf game suck?

We want you for an eight-week golf-conditioning course at *Your Gym* Golf conditioning, led by Tiger Woods and David Duval, has changed the golf world and it can change the way you play your game.

Take part in our program for only $429 for a full eight-week course, no membership necessary, work with area teaching pro John Smith, and learn how the power stretch, ply metrics, basic strength training and nutritional guidance can combine to improve your golf game before this year's season begins.

The course would be designed as an eight-week course, offered in late winter or early spring in most areas and that meets once a week for an hour and a half. The club could hire a golf pro who would take part every other week for one of the hour-and-a-half sessions. He would be there the first night, put clubs in their hands, and work them through why a good swing comes from a combination of factors, including flexibility (power assisted stretching), the ability to turn your body (nutritional guidance), balance (ply metrics and stability ball), and strength.

By having a club in their hands the first night and having a real pro guide them through a Tiger Woods swing, being in a gym feels like golf. *In other words, if it smells like golf, it is golf.* Instead of competing with a person's lifestyle, you are enhancing what they do in a gym setting without a membership requirement.

In other words, if it smells like golf, it is golf.

The person signing up for a portal should also have use of the facility for those eight weeks so the club would also gain more in profit center income. This could be tracked by simply issuing the person a short-term membership card. Allowing the person to use the club would also raise your conversion rate with the portal students. The club should target at least 50 percent of the participants as becoming full members after the course ends. As far as the numbers go, this program is based on $429 per person with 12 to a class as an ideal target goal. The numbers would look like this:

Revenues
>   12 @ $429 = $5,148

Expenses
>   Golf pro @ $100 per session, 4 sessions = $400
>   Training budget of $100 per session @ 8 sessions = $800
>   Payroll taxes @ 20% = $160
>   Marketing (direct mail) @ .30 x 4,000 = $1,200
>   Support materials @ $20 x 12 = $240

Total Expenses = $2,800

Revenues of $5,148 - $2,800 = $2,348, or a net of 45 percent

The golf pro would do this class at that time of year in hopes of developing summer lessons. The training budget could be allocated to one trainer or divided by more than one depending on your training rate.

The marketing would be directed to the top 40-percent demographic in your area. The $.30 each allows for a quality folded piece and includes mailing and the lists. The support material would be a handout developed by the trainers.

A net of 45 percent would give the owner a margin to put fewer students in the class, add more trainers, or put more in marketing and try and fill multiple classes.

A net of 45 percent would give the owner a margin to put fewer students in the class, add more trainers, or put more in marketing and try and fill multiple classes. The minimum target net would be in the 33- to 35-percent range.

Other Types of Portals

•   Women's makeover programs

This would be a six-week program including one training session per week, full nutritional guidance, supplements, and a workout book. It should also include a day spa package worth $150. If the club doesn't have a day spa, it could buy the package from a neighboring business at a discounted rate of $75 and promote off of the day spa's mailing list.

This portal could be offered as a 1-on-1 program with a price of somewhere around $329 to $389. Make sure you include a note that offers a second member combined rate. Women usually approach these things in pairs with some other support person in tow, so price accordingly. For example, one might be $349, or two can do the program together for $499. Your cost for the second person is minimal and you can still pay your trainer extra for two people.

Marketing to women is normally out of the realm of most male owners. A recommended read for any male-owned business is, *EVEolution: The Eight Truths of Marketing to Women*, by Faith Popcorn.

*   Other sport-enhancement programs

These would include tennis conditioning, running and racing preparation, softball shape-up programs, and other regional offerings depending on what people do in your area. These are all group programs built upon the same model as the golf program.

*   Specialty programs

Summer shape-up programs, Navy Seal conditioning classes, rock climbing, and mountain-biking enhancement using your studio bikes could all be channeled into portal options.

Don't Forget the Cash Flow

The purpose of this section was to discuss cash flow and portals, which are certainly a prime method of adding to your club's monthly cash flow. These can be offered about five times per year or roughly every other month. To make them work properly, portals have to be separated from the club's normal marketing and should be used in conjunction with your marketing program, not as a replacement.

The Key Points You Should Have Gotten from this Chapter

*   Cash flow is important because you need money coming through the register even when you don't have new sales.

*   You can reach the point that 50% of your monthly deposit comes from other sources than selling workout time.

*   Portals and profit centers provide cash flow from selling someone something on a daily basis.

*   Restructuring debt frees your cash flow from the bills you are already paying in the club.

*   Short-term debt must be kept to a maximum of 10% during the first three years of your business and then reduced to a max of 5% from that point forward.

Cash flow is important because you need money coming through the register even when you don't have new sales.

The Financial Foundation of a Fitness Business

The financial foundation in a fitness business is the combination of how you charge and how you collect from a member. The financial foundation is also where an owner can make the biggest mistakes in their business. Done correctly, an owner can still make mistakes and still stay in business. A financial foundation that is not done correctly is almost impossible to survive over time.

This section covers some of the foundational numbers and concepts that form the foundation of any good fitness business. The three most important areas are *the concept of price per month per member*, *the development of a strong and efficient receivable base*, and the *development of a pricing structure* that will give the club owner the highest probability of collecting the most money from the most members.

Pricing is discussed in Chapter 5 since it is the single biggest mistake any owner in the business can make. The other two components of the financial foundation, the receivable base and pricing structure, will be discussed in Chapters 6 and 7.

- **Chapter 5: The Right Membership Price Can Make a Business**
- **Chapter 6: Building the Club's Most Important Asset**
- **Chapter 7: Building a Price Structure that Can Make You Money**

5

The Right Membership Price Can Make a Business

The most important thing you should get from this chapter is:

The single biggest mistake you can make in the fitness business is pricing your membership too low.

Definitions and concepts you will need to know:

- The perfect price for a gym membership: something most owners look for but does not exist.

- Your club should be built and ran for the top 60% of the demographics by affluence in your area.

- Your price may be low enough that it actually keeps the good members out of the gym.

- You only have three decisions when it comes to setting your price: *lower than your competitors*, *the same as your competitors*, and *higher than your competitors*.

- Your price should be at least $10 to $15 per month per member higher than your competitor's price.

- Discounting lowers your return per member and will ultimately cost you your best members.

Getting Past the False Assumptions about Pricing a Membership

False assumptions are things we believe to be true because other people have accepted them over time without ever questioning what the assumptions was based upon. Pricing in the fitness business for most owners is usually done by lining up all the false assumptions you can find, and then combining them into a four-page price sheet and throwing it at their members.

Not true, you say? The industry has grown beyond that concept? Sad to say it hasn't because very few owners out there didn't set their first prices by gathering all of the competitors price sheets, doing a little averaging, and then opening a few dollars less in hopes of stealing all the potential members who are shopping around.

Who really sets your prices? Your competitors do. Was it based on positioning your club in the market? No! Was it based on expected yield and your cost of doing business? No! Was it based on capturing the top 60 percent of the market, or did you look for the perfect price that didn't irritate anyone who toured the facility? No, probably not.

The Search for the Perfect Price

In the fitness business, this has been better than searching for the Holy Grail, although there haven't been as many movies made about the fitness version. Every owner at one time or another in her career starts the search for the perfect price, the one that automatically closes every member through the door and reaches the happy compromise between the potential member and the sales staff. *It's not there and never will be.*

> **Pricing is part of the image of the club, and if done correctly, should irritate at least 20 percent of the potential members who enter the club because it is too high.**

Pricing is part of the image of the club, and if done correctly, should irritate at least 20 percent of the potential members who enter the club because it is too high. In other words, you want about 20 percent of your potential members to walk away from the club because they can't afford it.

The alternative in many owners' minds, of course, is to set it just perfectly that no one leaves but the club still makes money. While this sounds logical, it is a false assumption sprung forth from out of work consultants at trade shows who masquerade as seminar givers. There can't be a perfect price for many reasons.

First of all, the wrong percentile group of expected members normally dictates a club's price. Figure 5-1 divides a club into five groups of potential members.

20 — The top 20 percent of your club's demographic population
20 — The slightly above average demo group
20 — The average of your demo population
20 — Slightly below average of all your potential members
20 — The bottom of your economic potential (real cheap people with not a lot of money)

Figure 5-1.

It's the bottom 20 percent that complains the most in a club, wants $19 a month membership, and won't support the profit centers because they always complain you are ripping them off. Come on, every club has that aerobics member who has been there since the early 1990s, still wears a headband and leg warmers, pays $20 to $25 per month, and is the absolute biggest pain in the ass in the entire club.

The mistake made at this point is an owner lets the bottom 20 percent of the market drive the club's pricing plans. They complain and you react by lowering the price, or not pushing profit centers, or by running endless discounts as the foundation for your marketing program.

Keep in mind you don't have to be poor to act cheap. Some of our wealthiest members complain the most because we taught them to do that by letting them into the club at a cheap price.

The aerobics person who complains may have the money, but you taught her to complain and to expect everything else in the club to be cheap. How can you expect to sell a woman a $399 nutrition/training program who joined the club at $25 per month? Of course she will complain. You taught her to be cheap from the first day she was a member.

For a club to be successful, it should build a pricing strategy based on the top 60 percent of the market, not the bottom 40 percent. It's okay for potential members to walk out and complain about the price. It's okay to declare that this is a club that doesn't cater to people who join because you're the cheapest in town.

Another way to look at the perfect price is to analyze your price per month per member. Look at Figure 5-2 and try to find the perfect price where none of your members would complain because it's too high.

Every club has that aerobics member who has been there since the early 1990s, still wears a headband and leg warmers, pays $20 to $25 per month, and is the absolute biggest pain in the ass in the entire club.

$79 per month
$69
$59
$49
$39
$29
$19
$9.50

Figure 5-2.

The $79 per month represents what an upscale adult club should be charging in most major metro markets. The $9.50 price was advertised on television in Las Vegas during a trip in the early stages of this book. All the rest of the prices in between represent possible monthly prices for your membership.

It doesn't take long to figure out that you cannot find one single price on that list that will keep every potential member from complaining. Even the guy at $9.50 per month will have someone walk in and say, "Hey, the guy down the street is only $8.00 per month. How come you're more expensive?" What do you do then? You lower your price to $7.00 per month.

A very important number on the list, however, that owners need to consider is the *$39/$40 per month per member.* As of this writing, that number is still a barrier for many owners to cross but the theory would still apply in a few years if we were then looking at crossing the $49/$50 mark. The false assumption is that if you raise your price over the $40 barrier, your memberships will drastically fall apart. This is somewhat true in that you will limit your current market by moving over the $40 barrier.

The other side of that issue is that just as many potential members are out there who won't come into a club because it is too cheap, meaning under $40, than those who won't join a club because it is over $40. In other words, price can be a limiting factor to your more affluent, potential members and to the quality of members you attract. Too high and the bottom 40 percent won't come join the club. Too low and the top 60 percent will stay away from the club because of the expectations that go with that price, such as poor service, crowded conditions, and a dirty physical plant.

They know a club offering $25 per month memberships has to pack the place to make any money and an owner can't possibly keep the place together on that little per member per month. The problem is the owners need to learn they can't run a successful club on less than $40 per month per member ($39 being the low for you purists).

> **The false assumption is that if you raise your price over the $40 barrier, your memberships will drastically fall apart.**
>
> **The other side of that issue is that just as many potential members are out there who won't come into a club because it is too cheap, meaning under $40, than those who won't join a club because it is over $40.**

In the Real World, $40 Doesn't Really Get You Much

You might have heard an old investment adage that has been around for years concerning the price of gold and why gold is not a good investment for most investors. In the late 1800s, an ounce of gold would buy you a good suit. In that late 1900s, an ounce of gold wouldn't buy you a good suit. The truism in this is why invest in something that has lost its buying power over time.

In the gym business, the value of $40 has decreased since the beginning of the fitness clubs, but most clubs still can't cross that barrier. Take a look at Figure 5-3 to compare the risk of opening a club versus the money you can charge.

Pricing in clubs throughout the years
The prices described are illustrative and don't reflect exact pricing or costs from each era.
The club in this example would be a different size during each decade. An old Nautilus center
from the late 60s might only be 1500 square feet (just enough for the original circuit) and the club
in the year 2000 might be 15,000 square feet. The start-up cost for each year reflects a guess at the
size of that time and the equipment as it existed then.

The year	Cost of opening the club	Approx. monthly dues
1949	$1000	$29
1959	$10,000	$29
1969	$50,000	$29
1979	$100,000	$29
1989	$250,000	$34
2000	$1,200,000	$29

Figure 5-3.

This chart is a brief tour of fitness time. Not many fitness facilities were in the country in the late 1940s, and those that were established revolved around the physical culture movement, which promoted a healthy lifestyle that was startling new at the time. A gym in those days was a collection of mostly homemade or custom-made equipment. If you had a $1,000 to start a gym, you had a lot of money and were off and running. Members paid about $29 per month in those days, in equivalent dollars to today.

In the 1950s, fitness took hold and by the end of the decade there were hundreds of clubs in the country. Some of the legends got started in those days such as Jack LaLanne, Joe Gold, and Bill Pearl, all whom led the way into leading fitness into the mainstream. Equipment was still somewhat custom or homemade, although some early manufacturers were emerging. Only about $10,000 got you a gym and the memberships were still equivalent to about $29 per month today.

In the 1960s, fitness changed dramatically with the advent of the first generation of Nautilus equipment. This equipment brought fitness to the mainstream population in the form of early circuit training and Arthur Jones created a legend. You could get yourself a 1,500-square-foot facility and a line of Nautilus for about $50,000 and you were off and running. The members were still paying about $29 per month.

The 1970s brought more women into the gyms with the start of group exercise. Fitness was growing into the true mainstream and fitness facilities, spas and racquet centers were springing up everywhere. You could get yourself into a mainstream facility for $100,000, although the racquet facilities were usually land deals and more expensive, and have a decent competitive facility.

The facilities in the late 1970s were some of the first truly mainstream fitness businesses that began to accommodate the new breed of fitness

Some of the legends got started in those days such as Jack LaLanne, Joe Gold, and Bill Pearl, all whom led the way into leading fitness into the mainstream.

consumer -- the average American caught up in the first real fitness boom in this country.

This boom was fueled by a contribution of factors including the running craze of the 1970s, early aerobics programs, a young Arnold Schwarzenegger, the California lifestyle image, and the new-look female on television who was actually shown being fit. All of this was yours for a $100,000 investment and the right to charge $29 per month.

The late 1980s was another breakthrough period for the fitness business. Licensed gyms emerged in big numbers giving the consumer a new, trendier choice for fitness, chains started to make an impact on the market, and the concept of strip-center fitness was launched.

While branding had been around for a while in the fitness business, including early Vic Tanney gyms, Jack LaLanne, Gloria Marshall and European Health Spas, it's interesting to note that the licensed clubs in the 1980s gained a lot of their early success in reaching a younger market than the other brands had connected with in their businesses. Women may have grown up watching Jack LaLanne on television, but in the 1980s, if you were serious about fitness, you didn't go to your mama's club, you went to a licensed gym or to one of the new mainstream fitness centers that appeared in the 1980s.

Women may have grown up watching Jack LaLanne on television, but in the 1980s, if you were serious about fitness, you didn't go to your mama's club.

The breakthrough occurred, however, in the pricing of clubs in the 1980s. Memberships consistently broke the $30 barrier and many facilities were in at the $39 per month membership range. Membership was growing, the consumer had options, and the price was relatively strong for the time period.

During the 1990s, the fitness industry took a 20-year retreat into time. Because of the hardcore sales approach endorsed and practiced by the chains that artificially kept the price low and the independent operators need to emulate someone; price wars ripped the market during most of the 1990s.

Club owners in the Denver market, for example, built 50,000-square-foot warehouse-style gyms and then priced their memberships at $19 a month or $199 a year. Licensed players in this market fired back on everyone with an answering $199 a year or worse and the chains increased their pressure tactics by exploiting the member and the membership price. In the Las Vegas market during the 1990s, price wars became so vicious that several of the big players advertised $9.50–per-month memberships on television. By the late 1990s, a new 10,000- to 12,000-square-foot club could cost as much as $1.2 to $1.5 million to build — all for the right to charge the same price owners did in the 1960s.

While the prices in these examples are illustrative and show the relationship between a membership today versus early in our industry, if you looked at actual members and value of money versus the risk involved to start a facility, memberships today are worth relatively little compared against what guys got for a monthly membership to a 1,500- square-foot Nautilus circuit center.

Price wise, we've lost ground in the last 40 years. The risk to create a business is much higher but the return per membership dollar is substantially lower for most operators.

Where Should Your Monthly Price Be?

Price is part of your image. It defines a potential member's first impression of who you are and what your business is all about. This means that your price has to have some relative comparative value against the competitor's in your market place. If you don't have competitors, than your price should be used as a tool to set the consumer's level of expectation for expected service, who else will be a member of the gym, and for the intensity of the expected experience itself.

An insidious false assumption applies here that concerns your price set in comparison to your competitor's. Take a look at Figure 5-4 and a few typical price relationships between your club and your competitor's business.

Price choices an owner can make in relation to competitors	
Your competitor's price	Your options
	$34
$39	$39
	$49

Figure 5-4.

When most owners begin their businesses they all set their prices the same way. They tour the competitors in their area, gather the price sheets from each, and then pick a price in comparison to the other clubs.

Maybe an owner will make a magical guess, either picking a price lower than the competitor's, a price the same as the other prices, or one that is higher than every one else's. Each one of these choices has an immediate effect on the return per member and a long-term effect on the overall marketing and consumer image in the marketplace.

The Low Rate

In Figure 5-4, the owner just picked a price $5 per month per member lower that the average competitor's. This is a very common mistake and is based on one of the biggest false assumptions in the fitness business: the lower the price, the more members you will attract. In other words, when faced with a choice, the assumption is that all consumers will make their final buying decision based upon a $5 price differential.

In this example, the price is $34 per month compared to $39 down the street. The thought process here for most owners is that a potential member will visit both facilities and then be overwhelmed by that $5 difference in price.

When most owners begin their businesses they all set their prices the same way. They tour the competitors in their area, gather the price sheets from each, and then pick a price in comparison to the other clubs.

How stupid does this owner really think her potential members are? Remember that you concentrate your businesses on the top 60 percent of per-household income in the demographics of the area. This means that you are targeting a lot of people that just plain don't care about something as small as $5 over a monthly period.

Is $5 spread over 30 days an influencing factor? Is your club really $5 a month worse than your competitor's club? Would you, in your own life, really make any major buying decision, such as a fitness membership for a year, on $5 per month, or $60 a year? Most importantly, though, is the image you send by pricing below your competitors. Say the following lines out loud to yourself as you read along:

- I have the best club in the area.
- I have the best staff in the area.
- We give the best service in the area.
- We provide the best fitness experience in the area.
- And I am the cheapest priced gym in town.

The potential member is not nearly as dumb as you hope they are. They do realize that you can't be the best and the cheapest at the same time.

The potential member is not nearly as dumb as you hope they are. They do realize that you can't be the best and the cheapest at the same time. They also realize that you can't set an image or motivate anyone you would have as a member for $5 per month.

The Same Rate

This is the choice of indecision. Hey, maybe the other guy knows more than I do so his price must be right. After all, he's been in business longer than I have and must understand how to set prices for this market. No, all that owner knows is how to set a price that may match his business, may reflect his cost of business, and may be an indicator of his club's positioning in the marketplace.

Or it may not be any of these things. All his price may indicate is that he looked at all his competitors when he opened and made his best guest just as most other owners do.

Pricing the same forces the potential member to one simple conclusion: you are just the same as the other guy. Price again is part of your image and the image you want in the marketplace is that your club is different or of a higher quality than your competitor.

Pricing the club at the same rate as everyone else in town states that all the clubs are the same and it doesn't really matter which one you choose. You may feel you have the best club in the marketplace but you can't prove a better quality experience in just a 20-minute or so tour.

Someone Take the High Road

It's fascinating that so many young owners will put everything in their life into a club and then be afraid to price it as the top-end quality experience in the market place. By setting your price $10 to $15 higher per month than your competitors, you are making a statement to the potential buyer that you are the quality option.

By being more aggressive with your price, you are saying that you are the most expensive club in your market by choice. Being cheap means low quality, long lines, and a dirty club; assumptions potential members are already making about your business from just your price alone. Being aggressive also means you are making a statement that this club is not for everyone -- some people may not be able to afford a membership here. One constant you can expect about a price increase is that when you raise your price, memberships don't go away.

Being cheap means low quality, long lines, and a dirty club; assumptions potential members are already making about your business from just your price alone.

In most cases memberships will actually increase because the perceived value of your business becomes higher than it was before the raise. This means you receive a higher return-per-member without sacrificing the volume you may already have in your club.

Your large-volume clubs may actually want to limit your volume somewhat. For example, if you are living off of 150 new members a month all paying $34 a month, you will make more money in the long run from signing up just 120 at $44 a month. Most importantly, your cost of business also goes down too with decreased commissions, lower wear and tear on the club, smaller marketing budgets, and lower labor costs to service fewer members.

The Price Is Low Because You Force It to Be

Pressure sales create an artificial ceiling on what you can charge a member each month because of the member's inherent fear of risk. If you sell memberships too aggressively, trying to slam for that first visit close, you will create a price ceiling that the consumer will not cross because the risk is too high. The consumer has a point in his head where he'll risk the money, but only up to a certain cutoff, even if he makes a bad decision.

A high-pressure, first-visit closing puts all of the emphasis on the salesperson and takes it away from the strengths of your operation. In a typical sales tour in a high-pressure chain-style club, the consumer is only actually in the workout facility for about 15 minutes. After that point, she is held captive in a sales office for the remaining time she is in the club, or until she dies first trying to escape.

You can't sell an extraordinary fitness experience in 15 minutes. You can't sell legendary customer service in 15 minutes. You can't sell great staff in 15 minutes. Nor can you sell anything to a visual learner who needs something substantial to read and review before he buys.

A visual learner will only buy if he can read or accumulate information about the choice, or if he can spend enough time in the facility to get a visual feel for the club. This can't happen in a 15-minute club tour yet visual learners make up one-third of the population.

And you certainly can't sell a doer-type learner in one 15-minute tour. Doers only buy things or process information from the experience of how does it feel. They buy when it feels right and this comes from trying a few workouts and getting a feel for the club, the staff, and the other members. The again represents one-third of the consumers you face in the marketplace.

Wait you say, clubs sell memberships all the time, so someone must be buying on the first visit. Yes, clubs do sell memberships all the time. But the key questions are the sales at a volume that can be maintained and at what price per member.

Those clubs that have aggressive, first-visit pressure sales seem to average $34 per month per member or less. Clubs that use trial memberships or lower-key sales practices are the ones that get into higher pricing and break the $40-per-month barrier. It's almost impossible to find a fitness business that charges $49 per month per member or higher that also relies on old-style, high-pressure sales offices filled with sales-geek driven membership sales.

The prices in the fitness industry are low because too many clubs still force the consumer to make a buying decision during their first visit to the club. Some people will buy at this point and the price they will pay to keep the risk low will be $34 per month or lower.

Just take a tour from one of the big chains and get pitched, and pounded, by the pressure professionals. They only start you at a higher price, but the final membership quote going out the door, therefore reducing the average return per member, will be $34 per month or less.

Trial Memberships Are the Only Way to Drive Up the Price

Price-driven advertising and pressure sales, when combined as tools, lower the return per member by forcing the price down. Any traditional health club marketing that advocates some type of discount, special, or one-time offer is just another form of a sale meant to move memberships at a discounted price.

Pressure sales further lower the price by introducing risk associated with impulse, or on-the-spot buying. The higher the pressure, the more the consumer is overwhelmed by the feel of risk, or the *this-is-just-too-quick-what-if-I'm- wrong* sickening feeling in their stomachs.

Trial memberships are forms of exposure marketing where the potential member can experience the product before she has to make a buying decision. Memberships still have to be sold, but the significant difference with

> **Any traditional health club marketing that advocates some type of discount, special, or one-time offer is just another form of a sale meant to move memberships at a discounted price.**

trial memberships is, *when does the sale occur?* It may still happen on the first visit, but it might happen later in the trial membership.

With pressure sales, the potential member has no reason to come back to the club since all of the deals and specials are contingent on making a buying decision during the first visit. Trial memberships, however, coupled with positive incentives such as giving potential members something of value to make a buying decision rather than punishing him by costing him money if he doesn't do what we want. They allow the potential members to come back to the club, experience the services, and they make a decision when it is comfortable to buy.

Trial memberships, usually offered in five-day, 14-day, or 30-day increments, shift the emphasis away from sales and puts it on operations where it should have been all along. The belief is that if you meet the staff, try the classes, experience the energy and atmosphere, you'll want to join the gym. But most importantly, once you've had a chance to see what the business is all about, price is no longer an issue. It's the service and the quality of the experience that's important.

This concept allows you to charge a much higher price than a pressure gym because the risk factor is eliminated, they tried before they bought, and the gym owner has a chance to establish value for the price.

This is what is so hard for the chain clubs that still believe in aggressive first-visit closing: you never get a chance to assign any type of value to the membership price because the potential member has no experience with the quality of the service or appreciation of the club experience.

Tell Me Again Why that Second Member of the Family Gets a Discount

Most clubs discount for almost everyone including a second member of the family, senior citizens, students, firemen, teachers, or anyone else the club's salesperson can think of to move a few memberships.

Discounting has been a part of the fitness industry since it took a serious leap forward in the late 1940s and early 1950s. While many explanations as to why they were originally discounted as an industry are clear, absolutely no reason is valid as to why the industry still continues to offer broad-based discounting in the clubs.

One theory was that they offered discounts because no one used the club very long anyway. This was probably true, especially in the 1960s during the era of chrome equipment that didn't really work and before the advent of Nautilus and group exercise.

The club sold memberships in those days with the actual hope that no one would really stay around long. In this case it didn't matter what the

Most clubs discount for almost everyone including a second member of the family, senior citizens, students, firemen, teachers, or anyone else the club's salesperson can think of to move a few memberships.

second member of the family really paid since he was only going to be in the club a few months and then disappear anyway. Memberships were sold, usually two- or three-year contracts, no one was trained, and the club still collected money. And you still wonder today why this fitness business has such a bad image.

In today's market, people do train, service and member results in the clubs are better and members, if treated well in a club that provides an exciting and motivating fitness experience, will stick around for years training, and most importantly paying.

Your best members, however, are the ones who feel the true effect of discounting. It's that core group who renews year after year, supports the profit centers in the club such as personal training, paid full price for a membership, and takes the biggest hit from a club that offers endless discounts.

For example, the club has a member who has been with the gym for two years, pays $40 per month, and works out of his house. Explain each of these discounted groups to this member:

- Herds of college students who flood the club every spring paying $99 for four months.
- Senior citizens who work out during the day for a discounted senior rate.
- Five people from a small local company all paying $30 a month on a corporate rate.
- Police officers form the local precinct all paying $30 a month on a special rate.
- The second person in a couple who is paying $20 per month.

How would you explain to this person, one of your better members, who is paying full price and who supports the club's profit centers, that he is almost the only guy in the gym dumb enough to pay full price?

How would you explain to this person, one of your better members, who is paying full price and who supports the club's profit centers, that he is almost the only guy in the gym dumb enough to pay full price?

He will find out in the locker room, or in the cardio area, and he may never say a thing. But by renewal time he is gone without an explanation. And what are the chances this person ever recommending any friend to join the club since he felt he was just cheated as a member?

Discounting hurts the club in two ways. First of all, it lowers the club's retention rate by punishing the members who are paying full price and who resent all the club's discounts for what appears to be no logical reason. Second, it lowers the return-per-member for monthly memberships. The average of all those discounts previously listed is barely over $30 per month, not the $40 the club is allegedly selling and basing its business plan on today.

The goal with establishing a price is too gain a higher return-per-member on a monthly basis. In the past, you used to discount memberships because you had little in the way of expectations for member usage. Today, you want the members to train and get results because they will stay longer, pay longer, and support the club's profit centers each time they come to workout.

Discounts should either be eliminated or minimalized in a club's pricing structure as detailed in Chapter 7. You don't have to discount to sell memberships because few if any other service businesses discount. The member may ask for a discount if he has visited other clubs, but trial memberships will help here since using them will shift the emphasis away from discounts as sales tools to the service the club offers and the experience the potential member has during their visits.

You don't have to discount to sell memberships because few if any other service businesses discount.

The Key Points You Should Have Gotten from this Chapter

- Most pricing in the fitness industry is based upon false assumptions.

- The search for the perfect price causes many owners to substantially under-price their club's memberships.

- Your club should be built and run for the top 60% of the demographics in your area according to affluence.

- Many owners won't raise their price because they are afraid it will keep members out, but a price too low may also keep the better members from your club because it appears too cheap.

- Prices for memberships in the industry don't reflect changes in the cost of doing business and building clubs.

- When it comes to setting your price against your competition, you only have three choices.

- Pricing is artificially low in the industry because of the first-visit closing pressure you put upon potential clients.

- Trial memberships are the only way to drive up the price.

6
Building the Club's Most Important Asset

The most important thing you should get from this chapter is:

The most important asset a club owner owns is the club's receivable base, which is the total outstanding balance of all member payments who are on a contractual obligation.

Definitions and concepts you will need to know:

- *Receivable base:* Money you could count on collecting in the future from your current members if you never sold another membership in the club.

- *Loss rates:* Money the club owner should have collected from the receivable base but couldn't because the member elected not to pay.

- *Cancellation rate:* Cancellations are members who sign a contractual obligation with the club and then later cancel their membership due to moving, a medical problem, a death, or a three-day right of cancellation required by federal law for anyone signing a retail installment contract.

- *Obligation:* The member signs a contractual obligation to pay the club for a membership over time. The recommended time is 12 months. This membership tool has the lowest loss rate and will provide the club with the highest return per member.

- *Method of payment:* Method of payment is how the member elects to pay for the membership. Writing a check each month, or allowing the club to draft a checking account or credit card, are both methods of payment. Neither one of these methods infers any type of obligation from the member to the club. Obligation is a separate issue defined by a contractual tool such as a 12-month membership.

- *EFT:* Electronic funds transfer is a method of payment the member might elect that involves giving the club permission to automatically draft a membership payment from the member's checking account or credit card each month.

- *The yield:* The yield is what's left over from a member payment after allowing for a loss rate, cancellation rate, cost of collection, and the effect of any free services the club provides in the member's name.

Understanding and Developing a Membership-Receivable Base

Club owners should be seeking long-term stability, the ability to project revenues into the future, the capacity to have cash flow in slight downturns in the business, and most importantly, the ability to increase the worth of their business and sell it in the future at a gain if or when they decide to get out of the business. Only one method to accomplish all of these financial goals is possible, and that is through the development of a *strong receivable base* based on consistent member payments.

First of all, we need to understand just what a receivable base really is. A receivable base can be explained several ways but the simplest is thinking of it as how much money could you count on collecting in the future from your current members if you never sold another membership in your club.

The key words are *count on* and *future*. For there to be a receivable base there has to be an obligation between the member and the club. If no obligation exists, then the club owner has nothing to count on at a later date.

For example, an older-style club that sells the majority of its memberships as paid-in-full does not have a receivable base, since no revenue exists that can be projected into the future. The owner received cash today, spent the cash today, and must sell memberships in the future to have revenue in the future.

This same scenario applies to club owners who build their membership based upon open- ended, month-to-month memberships. These owners do have cash flow in the form of a monthly check from the total of their member payments, but they don't have a true receivable base since they can't count on revenue in the future. The nature of being month-to-month means if the entire membership decided to leave tomorrow, they could by simply call their banks and cancel their monthly drafts if the club was using some form of electronic funds transfer (EFT).

This type of club seldom loses its entire membership in one swift shot, but it can often lose 30 to 40 percent of its membership in a 90-day period if a fresh, bright competitor moves across the street. Without obligation, meaning the member has some type of commitment to pay the club in the future such as a 12-month contract, the club doesn't have the stability a similar club would have with a strong receivable base.

Another way to look at a receivable base is that the club sells memberships over time, meaning that each month its opened, and the accumulation of the monthly payments each member makes to belong to the gym grows to a certain point that provides stability for the club owner in the form of cash flow she can plan for in the future. This stable cash flow becomes the club's most valuable asset since it is something bankers will

This type of club seldom loses its entire membership in one swift shot, but it can often lose 30 to 40 percent of its membership in a 90-day period if a fresh, bright competitor moves across the street.

recognize and give loans against compared to equipment or the number of members a club claims to have, both which have little meaning to a bank since these things are worthless if the club owner should fail.

Apply the concept of receivable base to a typical club. A 13,000-square-foot club opens with a $59 per month membership and a 12-month obligation (annual contract) for a total annual membership of $708. In this example, ignore any type of one-time membership fee. This is only about the receivable base and not the money a club would get up front for its memberships.

If the club enrolled 90 members a month for 12 months, it would have a gross membership (yes, you owners who have been around awhile are chuckling at how gross your members are sometimes) of 1,080 at the end of the year. But, in real life, you never collect all of the money from all of the members. Loss rates will be there and these need to be subtracted.

Loss rates will be discussed in detail later in this chapter, but at this point look at the 1,080 members and how this number would be affected. First of all, not everyone pays as promised. This is one type of loss rate that will affect the total. By using 12-month contracts, which have the highest chance of being collected, this club would only lose about 10 percent of its membership due to nonpayment over a year's period of time.

The club would also lose another 12 percent due to cancellations. This type of cancellation would be due to either a member moving too far from the club, a medical problem, a death, or a three-day right of rescission, which is a cooling off period the members can use to escape any type of retail installment contract such as a 12-month membership on a contractual basis at a club.

The total of these two numbers is 22 percent. This means that there would be a 22- percent adjustment to the members paying the club:

1,080 gross members x .78 collection rate
= 842 members paying at year's end

When these members make their $59 monthly payment, the club would receive a gross check before collection expenses of $49,678. This gross check would be adjusted by about seven percent, which is the national average for clubs using a sophisticated third-party collection system such as ABC Financial Services in Little Rock, Arkansas, the category leader in club financial services. The net amount to the club would be:

$49,678 x .93 (7% collection fee) = $46,200

Projected as part of a total outstanding receivable base, which represents the total amount of member payments the club owner can count on being collected in the future (in the form of a 12-month contract between the member and the club), the total to be collected from all member payments

If the club enrolled 90 members a month for 12 months, it would have a gross membership (yes, you owners who have been around awhile are chuckling at how gross your members are sometimes) of 1,080 at the end of the year.

would be approximately $550,000 to $600,000. This $550,000 to $600,000 number would be defined as the club's total outstanding receivables or receivable base.

In actuality, this number would not be this high since the previous assumption is that every member is on full, 12-month contracts. In the real world, a club has members that have just signed up today and members who are a day from making their last payment. Over a number of years, the club's average outstanding membership will actually only average about seven to eight months in its receivable base. Allowing for this would mean that the club in the previous example would only have a receivable base of between $350,000 and $400,000. For example:

1,080 members x $59 = $63,720
$63,720 x 7 months average member contract = $446,040
$446,040 x .78% (22% losses) = $347,911

Going further, this club also has a monthly base operating expense (BOE) of $60,000. This includes all bills the club pays each month including payroll, taxes, cost of goods, debt service, and any other bills the club has to cover its monthly breakeven point. The exception would be if the owner is offsite and has a manager. In this case, the owner's salary would not be counted as part of the club's BOE. The relationship between the net-receivable check each month and the club's BOE is the most important thing to understand in a fitness business.

> The relationship between the net-receivable check each month and the club's BOE is the most important thing to understand in a fitness business.

The Single Most Important Number to Look at in Your Business

An important relationship coexists between the monthly operating expense (BOE) and the net amount of the monthly member payments, or receivable check. Once the net check gets to a point that a certain percentage of expense is automatically met each month, the club has reached a level of stability and maturity that will allow it to withstand heavy competition as well as any serious downturns in member sales.

Your goal is 70-percent coverage of your monthly BOE by your net-receivable check. Using this example, the club's BOE is $60,000 per month. A 70-percent coverage goal would mean that the club's goal for its net-receivable check would be $42,000 per month. The club in this example has a net check of $46,000, which represents a very stable and financially secure business.

This could happen as early as the 13th month for a new club and should happen no later than the 25th month. Existing clubs that are revamping their receivable base and pricing structure as discussed in this book should make reaching 70-percent coverage of their BOE by their net monthly receivable check as one of their prime goals for their business.

The ultimate goal, of course, is to grow your net-receivable check to the point that it covers 100 percent of your monthly expenses. In this world, you receive your check on the first of the month and your club is becomes profitable for the month. Every dollar you make from that point forward becomes profit. From our research at the Thomas Plummer Company, only about five to six percent of the clubs in the country reach this goal. It is, however, the goal to strive for in your club business.

The Difference Between Obligation and Method of Payment

A common point of confusion for many owners is the difference between setting an obligation for the member and the member's method of payment. The actual point of confusion arises when owners start to use electronic funds transfer (EFT) for collecting their member payments.

Method of payment refers to how the member actually makes their payment each month for their membership. A member may give a club actual cash, write a check, or allow the club to automatically draft (withdraw funds electronically from a checking, savings, or credit card) each month. For those of you in less sophisticated club states, the occasional chicken over the counter as a trade is not out of the question, but for the purposes of this book, please ignore farm goods as an accepted method of payment.

Having a thousand members on EFT each month does ensure good cash flow. EFT as a method of payment means that the member will, for the sake of convenience, allow the club owner to automatically take the payment each month electronically from his account or credit card. *This does not infer obligation*, unless the club has established a 12-month contract first and then let the member pay by their desired method of payment.

In other words, without first establishing a contract between the member and club that promises payment for a fixed period of time, such as 12 months, the club owner has not developed a strong receivable base by enrolling the member on EFT payments. The member can still walk away by simply calling his bank if he has not first signed a contract for obligation.

The rule of thumb at this point is to first establish an obligation (contract) and then let the new member pick his own method of payment. The contract builds a receivable base, the main goal of selling club memberships, and the member makes his payments using a method he that meets his individual needs. The right flow or order for a club membership looks like this:

- The club establishes a pricing system that is fair to the member yet allows the club to collect the most money from the most members while developing a strong receivable base.

- This pricing system is first built upon the 12-month contract, fair to the member yet collectable for the club since 12-month contracts only have

> For those of you in less sophisticated club states, the occasional chicken over the counter as a trade is not out of the question, but for the purposes of this book, please ignore farm goods as an accepted method of payment.

123

about a 10% national loss rate if collected by a strong third-party financial service company. This establishes obligation first.

- Once the new member agrees to the obligation, the club then offers method of payment. For example, the club's monthly price might be $49 per month if the club may automatically deduct the payment from the member's checking account or credit card (EFT). If the member wishes to write a check each month instead, the club charges $54 per month passing along the slightly higher charge of servicing a check as opposed to EFT.

- The club should have established a relationship with a third-party financial service company (data-management company) to be the hired *bad* person and separate the collection function from workout function. The third-party then becomes the power that collects money rather than hoping a member will pay the club since the club really doesn't enjoy any leverage for collections.

The issue is: Does EFT have a higher collection rate than people who simply write checks each month to pay their bills? The answer is yes and no. Overall, EFT payments are collected at an average rate of about seven-percent better than people who simply write checks each month. It seems that this number should be much higher since the club is automatically collecting the payments directly from the member's account each month.

It also seems that it should be higher since the companies that are EFT processors, as opposed to true third-party financial service companies, claim that by using EFT you will collect all the money from all the members every month.

No one collects all the money from all the members each month. No one will ever collect all the money from all the members each month. And anyone that claims to collect all the money from all the members each month is either lying or doesn't understand the concept of basic loss rates.

The illusion of EFT is that it is a magical cure for a club's collection woes. EFT is advertised directly at most clubs' weakest part: the back-shop business area. A club owner that has tried ineffective systems is drawn to the magic cure being offered by a system that claims to be so effective in solving the gym owner's biggest headache. These clubs often use EFT as the only method of payment, besides paying cash for the year, setting up an adversarial relationship between a potential member and the club.

According to the major business magazines, only about 50 percent of the people in the country are comfortable with EFT as part of their bill-paying routine. The exceptions are a person's insurances, car payment, and investments, which a slightly higher percentage of people are more comfortable in using EFT to pay.

Assuming that you build most of your clubs to appeal to the top 60 percent of the area's demographics, it can probably be estimated that the more financially sophisticated segment of the market might be more comfortable with having their accounts automatically drafted. You might then be able to project that at least 60 to 70 percent of your target market is likely to be okay with an EFT system.

That still leaves 30 to 40 percent of your market not comfortable with giving their checking account information or credit card numbers to a club. And if the potential member is not comfortable with giving out that information, then he will most likely not be happy with paying for a membership in full, which is often the only membership alternative a club that forces EFT will give.

You've probably heard a club owner say, "I have no problem with EFT at my club. Not a single member that enrolled complained about having to use it." In this case, it's not the members who enrolled that are the problem; it's the potential members who never even came in the club because they know they have to use EFT that is the problem.

Paying your rent or mortgage payment is a necessity. Making your car payment is something you just have to do. Joining a club is something a person can do without because they are using discretionary money, which is money left over in their life to do with as they please after they have paid all their other real-life bills such as the ones previously mentioned.

EFT does have a place in the club business as a method-of-payment option, but it does not guarantee collections — it just makes collections simpler in some situations. This is especially true if you aren't using a strong third-party collection company in conjunction with your EFT. Before EFT can be discussed, you need to have an understanding of the collection options for member payments open to most clubs.

> EFT does have a place in the club business as a method-of-payment option, but it does not guarantee collections — it just makes collections simpler in some situations.

Collecting Your Membership Money from Your Members

A number of ways to collect money from your members are available. Beating the members senseless who didn't pay was one of the more popular options in the old days, but as is most things in life, the good things are sometimes lost. A club owner's options are somewhat limited in scope and number, but not in the return that is possible if she avoids a few of the more common mistakes.

> Beating the members senseless who didn't pay was one of the more popular options in the old days, but as is most things in life, the good things are sometimes lost.

Doing It Yourself

Most owners like to brag that they are entrepreneurs. They hang out at family functions, or try and impress a new future significant other, and say, "Yeah, I'm an entrepreneur. I'm in business for myself."

What they don't know is that entrepreneur is French and means: *Get the hell out of the way. I'll do it myself.* In this business, too many control freaks

Many of you in the gym business are in it because you were such lousy employees in the real world.

are masquerading as gym owners. Many of you in the gym business are in it because you were such lousy employees in the real world. In other words, you are somewhat unhireable because since as a species, gym owners rather do things themselves rather than let people tell them what to do.

Collecting your own memberships is the ultimate example of trying to be in control. The problem with this scenario is that the more you try to do yourselves, the less control you really have in your business because of one of the true maxims in the business:

You can manage more than you can do yourself.

Collecting and serving your own memberships usually means higher loss rates, little economy of scale (even if you have multiple units you seldom get to the point that it's cost effective to establish your own billing and collection company), and higher risk because your most important asset is controlled and managed by too small of a number. In other words, if you have three units and a small office set up to service your own accounts managed by two to three people, you are only one car wreck away, especially if these two to three people go to lunch at the same time together, from being out of business. It is possible to collect your own memberships but the effectiveness is seldom there. Generally, two key things go wrong when you service your own accounts.

First of all, your effort is concentrated on the good members that would have paid no matter what you did to them, and not enough on the problem members who move, close accounts, are chronically late with their payments, get divorced, are overdrawn on their accounts, or any of the multitude of problems associated with trying to collect payments from hundreds of members. Even with an in-house system that forces EFT as the only membership option, you will still have problems with closed accounts and overdrawn accounts. Remember that no one collects all the money from all the members every time.

The second common issue with do it yourself collection systems is that the losses are too big too soon. The national average for the cost of collection with a major third-party financial service company should be about seven percent, as was mentioned earlier. This number represents the combination of the charges for the servicing and collection of EFT and the slightly higher charges for the servicing and collection of coupon/check payments.

Owners that collect their own memberships usually do a decent job of servicing and collecting from the members who willingly pay each month. The newer billing software available everywhere in the club industry gives the illusion that the better the software the better the collections. Good software can give you more options for collecting from the members and better tracking, but software alone cannot increase the effectiveness of your collections.

The difficulty arises from the problem members. Not everyone pays on time as promised and then the fun begins. These members take you out of the gym business and into the collecting-money-from-the-member business, something most gym owners are not very good at and don't want to be even if they had the time or courage. Problem accounts are going to average anywhere from a few percentage points a month to sometimes 10 percent or more of your member file. And these are not all just members who are late. Closed accounts, members that move, divorces, bounced checks, members who change jobs, and just plain members who like to pay late or not at all are just a few of the categories you would have to deal with on a daily basis.

Instead of collecting these payments for the seven-percent average, these problem accounts are turned over to an end-of-the-road collection company. Clubs don't normally do well in chasing down and solving member account problems. This is vastly detailed work and it's hard to develop a process that can systematically turn a troubled member account back into a strong reliable payment.

These companies specialize in hardcore collections on bad accounts and they usually charge somewhere between 33 to 50 percent of what's collected. They can do their job, but the problem is that most of the membership contracts they received as bad accounts should have never been turned over to them in the first place if the club would have been using a sophisticated third-party financial-service company.

Using EFT-Processing Companies

This type of company usually provides the software and systems to set up a more effective EFT processing for those clubs that specialize in just using drafts for their member payments. The company provides the software, the club sets up the accounts, and then the company actually does the draft for the club.

This is generally better than doing it yourself, but you still have the inherent problem of trouble accounts at an added cost to the club. If the processing company encounters a collection problem with a member account, again such as an overdraft, the account is sent back to the club to be solved, but not before the processing company adds on a service fee for resubmitting the bad account as well as other fees such as reporting fees, the cost of returning the account, etc.

These processing companies give the illusion that they are saving you money but on a national average the total costs of their extra fees often gets the club back to that seven-percent average or higher. The club still has to solve the account problems and the risk that the club's losses are going to be too big too soon are still there.

A common problem with this system is that the club doesn't do anything at all with the returned problem accounts except put them into a drawer.

These processing companies give the illusion that they are saving you money but on a national average the total costs of their extra fees often gets the club back to that seven-percent average or higher.

127

Since the accounts are normally returned slowly throughout the month to the club. The number seems small and the club usually doesn't do anything with them since it doesn't have an infrastructure in place to handle that small number of returns. Again, this translates into losses for the club; money the club should have collected but didn't because it was using a system that was never designed to collect future service-club memberships.

Using Third-Party Financial Service Companies

The name *third-party financial-service company* is in many ways not even a valid name anymore. This type of company has evolved into more of a *data-management provider* for clubs, providing much more than the servicing and collection of member accounts.

The name *third-party* came about because the club used the illusion of a strong outside company to collect its payments. It didn't take owners long to figure out that the club would be the last to get paid each month by the member since the club had no leverage to collect. What was the club going to do, kick the member out? He already wasn't paying and wanted out anyway.

Creative owners back in the 1960s formed their own outside companies, actually still the club itself, with strong sounding official names to scare the members into thinking they were paying someone who represented the club and that had the power to do something bad to you if you didn't pay. So would you make your payment on time to the small-time local club owner, or would you pay the World International Superior Collection Services?

This illusion worked but eventually club collections became too sophisticated and owners began wanting more reporting and more money from their memberships. Third-party collection companies became strong in the industry in the 1970s, but a series of very unethical companies that eventually failed, coupled with a number of third parties that were taken down due to cash advancing against membership contracts for gyms that crashed, decimated the number of third-party survivors over time.

Today only a few legitimate choices in the fitness industry for third-party financial service companies are available. Those that have survived and thrived have evolved into data-management companies that provide in-depth reporting, computer software support systems for the club, data manipulation, and other services that tend to give the gym owner more and better information for managing her club, as well as optimum collection power for the club's memberships.

> In essence, data-management companies become your partner in your business by allowing the club to totally concentrate on the production side of the business

In essence, data-management companies become your partner in your business by allowing the club to totally concentrate on the production side of the business while the third-party company concentrates on giving you management information and strong cash flow from the memberships the club sells over time. This partnership provides the long-term stability and planning ability a club owner needs to continue to grow a business over the years.

The Next Step

With the advent of the Internet, the third-party financial service/data management companies will have to evolve another step. The logical course is that all your data will be held, stored, and maintained in the data-management company's computers and you will access all of your account information online. Several companies, such as Aphelion, are leading the way into this area, but the exciting times when an owner can easily source and research all accounts and management data are still ahead.

There will of course be problems in the delivery system initially, but over time the club owner should gain quicker access and more pertinent information to make club management decisions. For example, a club owner might be considering a change in her marketing plan. A few simple key strokes on her computer and she should be able to access the demographics of her current membership including where they live, ages, usage in the club, income, e-mail address, average member payment and other information that would influence the type and amount of marketing a club would need to do to establish a niche or specialization.

Other information that would become available to the owner in this scenario would be the amount spent in profit centers during each member visit, renewal percentages, and daily cash flow from all sources. As financial service companies evolve in the next few years, their ability to help your business beyond just the collection of money and basic reporting should grow substantially.

Factors that Influence the Strength of Your Receivable Base

The following four major factors that influence the strength of your receivable base and the total money you will collect over time from your membership base determine the yield you can expect from an average membership over a year's period of time. The owner of any fitness business only has one main purpose: to strengthen and protect your most valuable asset, which is the receivable base. All of these factors can be controlled to some extent and an owner needs to do whatever it takes to minimalize the effect each of these have on the club's total outstanding contracts to be collected. These four factors are:

> The owner of any fitness business only has one main purpose: to strengthen and protect your most valuable asset, which is the receivable base.

- Loss rate
- Cancellations made by the club
- Cost of collections and servicing member payments
- Free enhancements added as part of the membership

The Loss Rate Has the Most Powerful Effect on Your Receivables

The simplest way to explain *loss rate* is to think of it as money you should have collected from the members but didn't because the member opted not to pay for some reason. For example, your club signed up 100 new members in July of last year. True loss rate would mean that you track those 100 members through their year and determine exactly when they stopped paying on their membership agreements.

In this example, assume you are using 12-month agreements, which should have an annual loss rate of about 10 percent. This means that 10 people will not pay for whatever reason but 90 will pay until the end of their membership term. This also assumes your club is using a strong third-party financial-service company to service these memberships.

Another way to look at this is that your club will lose slightly less than one percent of its 100 hundred members each month for 12 months. Where this gets complicated is that your club is also adding new members every month and there may be other reasons the member may not pay that will be discussed later in this chapter.

Applied to principal is another way to consider loss rate. This term means each month the total outstanding principal to be collected, which is represented by the amount each member has to pay on the remaining balance of his contract with the club (obligation) changes.

During each month the club adds new members to its total outstanding, but it also subtracts too in the form of members who make their last payment but don't renew, those who elect not to pay, members who have a legitimate reason to suspend payment such as a move or medical, or those who pay the balance of their membership in full when it gets down to the last few payments. You can then compare what should have been collected from your total outstanding against what is actually collected each month and figure loss.

However, the club doesn't need to have a true loss rate or the exact applied to principal to gain valuable information on protecting and strengthening its receivable base.

However, the club doesn't need to have a true loss rate or the exact applied to principal to gain valuable information on protecting and strengthening its receivable base. All you really need is to understand that each month a certain percentage of contracts will kick out of your system and then work with this average.

Three prime factors that directly affect how high or low your loss rate will be are:

- The higher the pressure at point of sale the higher the loss rate will be.
- Each membership tool you use has a loss rate associated with it.
- If you over promise and under deliver.

High Pressure Produces High Loss Rates

Some people just sign a membership agreement to get away from the salesperson in hopes of getting out of the club alive. Pounding people into submission — again read chain clubs here — results in higher loss rates, especially in what's called first-payment defaults.

First payment defaults are people who, after thinking about their sales experience in the club, feel that some slickster salesperson talked them into something they didn't really want. They then exact their revenge on the salesperson and the club by defaulting on the first payment on their membership agreement. It doesn't matter if the member writes a check or is set up on EFT; they will find a way to not make that first payment.

Clubs that practice strong first-visit sales closing should track their first payment defaults by the club total and by individual salespeople. A salesperson that claims an unusually high first-visit closing rate will almost always have the accompanying first-payment default number to go along with it.

Normally a good salesperson in a club will close about 30 to 40 percent of their first visits over time. If they are closing higher than this then their first payment defaults should be tracked monthly.

The element behind pressure sales is the term *buyer's regret*. These means somebody bought something and then had serious second thoughts immediately after the purchase. For example, you go to the mall to buy sandals and two hours later you're sitting in your living room feeling bad about that entire new outfit you just bought because some salesperson said, "Hey, you really look good in those shorts and they really go well with those sandals you were looking at." This is buyer's regret, or the, "What the hell did I buy this time?" feeling you get thinking of how you are going to pay for the purchase.

In most cases the club actually causes buyer's regret. Too much pressure is put on the first visit to sign today and the use of discounting at point of sale both add to high buyer's regret and higher losses than need be.

Trial memberships take a lot of the buyer's regret out of the picture since the consumer has an actual chance to try before he buys. With trials, the consumer also feels that he is in more control of the buying situation than he does when he forced to making a buying decision 20-minutes after visiting a club for the first time.

True trial memberships, coupled with a strong third-party financial-service company and 12-month contracts, can usually drop a club's loss rate to less than 10 percent annually. Most of this gain comes because the client felt he actually participated in the buying decision instead of being forced into something he didn't even know he really wanted.

Discounting Hurts You Worse than You Think Over Time

Discounting is a practice left over from the 1960s in the fitness business and may actually go all the way back to people selling dance lessons in the 1940s. No matter how old it really is, discounting is one of those things that

> This is buyer's regret, or the, "What the hell did I buy this time?" feeling you get thinking of how you are going to pay for the purchase.

this industry outgrew too many years ago and which still gives the fitness business a very bad name.

Discounting means that you offer a potential member one price today, but if he waits and comes back tomorrow, he'll lose that special price. The deal is for today only and is a tool to force the consumer to buy today or be punished for returning.

For example, during one trip to the Hyde Park area of Massachusetts, a visit to nine clubs in one day yielded interesting results. Every single club offered a discount if potential members were willing to makeup their minds right then and there that this gym was the one for them. The most outrageous discount was offered by the last facility visited and went something like this:

> "Sorry, you just missed our sale. This is the last day and we just sold our last membership at the sale price. But you may be in luck if the manager is in a good mood. Normally our membership fee is $350, but during the sale we were allowing new members to get started for just $50. Our manager is still here and if I can still get you that price, would you be willing to get started today, because I absolutely know he won't extend that offer to anyone tomorrow."

This discount, or take-away close, once worked in the fitness business but the consumer, at least those in the top 60 percent of the demographics you should seek, has grown too sophisticated and feels insulted by this type of practice.

This discount, or take-away close, once worked in the fitness business but the consumer, at least those in the top 60 percent of the demographics you should seek, has grown too sophisticated and feels insulted by this type of practice. If you're 20-years old and never been pitched before by anyone then you might fall for this nonsense, but the people most owners want in their gyms would find this type of discount very insulting.

The consumer knows that when she returns tomorrow she will get just about any deal she wants because she understands that the club is in the deal-making business. Buyer's regret pops in again when the consumer goes home, and then she questions the deal she got compared to what she thinks others may have gotten that were better than hers.

Discounting is based on the principle that you need to give the consumer a deal to get started and that the only way to do this is by taking away something. Actually, two ways are possible to get a consumer to do something you want them to do, but one of them takes more preparation and more follow through by the club. The rule is:

In the club business, the easy way is usually the wrong way.

- *Negative incentives:* An example of a negative incentive is discounting. Simply put, you punish a consumer for not making the decision you want when you want it. *Do it today or pay more later* is a negative incentive that works on an unsophisticated consumer and irritates everyone else. But it is the easiest way and doesn't really require anything more than a sales office and an old-style sales dinosaur.

- *Positive incentives:* Positive incentive means that you reward the consumer for making the choice you desire. For example, if you join the club any time during the first seven days (out of a 14-day trial) the club will give you a gym bag, water bottle, tee shirt, three free tans, one free sports drink, a free personal training session, and coupons for other discounts in the club. And if you decide to join during your first visit, you will also receive more loot in the form of an additional month added to membership and $50 in *club bucks* that can be spent any where in the club.

In this case, the positive incentive on validating the sale is based upon giving the consumer loot to join the club. In a club that uses negative incentives, the consumer may buy and then walks out with nothing more than a few pieces of paper and the receipt for a membership that he will have to pay for into the future. In a club using positive incentives, the person walks out with loot and has his buying decision validated.

The club using the positive incentive sends the new member home with a bag of stuff that goes far toward softening buyer's regret. Most importantly, however, is that the club using positive incentives has virtually guaranteed that every member pays the same price.

You're not giving a deal, which translates into fewer first payment discounts, lower loss rates because the consumer was rewarded for making the decision you wanted, and lower pressure because of the ability to make the buying decision during the first seven days of the trial, as opposed to being forced to make a decision during the first visit.

> **The club using the positive incentive sends the new member home with a bag of stuff that goes far toward softening buyer's regret.**

The Membership Tool the Club Uses also Influences the Loss Rate

Who collects and how the memberships are collected are factors in how much money the club will collect from its memberships through its receivable base. Using a strong third-party financial-service company will significantly increase the overall money you collect from your memberships.

The tool you use with the members also plays a factor in how collectable your membership agreements are too. *Tool* is defined as the agreement and term the club uses to define its relationship with its members. For example, one club might use a 12-month membership agreement, another a 24-month, and a third in the same area might use month-to-month, pay-as-you-go memberships. All of these are examples of tools and each tool has its positives and negatives as to their effect on the club's loss rate.

- The Month-to-Month, Pay-As-You-Go Membership

This tool was popularized by some of the club chains and was a fad seminar topic at the major tradeshows for several years. This type of membership means that the club does not establish any type of obligation with the member. The member can simply pay month-to-month and cancel any time she chooses.

This type of membership seemed to be a knee-jerk reaction to the clubs that forced long-term memberships upon their members and then suffered the wrath of State Attorney Generals all over the country. Instead of contracts, why not just let the members pay month-to-month and come and go as they please?

This type of membership is riddled with problems. First of all, the losses are about three and four percent per month or about 36 to 48 percent annually. This means that if a club signs up 100 members in January, by the next January it will only have somewhere between 52 to 64 members left. In other words, you could lose almost half your members over time just through the loss rates associated with this type of membership.

This type of membership seems logical but is actually not a good thing for the club. Clubs using month-to-month have to do the same work to sign up a new member as a club using a fixed obligation does, runs the same kind of marketing (if not more) because the losses are so high, has the same start-up cost per new member and the same labor cost to get the new member into the system. In other words, it has the same cost but has a much less likely chance to collect money on from the membership over a year's period of time.

Month-to-month memberships may work in very high-volume markets such as San Francisco or Manhattan, but the rest of the country should avoid month-to-month memberships because of the excessive loss rates.

Month-to-month memberships may work in very high-volume markets such as San Francisco or Manhattan, but the rest of the country should avoid month-to-month memberships because of the excessive loss rates.

It's pointless to offer month-to-month memberships as your only membership option. Clubs that feel they need to compete with other clubs that feature month-to-month can do so but offer at least two membership types and simply let the member decide. This type of club would offer month-to-month at a rate of about $8 to $10 more per month than its normal 12-month contract rate.

For example, if the club sold 12-month memberships for $49 per month, it could offer a month-to-month option for about $57 to $59 per month coupled with a slightly larger membership fee. Using the $8 to $10 spread, about 80 percent of the club's new members each month should take the 12-month membership, which provides more stability and lower losses than the month-to-month.

- The 24- to 36-Month Membership Tools

These were made popular by the big chains for several reasons. First of all, old-style owners believed that they didn't want the customer to have to make a second buying decision at the end of the first year. Second, two- or three-year memberships make for a larger paper receivable base, which was better with the banks at that time since the size of the receivable base was the important issue, not the effective return.

While on the surface, two-year and longer contracts look pretty good to a club owner because of the belief that once a member signs one, he is locked into the system forever. However, some misconceptions about this longer contract need to be addressed. This type of membership tool may look good, but in the long run using membership agreements this long may be really detrimental to the club's financial health.

Two-year contracts have an exceptionally high loss rate somewhere in the 35- to 50- percent range. If these losses were spread out over two years, and loss rate was the only negative attribute of this tool, using these wouldn't be a bad deal for the club. The problem, however, is that the losses for two-year contracts almost all occur during the first 12 months and are associated with three stages of loss. Buyer's regret over a two-year commitment leads to a high first-payment default, the glamour of working out fades during the first three months for clubs that don't have above-average member service, and the feeling that this membership will never end around the sixth month all add to high loss rates during the first year.

The chain clubs that sold two-year and longer memberships often experienced losses higher than 50 percent because of the added factor of heavy first-visit close pressure. Two-year contracts are obviously harder to sell than one-year contracts and require a more sophisticated salesperson to be effective using this tool.

Due to this difficulty, a much higher per sale occurs when a club uses two-year contracts as opposed to one-year. You have to dole out higher commissions and pay higher marketing costs for closing a two-year contract that then leads to the need for more marketing to buy a higher number of prospects than you would selling solely one-year contracts.

But because the total outstanding receivable base gets so high using 24-month contracts, they still persist in some markets. It's important to remember that it's not the total outstanding receivable base that is important, but the *return-per-member* that drives the club's income stream. An example of how a club tries to force 24-month contracts is by pricing them lower than 12-month agreements and of the return the club would get off of each tool.

The technology itself concerning two-year contracts is also dated. This type of tool originated over 40-years ago in the club business. The buyer at that time was not nearly as sales sophisticated as today's consumer and was much more susceptible to first- visit drop closes and signing long-term commitments for a membership.

A club owner could still sell long-term contract today if he wanted his club to be filled with everyone from the shallow end of the gene pool. Today's clubs should again focus on only the top 60% of the affluence in their demographic marketplace. A few gyms may specialize in nontraditional populations, but if you are going to risk investor money, or worse your own money and that of your family, do it by targeting the populations that are known to have money and who have the highest possibility of joining and supporting a fitness business.

> The chain clubs that sold two-year and longer memberships often experienced losses higher than 50 percent because of the added factor of heavy first-visit close pressure.

Sophisticated buyers want to buy a membership that makes sense. One-year commitments make sense. Two-year commitments do not make sense to a more affluent buyer who has been pitched on everything from life insurance to phone plans. This could be taken even further by asking the question, "Why use any contract at all? Why not just give everyone an open-ended option?"

Specific membership plans will be discussed in Chapter 6, but for the sake of this example remember that a strong receivable base gives the club stability, long-term planning ability, and raises the value of the club to a potential buyer.

Even club owners totally committed to open-end memberships could have the best of both worlds by simply giving the potential member a choice when choosing a membership type.

As mentioned earlier, a club could have an open-ended membership priced at $69 per month and a contractual membership at $59 per month and let the member decide which membership is best for him. If the price for an open-ended is about $8- to $10-per- month higher the contractual price, about 80 percent of the new members will pick the contract option. This give the club owner the ability to offer an open-ended membership while building a solid receivable base built upon 12-month contracts.

A final note on long-term memberships is that by using this tool you give an automatic edge to your competitors. If your club features 24-month memberships and uses the necessary pressure needed to sell this tool, you are opening the door to a competitor that offers 12-month or a combination of 12-month and open-ended memberships.

This type of club is also giving another advantage to the competitor in membership costs. Long-term memberships are more costly to sell and that club's cost per membership may be as much as twice as high as a club using 12-month memberships. For example, a club that is using primarily 24-month memberships may have commissions of $40 to $50 per sales because the total amount of the membership is larger compared to a standard 12-month membership. Losses are also higher because of the tool itself, and therefore the club owner must spend more on marketing because she is not growing her business, only replacing the members she lost.

Keep in mind that a club owner using a 24-month membership will have losses of about 36 to −48 percent, most of which will be incurred during the first year, as opposed to an owner using a 12-month tool that will have annual losses of only about 10 percent. A club that is using exclusively 12-month memberships will normally only pay $25 or so in commissions and should have lower marketing costs because the loss rates for the 12-month tool are so much lower than a 24-month tool.

• The 12-Month Membership Tool

This is the core element in any club's financial foundation. Low loss rates, highly collectable compared to long-term memberships, easier to sell to the

> If your club features 24-month memberships and uses the necessary pressure needed to sell this tool, you are opening the door to a competitor that offers 12-month or a combination of 12-month and open-ended memberships.

consumer, and a low cost per sale, all combine to make this tool the first step in building a solid financial foundation for a club.

The 12-month membership contract only has loss rates of about 10 percent per year or less than one percent per month. Again, compare this to a club using 24-month contracts that has loss rates of 36 to 48percent.

Another key to using 12-month commitments as your core tool is: *how does the money arrive?* For example, a typical club that uses 24-month contracts as its primary tool also has a 12-month tool in place as a backup in case the buyer balks at signing a 24-month contract. This alone should give the owner a hint that maybe the 24-month deal isn't acceptable to the consumer and does not meet the criteria for a win-win situation.

Take look at a typical pricing option for a club that uses both tools but prices each one so the 24-month is the most acceptable. These are only the actual membership numbers a member might commit to through signing a contract and do not include any upfront fees. The member may chose between these two options:

$49 per month for 12 months = $588
or
$39 per month for 24 months = $936

Many club owners would salivate at the $936 number. Why sell a smaller number when you can get the bigger number on the books. In fact, in this example the pricing is such that the club is trying to force the member to take the $39 per month option. How the money arrives is the key, but the effect the loss rates have on the net to the club is also significant. For example:

$588 x .90% (10% loss rates on 12-month contracts) = $529
The $529 arrives over a 12-month period.
$936 x .64% (36% loss rates minimum on a 24-month contract) = $599
The $599 arrives over a 24-month period.

In other words, the club makes approximately the same amount of money but the money from a 12-month contract arrives in half the time as the 24-month contract. Besides the false myth of building a more effective receivable base, the other popular defense for the 24-month contract has been that the member doesn't have to make another buying decision at the end of 12 months. This defense assumes that the members all stick around, but the loss rate difference invalidates that claim. A club using 24-month contracts versus 12-month memberships as its base tool is eaten alive by the excessive loss rates during the first year and never overcomes the deficit.

Put as bluntly as possible, you as an owner want to go back to the member at the end of one year and ask if she wants to go again for another year. If faced with the fact that you have to service your members and be attentive to their needs, including offering closed-ended renewals and asking for another 12-month commitment as opposed to auto-renewing as discussed earlier in the book, you will be forced to run a better club.

Put as bluntly as possible, you as an owner want to go back to the member at the end of one year and ask if she wants to go again for another year.

Hoping the member doesn't work out, but does continue to let the club draft his account after the initial 12-month period, is not a business plan for a million dollar or more investment for a competitive fitness facility.

Hoping the member doesn't work out, but does continue to let the club draft his account after the initial 12-month period, is not a business plan for a million dollar or more investment for a competitive fitness facility. You want to be forced to ask, "It's time for you to renew as a member. Did I earn your business for another year?" Ask that question and you run a better business. And most importantly, the statistics behind the 12-month membership illustrate that it's the most overall membership tool and effective way to run a fitness business anyway.

• Why Not Simply Go for the Cash?

You can't discuss membership options without discussing cash, or the more current term *paid-in-full,* since not many members actually give clubs cash anymore. They prefer instead to use credit cards or checks.

Why not simply go for the cash, eliminate all the hassle of collecting membership money from the members, and not worry about the loss rates at all? Cash is not king as proclaimed by the old health club and spa guys. Credit is the new ruler in America and is part of the American way. Virtually anything in this country can be bought over time either through credit cards or by signing some type of retail installment contract.

Plus, cash has several problems. First of all, it lowers the return-per-member. The false assumption is that if the club has a cash-only policy, every potential member that wants to buy a membership will simply agree and pay cash. But the amount of members who will pay cash is limited.

The club owner, in response to not enough members paying cash, lowers the cash price. Besides pissing off everyone who has joined already and who has paid a higher price, the return-per-member has dropped. It will keep dropping until it gets to around $249 to $299, which is the eventual ceiling for clubs that go after cash-only memberships.

These clubs all start with higher cash prices but they all also get back to the $249 to $299 number eventually. You won't see any loss rates with paid-in-full memberships since you get all the money at one time, but the return is too low over time since the number of members who will pay in full for any amount over $300 are limited except for maybe two or three of the richest areas in the country.

Paid-in-full memberships are still a part of a club's business plan, but a very small part. The rule is that if a club sells 100 memberships in a month's period of time, only 10 percent or less should have paid-in-full. This example assumes these are all annual memberships. These clubs will get full price, or at least close to full price, for their paid-in-full memberships as opposed to clubs that get cash only and have to lower the price to keep the volume coming in at a base rate.

Clubs that get over 10 percent of their monthly memberships paid-in-full have just received their morning wakeup call. The potential members who are joining the club took a vote and decided that the club's prices are too low. If you get over 10 percent paid up front, then your price is too low for the market. Slowly wean yourself off of cash by raising your cash price slightly each month over a year's period of time. Each raise will force a little more of that month's new business to take the receivable option (monthly payments) and eventually the club will fall under the 10-percent rule. Keep in mind that it's okay to have a few cash memberships for cash-flow purposes, but your real future will be in building the strongest receivable base you can by using 12-month contracts as your core tool.

Another important factor that has to be kept in mind for clubs getting too many paid-in-full memberships is that *cash in equals cash spent*. This means that the cash comes in and is spent at that time. In a perfect world, the club owner would be smart to allocate a percentage each month for club expenses from the cash taken in for that membership. In other words, the owner would try and achieve the basic rule: *The money has to arrive as the service is incurred*. Fitness businesses are more successful when cash flow arrives from membership payments each month in the form of a check collected by a third-party financial company each month comprised of all of the member payments, especially as expenses for that membership are incurred.

> The money has to arrive as the service is incurred.

Paid-in-full memberships may be tempting to a new owner, but the important thing to keep in mind is that a consumer will pay much more for a membership if she can pay over time, which in turn drives up the return-per-member. Paid-in-full memberships are still part of your business plan, but in a much smaller role, since a more sophisticated owner should only think of one thing: develop a strong, consistent receivable base that will net an amount of money from my member payments covering at least 70 percent of your monthly expenses. Going for the cash has never proven to do this over time in the fitness industry.

Cancellations Made by Your Club Are the Second Factor that Determines the Strength of Your Receivable Base

You spend money on marketing to attract new members by spending money on advertising. Your club's salesperson turns that potential member into a real member-- for a commission of course. Then the new member is turned over to a trainer to be set up on a new workout. Don't forget the specific costs to set up the new person and get her into the system, and the additional labor costs you'll incur during the first 30 days to get her fully acclimated into your club. Six weeks later your knuckleheaded, pork-chop-for-brains salesperson didn't you read the manual (what the hell was he thinking?) and the assistant manager lets this new member cancel because she mentioned that she moved and it had become more difficult to get to the club than before.

Canceling memberships is a necessary part of the business and most states have pretty clear laws that govern the cancellation of memberships.

Canceling memberships unnecessarily, however, can severely affect the strength of your receivable base. Members can cancel legally for clearly defined reasons. Examples would be: a move over 25 miles from the club, a medical problem where the member can't continue to participate in the club due to a note from a doctor, death, or the three-day right of rescission which states that a member has a three-day cooling off period and can walk away from any retail-installment contract she signed without penalty.

These are the major reasons a person would be allowed to cancel most health club contracts as stated in the health club laws in most states. If a club cancelled memberships by sticking to just what the law required, its losses against the receivable base would be about one percent per month, or 12 percent annually.

Where the trouble begins is when club managers and owners become creative. Look at the previous example where a woman wants to cancel because she moved. Too many owners and managers cancel because the move caused inconvenience for the member, not because the club had to legally cancel the membership.

Too many owners and managers cancel because the move caused inconvenience for the member, not because the club had to legally cancel the membership.

The proper response to a move should be, "We'd be happy to cancel your membership if you meet the cancellation requirements explained on the membership contract. First of all, did you move over 25 miles from the club? If you did, simply send a copy of one of your new utility bills to the club and we will be happy to cancel you immediately."

A lot of things happened in that paragraph. First of all, it's the law that state cancellation requirements are spelled out on the contracts. You can't enforce them if they are not in writing. Second, the club is happy to cancel the contract if you as a member can prove you actually moved over 25 miles from the club. Getting a copy of a utility bill is about the only way you can get true verification without getting stuck too often. The third factor is that the member is not cancelled until proof arrives and not a point of conversation as most clubs do. Prove it and you are gone, but you still pay until the proof arrives.

The club's loss rate from cancellations should only be about one percent per month. Again this means that for every 100 members a club signs up, about 12 per year will have legitimate excuses to cancel their membership at some point in time. Unfortunately, the true loss rate due to cancellations for most clubs is about three percent per month, or about 36 percent per year. If a club signs up 100 members in this example, it will only have 64 left at the end of the year from club cancellations alone, let alone adding in the losses from nonpayment as discussed earlier. These many cancellations, most of which were unnecessary, can put a serious negative effect on a club's receivable base. Keep in mind that this club also paid advertising costs, commissions, and other start-up costs to buy this member in the first place.

Clubs simply cancel more members then necessary. To build a truly effective receivable base, again defined as the club's ability to collect the most money from the most members, the owners and managers need to adopt the policy that memberships are only cancelled as the law requires.

It is a simple fact of life, though, that a club owner can run a marathon, lift weights for hours, teach three back-to-back classes if necessary, and then sit in the corner and cry like a baby if she has to talk badly to a member. Some club people just cannot handle cancellations.

If you are using a strong third-party financial-service company, consider letting those folks handle the cancellations for the club by first giving the company the parameters you want enforced and that are required by your state. Let it be known, however, that you will hear these words come out of a member's mouth the first week you start this arrangement with your financial company, "The billing company said they would let me out if you would, so they told me to talk to you."

If you are using a reputable company this was not said. What did happen is that the member is working the club, something any club owner in the business for over a week knows happens every day. Set the parameters and let the company do its job to keep the members away from the club.

On the other hand, if you are fairly strong and don't have a problem getting in a member's face, you have other options. The first one is to have the cancellations go to the financial company, but then have the company notify the club of all members who want to cancel. This system works well if the club has some strong people who can step in and attempt to save the cancellations by reselling the member on the club.

In this system, the member first starts with the third-party company where she understands that something larger is looming in the background if she doesn't pay. She is then turned over to the club where she might feel more at ease and more likely to make a deal if possible. If it is a true cancellation, the club can then handle it, but there might be a chance that it could be saved if it is just a member trying an easy escape on her membership.

Another option is for the club to handle all cancellations directly. Realistically, most clubs just don't have the people to do this, or the time. If you are going to cancel memberships at the club level you have to have someone who can decipher between a valid cancel and a simple escape. This person should also have the strength to resell those members who want out just because they aren't using the club anymore.

Keep in mind the big issue for the club owner: you have to build a strong, effective receivable base that provides stability for the club. To do that you have to keep the losses from cancellations at the club to about one percent per month of your membership file as compared to the national average of three percent. Pick the most effective system for your club that will gain you those two extra percentage points.

> **It is a simple fact of life, though, that a club owner can run a marathon, lift weights for hours, teach three back-to-back classes if necessary, and then sit in the corner and cry like a baby if she has to talk badly to a member.**

Charge what the state allows and follow your law exactly but don't forget that a cancellation fee is not a profit center.

A side issue that always comes up with club cancellations is the cancellation fee. Many states allow the club to use a cancellation fee to let the members out of their contracts. This fee might be anywhere from $25 to $150 depending on the state. Charge what the state allows and follow your law exactly but don't forget that a cancellation fee is not a profit center. Racking up a couple hundred dollars in cancellation fees that day is not a cause for celebration since you had to give up several thousand dollars in memberships to get that money.

An old concept dating back to at least the 1960s that concerns canceling members keeps circulating around the industry. This idea was to put the burden back onto the members to resell their memberships themselves instead of letting them out. If the member could find another person to take over the balance of their payments, they could walk and the new person could start wherever the old member left off at that time.

This sounds good in theory until the first time you see a local newspaper with 30 to 40 classified ads featuring your memberships discounted. This builds a horrible image for the club, enrages the members who have to sell their own memberships, and is probably illegal in most states today anyway.

Collecting Money from Your Members Has a Cost and Affects How Much You Ultimately Collect from Your Receivable Base

Collecting money from your members always has a cost associated with it, and while it does not directly affect the loss rate, it does have an effect on the strength of your receivable base. The cost for collecting money from your members is always going to be there; the key is how much money you collect for that cost.

The mistake usually made at this point is that many owners believe if they collect their own memberships, there won't be any cost of collection — the simple do-it-yourself, no cost theory.

It will always cost you something collecting money from your members. A rookie owner might ask what it costs to collect the money, and then complain about the cost being too high. An owner with business experience might ask what it costs to collect money from his members, and then ask the most important part of the question: what do I get for that cost?

The cost of collecting a membership payment can be as little as $0.25 per transaction from a low-end, get-what-you-pay-for, EFT-processing company, and as much as 16 to 18 percent of what is collected from the members. The high end is for club owners who attempt to do it themselves but then let the associated bureaucracy expand beyond control.

The benchmark fee for collecting membership payments should be at approximately seven percent of what's collected, which is the national average for a club using a reputable third-party financial-service collection that provides EFT, a check/coupon system for member payments, and full reporting. This fee should also include phone calls and past-due notices for delinquent members as well.

Can you collect your own payments for less? Yes, but what do you get for less? Remember, it is not what it cost you to collect; it's what you get for your money. For example, imagine a club selling 12-month contracts, which are known to have less than 10-percent loss rates over a year's period of time if collected by a strong financial-service company. Figure 6-1 will outline just the collections on the 12-month contracts and not any other associated losses such as cancellations.

Club A	$400,000 outstanding in receivables on 12-month contracts Collects her own memberships in-house Uses a prepackaged software system Averages about 5% cost each month of what's collected
Club B	$400,000 outstanding in receivables on 12-month contracts Uses a third-party financial-service company Averages about 7% cost each month of what's collected
Club A	$400,000 x .75 = $300,000
	This club has a 25% loss rate on 12-month contracts since no collection effort has extended beyond a few notices. Most importantly, this club has no leverage since they use nothing to threaten the member with except not letting them work out, something the member is probably already doing anyway. Without a third-party system, no leverage exists and no sense of power exists to apply to a member that is not paying.
Club B	$400,000 x .90 = $360,000
	This club, since it is using a third-party outside company, will only have loss rates of 10% on 12-month contracts. The losses are lower because the third-party company has the illusion of power that will leverage more members into making more payments. This is similar to an auto-finance company having the power to collect or you lose your car and your credit. In reality, who is the member going to be most afraid of not paying, a large national third-party financial company, or the club?
Club A	$300,000 after losses x .95 (5% collection cost) = $285,000
Club B	$360,000 after losses x .93 (7% collection cost) = $334,800

Figure 6-1.

Club A collected its memberships cheaper but only netted $285,000. Club B paid more in collection costs using a third-party but actually collected $49,800 more from its receivable base than Club A. Remember that it is not the cost of collection but what you get for the cost that is the most important issue.

In reality, most clubs spend a lot more than five percent to collect their own memberships. Add in labor, rising mailing costs, forms, and software, and it gets up around the 10 percent or higher mark for most clubs. Unless you are really good at collections and want to create the bureaucracy necessary to be effective, it is not normally cost effective to collect your own memberships until you have a number of clubs in your system.

Another hidden factor is that the losses are too big too soon for clubs that collect their own memberships using either a software program or an EFT-processing company. This means that when a membership payment can't be processed due to a closed account , most clubs are not very good at cleaning this membership up by getting new account information, or by switching the member over to a check system instead of the EFT draft.

Clubs then typically turn this problem account over to an end-of-the-line collection company that charges between 33 to 50 percent of what's collected, as mentioned earlier in this chapter. In other words, the club ended up paying at least 33 percent to collect a membership that should have been collected for just seven percent if the club had been using a third-party company that would have automatically gone after the member and made the save.

A club owner should be allowing for about a seven-percent cost to collect memberships. For that cost, the club owner should expect to lose about 10 percent of all 12-month memberships through acceptable losses and another 12 percent through normal cancellations.

Remember, in the fitness business, it's not the one who collects the memberships for the cheapest that wins, it's the one who collects the most money from the most members that wins the business game.

Free Lowers the Return-Per-Member

The final factor that affects your return from each membership dollar is the effect of so called *free* stuff in the gym. Always remember that *you never get anything for free.*

The final factor that affects your return from each membership dollar is the effect of so called *free* stuff in the gym. Always remember that *you never get anything for free.*

You see it everyday in gyms everywhere. Free coffee for those morning members, free towels even for the members that don't ask for or need one, and the all-time favorite, free childcare for the members; everything's free everyday of the week. This is a fallacy. Each of these items has a cost and this cost directly affects your return-per- member. For example, an average club spends:

- $700 to $900 per month on free coffee for those morning members.

- $1,200 to $2,500 per month for childcare with an average negative cash flow of minus $1,500 for that nonprofit profit center.

- $600 to $900 per month for a towel service and sometimes more if the club attempts their own laundry service.

Member service ends where bad business begins. The member is not always right or we couldn't even charge for a membership. People that believe the member is always right aren't around long enough to get the point across because they have gone out of business, leaving no trace except a stupid sign hanging on the wall stating the member is our number one priority.

Yes, you have to have member service, and yes the member is obviously what makes the business work, but you have to draw some type of line between giving outstanding member service and losing money. The rule should read: *Our members are always right -- until he wants something totally stupid that is going to lose me money, and then his ass is wrong.*

Many rookie owners associate free with member service. Thank you for being a member -- here's a free shake. No, don't worry about that personal training -- let me give you a few workouts free. Hey, here's another shake, thank you for coming in today. All these are associated with member service in that type of owner's mind.

What member service does mean to a member are options. It's not the free coffee that excites him. It's being able to get a good cup of coffee at a reasonable price without having to make a second stop on the way home or on the way to the gym at a drive-up window.

Member service is not free childcare, it's childcare for a reasonable cost that is safe, has planned activities, computer games, study areas, and adult supervision, as opposed to some tattoo-covered, 17-year-old babysitter that scares the hell out of you and your kids. Childcare is one of those hidden landmines that slowly erode a club financially over a long period of time. For example, a smaller club has the following:

- 2,000 members either actively paying or paid in full that could use the club.

- Childcare that is open at least partially seven days a week for a cost of $2,500 per month (hard cost), but not including soft costs such as rent for the space, utilities, supplies, or any additional insurance requirements.

- Over a 30-day period of time, about 6% of the club's membership, or 120 members, use childcare.

- The club has about 60% usage from its membership, meaning that about 1,200 members out of the 2,000 who use the club over any 30-day period.

Member service ends where bad business begins. The member is not always right or we couldn't even charge for a membership.

Our members are always right — until he wants something totally stupid that is going to lose me money, and then his ass is wrong.

145

- In this example, childcare costs the club over $2 out of every member's payment of those actually using the club ($2,500/1,200 = $2.08).

- Cost-per-member for those members actually using the childcare is $20.83 per member per month ($2,500/120 = $20.83).

In this example, an owner would justify the program as a way to attract members (120) or as a sales tool (childcare sold the membership but the person didn't really use it). In reality, 94 percent of the club's membership doesn't use the program. With total costs figured in for the childcare area, the club is probably losing money on those 120 members who actually use the program over a month's period of time.

In other words, the payments from the 120 members don't cover the cost of the childcare program. This means that the club owner has to struggle to find childcare workers, provide coverage, take the risk of having children in the club, all to maybe breakeven or at most make just a few dollars.

Charging for childcare might help the program breakeven, but is it worth the effort since less than one out of 10 members use the program. The club could actually cut the childcare program and lose every member of the 120 and still be ahead financially.

In reality, however, the club could offer some type of compensation to the 120 members actually using childcare, such as a personal training package and a few months added to the person's membership, and probably only lose about 40 percent of the 120. The rest would take the buy off and stay giving the club owner a positive swing financially for a losing program.

The same losses exist in free coffee, free towels, and all of your other freebies that you equate with member service. What other business gives a person this much free stuff when he is paying so little per visit? A car dealership might give you free coffee and a donut when you are waiting for service, but you are spending $50 to $100 per hour while you are enjoying that horrible, cheap coffee and bad-for-you donut. Your gym members are only paying a buck or two a visit, and it doesn't make sense to give that person something costing the club $0.30 to $0.50 per visit as a perk. Freebies don't affect the receivable base directly, but they do affect the yield from each member payment, which is the next issue to be covered.

What other business gives a person this much free stuff when he is paying so little per visit? Your gym members are only paying a buck or two a visit, and it doesn't make sense to give that person something costing the club $0.30 to $0.50 per visit as a perk.

The Loss Rate, the Cancellation Rate, the Cost of Collection and Club Freebies All Combine to Lower the Yield

Very few club owners ever consider the *yield* they generate from each member payment. The yield can be simply defined as what's left over from each member payment to pay the bills with a little left at the end for profit.

The members think most club owners are rich. The parking lot is full with 200 members in the gym all paying $49 per month. A quick calculation in a greedy member's head says that 200 members times $49 per month is a lot. Of course this member does the count every time he comes in not realizing that every time he works out, it might be many of the same members from yesterdays count paying $49 for the month.

What this member doesn't realize, and few owners do either, is that a member payment is affected by four factors before the owner ever gets a chance to get her hands on it. In other words, the payment may be $49, but a portion of that disappears due to loss rate, cancellations, cost of collection, and club freebies before a club owner sees any return on that membership.

The yield for a club can't be figured, however, until the average member payment is calculated. The previous example uses $49 per member, but that assumes that every member in the club is paying exactly the same amount, something that rarely if ever happens in the club business.

In the real world, a club that has been open for a few years has original members paying less than the current rate, corporate discounts, second-member-of-the- family rates, and other ways into the club without paying the regular advertised rate. All of these factors combine to lower the club's average member payment.

For example, a club owner has set her prices at $49 per month, but gives the second member of the family a $5-per-month discount, or $44 per month. Even just these two memberships have lowered the average member payment from $49, which is the current rate, to $46.50 ($49 + $44 = $93, $93/2 = $46.50).

Existing clubs that have been in business for a while should review 200 or so memberships and get a broad average. If you have paid-in-full memberships, simply divide by 12 months to get a monthly average. Once you know your average monthly payment you can then figure the club's yield from membership payments. Figure 6-2 illustrates an example of what a typical yield might look like for an average club.

Please note that the club in this example has an average monthly payment of $40. In the previous example, the club has a monthly payment of $49. Again, your average monthly payment is not your current list price on a membership unless you are a brand new club and every member is paying the exact same rate.

What does this mean for a club owner trying to operate a business in the real world? First of all, this club is doing a lot of things right. It has lower than average loss rates because it is using 12-month contracts exclusively for its memberships. This means that if this club signs up $400,000 in memberships it will only lose about $40,000 in losses because of its membership tool. This club also has a low cancellation rate of only 12 percent per year or one percent per month, which is several points per month lower than a typical club. This club is also using a third-party collection effort for its memberships with an average cost of only seven-percent

The payment may be $49, but a portion of that disappears due to loss rate, cancellations, cost of collection, and club freebies before a club owner sees any return on that membership.

annually. Using a strong third-party is also why the club's loss rates are so low on its membership collections.

The club's average monthly payment is $40

- *Loss rate*
  $40 x .90% (10% loss rates on 12 month contracts) = $36
  $40 - $36 = $4 loss from every member payment

- *Cancellation rate*
  $40 x .88% (12% of club files cancelled per year due to normal club cancellations as required by law) = $35.20
  $40 - $35.20 = $4.80 loss from every member payment

- *Cost of collection*
  $40 x .93% (7% average for third-party collections) = $37.20
  $40 - $37.20 = $2.80 cost from every member payment

- *Club freebies*
  $2 per member per month for combined cost of childcare, free coffee, and free towel service
  $2 cost from every member payment to support the freebies

- *The total yield from this club's average member payment*
  $40.00
  -$4.00
  -$4.80
  -$2.80
  -$2.00
  $26.40 or 66% of the average member payment equals the *yield*

Figure 6-2.

The club has made a mistake, though, by giving away too many free services and goodies in the club.

The club has made a mistake, though, by giving away too many free services and goodies in the club. This club could raise its yield and increase its overall cash flow by switching away from free to a better quality product in each area that then generates revenues, such as a towel-rental program, a profitable coffee/juice bar, and by either charging real rates for childcare or by eliminating it completely.

What to Do with the Yield Once You Find It

The yield should be figured once or twice a year with an overall goal of driving the number continually upward. Your immediate goal is to keep your yield within a 60- to 75-percent range of your current price.

As a club owner, you can change the yield giving you a higher return-per-member per month. For example, switching to a more productive membership tool such as a 12-month membership contract as opposed to a 24-month would make a dramatic difference in the long run because of the difference in loss rates.

Constantly analyzing your working cancellation rates would also lead to a higher yield over time. Setting tight cancellation procedures, better training with the staff, and involving your third-party collection company could all decrease losses in this area.

Collecting your own memberships is a true rookie mistake for almost every club. Getting a consistent collection cost tied to a strong collection effort will reduce unnecessary losses and allow the club owner to concentrate on making money, not building redundant systems that can be better farmed out to major players in that area of the business.

The Yield Provides Membership Sale Insight for Your Business

The most often-asked question by new owners is, "How many members will I need to make this club work?" The yield, or anticipated yield for a new club, can answer this question. For example:

- An anticipated start-up has an estimated base operating expense (BOE) of $60,000.

- The club owner expects to open with an average monthly payment of $40 after allowing for all discounts.

- This club has an estimated yield of $28 after allowing for loss rates, cancellation rates, and cost of collection. The club anticipates few freebies.

- To figure the estimated new members divide the BOE by the yield:

    $60,000/$28 = 2,142 new members needed by month 25
    2,142/24 months = 89

This club has to write 89 new members a month to be profitable during month 25, the pivotal month for a club's business plan.

In this example, the club has to write 89 new members a month to reach 20-percent profitability by the end of its second year. This amount of memberships is the target number for this club to average each month for the preceding two years. The key word is *average* since it may write 150 memberships in February and 50 in July. Another key formula that affects a club's targeted membership sales is the one-per-thousand-dollars-of-expense method of determining the minimum number of memberships a club can do and stay in business:

Minimum memberships = One annual membership per thousand in BOE

Using the previous club example:

- The club has a BOE of $60,000.

- One per thousand means that the club has to do one annual membership per $1,000 of expense.

Collecting your own memberships is a true rookie mistake for almost every club. Getting a consistent collection cost tied to a strong collection effort will reduce unnecessary losses

149

• This club has to write a minimum average of 60 annual memberships per month to survive.

Combining the yield membership number and the one-per-thousand formulas, this club has to do the following membership numbers:

Minimum number of sales for the business plan for club survival = 60
Targeted, or ideal, number of memberships for the business plan = 89

This club has to do between 60 and 89 annual membership sales per month to survive and ultimately thrive with a 20-percent net going into its third year of business. These numbers are based solely on membership sales and do not include any profit center calculations, which would provide profits beyond the money generated just from membership sales.

What Does the Yield Mean in Profits for the Club?

What does a club actually profit from each member payment after all expenses and after adjustments for losses and collection costs? Typically a club can anticipate a net of 10 percent of the yield. Again using the previous example, a club that has anticipated yield of $28 will net about 10 percent of that, or about $2.80 per member payment, which reflects the anticipated profit per payment.

Of course, the club will have other areas that can drive the profitability of the business such as profit centers or rental space. But just considering membership payments alone, a club will net about 10 percent of the yield from each member payment per month. This should be an obvious signal to an owner to determine the club's yield. He should then do everything to keep that number as high as possible since profitability comes from the total yield.

The Key Points You Should Have Gotten from this Chapter

• A strong receivable base that provides stability and long-term planning ability should be the goal of every club owner.

• The single most important number to look at in a club business is the relationship between the base monthly operating expense (BOE) and the net check collected each month from all member payments. The goal is 70% coverage of your BOE.

• The club sets the obligation for the membership term (12-month contracts) and the member has the right to determine method of payment (EFT or paying each month by check).

• Clubs will collect more money from more members by using a strong third-party financial-service company to handle its member payments and software needs.

The club sets the obligation for the membership term (12-month contracts) and the member has the right to determine method of payment (EFT or paying each month by check).

- Your receivable base, meaning how much money you actually collect from your members, is affected by four factors:
  - √ Loss rate
  - √ Cancellations made by the club
  - √ Cost of collection
  - √ Free services
- These four factors determine the yield from each member payment.
- The club owner's goal is to keep the yield in the 60% to 75% range of the average monthly payment.
- The yield can be used to set a goal for the ideal number of annual memberships the club should write each month.
- Using a formula based on one annual membership per thousand dollars of expense gives the club the minimum number of new annual memberships it needs each month.
- The yield can also give an indication of net-per-member payment with a typical club netting about 10 percent of the yield.

7

Building a Price Structure that Can Make You Money

The most important thing you should get from this chapter is:

The right pricing structure will allow you to get the most money from the most members.

Definitions and concepts you will need to know:

- *Pricing structure:* How the club's membership prices are offered to a potential member.

- Four core principles that will help you get the most money are: *make decisions that enhance the club's receivable base, the optimum length of a membership contract is 12 months, there has to be an established obligation between the club and the member,* and *use a third-party financial-service company.*

- *One-time membership fee:* The money we get the day the person becomes a member. The ideal range is between 10% of the value of the contract and $90.

- *Payment in arrears:* The member makes a payment after the service is incurred. For example, the member signs today but his first payment isn't due until 30 days from today's date. This allows the club owner to build a stronger receivable base over time.

- *The 90/10 rule:* Less than 10 out of every 100 members should pay in full for their membership. Over 10% and the members are telling you that you are too cheap.

- You should raise your prices every 12 to 18 months.

The Right Pricing Can Give You a Higher Return-Per-Member

All the new sales and all the new equipment can't offset a bad pricing system or a club's inability to collect from the members it does sign up.

How you charge for your club's memberships and how you collect from your members comprises the club's *financial foundation*. These two issues are the most important decisions a club owner will make because all the new sales and all the new equipment can't offset a bad pricing system or a club's inability to collect from the members it does sign up.

In the previous chapters, several factors were discussed that form the financial foundation for a club. These factors were developing a receivable base, the optimum length of a membership contract, electronic funds transfer (EFT) as part of the club's membership program, and using a strong and efficient third-party financial-service company to ensure that what memberships you do write you can collect on. A club's goal is to collect the most money from the most members. If this is to get done, you should start to build your club's financial foundation around the following principles:

- Set your financial plan for your club around developing a receivable base that provides a steady income for the club that can be predicted into the future. This system eliminates cash memberships, which lower the return-per-member, or open-ended, month-to-month memberships that don't provide any stability and have high loss rates.

- The optimum length for a membership is 12 months because it provides income into the future but only has loss rates of less than 10% on an annual basis.

- There has to be an obligation for the member to pay the club in the form of a 12-month contract. Electronic funds transfer (EFT) is a method of payment and does not guarantee obligation. The member should have the option of which type of method of payment she chooses, but the club maintains the right to set the obligation in the form of the contract.

- Using a third-party financial-service company gives you the highest expected return-per-member because of the leverage it has over your members in the form of a powerful outside entity.

Building a price structure that works, and giving the club the highest return-per- member, have to be based on the previously listed assumptions. In other words, if you want to collect the most money possible from the memberships you do sell, you have to establish a membership program that uses 12-month contracts as its core element, offers the member a choice of either EFT or the ability to write a check each month, and then turns the membership over to a third-party entity for servicing. These factors would then combine to give the club a very strong receivable base providing stability and a long-term planning ability for the club owner even in months where new sales may be slower.

The Components that Make Up an Effective Pricing System

An effective pricing system should have a combination of these components that match the club and the competition in the area:

A one-time membership fee—This is the money a club gets up front from a member when she signs an agreement to be a member. For example, a club might have a membership with a $69 one-time membership fee and a membership of $59 per month for 12 months. Other names for the one-time membership fee you might have heard are initiation fee, down payment, or the down.

The monthly dues—This is the monthly payment a member would make as part of the membership. In the previous example, the monthly dues or payment would be $59, which would be if the member elected to pay by EFT. The club would also offer an optional method of payment in addition to the EFT. If the member wanted to pay by check each month using a coupon system, then the club would simply charge $5 more per month since it cost the owner slightly more to process a check then it does to accept an EFT.

The obligation—The member in this example has a choice of paying either $59 per month EFT, or $64 per month for the right to send in a check with a coupon to the third-party financial-service company each month. These are examples of method of payment. The membership, however, is based upon a 12-month contract that establishes obligation and builds a receivable base.

The membership agreement—This is club talk for a contract, which is a legal document the club uses to establish obligation between the business and the individual buying a membership to the club.

The open-ended option—In some highly competitive major metro areas, some clubs are forced to offer an open-ended payment option with no contract. This can work well if used in conjunction with a normal contractual obligation priced slightly lower. For example, the club might charge $59 a month for 12 months for an EFT membership, but offer an open-ended membership option based on $69 per month. If the club keeps the open-ended option priced at about $8 to $10 higher than the 12-month contractual option, about 80 percent of the consumers who buy memberships will pick the 12-month plan. The club can, however, still offer an open-ended option to be competitive.

Discounts—Clubs have historically offered discounts from everything for the second member of the family, to high school students, to police officers and corporate sales. Discounting is losing favor with more sophisticated owners as the cost of business increases and the cost of servicing a membership is also on the rise.

Discounting is losing favor with more sophisticated owners as the cost of business increases and the cost of servicing a membership is also on the rise.

Short-term membership options—Most clubs have to offer options for memberships less than the 12-month option. These are always priced higher than the equivalent period of time when compared to a regular membership, but still sell in markets that have people who are in the area for briefer terms.

> **A club must always have a daily drop-in fee for the day guest. This is also where club owners have traditionally made major mistakes by pricing this fee far too low.**

Daily drop-in fees—A club must always have a daily drop-in fee for the day guest. This is also where club owners have traditionally made major mistakes by pricing this fee far too low. If used correctly, the daily fee can generate decent revenue for the club from transient traffic, yet still provide a way to reward members for their patronage through a guest program driven off of the daily fee.

Resort and tourist exceptions—Clubs in high-traffic resort areas or tourist destinations have to learn to have a dual membership strategy: one based on the locals that support the club throughout the year, and one for those folks who may be in the club for anywhere from one day up to a month or two.

Renewal options—A club has to have a predetermined strategy for members who complete their first year of membership. In the past, club owners have devalued these renewal memberships by discounting them for future use. A more sophisticated approach is to lock the member in for her current rate for as many years as she would like to be a member. For example, the new member might pay $59 a month for 12 months and then be guaranteed that $59 rate for any successive years she would like to be member. Her rate is guaranteed to never increase no matter what the club's current rates climb to as long as she renews each year for 12 more months within 30 days of her expiration date.

Building a Membership Structure Using These Options

The core of the membership system is the *12-month membership* coupled with a *one-time membership fee*. An example might look like this:

To join the club the member pays a one-time membership fee of $69.
The member then would pay $59 per month for 12 months.
$69 + ($59 x 12 months)

While this looks simple, several important things are happening in this system that affect the return-per-member and how effective an owner is going to be in collecting this membership. First of all is the issue of the one-time membership fee. A trend in the industry is to get a smaller, one-time fee and get the first month's dues up front. That would look like this:

$69 + $59 + ($59 x 11 months)

However, this is an undesirable option for the club owner. The owner's future is in building a strong receivable base. This owner is weakening that base by on going for 11 payments instead of 12, which over a year's period of time for new membership traffic for a typical club can add up to a significant number.

If the owner is good enough to get that much money up front, why not just go for a slightly stronger membership fee and still get the 12 payments? In this case, it's just a matter of semantics. The owner is getting a pile of money up front and other little piles for a defined amount of months. It doesn't matter what you call the upfront money, or how you get to the total, but more of it how it's done.

How much money do you have to get up front to make the contract collectable is also an issue. Contracts are much more collectable if the owner gets at least 10 percent of the value of the membership up front. In this example, $59 x 12 months = $708. Ten percent is enough money in the member's head so she feels she is invested and has a lot to lose if she doesn't pay.

To ensure that this membership contract has the best chance of being collected by the financial-service company, the club would have to ask for at least 10 percent of that amount, or about $70. In the previous example, the club is getting $69 as a one-time membership fee, which would be close enough to increase the chance of collections.

You can charge too much up front, however, which kills the impulse aspect of a membership sale. Groups that do consumer research as to how people buy have found most people will impulse purchase if the money involved is $90 or less. Anything over that amount and the impulse turns into a family-buying decision for those folks, or to an I-need-to-think-about- that-overnight decision.

> You can charge too much up front, however, which kills the impulse aspect of a membership sale.

Translated into something that can be used in the club business, a club pricing system must feature at least one membership where a consumer can get started for at least 10 percent of the value of the contract as the minimum and up to $90 as the maximum so as not to eliminate the impulse sale. In other words:

One-time membership fee = 10% of the value of the membership up to $90

The membership fee is also something the average club owner has trouble explaining to the member who asks, "Hey, what's this membership for anyway?" You might have heard this old adage in the gym business that fits well in this case: *when all else fails, tell the member the truth.* In this case, the membership fee is simply explained as offsetting the cost of getting a new member started.

> When all else fails, tell the member the truth.

A lot of cost goes into getting someone started during her first 30 days as a member, including fees to set the account up with the financial-service company (these should not really exist except in the cost of the contract itself), labor costs to make sure the person has the right workout setup for her, and the cost of the sale itself through commissions and marketing expense, as well as minor expenses such as issuing a membership card. All these are incurred during the first 30 days and the club passes those through to the member in the form of a one-time membership fee.

Payment in Arrears

Again, look at this example:

$69 + ($59 x 12 months)

In this scenario, the club is getting $69 up front in the form of a one-time membership fee. But when does the club collect that first payment if it is not getting it today?

The answer is *payment in arrears*. This means that the club will collect the first payment after the service is incurred. If you rent an apartment, for example, you pay on the first of the month and then get to use the apartment for the next 30 days. With payment in arrears, you use the service and then pay at the end of the 30 days.

> If you rent an apartment, for example, you pay on the first of the month and then get to use the apartment for the next 30 days. With payment in arrears, you use the service and then pay at the end of the 30 days.

This enables the club to charge a one-time membership fee in addition to the 12 payments and to keep the renewal payments sequential when they begin at the end of the member's first year. Look at Figure 7-1 to help clarify the concept. In this example, the potential member decides to buy during her first visit to the club using the membership previous example.

- Today's date is March 1, 2003.
- The date the new person's membership begins is March 1, 2003.
- This person will give the club $69 today in the form of a one-time membership fee.
- The person's first $59 payment is due on April 1, 2003, or approximately 30 days from the date she signs the contract.
- The person's last payment is due on March 1, 2004.
- The date the member makes their last payment is the date the membership expires. Using payment in arrears means she does not have 30 days after the last payment since that payment covered the previous 30-day period.
- The person would then make her first renewal payment on April 1, 2004.

Figure 7-1.

In this example, the new member pays a one-time membership fee and then 12 payments of $59. At the end of those 12 payments, she then renews for 12 more months and just keeps paying that $59 since it is already in her budget. The date of her last payment is the date her membership expired and no, members don't skip that last payment. They have made the previous 11 and will make the last, and most don't realize it is in arrears anyway.

Another important note is that the member's first payment is not due for 30 days from the date she signs the membership agreement. It is important to note that if you are using the recommended third-party financial system, then you will have the ability to set the payment for the member on any day of the month the member wants. In Figure 7-1, the payment was due 30 days out which put it on the first of the following month, but the club could have rounded it off a few days either way to accommodate a certain time of the month for the member to make that payment.

The only legal aspect to consider is that when a member signs a retail-installment contract (the contract), which is regulated by the federal law governing said contracts, the member must make their first payment within 45 days of the date she signs the contract or it is void. Very few people ever really care about that but it is important to note so you can make sure the first payment falls no more than 45 days from the date the membership agreement is signed.

It is important to note so you can make sure the first payment falls no more than 45 days from the date the membership agreement is signed.

Introducing the Second Method of Payment for the Member

The example that's been used is generic and helped to point out the different components of a membership system. Next, take a look at an actual membership-system core a club could use in the real world. For example:

- $69 membership fee and monthly dues of $59 for 12 months on EFT

- $69 membership fee and monthly dues of $64 for 12 months on payment coupons

At this point the club has set an obligation for the member designed to build a receivable base for the club, but has given the member an option of paying either $59 or $64 per month. This pricing depends on whether the member will give the club the option to electronically draft the member's checking account or credit card each month.

If you are using a strong third-party financial-service company to service your memberships, it will allow you not to force the EFT and yet build a collectable receivable base. This is explained to the members as, "Our membership is $59 per month for 12 months, and that is based on allowing the club to automatically draft your monthly dues from either your checking account or credit card each month. If you would like to write a check each month, we simply add $5 per month to your dues since it does cost the club more to process checks. Which is best for you?"

Short-Term Membership Options

The legitimate reasons as to why a person wouldn't want to join a club based on 12-month memberships alone are many. For example, a person might only be in town for a few months or might want to try the club for a shorter period of time before committing to a regular membership. Whatever the reason, the club should have several *short-term options* available for membership.

The Short-Term Membership

This would be your primary tool to be used in conjunction with your regular memberships. The short-term membership is good for up to three months and includes full use of the club just as in your regular memberships.

Do you have one-month memberships? the potential member asks.
Yes we do, the club answers, *and it's our short-term membership and it is good for up to three months.*

Do you have two-month memberships?
Yes we do, the club answers, *and it's our short-term membership and it is good for up to three months.*

Do you have three-month memberships?
Why yeessssss wweeeee dooooo, the club answers.

As you have guessed from this example, the short-term membership is good for up to three months. A few other options are possible if the person doesn't truly want this membership, but this is the all-purpose short-term tool for those people not wanting a regular membership.

The short-term membership should be more expensive in comparison to a regular membership. Some members will simply repeat the short-term over and over again, but then it should be priced to penalize those people to make the regular memberships more attractive. To properly price a short-term membership, add $150 to your regular membership, divide by four, and then round the new total off. For example:

$69 membership fee
$59 x 12 months = $708
Add $150
Total is $927
Divide by four = $231.75
Round off for salesmanship = $229

In this example, the club would have a short-term membership priced at $229 per three-month period. If the member purchased four of these he would pay approximately $150 more than a regular membership. If the

> *Do you have one-month memberships?* the potential member asks.
> *Yes we do*, the club answers, and it's our short-term membership and it is good for up to three months.

member decides to buy a regular membership, simply subtract what's already been paid from the regular membership and go on from that point.

The Daily Drop-In Fee

You have to have a system in place that allows the club to charge a person for using the club just once, or on an occasional basis, without purchasing some type of longer-term membership. For example, if someone is staying at the Holiday Inn down the street, they should be able to work out for a single visit or be able to work out several times if they are going to be in town more than just a few days. Club owners err here, however, by lowering this fee so low that the club may actually lose money on that visit.

The daily drop-in rate has several purposes. First of all, it establishes a daily value for your club that makes the membership options appear to be much more attractive. Second, it punishes the poor idiot who is actually staying at the Holiday Inn down the street. This person should be allowed to work out but it shouldn't be cheap. This traveling businessperson is not your future and a single visit to the club should be aggressively priced.

The most important aspect of using a daily fee, however, is establishing a show rate that will allow you to maximize a single visit for outsiders that won't be a part of the club in the long run, but will still allow you to reward your members and those folks who will be part of the club's long-term business plan. *Show rate* means that the number is set high as a reference point. If someone pays it, then fine, but a high show rate allows the owner to come off of that number if needed for other reasons.

For example, the lowest daily fee a typical club should offer is $15 per visit. The owners laying on the floor choking at this point because their fee is still a born-in-the- Midwest $5 should keep in mind that your future is not the single visit. If someone wants something beyond a single visit, but not any type of longer-term membership, you'll find other options that will be discussed later in this section. Establishing a $15 daily fee also allows you to come off of that number for your special guests brought in by your members. For example:

- The club's daily drop-in fee would be $15.
- The guests who come in with a member would be charged $7.50.
- The poor guy at the Holiday Inn who you will never see again after that single visit would be charged $15.

The show rate of $15 then gives the club owner an option of giving her members a special benefit of membership. Most owners are terrible about charging a good member for his guest and usually end up getting stuck for free. This system allows the owner to say, "Normally our single visit fee is $15, but since you are a guest of one of our good members, your fee will only be $7.50."

> **The lowest daily fee a typical club should offer is $15 per visit. The owners laying on the floor choking at this point because their fee is still a born-in-the- Midwest $5 should keep in mind that your future is not the single visit.**

The club owner is happy because she made $7.50 and didn't have to give away a free visit. The member is happy because he felt special by being able to get his guest a deal. The guest is happy because he didn't have to pay full price. Everyone wins and everyone is happy.

The guest might have been a local and would have qualified for a trial membership, but in this case you assume that it is someone from out of the club's immediate area. The member can bring this person as a guest as many times as he likes since the club is getting at least $7.50 per visit and is making the member happy at the same time.

The Punch-Card Option

If your club has a large amount of transient members, either through business people passing through the area or tourists, you have several options beyond selling a typical week membership. The first option is the *standard punch card*. This allows a transient member to buy more than one workout at a discount without buying a longer-term membership of any type. Punch cards are perfect for folks who might be in and out of town on a regular basis and are more interested in the number of workouts they receive rather than having use of the club on a daily basis.

Using the previous example, the club has established a daily fee of $15. An example of a punch card based on this number would look like this:

- The club has a daily fee of $15 for one visit.
- The club offers a punch card at 10 visits for $120, and the short-term member receives a discount of $30.
- The club sets an expiration date of 60 days on the punch card.

In this case the club has established a daily fee of $15. The short-term member wants to use the club more than once, or perhaps travels extensively and is afraid of not using time that is paid for through a regular type of membership. The club offers a punch-card option that allows the person to purchase multiple workouts at a discount, in this case saving $30 for 10 visits. The expiration date allows the club to raise rates easily on a regular basis and force the person to either use it or lose it.

The Premier Week or VIP Week

Many clubs are in tourist areas. In these clubs, it's not just about the workout; it's about getting the tee shirt too for the short-term member.

Many clubs are in tourist areas. In these clubs, it's not just about the workout; it's about getting the tee shirt too for the short-term member. This type of club usually loses money by selling weekly memberships even if those memberships are priced in the $25- to $45-per-week range. By packaging the weekly a little more effectively, the club can get a higher dollar per visit and drive the profit centers in the club as well.

Premier week is a one-week, all-inclusive membership priced at about $69. The week includes a club tee shirt, full use of the facility for the week, a free tan, free shake, and free soft drink. Throw in a mini-massage if possible and perhaps a studio cycling class, too. The goal is to add value to the week in profit center items that don't really cost the club too much money. This also gives an owner the ability to charge far more than a typical club could get from just charging for the week alone.

You May Have to Consider a Month-to-Month Option

As previously mentioned, some club owners may be forced to offer an option beyond their core 12-month contractual membership. In areas that are extremely competitive with clubs that offer no contracts but instead rely on month-to-month, pay-as-you-go memberships, an owner may want to consider offering the *month-to-month option* in addition to her regular membership offerings. In the example that has been previously, the club has set it core membership offering at:

$69 + ($59 x 12 months)

Again, this club is asking for $69 up front in the form of a one-time membership fee and is getting $59 per month for a 12-month membership. In an overly competitive market, the club owner still wants to establish a strong financial foundation in the form of receivable base, yet still be viewed as competitive in the market place by the potential consumer. To do this, she must offer an alternative to the 12-month contract.

$69 + ($59 x 12 months) *or*
$69 + $69 on a month-to-month basis

In this case, the club offers the member two choices: he can either join for a 12-month commitment at $59 per month, or for $10 more per month he could have the option to go month-to-month and quit any time he pleases with just a 30-day written notice while being current at the time of withdrawal from the club. If the club owner prices her month-to-month option at least $8 to $10 per month higher than the core 12-month price, about 80 to 85 percent of the new members will pick the contractual option. This pricing variation allows the club to be competitive in the marketplace yet still build a strong receivable base established on 12-month contracts.

A common mistake many owners make at this point is to price the open-ended membership lower than the contractual option. The goal is always to build the most solid long-term receivable base possible, and to do this you must drive the new members toward the contractual obligation.

In the month-to-month option, the club could present the 12-month as an option available for members who know they will be in the area long-term and who are able to support the club on a year-round basis. This makes it seem more like a reward for loyalty rather than a punishment.

A common mistake many owners make at this point is to price the open-ended membership lower than the contractual option.

Some club owners become too reactive and completely abandon the 12-month contractual obligation in favor of month-to-month.

Some club owners become too reactive and completely abandon the 12-month contractual obligation in favor of month-to-month. The thought on this is that those owners will run better businesses because the members could leave at any time. First of all, these owners should be running the best business they can anyway, so seeking an internal gimmick that allows them to claim they are working harder doesn't make sense to the consumer.

Second, it's not necessary to only go with a month-to-month. Give the consumer two choices and let him decide. In the previous example, the club is getting $10 less for the contractual obligation, but with a drastically lower loss rate will make more money than using open-ended memberships. Give the member the choice but always go for establishing a strong receivable base as your ultimate goal.

Going for the Cash

As was mentioned in Chapter 4, the old lesson in the gym business was, *cash is king*. Although cash memberships have already been briefly discussed, it's worth taking another look at this membership tool in relation to this section.

In the early days, those salespeople who could generate the most amounts of paid-in-full memberships were the kings and queens of the club business. People actually paid for their memberships in those days with cash instead of credit cards and checks, and whoever could get the most cash from the most people ruled in the sales world.

Paid-in-full memberships started to lose their luster in the 1980s as many clubs were able to raise their total memberships to at least the equivalent of $34 per month. Paid-in-full, or using the generic term cash deals, lagged behind because the consumer started balking even in those days at paying more than $249 to $299 cash for a membership.

Those old cash guys who are reading this are screaming about all the cash deals they sold -- but the key to remember in today's market is that although you can still sell cash memberships, how many can you sell and at what price?

Cash as Your Primary Membership

Although you don't see it too often anymore, some club owners still insist on building their membership plan around going for paid-in-full memberships as their primary tool. Several things usually happen to these clubs over time. First of all, the club starts out aggressively at a higher paid-in-full rate, perhaps at around $449 for a year's membership. A certain percentage of people coming through the door will pay in full for a year's membership at this rate, but not enough to support the club over a moderate period of time, which in club time would be about 18 months to two years.

Somewhere during the second year of operation the club's expenses surpass the club's ability to generate enough new paid-in-full memberships at the $449 rate. At this point the club owner makes his first mistake by lowering the rate *temporarily* to drive new sales in the door. This may work on the short-term basis but what happens to the club during the long-term?

When the club lowers the rate, new sales may increase for a short period of time. The existing members, however, who have paid the higher $449 fee, are at this point very upset with the club since new members coming into the door are paying a lower rate for the same service.

The club also has another problem to deal with concerning the new rate. Since the club is charging less for its membership, using a new rate of $379 for example, the club then has to do greater volume to meet its overhead. This requires more marketing, higher commissions paid out to the salespeople, and more wear and tear on the club due to the short-term increase in traffic from the lower rate. This club will continue to lower its rates until it hits the magic $249 to $299 range where most people coming through the door will pay because the risk factor for joining has been reduced to a very low number.

At this point the club has a membership that is totally price driven and is filled full of folks because the club truly is the cheapest deal in town. This type of member will not support club profit centers because they are paying so little per month on average, and will be the first person out the door to join another club if the price at the business is even lower than the member is paying today.

Going for cash membership, including paid-in-fulls generated through credit cards or checks, will ultimately lower the club's return-per-member since not enough potential members will pay a rate significant enough to support the club. Most importantly, using cash deals as your primary membership will only attract those members you didn't really want in the first place; the one's who are there because you have the cheapest deal in town.

Discounting for Cash as Part of Your Normal Membership

The most common membership structure in today's marketplace uses a core contractual membership such as the 12-month tool, yet still offers some type of discount for paying in full for your membership. The question is why? If someone wants to pay in full for his membership, then the discounting tool probably doesn't match that person. In other words, the potential member with the most money, one who is able and willing to write a check for the full amount, is the one that will pay less for his membership.

Discounting is part of our past but should not be part of the future. In the past, discounting was used to drive membership sales for a not-so-sophisticated consumer. Today, the consumer may be able to pay in full, but

This type of member will not support club profit centers because they are paying so little per month on average, and will be the first person out the door to join another club if the price at the business is even lower than the member is paying today.

the tool doesn't match the increased sophistication of the clientele you seek who is in the top 60 percent of your club's demographic drawing area.

For example, Jason is a member who is in his late 30s, works in a small company 30 minutes from the club as a computer person, is single, and has belonged to the club for two years. Jason pays $40 per month for his membership and never misses a payment. He is also the type of member who stops by the juice bar for a shake everyday and can be counted on to buy the occasional shirt or hat, supplements, and just about anything else in the club at one time or another.

In other words, Jason is the perfect member since he supports the club beyond his basic membership and pays his membership regularly without a lot of maintenance. This is also the type of member that regularly disappears from clubs and the owners never know why. This member will disappear because the trust and loyalty he felt for the club was broken due to the club's membership options and how these options affect your better members. Jason's club has the typical options in its membership structure the owner feels will drive memberships and increase the club's revenues.

The problem is that these options were developed 30 to 40 years ago when the consumer didn't stay in the gym and advanced sales techniques in general were new to the public and far more effective then they are today. For example, this club offers half-price memberships to the second member of the family. Jason pays $40 as a single, but his friend Steve and his wife pay only $60 for the two of them, or $30 apiece. Jason has also met several folks from a small company near the club that received a corporate discount. They signed up in a group of five and only pay $29 per month per member. Every spring the club offers a summer student special where college students who are home for the summer can work out for three months for only $99, or only $33 per month.

Jason is a nice guy who doesn't complain, but when he gets to the end of his membership, he simply goes away and tries another club. Why? Because Jason, who most owners would agree is the club's best member, is the only idiot who is paying full price and knows it.

All of these other people could still have been sold memberships but none had to be sold at the expense of losing your best member. In fact, every membership sold should be bent on the idea of protecting Jason, not irritating him to the point that he goes away quietly at the end of his time.

For example, the club could have offered the second member of the family a discounted membership fee making it easier to get started, but she still should have paid the full monthly membership. Remember, you are building clubs for the top 60 percent of demographics in the club's area. Discounting for a second member of the family doesn't necessarily make sense to the people in this group although the ease of getting into the club is important.

> **Because Jason, who most owners would agree is the club's best member, is the only idiot who is paying full price and knows it. In fact, every membership sold should be bent on the idea of protecting Jason, not irritating him to the point that he goes away quietly at the end of his time.**

The small company could have still been offered a corporate deal, but instead of lowering the monthly, the club could have waived the membership fee and added two months free to the 12-month membership, giving added value in the form of 14 months for the price of 12.

The college students should pay more than Jason, not less, and the club should not have been opened up to the general returning college population at all. For example, the club could have offered a special incentive package for students restricted to the sons and daughters of the club's membership. That could have been done like this:

- On May 1, the club would mail a letter to all members stating that the club will not be opened for college students for the summer due to the problems they cause for our existing members. However, the club is going to offer a special summer opportunity for the sons and daughters of the members.

- The club has a regular short-term membership (good for up to three months) it sells for $219. The members may buy one of these memberships for only $149 for their sons or daughters only.

- The members have to pay in full for this membership prior to June 1.

- Jason is happy because the club is not packed with low-paying college knuckleheads paying $33 per month. He is also happy and understands that the members are receiving a discount for their kids, especially since that discount amounts to $49.66 per month as compared to his $40.

- The club's members are happy because they received a deal for their kids, and the deal was also somewhat exclusive too since it was restricted to the families of the membership.

In this example, everyone wins and Jason feels more value in his membership. When everyone is discounted but him, the membership loses value, the trust between someone who invested in a membership and the club is broken, and he then feels that since the club owner is showing him no loyalty, he shows none back and is free to shop elsewhere.

This discounting also applies to a club that is discounting paid-in-full memberships for the year. Even if the club only discounts $50 to $100 off of the regular membership, it is still setting up an adversarial relationship between the members who paid in full for the discount and the ones who paid more but elected to pay over a 12-month term. The club could still seek a paid-in-full, but it should go for the full-price equivalent of the membership fee and the 12 payments. For example:

A $69 membership fee + ($59 x 12 months) = $777
Paid-in-full for the same membership = $777

In this example, the club can take the paid-in-full but shouldn't discount off of the total. As an incentive to get the member to pay for the membership

> When everyone is discounted but him, the membership loses value, the trust between someone who invested in a membership and the club is broken, and he then feels that since the club owner is showing him no loyalty, he shows none back and is free to shop elsewhere.

up front, the club could offer a bonus month added to the membership giving 13 months for the price of 12, and also perhaps throw in a gym bag, water bottle, and tee shirt combination retailing at $90 but costing the club only about $30. In other words, the club is offering $90 plus a month valued at $59, for a total of $149, if the person wants to pay in full for the membership.

The 90/10 Rule

How many paid-in-full memberships should a club do? To answer this, review the following paid-in-full guideline mentioned in an earlier chapter called the *90/10 rule: Out of every 100 annual memberships sold, less than 10 should pay in full using either a check, credit card, or real cash.*

These means that out of less than 10 members in a 100 who join the club on an annual basis should pay for their membership up front. If more than 10 pay that is an indication that the club's prices are too low and it's too easy to pay for the entire thing at once. It is okay to get a little cash flow from member's paying for their membership up front, but the real future of a club is to go for a strong receivable base and get that steady monthly income from the member payments.

Working Your Way Out of Depending on Paid-in-Fulls

Don't switch too quickly from being a club dependent on paying its bills with daily cash flow from paid-in-full memberships to one that has a core receivable base income. This switch has to be done slowly, over a year's period of time in order not to hurt the club. Take a look at an example of a club that is dependent on cash:

- The club sells a base annual membership of a $49 membership fee plus $34 x 12 months equaling $457.
- The club has a paid-in-full price of $349.
- This club sells approximately half of its memberships in paid-in-fulls.

If this club switched to all receivable-based memberships and eliminated the cash membership, or moved it up too quickly closer to the annual contractual membership, the club would hurt financially because its daily cash flow would virtually cease.

This club should make the switch slowly over a one-year period of time by slowly raising the paid-in-full price by $20 every two months. Each time the paid-in-full rate is raised, a few more of that month's members would choose the payment option and less would elect to write a check or put the membership on a credit card. By the end of one year the club would have raised its cash price to at least $419, although it could go higher and closer to the contractual total if the cash flow was enough not to hurt the business.

> Out of every 100 annual memberships sold, less than 10 should pay in full using either a check, credit card, or real cash.

Somewhere in the middle of this plan the club owner could also raise his rates to $39 per month, getting more for his membership without disrupting sales. This would allow driving the paid-in-full price even higher. The key is to slowly work your way out of the dependency on cash while still giving the club enough cash flow to survive the transition. Going too quickly would leave the club in a cash bind that it may not recover from even if sales increased because there would be no receivable base to sustain the transition.

Raising Your Prices

Most clubs usually handle price raises for memberships very poorly. Raises are not planned, are done during the wrong months, and are not used as a leverage tool by the club owner to drive new business in the club.

A club owner should plan to raise prices at least once a year, but should not wait any longer than 18 months. Raising the prices sets a value to the new members coming in, but most importantly enhances the value of existing members in the club.

Never raise the existing member's rates. There will be exceptions to this rule discussed later in this chapter, but at this point just use an example of a club owner who is getting decent rates for her memberships and who doesn't have any of those $19-per-month members either from her earlier days or from buying an existing membership in a used club. Her current membership structure looks like this:

> **A $59 membership fee + ($42 a month for 12 months)**

This is her core annual contractual membership based on EFT. She is charging $5 more per month for the coupon/check people, but that is not relevant for this example. The first thing she should do today is raise her rate to $44 per month. She does not have to wait for any special time of the year to do a simple raise like this one. The goal is to get a price of $44 and then raise her rates to $49. This raise gives her a $60 per year increase, or about 11 percent. No research is available to back this up, but by setting prices according to the $34-to-$39-to-$44-to-$49-to-$54 scheme, the club can clearly identify a raise to the members, gain an 11-percent increase per year, and pick up $60 more per year for the same membership.

Again, this increase is for new members just joining the club and would not affect existing members. Fee increases can be used as a leverage tool for existing members to ensure a stronger renewal and retention rate, however. For example, the club owner in this example can tell her members that the club is going to have a price increase, but as a way of saying thank you for being a member she is not going to raise existing member rates. Simply renew your membership each year within 30 days of expiration and the club will never increase your monthly rate.

Raising the prices sets a value to the new members coming in, but most importantly enhances the value of existing members in the club.

In this example, the owner is going for a raise increase from $44 to $49. Her core membership is paying the $44 rate, which is significant in today's market. The rate increase is passed on to new memberships only that automatically builds value into an existing membership.

Target Three Specific Populations with Every Raise

Don't target your price increase on only one population: the new member joining the gym after the increase takes effect. Instead, target four distinct groups as part of each raise:

- New members who will pay more after the increase.

- Existing members who can be leveraged to bring in guests in conjunction with the price increase.

- Missed guests who have visited the club during the last year but who have not made a buying decision.

- Former members who have slipped away during the years but who would come back if given a chance and a price break that reflect their past support of the club.

New business and additional revenue can be driven from all of these populations in conjunction with an effective price increase, especially if this increase is tied to specific times of the year.

Target Two Optimal Times to Raise Your Rates

Don't just stick to the highly unoriginal and unimaginative January 1 to raise your prices.

Don't just stick to the highly unoriginal and unimaginative January 1 to raise your prices. The obvious goal of a price raise is to generate more money per new member who joins the club. The less obvious reasons are more varied, and valuable, than most owners consider:

- A price raise can be used to leverage existing members into bringing more guests into the gym.

- A price raise can be used to keep a significant number of potential members out of the marketplace during key times of the year.

- A price raise can be used to bring former members back into the gym who have slipped away.

- A price raise can be used to leverage accumulated guests who have visited the club in the last year but who have not made a buying decision.

All of these reasons combined point to giving the *time* and *psychology* behind raising your prices more than just a little thought. With all of this in mind, the two optimum times to schedule price increases are October 1 and February 1.

The Psychology Behind a Price Increase

A price raise is nothing more than a leverage tool to get more money and to drive business from existing members. To get the maximum leverage from the raise, certain times of the year are better than others and will gain better results for the club.

To get the maximum leverage from the raise, certain times of the year are better than others and will gain better results for the club.

The October 1 Price Raise

September usually kicks off the fall selling season, which in many markets can be equal to the February through May stretch. The key to making this time of year effective is by laying the proper foundation over the summer. Most owners, especially those somewhat out-of-date male owners who don't understand the power of the back-to-school special, neglect getting the right marketing foundation in place during August to help drive the big number into the club during late September, October, and November. The back-to-school special might look something like this, and could be used in coed clubs as well as women's only businesses:

Your last excuse just got on the bus.

Now it's time for you.

We're your *back to school*. The kids are gone and now its time for your *10-pound, two-dress-sizes, am-I-ever-glad-summer-is-over* solution.

This type of marketing could be started in August, but the results aren't usually seen until late September or early October. In other words, by laying a foundation in the summer, you won't see the results in the club until October. Why? Because it's summer and no one wants to start a serious fitness program until after the first of September. A potential member may make her mind up to join a gym in August but won't make the move until the end of September or beyond.

A price increase on October 1 allows the club owner to leverage the increased traffic flow late in the month of September, with the thought of having a price increase looming in the near future. Additional traffic will also flow into the gym from the members the club already owns, usually coming back in more steady numbers after September 1.

September is also a time of year that many former members start to think about joining a gym again, especially after a long summer of too many barbecues or too much beer. These old members will come home again given the right incentives and are most susceptible to an offer during late August and September. They might not do anything about it until late September, but with the proper encouragement they will make up their minds in August.

For example, a former member might get a letter from the club in early August offering him a chance to join the club again at his old rate. He can take advantage of this offer at a party in the club late in September. This former member, on vacation in August and who absolutely has no inclination to join a club again today, might say, "Yeah, I'd love to go back to the gym in late September after the kids are back in school and we're back to our normal routine in the fall."

This member makes up his mind to go back, hangs the letter on the refrigerator, and then enjoys the rest of August and his vacation. But since his mind is already made up to join the old gym again, he will not even consider shopping for another club since he has a deal at his old one he capitalize on later at a time that makes more sense to his lifestyle. This same *make-up-my-mind-today-but-take-action-later* psychology also works for former guests that may not have yet purchased a membership, and for existing members who might want to bring someone to the gym but probably won't until they are actually back working out themselves and back in their routine.

> This same *make-up-my-mind-today-but-take-action-later* psychology also works for former guests that may not have yet purchased a membership.

The February 1 Price Raise

The same psychology applies here, although it might be more intense with the holidays and guilt over holiday eating and partying. People want to join a gym and get in shape but they probably won't do it until late January and even into February. This is validated by an unusual trend going on in the business for the past seven years or so in a large percentage of clubs in all regions of the country. Februarys are better business months than Januarys, and have been for a number of years in a row.

January used to be the big month but it seems many potential members keep delaying their joining dates later and later each year. A typical club that had a strong January in the early 1990s today has a slow first two weeks, greater traffic and more new members during the last two weeks of January, and then a big-business month in February.

There might be several reasons for this that would interest a club owner. First of all, the average person is working more hours per week, for the same pay, than she did in the mid 1990s. According to several of the prominent business magazines, the average working person used to work 47.5 hours per week, but today works 57.5 hours per week for the same money. If you worked this hard, and had the anticipated stack of work waiting for you in your office when you returned after the holidays, joining a gym may be something you get to later.

Another reason might be what people spend at Christmas these days. Christmas and holiday shopping gets more expensive every year, and when those bills arrive in early January the shock alone may keep most people out of a gym, especially if they have to spend money to do so.

The temptation here would be to give these people some type of deal to get them into the gym earlier. Keep in mind that it may not be the money alone, but a combination of time and money that is keeping them from being a gym member. Wait patiently, schedule a price increase on the first of February, and then get the same people anyway for full price.

A Sample Price Increase

The following is a sample price increase, the steps necessary to get the most revenue from the most members, and the timing needed to make it effective. Use this premise for the example:

- The club has a current monthly rate of $49 for 12 months.

- On February 1, the club wants to raise its rates to $54 per month per member for the new member.

- These are the club's EFT rates. The member can write a check instead each month for simply $5 more per month.

- The club will hold an Amnesty Night Party on the third Thursday of January.

The following steps detail everything a club owner would have to do to pull off a successful price increase. When compared to the steps a typical owner might take, most will find that they aren't doing enough to drive the revenues, nor are they starting early enough to get everything done that will make the club more money.

These steps have become so complicated over the years that The Thomas Plummer Company has found it necessary to package this process into a coaching package sold to clubs in a kit form. For more information on coaching kits for club owners, see the resource guide at the end of the book.

When compared to the steps a typical owner might take, most will find that they aren't doing enough to drive the revenues, nor are they starting early enough to get everything done that will make the club more money.

Things to Be Done on December 1

Post Sign in Lobby

The club posts a very large mounted letter, perhaps three by four feet, from the owner in the lobby of the club. This letter is an open letter to the members announcing a price increase on February 1. The letter should contain these points:

- A price increase will take effect on February 1, raising the monthly rate from the current $49 per month per member to $54 per month per member.

- This price increase will not affect any current members. The club appreciates the long-term support of its members and will never raise their existing rates as long as each member renews his membership within 30 days of expiration.

- A notice of any expected improvements the club will be making in the coming year.

- An invitation to a special party, called *Amnesty Night*, which will be held on the third Thursday of January. Existing members can receive great incentives for bringing guests who become members on that night. More information is available at the front desk and you will also receive a special letter in the mail.

Mail Invitations to Amnesty Night Party

The club sends letters to three distinct populations in the club: existing members, guests in the club who did not join at the time, and former members who have not renewed at any time in the club's history.

The existing-member letter—This letter goes to all existing members in the club offering them special incentives to bring guests during the Amnesty Party and who join the club that night. When a club focuses on the top demographics in its area as its target population, it will find it harder to get the members to bring guests for the normal club incentives, such as a month free added to a membership or a ball cap or tee shirt. These members will, however, bring in their friends if the incentives are more enticing. *One night, and one night only at Amnesty Night, bring in a friend who enrolls that night and receive one of the following:*

- *A $150 personal training package*
- *A $150 shopping spree in the club*
- *Three months added to your membership*

> **Members won't trap their friends for a ball cap or tee shirt, but you will roll your buddy in for a $150 personal-training package.**

Members won't trap their friends for a ball cap or tee shirt, but you will roll your buddy in for a $150 personal-training package. Since this is somewhat passive advertising, the club can afford to give up $75 to $100 in hard costs to buy a membership that night.

The missed-guest letter—This letter goes out to every missed guest the club has had during the last year. Think of this as one last closeout for everyone who didn't buy at that time. *One night, and one night only at the Amnesty Night, simply bring this letter to the party and sign up that night to beat the club's price increase, as well as receive a gym bag, water bottle, tee shirt package with other added extras such as sport drinks and bonus months added to the membership valued at say, $250.* Remember that you can spend up to a $100 to buy a membership that night in hard costs so make the incentives strong. It is also good to keep in mind that these folks may have joined another gym, but either don't like it or are near their expiration date, and a strong incentive aimed at former guests might bring a few home to your gym.

The letter for former members, or non-renewals—This is the most important letter and what the Amnesty Night promotion is really all about anyway. Amnesty Night means *come home, all is forgiven*. Many of a club's form members drift away for a variety of reasons. A new job, new kids, divorce, stress in their lives can all lead to dropping out of the gym.

For most members, once they're gone even for a short while it's hard to come back and start all over again. Some of these old members might have paid for several years or more, and since they might want to come back, they won't because they simply don't feel they should have to pay full price again as a former loyal member. *One night, and one night only at the Amnesty Night party, bring this letter into the club and get your old rate back one more time. The club is increasing its rate to $54 per month per member, but as a way of saying thanks for your support in the past the club would like you to come home. As an incentive to help you, the club will honor your old rates one more time. If you were paying $34 per month when you left, you can come home one more time, without penalty, and simply pay $34 down and $34 per month for 11 months.*

These members paid you once already in the past and deserve some type of incentive, especially since they were probably there when you were just getting started. The current members can't complain since these are people who were already in the club ahead of them. Someday their present rate might be an incentive just like the old rates were for your former members who come back during Amnesty Night.

These members paid you once already in the past and deserve some type of incentive, especially since they were probably there when you were just getting started.

These letters work better if they are hand addressed and mailed approximately two months before the Amnesty Night Party. Make sure you've put a club return address on the envelope so the members aren't afraid of opening up your letter.

The Amnesty Night Party

This party works best on the third Thursday of January in this example. The purpose of the party is to gather your members one night in the club and write business based upon the leverage garnished from the price increase. Your goal at the party is to write one month's business in one night in memberships. If you normally write 80 memberships, for example, you should write 80 that night as well as your normal for the month.

The party works best with music, drinks and food, and a full party theme. This is also the night to put everything in the club on sale and blow out existing inventory and services with special pricing for that night only.

Many of the letters will appear in member hands early or after the party. Honor any deal from the time the person gets the letter through February 1. In other words, if someone shows up early or late, take the money since that is what this special is all about anyway.

Tips that Will Help

- Work the event hard, including calling old members in December and inviting them to the party.

Consider bartering for something big, such as a big screen television or something similar to raffle off that night. The odds will be good but the winner must be present to win.

- Promote the event using electronic marketing and through your web page and electronic newsletter.

- Consider bartering for something big, such as a big screen television or something similar to raffle off that night. The odds will be good but the winner must be present to win. This will bring in extra traffic that night and add to the profit centers. Extra tickets can be given for anyone who buys a membership that night including former members who turn themselves in.

- Staff the party with extra help since you need to be able to take advantage of the situation and write some serious business that night.

Putting It All Together into a Pricing Structure for Your Club

All of the basics have been covered, so it's time to put everything together into a pricing structure that can be used as a core-starting place for most clubs. Figure 7-2 may not include your exact pricing structure, but use it as a reference point to leverage and strengthen what you are already doing.

- The club offers a one-time membership fee of $65.

- Offer monthly dues of $49 per month for 12 months on EFT.

- Offer monthly dues of $54 per month for 12 months on coupon/check.

- Renewal rates are guaranteed: simply renew your membership for 12 more months within 30 days of your expiration and your rates will never go up as long as you are a member. Members renew at $44/49.

- Second member of the family/other receives discounts of $5 per month.

- Paid-in-full memberships are the same as the total of your EFT membership, including your one-time membership fee of $65. The paid-in full rate would be $653 ($65 + $49 x 12 = $653).

- An open-ended, month-to-month option is offered if necessary in your market:
  √ One-time membership fee of $75
  √ Monthly dues of $59 per month open-ended with 30-day cancellation

- Other membership options:
  √ Short-term membership (good up to three months) of $219
  √ Daily drop-in rate of $15
  √ Guest/member discount of $7.50
  √ Punch card of 10 workouts for $120

Figure 7-2. Pricing structure example

The Key Points You Should Have Gotten from this Chapter

- Seek a higher return-per-member through an effective pricing structure.

- A receivable base, meaning members who owe you money that can be collected in the future, is the most valuable asset your club owns.

- Twelve-month contracts are the core of your financial foundation.

- Using a strong, third-party financial-service company will give you the highest return-per-member.

- Keep your pricing system as simple as possible.

- Discounting everything from the second member of the family to paid-in-full memberships is something most clubs no longer have to do.

- Payment in arrears gives you a chance to get more money up front and yet build a stronger receivable base.

- You must get at least an equivalent of 10% of the total of the monthly payments up front to increase the collectibility of your membership.

- The club sets the obligation (12-month contract) and the member picks the method of payment (EFT or writing a check and using a coupon system).

- Short-term membership options should enhance your long-term receivable base, not distract from it.

- Avoid using a month-to-month membership option unless you have to be competitive in the market place.

- Paid-in-full memberships often lower the return-per-member and are not part of a club's long-term financial plan. A typical club should write less than 10% of all its annual memberships as paid-in-fulls.

- You should try and raise your prices every 12 months, but don't wait longer than 18 months.

Keep your pricing system as simple as possible.

The Operational Numbers and Concepts of a Fitness Business

Club owners can learn to drive the revenues in a club by understanding the operational numbers of their day-to-day business. Understanding these numbers will give an owner an expected outcome or target to achieve in the business, as well as the ability to trouble- shoot things more effectively when the business is not performing as expected.

This section covers the base operating numbers that reflect your business as it occurs on a daily basis. Operational numbers can be used to problem solve, track revenue in a more efficient manner, develop target numbers that reflect where the club owner should focus the team's energies, and increasing return-per-member by targeting weaknesses in the club's profit centers.

This section also includes a number of reports that can be adapted to the daily running of a fitness business. Evaluation sheets could also be developed for an owner looking to purchase an existing business, or who is unhappy with the performance of their business but is not sure just where to start fixing it.

- **Chapter 8: Using the Numbers to Find and Solve Problems in the Club**
- **Chapter 9: Driving the Revenue Through Daily Number Tracking**
- **Chapter 10: One Simple Daily Report Can Keep You Focused**
- **Chapter 11: Learn to Save Money Before It's Spent**
- **Chapter 12: Increasing Return-Per-Member Using Multiple Profit Centers**

8

Using the Numbers to Find and Solve Problems in the Club

The most important thing you should get from this chapter is:

When a business is not performing, the answers are in the numbers.

Definitions and concepts you will need to know:

- Most methods of business valuations can tell you where a business is, but not where it should be going.

- *Expected outcome:* Working backward from the business potential.

- Clubs should close a minimum of 55% of their potential member traffic over a 30-day period of time.

- Your goal as an owner is to get to a 20% pretax net

- When rebuilding a faltering club, start with the payroll. Payroll, payroll taxes, bonuses, and commissions should be 37% to 43% of the club's BOE.

- A club that is in transition from flat to production-based usually has to get a new staff. In the gym business, 95% of what you do every day is selling somebody something every day.

Analyzing Your Key Numbers Can Lead You to Weaknesses in Your Business

It is a lot easier to fix a problem if you can first identify it as something that is not working right in the club. Typically, many of a club's problems that could be fixed go unsolved because an owner hasn't identified just what the specific problem is. Just as common and as detrimental to success is an owner that gathers data, but then doesn't know what the data means and what the standard of comparison should be. For example, just what is a good closing rate for a club using a trial membership? How many sales does a club need to stay in business over the long-term? And how much is enough when it comes to growing a net-receivable check compared to what it cost to run a fitness business?

Finding out where you're at and how your business compares to some standard or number gives you as an owner a chance to focus on what is fixable and ignore the rest. The numbers in this chapter will help determine where you are, and perhaps where you need to go, when it comes to putting together a plan that will allow you to drive the maximum revenues from your fitness business.

This chapter focuses on the big-picture numbers, the ones that can show an owner where exactly the club is today. Chapter 9 goes on to discuss what it takes to run a club by the numbers on a daily basis, and how to drive revenues by building a daily plan around the numbers you must reach each day.

Getting the Big Picture Using the Numbers

After years of consulting and visiting every type of fitness business imaginable, it has become relatively easy to walk into a business and get a quick snapshot as to exactly where that business is today and where the owner needs to fix it. Some of this ability comes from experience and being able to *feel* if a business is right or not. A dirty physical plant, out-of-date colors, broken or run-down equipment, a staff that is too young, and a club atmosphere permeated by the feeling of death and dying in the air all add up to a business in decline.

Businesses either feel right or they don't, and very seldom do you see any contradiction between the feel of a business and its performance. A business that is flat and on its way down gives off the stench of death even a potential member can feel and react to when it comes to not buying a membership.

The weakness to approaching a business in this manner is it becomes an emotional journey easily affected by the owner's story and situation. Fitness businesses that are flat but not dying are the majority. These businesses hang on year after year being worked hard by passionate people who just don't yet have the business skills to grow their business beyond the survival stage.

Helping this business get past survival is difficult because this type of owner will usually place the blame for the lack of success anywhere but where it should be, which is with his lack of business skills to get the job

> Finding out where you're at and how your business compares to some standard or number gives you as an owner a chance to focus on what is fixable and ignore the rest.

done. He may have the talent, but not the skills to analyze and focus on the real problems of the business.

The difference between a dead and dying business and one that has potential to survive can be felt, but more importantly, the numbers can better tell the story in a very short period of time. Using broad-based big-picture numbers to analyze a business takes the emotion and subjective approach away and moves the analysis to an objective, unemotional approach that can help an owner focus on the few key things he can do to start seeking change.

Analyzing a Business from the Big-Picture View

You have two ways to approach an underperforming business analysis: the traditional financial statement/cash flow approach, and the non-traditional approach that looks at key indicators as signs of performance and of expected outcome.

The Traditional Approach

The traditional approach to analyzing a business involves pulling out a year's worth of financial statements, doing some type of basic EBITDA (earnings before income taxes, depreciation, and amortization) formulation, and then digging into the business. The major problem with this type of approach is that all you get is a snapshot of where the business is today, but not of the potential of the business.

Another shortfall of the EBITDA method is that it may also tell you that you are not doing enough sales, but you won't be able to figure out how many sales the club has to close to survive. Another example is that this method may tell you what the cash flow is from the net membership dues collected from the club's receivable base, but it can't tell you what minimum cash flow has to be reached where the owner can then begin looking elsewhere in the business for other problems.

EBITDA formulations will again be discussed in Chapter 16 as a method of selling or buying a business, but today many consultants are applying this method of analysis too broadly and using it in areas that it is not suited for in the fitness business. The traditional definition of EBITDA is earnings before interest, taxes, depreciation, and amortization, but this definition does not apply well to businesses with gross revenues of less than $3,000,000 per year because debt is either replaced or assumed and usually the interest remains constant. Since most fitness businesses have less than three million in annual revenues, we will use earnings before income taxes as our reference. Chapter 16 is about valuations and further explains this term.

Another way to think of EBITDA is what the club makes in pretax net income. For example, a small club might have annual gross expenses of $500,000 and deposits in gross revenue $600,000 for the year giving the business a 20-percent pretax net.

The difference between a dead and dying business and one that has potential to survive can be felt, but more importantly, the numbers can better tell the story in a very short period of time.

Depreciation is a non-cash expense, and if you are buying a business this is a deduction applied against all earnings that lower the club net for tax purposes. But since you don't really have to pay depreciation with real money it becomes cash flow you actually get to spend if you buy the club. In other words, if a club shows $3,000 per month depreciation on its statements, then the club is declaring a $3,000 expense per month against the club's revenues effectively lowering the club's net profits. But since this is a non-cash item, the club actually has $3,000 more in cash flow than is actually reflected on the statements for tax purposes.

Amortization usually is defined as things such as intellectual properties including patents or rights to certain parts of a business and is something that seldom applies to a fitness business to any great extent. In the gym business you seldom have any long-term intellectual properties that decline in value over time as they come closer to becoming public domain. Amortization can also apply to a franchise fee or the purchase of a member list from a failing club.

When analyzing an underperforming business, pretax cash flow and depreciation can tell you where the business is at this point in time, not what the business can do in the future.

When analyzing an underperforming business, pretax cash flow and depreciation can tell you where the business is at this point in time, not what the business can do in the future. This type of method is a very good indicator of past performance but a very poor indicator of future potential in the business.

In addition to analysis limitations, another issue with trying to problem solve in a fitness business using tools such as financial statements is that the statements are so easily manipulated as to what an accountant or owner wants to accomplish tax wise, or worse yet, what he wants to accomplish with a bank or other lender. The Enron scandal during early 2002 clearly defined what accountants and owners can do to a financial statement.

Even if the statements are valid and actually represent the true state of the business as it is operated, this tool only reflects what the business did. It can't help in determining the potential of the business and what needs to be fixed to reach that potential.

When buying a business for example, it is always recommended that you start with the tax returns and statements, and then set these items aside and really dig into the business. The standard recommendation is to reconstruct the business from scratch going back at least one year by using the checkbook and bank statements. Buying a business is much more extensive than this and will be discussed in Chapter 16, but a simple reconstruction of the business from the cash outflows and inflows will give a vivid picture of where the club's money came from and how it was spent.

A Non-traditional Approach to Fixing a Business Begins with Determining Its Potential

It's hard to get anywhere if you don't know where you are going. If you are going to rebuild and then grow a fitness business, you first need to know where you want to end up. This is the concept of *expected outcome*, or beginning at the end and then working backward.

Expected outcome = working backward from the business' potential

If you know the numbers a business can do, you can then take steps to work toward those numbers. Numbers analysis can be applied to a fitness business to gain the expected outcome, which is really nothing more than achieving the potential of that business.

Each one of the following numbers or ratios should tell you where the business is and where it should be. Most of these numbers and formulas reflect a standard of comparison to see if the business is where it should be, but also reflect where the business should head if it is not yet at the prescribed number. While exceptions to every rule are always there, by applying these numbers across the entire spectrum of a club business, you should be able to paint an accurate big-picture view of just where to begin your problem solving.

The rules, formulas, and ratios are listed by number. If each one of these were applied to a business it would be in the following order. You will get a much better idea of how to use these numbers if you apply them to an actual business. The business in Figure 8-1 is an actual fitness business that encountered problems, was analyzed and set on a new course, and eventually reached a strong profitability.

This owner knew how to make money and was profitable for a number of months. It was her dream to start the business. The husband was in another business, and while he also liked being in the fitness business, he had very little effect on the day-to-day operations.

It is unusual to cover the operating expenses each month from the day you open a club. It was discussed in Chapter 6 that a typical club will burn through at least two months of operating expenses before the club can consistently cover its base operating expense (BOE). Breaking even normally takes about seven to nine months for most clubs and that is why the club in this example is so unusual.

As the old adage goes, it is a lot easier to get to be number one than it is to stay number one. Divorce, drugs, complacency, or new competition can bring an owner's lack of business skills to the forefront or simply a lack of continuing focus all can lead to a healthy club taking a downturn.

This club had strong demographics, a decent design, and an owner that knew how to make money. During her divorce she lost control of her business and its profitability was lost in just a few months. When the business began to lose money was when she called.

If she had stayed on top of the numbers she could have predicted the downturn a few months before it happened and then taken a more proactive approach at an earlier time. Most people don't, however, feel very proactive when they are in the middle of life-changing circumstances.

Divorce, drugs, complacency, or new competition can bring an owner's lack of business skills to the forefront or simply a lack of continuing focus all can lead to a healthy club taking a downturn.

The club history and status at the time the owner realized there was a problem

- The club is a 14,000-square-foot club, coed, that was started by a couple, but ran and operated by the woman.
- The club has approximately 50,000 people within three miles, each with an average household income of $65,000.
- The club was designed as an upscale adult-fitness center concentrating on the top 60% of the demographics in the area.
- It opened with 50 pieces of cardio, a full workout facility, a group exercise room, studio cycling, a nutrition program, and childcare.
- The facility was profitable for 15-consecutive months beginning with the first month it opened and was netting 17% pretax during those months.
- The club income flattened during months 16 through 20 and it began to lose money during the 21st month.
- The club had a monthly net check from its third-party financial-service company of $35,000.
- The club used the largest third-party financial-service company in the country, therefore lowering expected losses from its 12-month memberships.
- The club owners separated and pursued a divorce around the 15th month.
- The club's expenses are currently at $63,000 per month that includes all operating expenses, payroll, and debt service. This is the club's breakeven point, which the club was falling short of at that time by about $2,000 per month.
- At the time of review, which was at the 20th month, the club had 1,400 members and daily traffic on a Monday of about 200 workouts.
- The club charged $59 per month per member on a 12-month contract in addition to an $89 membership fee. The marketing for the club was primarily direct mail, using a 14-day trial as the incentive, restricted to local residents with valid ID and credit card with a 21-year-old minimum, which allowed the club to attract qualified leads without becoming price driven.
- The club was analyzed in May. At this time the owner knew the expense numbers but could not determine potential sales traffic in the club, closing rates, or usage rate from the profit centers (The usage rate is the relationship between the number of workouts a club does a day and what those workouts spend in the club's profit centers. The national average is less than $1 per day per member visit where as the target for a club with four profit centers is $5 per day per daily visit.).

Figure 8-1.

Initial Assessment

The first step in fixing this business was to give an assessment and determine just how far it was out of whack at the time. The following steps were the first ones done, and in the order they were presented, to find out where this business was at the time and what it needed to do. Some of these rules and numbers are mentioned in other chapters but will be reviewed here.

- Step 1: Application of the 1/$1,000 rule

This is a basic sales/production rule and is the first place to start when you are troubleshooting a club. The rule states that a club has to do one new annual membership per $1,000 of expense or it will eventually fail, assuming that the club's membership price is at least $39 per month per member. In this example, the club would have needed to average 63 annual sales a month to hit its minimum number. At this point in time, the owner couldn't determine where exactly she was in relationship to the desired sales number. The analysis was done in May and she had no real sales numbers since the first of the year. Her sales manager was keeping sales information, but after a few minutes of examination it was clear to see that the numbers didn't really match what was truly happening in the club since they were so poorly kept. Sales were decent but she didn't know if she was hitting this minimum. After reconstructing the business back through the first of the year it was figured that the club was averaging only 48 new memberships per month, 15 short of what was needed. Note here that this club hadn't died yet, but was bleeding to death slowly to the tune of about three to four new memberships a week, a number much easier to focus on if the owner realizes the problem.

- Step 2: Traffic and closing rates

Since the sales manager did such a poor job of tracking the new sales, it only followed that he had no idea of how many leads had come into the club during that five-month time period. After a brutal manual reconstruction of guest slips and daily logs, the owner was surprised to learn that she had been averaging around 200 leads in the club per month since the first of year. The 48 new annuals, compared to the 200 leads, resulted in a demoralizing 24% closing rate. Clubs using trial memberships as the primary marketing method should close 55% of all trial members over a 30-day period of time. Out of that number, 30%, or about 16 to 17 in this example, should buy the first day. Put another way, if this club had 100 trial members a month it should write 55 new memberships with 16 to 17 of those memberships closing the first day. This club had no data that could be obtained on the number of first-visit closes and no assumptions could be made from the data at hand.

> Since the sales manager did such a poor job of tracking the new sales, it only followed that he had no idea of how many leads had come into the club during that five-month time period.

- Step 3: Cash flow

The club had average deposits in the $75,000 to $85,000 range for most of its existence giving it an average pretax net of 17%. The goal of every owner should be to get the club to a 20% pretax net as its minimum standard. Expenses had averaged in the $65,000 to $70,000 range depending upon profit centers and the time of year. Current deposits had dropped to a

$63,000 average and the club was either in a breakeven or slight-loss mode on paper, although as noted later it wasn't paying all of its bills on time.

- Step 4: Application of the 90/10 rule

This rule applies to the number of paid-in-fulls a club should write in relation to all of its total sales each month. For example, if a club signs up 100 new members per month, less than 10% of those should pay in full for their membership using credit cards, checks, or actual cash. If more than 10 pay in full, it's a sign that either the membership is too cheap for the market and too easy to pay in full, or the salesperson is slamming for cash and discounting too much. Out of the club's 48 average new memberships per month, about 25%, or 12, were paid-in-full. Following that clue another step further we pulled up those memberships and found that the salesperson, and current club manager, were discounting somewhere between $100 and $150 per membership, dramatically lowering the club's return-per-member.

> **We pulled up those memberships and found that the salesperson, and current club manager, were discounting somewhere between $100 and $150 per membership, dramatically lowering the club's return-per-member.**

- Step 5: Application of the 70% rule

This rule states that a club should have 70% of its BOE (base operating expense or breakeven point) covered each month by the net payments received from the club's third-party financial-service company. This club had expenses of $63,000 and a net check of $35,000 for a percentage of coverage of 55%. A scan from the reports sent by the third-party company showed that the club had achieved 70% coverage in the past with net payments totaling $44,000 to $45,000 during the later part of the previous year.

- Step 6: Analysis of cash flow from receivables

Since this club was using a third-party financial-service company, it was relatively easy to verify its cash flow from the member payments collected through the club's receivable base. The club had a moderate presale of about 150 members that allowed it to open with good service and good word-of-mouth in the community. The club averaged about 75 to 85 sales per month for most of its first year enabling it to reach 70% coverage of its BOE around month 10. The club had a high net receivable base check of $49,000 late during the first year, but by the 15th month the check had started to deteriorate and the net collected per month had dropped to approximately $35,000, which appeared to be the lowest point in consideration of the current monthly membership sales.

- Step 7: Analysis of loss rates

The club was using a category leader in third-party financial-service companies and a 12-month contract as its core membership. The combination of these resulted in loss rates of only about 10% annually for the memberships. If a club was using 24-month contracts, for example, the loss rates would be at least 35%, and most of those are incurred the first year of the membership.

- Step 8: Analysis of cancellation rates

Cancellations are memberships cancelled by someone on the club staff. Cancellations are due to the three-day right of rescission, which is a federally mandated cooling-off period for consumers who buy retail installment contracts; a medical problem; a death; and in most states a right to cancel if the member moves over 25 miles from the club. Normal cancellations amount to about 1% per month, or about 12% annually. This club was averaging about 3% per month, or about 36% annually. This meant that this club was giving away about 24% of all the members it had enrolled due to the manager and salesperson letting people out of their membership agreements too easily.

- Step 9: Analysis of the club's debt structure and balance sheet/using the short-term debt ratio

The club was financed with a conventional bank loan with long-term debt service of about $5,500 a month, or about 8.7% of the club's monthly BOE. The original note was for approximately $260,000 over five years at 9.5% interest.

The goal for club owners is to keep the club's long-term debt service at less than 10% of the BOE. Long-term debt is anything that is longer than five years.

The club's short-term debt structure, which is usually high-interest debt with a three-year or less payout, was only $1,260 a month representing a small equipment lease. The goal with short-term debt is to keep the total less than 5% of the monthly BOE. The ultimate goal for a mature club going into its third year is to have a combined debt structure of less than 15% of BOE. This club was nearing its second year and had a combined debt structure of around 10%.

Clubs can handle long-term debt of about 10% or less as an ongoing part of its operational expense. The short-term ratio, however, should be limited to about 5% of the BOE during the first three years of operations and then be reduced after that point as the club gains the ability to obtain long-term financing.

However, the club had a problem with its balance sheet. Due to lack of owner attention and a recent cash-flow problem, the club was showing payables of about $50,000, most of which were somewhere around 45- to 60-days past due. The club's cash reserves were also dwindling and were less than $30,000 since the owners had taken most of the cash during the divorce.

- Step 10: Percentage of deposits from multiple profit centers

This club had done well with profit centers, especially in personal training, nutrition, and supplements. During its first year the club had averaged between $4.50 and $7.00 in profit center revenue per member workout, exceptional numbers for a club of this size. These numbers had started to decline, however, with personal training dropping from a high of $20,000 per month to less than $12,000. Supplements, munchie-bar sales, and nutritional programs had dropped accordingly as personal training declined. The club was currently averaging less than $2.00 per day per member workout in profit center income.

> **The goal for club owners is to keep the club's long-term debt service at less than 10% of the BOE. Long-term debt is anything that is longer than five years.**

- Step 11: Positioning in the marketplace and other factors

No new competitors had come into the market since the club had opened. The club had three other coed facilities in its five-mile ring and one women's facility. The club's lease was below market value and had five years remaining on the initial lease as well as two, five-year options at CPI with a cap of 3%.

- Step 12: Payroll and operating costs

The club's payroll was running at 48% of BOE. Payroll, payroll taxes, bonuses, and commissions should be in the 37% to 43% range of the club's total operating costs depending on the type of club and the strength of the group exercise and training programs. The club's manager had not cut any expenses in payroll since the club's revenues started to decline and the club was overstaffed during most of the operating hours.

> **Payroll, payroll taxes, bonuses, and commissions should be in the 37% to 43% range of the club's total operating costs depending on the type of club and the strength of the group exercise and training programs.**

Other Numbers to Consider

Two other ratios to look at that can add more depth to your analysis are the *receivable/strength ratio* and the *current ratio*, or *quick ratio*. Both of these ratios give a simple reference point as to where the business is on a risk scale. Heavily leveraged businesses, for example, have a much higher risk factor than those with less leverage in the form of debt. Businesses that have a solid receivable base in relationship to the monthly base operating expense (BOE) are also at less risk than those gyms dependent on cash sales or high numbers of new memberships each month. Let's look at both:

- Receivable/strength ratio

Comparing the club's total outstanding receivable base and its monthly base operating expense can give an indicator of staying power in the marketplace. Again, the receivable base is defined as outstanding memberships to be collected in the future that are tied to some sort of obligation such as a 12-month contract.

Above a certain ratio and the club has long-term strength, meaning it has enough reserves to count on to give the owner time to change the business plan and rebuild a weak club, or to fight a particularly tough competitor that suddenly pops up in the market. Below a certain ratio may mean that the club is too dependent on paid-in-full memberships or is writing weak, uncollectible memberships. For example, this club's receivable base had dropped from a high near $350,000 to a current base of only $290,000. Compare this number to the club's base operating expense, which is currently $63,000.

$$\frac{\$290,000}{\$63,000} = 4.6$$

The target is to have a ratio of at least *five times or higher*. In this case the club has a ratio of 4.6, or in other words, its receivable base is only 4.6 times bigger than the monthly base operating expense. The goal is to achieve an outstanding receivable base that is five times bigger than the cost of operating your gym each month.

This gives an owner a huge advantage if trouble arises since she can count on a steady cash flow months into the future from the strength of the receivable base. Another way to look at it is that if new sales decline dramatically because of a new competitor, or if something happens such as a divorce or personal tragedy, the owner has a certain amount of cash flow she can count on to carry her through while she scrambles to fix the problem or rebuild the business plan.

- The current ratio

It is not unusual for a club owner to be stuck in a quagmire of debt and not realize that it may be life threatening to the business. If nothing else in this industry, as a group we are optimists. Work harder, although seldom smarter, and you can work your way out of almost anything. This could be on the flag for the fitness industry because so many owners believe it to be true.

The problem is that these owners often get close to financial nirvana and sometimes the fates even let them win for short periods of time, but in the long run the businesses eventually wear the owner down and the club is lost. The reason behind this is that often the clubs were financed incorrectly resulting in too much debt that has to be paid off too aggressively.

As previously noted, a club should have 10% or less of its BOE in long-term debt and less than 5% in short-term debt during the club's first three years. After that period of time, the short-term debt ratio should drop to less than 5% as the club gains the ability to refinance necessary debt through long-term means, such as SBA or conventional loans that are least five years or more.

A club will always have a certain amount of debt and in fact, if a club doesn't have debt, it usually is not competitive in the marketplace because the owner is attempting to reinvest by using all of the club's cash flow. Debt is good, but only if it is controlled debt and as part of a long-term plan to reinvest in the club and keep it competitive.

The current ratio, or quick ratio, is an old accounting tool that has been modified to match what you need to find out about any fitness business you are analyzing. The goal with the current ratio is to find a reference point as to how much debt exists in relationship to a club's working assets, which are its receivable base and cash on hand.

Step one — List the club's assets:
- List the club's total outstanding receivables.
- List the club's cash on hand including checking and savings.

Step two — List the liabilities of the club:
- List the club's outstanding balances on all leases.
- List the club's outstanding balances on all loans.

It is not unusual for a club owner to be stuck in a quagmire of debt and not realize that it may be life threatening to the business.

- List the club's outstanding balances on other debts such as investor. paybacks. Do not list your lease or mortgage as part of your debt.

Example:

Assets

> Receivables: $290,000
> Cash on hand: $30,000
> Total = $320,000

Liabilities

> Leases: $90,000
> Loans: $150,000
> Other debt (investor): $50,000
> Total = $290,000

The ratio

$$\frac{\$320,000}{\$290,000} = 1.1$$

In this example, the club has almost as much debt as assets with a ratio of 1.1. Clubs with a ratio less than two usually are choking on their own debt. In other words, these clubs might have decent cash flow for their current level of maturity, but because of an aggressive payback of the debt, all the cash has to go for debt reduction rather than a more moderate payback that services the debt but still allows the business to get healthy with cash flow.

This club owner also made another key mistake in trying to pay down the bank loan too quickly. She paid at least a payment and half during the first year and sometimes more if the cash was available. At the end of the tax year she received a common surprise in that this debt reduction beyond the payment was declared phantom income and had to be taxed. She thought she was saving tax money by paying the debt, but this extra cash was from the profit side of the business and was declared taxable income.

She would have been better off to let the business get healthy and reduce some of the short-term debt instead of the long-term, and then refinanced the long-term debt into the future during the second or third year.

The goal with the assets to liability is to get at least a 2:1 ratio. When this ratio is achieved the cash flow from the receivable base can usually handle the club's debt service. If the club's ratio is under 2:1, the owner should consider refinancing if possible and especially should review the club's financial foundation, including how the club charges and collects from its members. Obviously, building a stronger receivable base would help strengthen this ratio.

Always start with the numbers. The numbers don't lie. But sometimes you use the wrong numbers to analyze the problems.

An Analysis Using the Numbers We Have Derived

Always start with the numbers. The numbers don't lie. But sometimes you use the wrong numbers to analyze the problems.

According to an EBITDA application, the club is flat and not worth very much if sold. It has no pretax profit at this time, although doing a weighted average of pretax revenues since the club was open would add to its worth. The owner has reduced her salary and other forms of owner compensation leaving very little to add back to any formulation. If you take a $0 current pretax, a moderate depreciation and the owner's compensation, you might value the club at maybe $250,000 to $300,000 if it was sold. Again, for a more detailed look at using EBITDA, review Chapter 16 on valuing clubs.

As stated earlier, the problem with this type of valuation formula is that it doesn't reveal the potential of the business nor point anyone where to look for solving the problems in the business. Without numbers and ratios relevant to your specific business, it's hard to get a true picture of the potential of the business. The evaluation points to consider about this business are:

Without numbers and ratios relevant to your specific business, it's hard to get a true picture of the potential of the business.

Looking at the sales picture—The club is averaging only 48 new memberships a month but it needs a minimum of 63 according to the 1/$1,000 rule. The club's price of $59 is viable since the club had achieved an average of over 63 new annual memberships a month in the past and no new competition had entered the marketplace. Potential member traffic had also stayed high at around 200 leads per month although the marketing had been cut back several months ago. This amount of traffic validates the location and concept since such a high natural flow to the club occurs. The club was less than two-years old and although it was showing its age, the physical plant was not yet a deterrent to new sales.

Cash flow—Cash flow was tight because the profit centers had dropped off and new sales cash had fallen away. The potential for increasing cash flow was high because the daily workouts had stayed high and enough leads came in to turn the sales effort around in a short period of time.

The club's reputation—The club's reputation was damaged because of the discounting for prepaid memberships, something the owner had never done in the past. This could be fixed, but slowly over time by eliminating the discounts.

The receivable base—The club had once covered over 70% of its BOE from its net check from all member payments. The check had fallen significantly because the new sales had been so low for an extended period of time.

Stop the bleeding through cancellations—Since the owner had somewhat removed herself from the day-to-day operations of the club, her manager had taken it upon himself to run the club. The club manager was canceling 2% per month, or 24% annually more memberships than was necessary costing the club one quarter of all the memberships sold through unnecessary loss.

Consider the debt—The owner had not missed any bank payments or loan payments, and although she was behind, had not yet taken a beating on her credit. She should consider refinancing the existing debt by rolling the loan, leases, and back due bills into one seven-year loan. This would actually lower the entire debt payment each month by about $2,000 to $2,500 per month depending on the current interest rate and outstanding back debt at the time of refinance. This would free up immediate working cash flow allowing the club to market again and replenish the profit centers

The workout traffic—Workouts continued right along during the entire process, but the profit center income had dropped for several reasons. First of all, the club had stopped promoting the profit centers on a regular basis since the owner was not in the club as much as she had been in the past. Second, the manager had stopped reordering profit center stock in an attempt to cut costs, so all cash flow from these areas had virtually stopped.

Waste in payroll—When rebuilding a club one of the biggest mistakes any owner or buyer of a club can make is to try and work around the existing staff. In this case, the salesperson can't sell, the manager can't manage, the profit center person is not profiting, and the head trainer is not producing the training revenue once generated by that department. This club turned around when the owner decided to get back into the game. She did so by firing the manager and the salesperson and then began driving the numbers herself, just as she did in the past when the club did make money. The head trainer ultimately stepped aside and was replaced by someone who understood programming and revenue production and that department was ultimately rebuilt beyond its old numbers. When staff people work in an environment where they don't have to produce it is very hard to move them back into one where they have to perform.

> When rebuilding a club one of the biggest mistakes any owner or buyer of a club can make is to try and work around the existing staff.

Where the Numbers and Changes Lead

The final outcome of this club was that the owner rebuilt it beyond its former production numbers in about four months by cutting payroll immediately, replacing the salesperson with someone who could take advantage of the immediate traffic, and ultimately refinancing the club's debt to free up cash flow.

By using the right numbers, the owner could set targets and understand what had to happen to turn her business around. Imagine how frustrating it would be to attack the problems this club had without having some type of expected outcome. How would you know you were on track? How would judge the salesperson or profit center manager? And most importantly, how would you analyze your receivable base and its strengths and weaknesses?

The right numbers allow an owner to set a course and rebuild according to an attainable expected outcome and minimum standards that have to be reached to be successful, such as the 1/$1,000 sales rule. Without these numbers, a lot of effort could be directed toward the wrong parts of the business and the chance to turn this business around might be lost.

Other Problems You Might Encounter in a Club

This entire book could be dedicated to the problems an owner might encounter in a club and the possible solutions to fix them, but in many ways everything in this book is designed for an owner to problem solve in his own gym. When an owner or potential owner has to problem solve a nonperforming club, always start with the financial foundation and work up from that point. If a proper financial foundation is laid, an owner can make a lot of mistakes and still stay in business. If an incorrect foundation is setup, it becomes almost impossible to sell your way out of trouble.

The financial foundation is always defined as how you charge and how you collect from the members. Most problem clubs can be fixed by starting with the financial foundation and rebuilding it along with the sales department. If you can sign up enough new members at a decent price, remembering the 1/$1,000 rule as the minimum standard for sales, and then have a reasonable chance to collect the memberships through a solid third-party effort, you can usually save most club businesses. The following are a few typical problems and some simple solutions to apply:

- *You bought a used club and the memberships are all over the board with members paying anywhere from $19 per month to $39. How do you raise the existing member prices and not make them mad?*

The rule of thumb is not raising the existing member prices if you can avoid it. The revenues increase from the raise is usually cancelled out by the fall off of pissed-off members who quit. If possible, honor the existing memberships, and get credit for this by sending a letter to every member telling them you could have, but didn't raise their rates, and then pass the rate increase along to new members joining your club.

However, if you have memberships in the file that are too low, which is probably less than $24 per month on an average in most clubs, you can only target those members for an increase and not the higher-priced ones. If you do this, always give them somewhat of a break by not raising their rates all the way up. In this example, the new owner might establish a new rate of $44 and bring all the current members who are less than $29 up to the $29 mark. Ignore the rest of the current members and honor their rates forever, as long as they renew within 30 days of expiration each year.

This is very controversial and most owners can't stand the thought of not raising existing member rates at some point. Consider honoring the old members by locking in their rates if they stay current and don't drift away, and then pass all increase to new members joining the club. The word-of-mouth is better and the fallout amongst the old members as they move away or dropout over the years will eventually cancel out their lower rates.

> Consider honoring the old members by locking in their rates if they stay current and don't drift away, and then pass all increase to new members joining the club.

The assumption at this point is that you are already using a strong third-party financial- service company. If not, switch the club's receivables there first before you make any changes and clean up the accounts. You don't want to add more volume to an already bad system.

- *Too many of your members are paid-in-fulls. How do you get away from being too dependent on cash and build a receivable base?*

Slowly! You have to work your way out of a paid-in-full dependency very slowly over at least a year's period of time. In this case, raise the paid-in-full price by about $20 every other month. This should force a few more people each month to pick the credit option, meaning the 12-month contractual obligation.

Over a year's period of time, the club should ease its dependency on cash flow from paid-in-fulls and shift it toward cash flow from a receivable base.

Over a year's period of time, the club should ease its dependency on cash flow from paid-in-fulls and shift it toward cash flow from a receivable base. Somewhere during that year the owner would probably be able to raise the monthly dues by at least $5 per month as the paid-in-full price started to creep up. Your ultimate goal is to have 10% or less from your new memberships opt for the paid-in-full option.

- *You're with another third-party company that doesn't seem to be doing a good job. How do you switch companies without hurting yourself?*

It depends on the mess and number of memberships in the file. Most owners wait too long to make this decision to switch because they worry about the pain of the transfer. You have several options to consider here.

First of all, if your current company is a complete mess, then you may have to transfer your existing file. Signs of a mess are poor customer service, lost members or accounts, too many mistakes, money that doesn't balance, software or hardware problems that can't be fixed, or high turnover at the company that affects your business. The company that is losing the business seldom likes this and will not make the transfer easy although you may have to force the issue if the accounts are truly in a mess.

The safer way for most owners is to run dual systems for about six months. This means that you start with the new company for all new sales moving forward so there won't be any more memberships being fed to the old company. This also means you might have to run dual check-in computers for about six months, but that is less trouble than you might think.

In conjunction with the new system simply let the old file pay itself down over six months. Members will renew and be put in the new company and the file will start to deplete itself over time as everyone is slowly shifted toward the new company. At the end of the six months, consider transferring the remaining members with the old company or simply let the system play out for the remainder of the year.

- *If you had to narrow it down, what are the simplest things to do to fix a club in the shortest period of time that will have the greatest positive effect on the business?*

√ Switch to a third-party financial-service company.

√ Use 12-month contracts as your primary membership tool.

√ Use closed-ended renewals as opposed to open-ended, auto renewals.

√ Establish at least four profit centers in the club that net a minimum of 20% each.

√ Get away from price marketing by using trial memberships as your primary way to attract new potential members. Trial memberships will switch the emphasis away from sales to service and the person's experience in the club, which is where it should have been all the time.

√ Price the monthly memberships at least $39 per month per member no matter where your competition is. By using trials, you can get a higher price than you can by running price ads.

If you do these six things you have a very good chance of turning any business and very high percentage of making a new business successful in the shortest period of time. Ignore these, especially in regards to the financial foundation, and you will have a hard time selling enough memberships to overcome your mistakes.

The Key Points You Should Have Gotten from this Chapter

- Most club owners can't fix the problems in the club because they can't identify what is really happening. To grow a business and fix problems in an existing business, you have to use the right numbers.

- Traditional number analysis only gives an owner a snapshot of where the business is today and doesn't lead to achieving an expected outcome by establishing the club's potential.

- The 1/$1,000 rule establishes the minimum number of new memberships a club has to sell each month to stay in business.

- Clubs should close a minimum of 55% of their potential members, of which 30% of all sales a club does get should be the first day.

- Your goal as an owner is to get a club to a 20% pretax net.

- The 90/10 rule is a simple gauge to determine if a club is selling too many paid-in-full memberships. The goal is to build a strong receivable base not be dependent on paid-in-fulls.

- The 70% rule is the first step in determining the strength of your receivable base. Your goal is to have 70% of your monthly base operating expense (BOE) be covered by the net payments from your members.

- Loss rates are reflected by the length of the membership agreement and whether you use a strong third-party financial-service company. Your primary membership tool should be a 12-month membership, which only has losses of about 10% annually.

- Short-term debt can choke a business to death. Clubs can handle about 10% of their BOE in long-term debt and less than 5% in short-term debt.

Most club owners can't fix the problems in the club because they can't identify what is really happening. To grow a business and fix problems in an existing business, you have to use the right numbers.

- Profit centers drive cash flow. A well-balanced club should have at least four profit centers that net at least 20% each and strive for $5 per day per member visit in gross income from the club's profit centers.

- When rebuilding a faltering club, check the payroll. A club's total payroll, including payroll taxes, bonuses, and commissions, should be in the 37% to 43% range.

- A staff that has worked for an extended period of time in an environment that has not called for individual performance usually can't make the cut when an owner switches to a production-based business plan. In the fitness business, selling somebody something every day is 95% of what you do with operations being only 5% of the business.

9

Driving the Revenue Through Daily Number Tracking

The most important thing you should get from this chapter is:

Understanding the numbers that drive the revenues in the business is the difference between working hard and working smart.

Definitions and concepts you will need to know:

- The minimum number of annual memberships you have to sell each month is one per $1,000 of expense. For example, if your BOE is $60,000, then you would have to sell a minimum of 60 new annual memberships.

- You should close 55% of your total potential prospects over a 30-day period.

- *The daily number:* The amount of revenue you have to run through the club for the month needed to hit your target deposit minus the club's expected receivable- base revenue.

- *The usage rate:* The relationship between the amount of workouts a club does a day and the amount of revenue those workouts spend in profit center income.

- *Profit mode:* The day of the month the club owner deposits enough accumulated money to cover the club's BOE. Your goal is to go into profit mode as near as you can to the first of the month.

- *Action plans:* All expected income for the club is assigned to individuals on the staff through action plans. Action plans are production-based management tools that keep staff members focused on selling somebody something everyday.

- *Bag of tricks:* Things you have learned over the years you know will generate income when needed on a slow day.

You Can Make More Money Every Day Running Your Club by the Numbers

When you come to work each day, do you have a written plan to make money? Do you actually have a plan anticipating exactly where every dollar of expected income is coming from in your business? This written plan does not mean a simple checklist of things to do. Nor does a written plan mean writing a dream number on a sheet of paper and then hoping that number comes true; a plan often used by young club owners during their first several years in the business when they really don't know what else to do but watch the front door and hope. In the fitness business, you can take what you get or you can learn to get what you want. The difference between these two philosophies is the difference between being a reactive owner or a manager dependent upon whatever flow of business that may exist at the time, or a proactive owner who establishes an expected outcome and then builds a daily, monthly, and yearly plan to reach that outcome. This difference could also be translated into owners who make money by driving the revenues in their club every single day, and those that wait until the end of the month to find out what really happened in their business after it's too late to affect the outcome.

> Nor does a written plan mean writing a dream number on a sheet of paper and then hoping that number comes true; a plan often used by young club owners during their first several years in the business.

Many owners work hard in their businesses, but in some cases they work hard at doing things that don't make them any money. Putting in 15 hours a day can make you a certified pudding head, but working this many hours on the wrong things can also make you very poor. Knowing and tracking the right numbers on a daily basis can provide a guideline for planning to make the money you want rather than accepting the cash flow that normally flows through your business. In other words, the money you make can be altered each month by learning to drive the revenue. This comes from running your business by the numbers.

> Putting in 15 hours a day can make you a certified pudding head, but working this many hours on the wrong things can also make you very poor.

Figuring Out the Right Things to do Is in the Numbers

Most owners believe they are doing the right things but still end up without the desired results. A good example is an owner that believes he is running his business because he looks at sales numbers each day and at the total deposit, and then compares these numbers to what happened last year. This system only can show him where he is and not what he could be doing in his business because he is merely recording the number; he is usually doing nothing on a daily basis to drive the business toward some type of expected outcome.

The total amount of new memberships by itself tells you nothing about your business unless this number can be related to other information about your club. It is not unusual for a club owner to work under the *I-have-bills-so-I-need-a-lot-of-new-memberships* operating system. This is situational management and relates the number that month to an immediate need and not as part of a planned expectation based upon the past and current performance of the business. Just because this number of new sales might be better than last year's number does not mean it is the right number or that it reflects the potential of the business.

An owner can look at a total deposit for this month this year and say that it is better than what he did during the same month last year. But was this month's deposit the real potential of the business, and could the club have done better if a different number was targeted with an entire business plan built around driving the revenues on a daily basis to hit that number?

Fitness-business owners can make more money by running the club each day based upon tracking and then reacting to specific expected numbers. These numbers have a relationship to what happened during the same month last year and what is happening during the preceding three months this year. By projecting numbers based on these two relationships an owner can compare history, which is what happened last year at this time, and trend lines, which is what happened during the preceding three months this year.

Establishing an expected outcome also gives an owner a chance to break this number into smaller segments such as a daily number for sales or profit centers, and then assign this number to a member of the staff. For example, an owner might look at cooler-drink sales from the same month last year and then compare that number to the preceding three months this year. Since this particular owner added another cooler to the gym, the preceding three months showed a trend line greater than the same month last year.

Based upon this, the owner can then make a projection for the coming month. He can break this number into daily segments for the entire staff, and a good owner can even break this daily number into what each individual counter person has to contribute during their shift. Instead of having a counter person just show up for her shift with no expectation of production, the owner can say that since today is Monday, and you are working from 4:00 to 9:00 p.m., you should be able to do $84 in cooler drinks during your shift.

In this example, the owner can run the employee by expected production numbers and then compare her hourly performance against an established financial expectation. Most importantly, this type of tracking also gives the owner a chance to react today to numbers that aren't being reached by making changes in the business in a timely fashion. By reacting today when a number is not met ensures production numbers will be hit on a daily basis instead of waiting until the end of the month, and then wondering what in hell happened to the business and why didn't he react faster to save it?

The owner can run the employee by expected production numbers and then compare her hourly performance against an established financial expectation.

What Are the Numbers You Should Look at Each Day and What Do You Do with These Numbers Once You Have Them?

Target an expected outcome, break all the numbers that comprise this outcome into daily chunks, assign these chunks to teams and individuals on the staff, and then post the numbers on the wall each day as a form of visual management. On the first day you don't hit one of your daily goals, react at that moment, not at the end of the month, to fix the problem and get back on track. In other words, you run your club each day by the numbers based upon an anticipated outcome.

Another way to look at it from a management viewpoint is that you learn to *run the plan and not the man* (or woman). Each day each member of your staff has production numbers to reach. You should run your day by coaching your staff to hit these numbers. If the person is not on track, you problem solve at that moment to get the person back focused on hitting their daily goal. At the end of the month, if everyone hits their assigned goals, then the club will hit its anticipated outcome, meaning its targeted numbers for the month such as total deposit, sales numbers, and profit center income.

The whole concept sounds so simple yet to many it is so hard because most owners don't run their businesses this way. A typical owner might run a little marketing, do a little sales training, track a few simple numbers, and then hope that business happens. Moving away from a reactionary management style into a production-driven, proactive system begins with a few simple steps:

A typical owner might run a little marketing, do a little sales training, track a few simple numbers, and then hope that business happens.

- Identify the numbers that will make a difference in the business.

- Set up anticipated outcomes for each category for the coming month.

- Break these numbers into daily and weekly goals if the category allows it. Some of the numbers only need to be tracked once a month and then compared to what happened during the same month last year.

- Track these numbers on daily basis.

- Assign portions of these numbers to individuals and teams on the staff by using daily action plans for every staff member.

- Learn to run your club's production by driving the numbers instead of the people.

- If a number isn't hit that day then go proactive and come up with solutions that will get you back on track for that category.

- Never forget the primary rule of owning a fitness business: 95% of what you do is production based, meaning that you have to sell somebody something every day.

Step One — Identifying the Numbers that Will Make a Difference in the Business

Each one of these numbers represents a production category for different parts of a fitness business. Several of these numbers have been mentioned elsewhere in this book but they are reviewed here in a different light and different application.

If an owner is going to drive the maximum revenue from a business, then she needs to set goals for each of these categories for the coming month (expected outcome) and then build a plan for the month that will make these numbers happen. What these numbers or categories are will be discussed first followed by how to target each one for a typical month.

Total annual memberships sold—This category only represents annual memberships. These might be either paid-in-full or annual contractual memberships but not anything shorter. Many owners count all new memberships that give a false sense of the business since many of these might be short-term memberships that are just a few months in length. They should also resist adding together their shorter-term memberships and then count them as one annual. Do not count three-month memberships as one annual if you are trying to build a strong long-term receivable-based business. How many memberships a club has to do is discussed later in the 1/$1,000 rule.

Closing rates for the teams and individuals—As an owner you have to sell memberships to stay in business. You buy or rent large spaces, fill it with equipment, and then rent this space in the form of group classes or equipment back to the consumer. That is the business you are in. If you are going to stay in business you have to sell memberships for this space to someone each day you are opened. How many of these you sell are affected by how good you are at closing prospective members. Closing 55% of all prospects through the gym over a 30-day period is the target number no matter what type of marketing or sales system you are using. This should be tracked daily and applied to the total sales team and individuals on the team.

Closing 55% of all prospects through the gym over a 30-day period is the target number no matter what type of marketing or sales system you are using.

The daily production number—The daily production number is the single most important number an owner needs to know each day because it reflects the total revenue needs for the month from all sources in the gym divided into small, daily increments.

Another way to understand the daily number is to think of it as a way to set your cash-flow goal for the day that includes all sources of income in the club adjusted for anticipated income you can already count on each month, such as a receivable check representing member payments. Typical sources of income are cash flow from new memberships, daily workouts, multiple profit centers, or renewals paid at the club.

The usage rate—The usage rate is based upon two factors: the total number of daily workouts and the total daily deposit from all of the club's profit centers. By dividing the profit center income by the number of workouts will get you a return-per-member number for each workout through the door, or what is called the usage rate.

The anticipated renewal percentage—If you are using a closed-ended renewal system, meaning the member renews for another year at the end of their annual membership rather than going open-ended or month-to-month, you can target a percentage of members that will stay in the system by renewing another membership for an additional year. Since members enroll each month they will also renew each month and a club can set systems in place that will increase their renewal percentage. An owner should target 65% as an achievable renewal percentage. In other words, if 100 members buy memberships based on an annual basis, at the end of one year, or going into the 13th month, 65 should buy another year's membership.

If the club is using open-ended memberships, meaning that at the end of their first annual membership they simply keep paying until they quit, the club can track loss rates from those members that drop out each month after their first year. The club owner's target at this point is to keep the loss rates at less than 2% per month, or 24% annually.

> **Profit mode occurs when a club has enough income to pay all of its bills somewhere before the last day of the month.**

What day the club goes into profit mode—Profit mode occurs when a club has enough income to pay all of its bills somewhere before the last day of the month. For example, a club might have base operating expenses (BOE) of $60,000. Don't forget here that BOE is the breakeven point for a club if it pays all of its bills, including rent or the mortgage, debt service, and salaries. If the owner doesn't work full-time in the business then the money she takes out doesn't count.

If the club makes a deposit that brings the monthly running total to $60,001 on the 20th day of the month, this means that this club went into profit mode on the 20th. The goal is to obviously go into profit mode on the first day of the month by establishing a large enough receivable check from the total of all member payments that can more than cover the total base operating expense for the business.

The 70% rule—The relationship between the BOE and the net-receivable check, represented by the accumulation of all member payments, is the single most important percentage to track in the entire business because this represents the point that a fitness business has become stable.

The goal for the owner is to cover 70% of the BOE with the net check from member payments. For example, if a club has a BOE of $60,000, then the owner's goal is to achieve 70% coverage or work toward a net check of $42,000.

The one per $1,000 rule—If you don't hit this number then your business bleeds to death slowly over time. This rule states that you have to write at least one annual membership per month, either paid-in-full or on an annual contractual basis, per every $1,000 of operating expense the club has if the club's memberships are at least $39 per month per member. For example, if a club has a $60,000 BOE, then the owner has to put a minimum of 60 annual memberships in the bank each month to survive. Again, this is the minimum number the owner needs to survive not the maximum or ideal number.

Step Two — Setting Up the Expected Outcomes

Setting up anticipated or expected outcomes is done by either one of two methods: looking at available history and trend lines or by swagging, which is the common practice used by most owners and means systematic, wild-ass guessing. You need a combination of both of these to properly set expected outcomes for your business.

Looking at the same month last year gives you a historical perspective since you can compare the numbers you generated back then versus the numbers you anticipate hitting this year. This works great unless something changed in your business, and something always changes in your business. You might have a new staff, a better sales approach, new equipment, you're better because of new education or more experience, or you might have simply added a new profit center that is working wonders for the cash flow. In the gym business, history is relative and as a stand alone indicator seldom indicates future performance.

History can be coupled with trend lines, however, which gives more depth to your projections. Trend-line analysis is looking at the last three months of your business prior to the target month, and then comparing these numbers with your historical data.

For example, say you are trying to project a target deposit for the month of October. This target deposit represents all money deposited from all sources for the entire month. During October of last year, the club deposited $55,000. The goal in the fitness business is to maintain steady consistent growth over time; therefore, the club owner should strive to:

Grow the business each year by three to five percent.

This means that during October this year you want to *minimally* grow the business by three to five percent. In this case if you just used October of last year as the basis for your projection, you would be looking at a targeted deposit in the $56,650 to $57,750 range.

This changes though if you look at the preceding three months for this current year. Since last year this club has added several new profit centers, used more effective marketing, and has instituted better staff training and development, all reflected in the increased deposits during the last three months. Put all together, the numbers look like Figure 9-1.

> In the gym business, history is relative and as a stand alone indicator seldom indicates future performance.

Total deposits for last year	Total deposits for this year
October last year $55,000	October this year (not yet projected)
September last year $53,000	September this year $58,500
August last year $53,000	August this year $59,000
July last year $49,000	July this year $54,000

Figure 9-1.

In this case, the preceding three months before your target month are all strong months compared to the same period last year averaging $57,100 per month. When compared to the same month last year, you are averaging around 10 percent more in deposits. The comparison looks like this:

Projection if based upon 3% to 5% over last year = $56,650 to $57,750

Trend line indicates approximate 10% growth

New projection = $55,000 x .10 = $5,500

The projection for this year is $60,500

A *swag factor* here should also be considered. Swag is systematic, wild-ass guessing, or in more literate terms, an educated guess. Starting with the numbers and projections previously figured, you could also look at an educated-guess factor. During October this year you are starting the month on a Monday and have an extra Monday in the month as compared to October last year. This year the club has also increased its marketing during September and October by sending out 15,000 direct-mail pieces a week. Based on these considerations, and looking at the history and trend-line indicators, the owner could swag a little and do a projection at perhaps $63,000 and have an excellent chance of bringing the club in at those numbers.

Why is this so important? Because you are going to break that number down into department segments and then again into daily numbers and assign these numbers to individual team members. Every one on the staff is going to be accountable for bringing in some portion of that number. Every one on the staff contributes.

Most club owners target a number and maybe assign some part of the number to departments such as sales or personal training. In this system, every single staff member knows when they come to work what is expected of them and what they have to contribute that day toward the overall target goal. Each day the owner then has to make sure that the individual staff members are on track to hit their goals. If this happens each day, then at the end of the month the club will have a much better chance of hitting its overall target projection.

> A *swag factor* here should also be considered. Swag is systematic, wild-ass guessing, or in more literate terms, an educated guess.

A final point to consider when projecting a target deposit is to be sure and figure in a net profit. Your ultimate goal is to hit a pretax net of 20 percent. When you first start to build the business, or rebuild in some cases, the profit will be smaller. No matter where you are at this moment, even if you are just showing your first point or two of profit in the business, be sure and include a profit as part of your monthly target projection for your total deposit.

Setting Expected Outcomes for Your Daily Numbers

Each of the tracked numbers listed in *step one* has to have an expected projection for the coming month. Each number is listed along with a hint on how to project that number. Most of the numbers can be projected using the method previously described. Those that need to be figured in another method are discussed separately.

Total annual memberships sold—History and trend line keeping focused on the 3% to 5% minimum growth. If you increased your price you still win if you sell the same number of memberships this year as you did last year. This category is also hard to keep increasing over time since you may eventually hit a number that is sufficient for the club and still allows you to provide great member service.

The 1/$1,000 rule tells you the minimum you have to hit each month on an average for the club to survive, but strong clubs will often surpass this number virtually every month. The most important aspect of applying this rule is that the one sale per $1,000 of base operating expense is a net number and has to be adjusted for cancellations. Cancellations that should be included in the adjustment are: three-day right of rescission, death, legitimate moves as mandated by your state law, and medical cancellations that prevent the member from continuing their membership. Most clubs using 12-month contracts as their core tool should average about 1% a month of their member file lost to these types of cancellations, or 12% per year, but clubs that cancel too easily will find their numbers in the 33% to 48% range.

Closing rates—Track these as a team and again for the individuals that sell memberships. Compare the actual percentages and move toward the overall 55% closing rate for your sales team.

The daily production number—This number has two steps. First of all, you have to figure the target deposit previously described. Once you have this number you can then figure the daily production number.

The daily number is figured by projecting a target deposit for the month and then subtracting the estimated receivable check. The receivable check again is defined as the net monthly amount of all membership payments. Normally this is called your net draft or billing check. If your club sells mostly paid-in-full memberships, then the daily number for that club would be

> The 1/$1,000 rule tells you the minimum you have to hit each month on an average for the club to survive, but strong clubs will often surpass this number virtually every month.

much higher than a similar club that has a strong receivable base reflected by a large net check from member payments.

The remaining number after the receivable check is subtracted is the club's daily cash flow needs that have to be met to hit the target deposit. For example, look at these numbers from a typical club. In Figure 9-2, the owner used the previous information mentioned to project her target deposit for the coming month.

Target deposit
  $60,000

Anticipated net check from receivable base
  $30,000

This is figured by averaging the last three months of net checks received from your third-party financial-service company. This is money that the club owner can count on as already having in the bank so she doesn't have to worry about collecting it on a daily basis.

  $60,000 target deposit
  -$30,000 receivable check
  $30,000 needed in daily cash flow to hit target deposit

Taking the $30,000 and dividing by the days in the projected month will equal the daily cash flow needs from all sources for the club.

  $30,000/31 days of the month = $967.74

This is the club's daily number it has to average from all sources including the profit centers and sales income to meet its target deposit and profit goal for the month.

Figure 9-2.

The usage rate—The usage rate is also based upon two factors: the total number of daily workouts and the total daily deposit from all of the club's profit centers. By dividing the profit center income by the number of workouts, you will get a return-per-member for each daily workout.

For example, if a club took in $1,000 from all profit centers on a Monday and recorded 400 member workouts, the usage rate would be $2.50. In other words, every member in the club that day spent an average of $2.50 beyond their membership in goods and services the club had for sale.

Your goal is to hit the magic $5 per day per member workout. This number can be reached if the club maintains at least four profit centers all netting a minimum of 20%.

Your goal is to hit the magic $5 per day per member workout. This number can be reached if the club maintains at least four profit centers all netting a minimum of 20%.

*Projecting renewal percentages or loss rates—*Clubs using closed-ended renewals should focus toward reaching a 65% retention rate. This category is a perfect example of why running clubs by the numbers is so important. An owner might look at her numbers for last year and realize that she is only renewing 44%. Part of her business plan this year, since she has a base point of 44% and a target number of 65%, would be to rebuild her renewal system and drive that 44% number higher.

*Having a base point and target number gives her a focal point for making changes in her business—*Whatever she is doing isn't working and the 44% proves it. She might try better follow-up, better tracking of upcoming renewals, using her third-party company to help her reach out prior to a member's renewal, or any number of things that could improve the 44%. *If you don't have a base point and a target number, then change does not happen unless it's accidental, which is not a proven long-term business plan.*

If the club doesn't use closed-ended renewals, but rather an auto-renewal system that lets members become month-to-month after their first year, then the owner should focus on loss rates each month for members who are beyond their first year. Your goal as an owner, which was mentioned earlier, is to keep this the loss rate number less than 2% a month or 24% annually.

Again, this is an example of a focal-point tool for the owner. If her current loss rate for her open-ended renewals is 3% per month and she has a target of 2%, she should know where to start improving her business.

*Profit mode—*Profit mode is an easy one. Simply look at your history and trend line and make a projection tied to your total deposit and anticipated receivable check. Again, your goal is to move the day the club goes into the black earlier into the month. Your ultimate goal is to hit the first of the month and go profitable with a large receivable check that covers your entire BOE.

*The 70% rule—*This number can be tracked using history and trend line, but it also has a few quirks of its own. A new business should target covering 70% of the BOE with its net-receivable check for the month somewhere between the 13th and 25th months of operation. When you rebuild a club or make major changes, you should target hitting this number in less than 13 months, meaning you should be able to build a strong receivable base built upon some type of existing base in less than one working year in the business.

This goal also has two parts. Covering 70% of your BOE is the first step, but once that is achieved you then want to work toward covering 100% of the BOE with your net-receivable check. Less than 5% of the clubs ever do this, but it is a great indicator of stability and success in the club business.

> **If you don't have a base point and a target number, then change does not happen unless it's accidental, which is not a proven long-term business plan.**

The one per $1,000 rule—The only target necessary for this rule is to get enough sales to keep the club on course. To maintain the minimum, always look at the last three-month average of new annual memberships. The goal is to keep the minimum amount of new business at one per $1,000 of BOE.

Step Three — Breaking Your Expected Outcomes into Daily and Weekly Goals

Some of the previously mentioned numbers don't need to be broken into daily or weekly goals, such as the day the club goes into profit mode. Those that do, such as the daily number and the usage rate, need to be tracked and worked each day to get the maximum revenues out of the club. In this step you will only review new sales, the daily number, and the usage rate.

New Sales Goals Have to be Adjusted for Cancellations

The sales goal for a club is based on how many annual memberships, either contractual or paid-in-full, it has to do during the target month. Once this number is established, it then has to be adjusted for cancellations. As previously mentioned, you are adjusting for member moves, deaths, the three-day cooling off period, or medical problems. Members that don't renew or who walk away from open-ended memberships are not included.

To get the cancellation factor, take a 12-month average and use that number as your adjustment factor. For example, if your club has 2,000 members in file and you are losing an average of 22 members a month due to these reasons, then your annual average is 13.2 percent. To build cancellations into your new sales goals, simply add the 22 to the projected annual sales goal for the month (See Figure 9-3).

For example, if your club has 2,000 members in file and you are losing an average of 22 members a month due to these reasons, then your annual average is 13.2 percent.

- The club wrote 70 annual memberships in April of last year.
- This April begins on a Monday and you'll have five Mondays in the month as compared to only four last year.
- The preceding three months of this year were running at about 5% higher than last year indicating a trend line that could be maintained into April of this year.
- Based on these numbers the club owner and manager target 74 sales for the month of April.
- 74 new sales
  <u>22 needed for cancellations</u>
  96 total needed to maintain the target
- The club's BOE is $60,000 per month meaning that this club has to do at least 60 annual memberships per month to survive.

Figure 9-3.

In Figure 9-3 the club could be in trouble and not know it. The owner and team may well write 70 or 80 new memberships a month, but if this owner is like most then she usually doesn't make adjustments for the cancellation. If she writes 70 new sales, but has 22 cancellations, she only nets 48, which leaves her below the 60 minimum average.

She obviously needs to attack the cancellations and work to keep those below her average of 22, but she also needs to do enough marketing and write enough sales to maintain her minimum as well as giving herself a chance to hit the target. In this example she needs 96 new sales to hit her target of 74 for the month. Her daily number would then be:

96/30 days in April = 3.2 a day average

The 3.2 represents the daily average she needs to hit to achieve her target of a net 74. But in the fitness business you don't write your sales in a nice and neat linear progression. To give the team a clearer picture of what they have to do, it helps to adjust the daily number into a weekly target. To do this the owner can use a weekly planner.

- Using a Weekly Planner to Drive Daily Goals

As mentioned elsewhere in the book, the fitness business thrives off of primetime periods. Coed clubs write about 65 percent of their business Monday through Thursday nights from about 4:00 to 9:00 p.m., and on Saturday mornings up to about 1:00 p.m. Some clubs might have a later primetime using 5:00 to 10:00 p.m. as their happening hours but the concept is still the same.

Women's-only clubs have a secondary primetime in the mornings that lasts from around 8:00 to 11:00 a.m. and then have a second surge in the evenings. Saturdays are still good business days for these clubs too, with a steady stream of traffic that might last into the afternoon.

Fitness businesses also write a large majority of their sales earlier in the week with Mondays through Wednesdays being great days. Fridays, however, are usually the day to host the Frisbee golf tournament in the club since so few members are around after the morning rush. A few exceptions might occur of course, but usually you load up the front of the week and struggle the closer you get to the weekend, except for that small savings rush on Saturdays.

When you start to use numbers to drive your revenues, begin by thinking in terms of blocks of production time starting with Mondays. Plan your production using Mondays through Sundays as your working time periods. Allow the days earlier in the week to pick up the biggest numbers and then adjusting downward toward Sunday.

For example, a typical club might do four to five memberships a day Mondays through Wednesdays and be happy if the Sunday guy pulled down

But in the fitness business you don't write your sales in a nice and neat linear progression.

When you start to use numbers to drive your revenues, begin by thinking in terms of blocks of production time starting with Mondays.

one membership. In the previous example, a club won't write 3.2 sales per day every day, but will probably follow something similar to the pattern cited next.

Continuing with the same example, this club has to do 3.2 a day or 22.4, rounded off to 23, over a seven-day period. To give the club sales manager a better idea of what's expected from him, he can track sales daily and then use the weekly planner to give him a better overall view (See Figure 9-4).

To give the club sales manager a better idea of what's expected from him, he can track sales daily and then use the weekly planner to give him a better overall view.

	New sales	Running total	Needed for goal
Monday	5	5	23 – 5 = 18
Tuesday	6	11	18 – 6 = 12
Wednesday	3	14	12 – 3 = 9
Thursday	2	16	9 – 2 = 7
Friday	2	18	7 – 2 = 5
Saturday	4	22	5 – 4 = 1
Sunday		we need one for goal	

Figure 9-4.

In Figure 9-4, the Sunday guy can do one sale and be a hero instead of having a false expectation of having to do 3.2 memberships. Tracking the numbers this way also helps the owner get a better sense of staffing and how business flows through the gym, especially if she tracks the time of sale for any extended period of time.

The Daily Number

In the example used in Step 2, the daily number is what the club has to collect each day from all sources adjusted for the club's receivable check, which is considered already in the bank since it is a constant and can be predicted. The sources left for the owner to work with are new sales income and revenue from the club's profit centers. The club being used in the example had a target deposit of $60,000 and a net-receivable check averaging $30,000 over the last three months.

> **$60,000 target deposit**
> **-$30,000 net receivable check**
> **$30,000 needed through the register that month from new sales income and profit centers**

In a 30-day month, this club has to do a $1,000 per day to make its target. However, the same rules apply here that were used previously in the new sales example. The club is most likely not going to average a smooth $1,000 per day and needs to use the weekly planner.

In this example, the club has to do $7,000 over a seven-day period, but as you already know most of the income will come early in the week and then again on Saturday morning. By using the weekly planner you can adjust the goals for your Friday and Sunday staff and realize that $400 on Sunday is a good job for that week and that month.

The Usage Rate

The usage rate, again the ratio between workouts and the amount spent in the profit centers that day, is more consistent in the way the money arrives in the club. For example, the club may do 400 workouts on Monday and $1,000 in profit centers for a $2.50 average, or 100 workouts on Friday with $300 from profit centers for a $3 average. On Friday one person went wild and purchased a nutritional program for $299 and kept the average alive.

The usage number can be kept daily with a daily number and a running total for the month, but it still works best when kept with a weekly cash-flow planner since most of the club's promotional events for profit centers will be held earlier in the week. Figure 9-5 is an example of a weekly cash-flow planner that could be used for sales, the daily number, and the usage rate.

Step Four — Tracking the Numbers on a Daily Basis

How hard can this be? Simply put the numbers on a spreadsheet and then pull the program up once a day and update as you go. Any *limited-output, I-dropped-a-weight-on-my-own-head, one-group-class-too-many* gym owner or manager should be able to do this once a day with little practice.

Unfortunately, two inherent problems with this system occur. First of all, if it is out of sight, it is out of mind. You have to call it up to use it and then you only get a small picture or a small piece of what is really happening.

The second flaw is that 95 percent of what you should be doing every day in your business is selling somebody something every day. If you owned a retail store at the mall you would quickly realize that you don't make money in the backroom looking at a computer. Sure you need to do the books, pay the bills, and study loss analysis and inventory, but if you want to stay in business somebody has to buy something.

If you want to make money you have to realize that you aren't in the business of selling fitness. Fitness doesn't sell, has never sold, and will never sell in the future. According to an IHRSA booklet (International Health, Racquet & Sportsclub Association), *IHRSA's Guide to the Health Club Industry for Lenders and Investors* (written by John McCarthy, executive director and one of the most influential leaders in the club business since 1981), the health club business is a unique combination of distinctive characteristics.

> Any *limited-output, I-dropped-a-weight-on-my-own-head, one-group-class-too-many* gym owner or manager should be able to do this once a day with little practice.

A Weekly Cash-Flow Planner

For the week of: _____   Club: _____

Daily sales target for the month: _____
Daily number target for the month: _____
Daily usage-rate target for the month: _____

Sales needed for the week: _____
Daily cash flow needed for the week: _____
Daily profit center income (ratio/daily cash flow for the week): _____/_____
(Example: $2.50 daily target = $2.50 x 2,400 anticipated workouts for the week = $6,000 in
    anticipated profit center income for the week or a goal of $2.50/$6,000)

Monday
Sales_____   +/-_____
Usage rate_____/_____   +/-_____/_____
Daily number_____   +/-_____

Tuesday
Sales_____   Week total_____   +/-_____
Usage rate_____/_____   Week total_____/_____ +/-___/_____
Daily number_____   Week total_____   +/-_____

Wednesday
Sales_____   Week total_____   +/-_____
Usage rate_____/_____   Week total_____/_____ +/-___/_____
Daily number_____   Week total_____   +/-_____

Thursday
Sales_____   Week total_____   +/-_____
Usage rate_____/_____   Week total_____/_____ +/-___/_____
Daily number_____   Week total_____   +/-_____

Friday
Sales_____   Week total_____   +/-_____
Usage rate_____/_____   Week total_____/_____ +/-___/_____
Daily number_____   Week total_____   +/-_____

Saturday
Sales_____   Week total_____   +/-_____
Usage rate_____/_____   Week total_____/_____ +/-___/_____
Daily number_____   Week total_____   +/-_____

Sunday
Sales_____   Week total_____   +/-_____
Usage rate_____/_____   Week total_____/_____ +/-___/_____
Daily number_____   Week total_____   +/-_____

Sales for the week_____   Goal for the week_____ +/-_____
Usage rate for the week____/_____ Goal for the week____/____ +/-___/_____
Daily # for the week_____   Goal for the week_____ +/-_____

Figure 9-5. A weekly cash-flow planner.

According to McCarthy, one of those distinctive characteristics is that the fitness business is a retail business. The vast majority of your business is transacted on a walk-in basis, meaning that it may or may not come in the door every day. As such, all of the rules of retail apply to how you run your business, including location, visibility, accessibility, and appearance, which are all critical factors to your success.

The second flaw then is that you don't want to create more and more office time. You have to create a system that can give you the big picture and then force you into action each day. Somewhere during all of this the staff needs to get motivated and should want to jump in and start selling people stuff every chance they get.

The solution is to start with a *visual tracking system*. This is a retro approach, but it still works and the staff buys into the concept by getting behind the numbers. In a visual management system, you should post the most important numbers you track each day on the wall in a common area such as the manager's office. Obviously you don't hang all of your numbers on the workout floor so the members can share in the fun, too. The numbers do, however, need to be posted somewhere where the staff can have easy access and most importantly forces you to stay focused on them the entire time you are sitting at your desk.

A good preference is to post them on the wall in front of the owner's desk and again on the wall in front of the manager's desk. Think of it as a *war room* where all you have to do is look up and get a complete overview of exactly what is happening in all of the important areas of the business as of close of business yesterday.

Most owners don't usually have a complete current picture of what is happening in their business at any one time. They are then forced to make decisions based upon incomplete or dated numbers, such as financial statements from the preceding month. To make the most money possible in your business you have to make decisions based on the most current numbers possible, preferably current as of the last completed business day.

Imagine sitting at your desk on the 5th of the month. You glance up, check the visual management system on the wall, which for most of you artistically challenged owners and managers is nothing more than sheets ripped off a pad of flip charts, and notice that the sales numbers are on track, but the usage rate is off by $0.50 a day. You were projecting $2.50 a day and your five-day average is only $2.00.

What does this tell you? Your business plan for the month is not working, and if things aren't changed, then you will not hit goal nor make the targeted deposit for the month. In this case there should be nothing more important in your life than concentrating on getting that number back on track. And that means today, not waiting until the end of the month to see if the number self-corrects.

> The vast majority of your business is transacted on a walk-in basis, meaning that it may or may not come in the door every day.

If it can be quantified, it can be tracked. If it can be tracked, it can be turned into a visual management tool. If it is on the wall, then it can be fixed, which means that you can work to get the numbers you want from your business.

Visual management systems forcibly point out what is wrong with your business today and then forces you to react to those weaknesses as they occur, not after they occur when it is then too late to do anything to fix the problem. If it can be quantified, it can be tracked. If it can be tracked, it can be turned into a visual management tool. If it is on the wall, then it can be fixed, which means that you can work to get the numbers you want from your business.

Involving the Staff

Your staff works better when they know what is expected of them each day. They also work better when they have some system that they can compare their performance against to see how they are doing in their jobs each day without having to ask or be told.

Most people want to do a good job, but managers seldom define just what good work is in that job and during that time period. To get the most out of your people incorporate a visual management system into your overall staff-development program. For example, the following are some sample steps that will help you focus your staff on the production side of the business:

- At the end of the month, sit down and set goals for the coming month with each staff person on your team. Don't forget that some of the team will have production numbers that don't involve selling memberships, such as a trainer or front-counter person.

- Also let the employee know what team goals they will be involved in during the coming month. If you are one of three salespeople for example, you will have an individual goal, be part of a team goal for sales, and also be accountable for your closing rates.

- Write a performance contract with each employee stating what is expected of them individually and as part of a team. These are simple one-page documents that state expected performance for the coming month. The employee signs a copy that is put into her file as well as receiving a copy for her use. The act of signing a contract based on set expectations creates a *transfer of ownership* from the gym owner or manager to the employee. As an employee, when you sign a paper agreeing to do a certain amount of work, you are accepting the responsibility for that work.

- Let the entire team know the goals for the month by hanging them on the wall. Individuals should post their own goals on the wall in addition to having access to the overall company goals for the month.

- Keep the numbers current as of the end of the previous business day. Some owners keep daily sheets and update their numbers hourly, but at least start with keeping your numbers current as to the end of the previous business day.

- Learn to run your club by the numbers. Base your business plan for the month on hitting the numbers that are important and the rest of the business will usually take care of itself.

As a review, the numbers that should be tracked on a daily basis are:

- New sales for the month adjusted for cancellations.
- Renewal memberships or loss rates depending on the retention system being used.
- Closing rates for the team and individuals that sell memberships.
- The daily production number.
- The usage rate.
- The one/$1,000 rule. This differs from the sales number for the month in that the one/$1,000 rule is the overall sales average for the year as a minimum, and the sales number for the month is situational for that time of year and previous sales history. The one/$1,000 rule is a minimum-maintenance rule and the sales for the month is a production number.

Of course, many other numbers can be tracked, and most owners will add to the system as they progress, but starting with these basic numbers will at least allow you to grow your business by focusing on the basic production numbers that drive revenues in most fitness businesses.

Steps Five and Six — Assigning the Numbers by Using Action Plans and Learning to Run Your Club's Production by Driving the Numbers Instead of the People

Action plans are tools used by managers to drive revenues. Action plans are also an extension of setting goals for employees and using visual management systems. A manager would use an action plan to translate an overall production goal for a club, such as a daily number of $1,500, into a specific number an individual employee would have to contribute to help make the big-picture numbers.

For example, a club manager might have a sales target of $2,000 from all sources on a Monday. The front-counter person needs to have an idea on how she contributes to that number. She may work from 9:00 to 4:00 p.m. on Monday and through action plans know that she needs to sell $120 of products and services while on duty in the club. If you are going to drive production, you can't have a club employee on duty and not have a production goal to hit during her shift.

Using action plans in this manner also gives the manager a different way to manage. Instead of managing the employee, you *manage the numbers*. Another way to look at this is that you run the plan instead of the man (or woman). Action plans enable you to coach performance on a daily basis by keeping yourself and the employee focused on selling somebody something each time she works.

Of course you still have to provide good service and support for the members, but if you don't have production, you won't have a club very long

> Action plans enable you to coach performance on a daily basis by keeping yourself and the employee focused on selling somebody something each time she works.

and service won't matter at that point. And even components of good service, such as answering the phone by the third ring, can be translated into quantifiable numbers that can be charted on the wall and then managed through action plans.

The Basics of Action Plans

- Run the club by the numbers each day

Get in the habit of running it by the numbers and moving to a production-based mindset. Running it by the numbers means you target an overall number and then build a plan to hit a portion of that number on a given day. If the number is not hit, then the owner and manager are forced to react to what's happening today and not waiting until the end of the month to see if the number corrects itself.

All this means is that running the club by the numbers forces an owner and manager to become *proactive* in the business instead of reactive. Proactive means you set targets and make the numbers happen. Reactive means you are often surprised by the numbers you hit in the business and then you react to those numbers too late to make a change that would positively affect the business.

- It's not enough to know the numbers

You must have a plan on how you're going to make money each day. Anyone can know the numbers, although the majority of the owners in the business don't know the numbers that drive their business. Knowing the numbers is the easy part. Knowing how to change the numbers when the target isn't met is often the difficult part.

> **Knowing the numbers is the easy part. Knowing how to change the numbers when the target isn't met is often the difficult part.**

This means that you may know the numbers, but you also must have a plan for the year, the month, the week, and the day as to how you are going to hit those numbers. Every dollar you anticipate making in the business must be assigned to some individual on the staff and to a team.

- Each employee should have an action plan for each day they work

This plan is different for each day since the numbers change throughout the month. No employee should work a shift without having some written plan on how they are going to contribute to the club's numbers for the day. Even the traditionally nonproductive people in the club, such as the childcare providers, can have quantifiable goals.

For example, your childcare provider on Monday night might have a scheduled event such as a clay or finger-painting session and have a targeted number of kids she wants in the class. She affects this number by inviting and reminding the parents of the event. If she fills the class the club will have extra members in that day who will buy something in the club's profit centers. The childcare person is not thought of as a production person but she can, through goal-setting and action plans, affect the club's production for that day.

- Each employee should meet with their supervisor for five minutes when they start their shift, receive their action plan for the day, and then report their numbers each hour.

If you are ahead of your numbers with that employee, you can then focus on those employees who aren't hitting their numbers that day. If an employee isn't hitting her numbers, the supervisor can coach and train that person specifically to her job and situation. Doing it this way allows the manager to run the plan not the man (or woman) and keep focused on the numbers that drive the business.

- At the end of the day the employee should meet for a few minutes with her manager to review and see what she contributed to the numbers for that day.

This allows for more individual coaching and training and to get a sense of what this employee can really do or not do. Working just a few minutes a day with each employee adds up to a lot of training and development in a very short period of time.

- The upper-level managers should not leave the club without writing a plan for what they are going to do for the next day.

Sketching out a plan today gives them time to casually think about how they are going to hit those numbers tomorrow, and the better managers will come to work prepared to get things done since they have has a full night to think about what has to get done.

The last thing an owner should ask an employee before they leave for the day is, "What did you do today to make this company money?" Don't ever forget that 95% of what you do in the gym business is selling somebody something every day.

Action plans work better if they are part of a long-term marketing and promotional business plan for the club. If you want to hit $5 a day in profit centers, for example, you have to plan events, sales, and marketing for the year so you can effectively promote those events. Most club promotions fail because the owners and managers started two weeks out to promote them as opposed to the necessary two or three months, which is the type of planning and effort it takes to properly promote most successful club internal events and promotions.

Action plans force the owner and managers to be proactive, which is just another way of saying you drive production by *making* the numbers happen each day instead of waiting to see if they happen. Action plans are simple tools that are effective because they are used every day with each employee. A key to using action plans with the staff is to give the lower-level employees more detail and a more complete plan, but let the upper-level managers and employees participate more in making their plan each day. Figures 9-6 through 9-8 are several examples of action plans for a few positions in a typical club.

The last thing an owner should ask an employee before they leave for the day is, "What did you do today to make this company money?" Don't ever forget that 95% of what you do in the gym business is selling somebody something every day.

Front-Desk Action Plan

Name of employee_____   For the day of_____

Club_____   Shift_____

Basic tasks you are responsible for each day:

• Greet every member by name and welcome him (or her) to the club today.

• It is your responsibility to make yourself aware of the daily promotions and your roles during your shift. Refer to the employee continuity book (a notebook kept at the front desk with notes from the manager and previous shift workers telling the next person coming into work what is happening today in the club) before you begin your shift.

• You should always answer the phone within three rings using the company greeting.

• Check members in with promptness and courtesy, but make sure the photo always matches the person. If you cannot find a photo in the computer, make sure one is captured during that member's visit to the club.

• Promote house charges and the club's credit systems to all members who buy something from the club's profit centers.

Today's promotions and sales:

The daily sale is:

_____

_____

The weekly special is:

_____

_____

Your daily goals are:

1). _____

2). _____

3). _____

Your plans to achieve these goals _____

_____

Summary of your day:

Daily goals hit _____

_____

Missed goals today _____

_____

Figure 9-6. Front-desk action plan

Trainer's Action Plan

Name of employee_____   For the day of_____

Club_____   Shift_____

Basic tasks you are responsible for each day:

• You are responsible for checking with the front desk and your supervisor to verify your schedule for the day.

• Every trainer in the club is assigned floor hours so the members can meet the staff, sample a variety of trainers, and so the trainers may have an opportunity to develop future business. Check when you start your shift for possible floor hours today. During floor hours you are part of the *first line of member service*. If you are not working out trial members or assigned to reviews, have a presence on the floor by talking to members, checking form, and reviewing exercises. Always strive to leave members better informed and safer after you finish your shift in the gym.

• Every trainer must sell a minimum of $750 in supplements each month and $250 in meal-replacement bars.

• Every trainer must be professionally dressed and ready for business. Check before you begin your shift for the uniform of the day.

Revenue from existing clients for today: $_____

Revenue from new clients for today: $_____

Special assignments for the day: _____

_____

(example: assigned to women's seminar from 6:00 to 7:00 p.m.)

Your plans to achieve these goals _____

_____

Summary of your day:

Daily goals hit _____

_____

Missed goals today _____

_____

Figure 9-7. Trainer's action plan.

Manager's Action Plan

Name of employee_____ For the day of_____

Club_____ Shift_____

The usage goal for the day: $_____ For the month: $_____

The daily number for the day: $_____ For the month: $_____

New membership target for the day: $_____ For the month: $_____

Revenues sources:: Promotions for the day:

1). _____ 1). _____

2). _____ 2). _____

3). _____ 3). _____

The manager's basic review of the day:

- Set the daily production with management team members or the staff.
- Coach performance by using the action plans.
- Train and coach throughout the day as the numbers dictate.
- Finish your daily production sheet through the previous day before you begin your new day.
- Walk through the club for an *atmosphere check* at least once an hour concentrating on the music, temperature, cleanliness of the club and the locker rooms.
- Set three staff training sessions for the day.
- *95% of what you do is selling somebody something every day.*

Summary of the day:

Daily usage number hit: $_____

Daily number hit for the day: $_____

Daily sales goal hit for the day: $_____

If these numbers were not reached, what is the plan to achieve these goals tomorrow: _____

_____

_____

_____

Supplies needed: _____

_____

Figure 9-8. Manager's action plan.

Action plans can change how you run your business because they force you and your staff to focus on the important revenue drivers in the business. Each employee should have an action plan as part of his daily routine. How can you let an employee, such as a front-counter person, actually work a shift and not have set revenue projections for the time she spends in the gym? Very few successful, real world businesses exist that don't have fixed revenue expectations for each employee in the company.

As a review of this step, keep these factors in mind:

- Project your numbers for the coming month during the last week of the present month.

- Break this anticipated number down into components that can be assigned to individual team members.

- Build daily action plans for every member of the staff. Remember that some staff may have non-monetary goals.

- Run your club by the numbers by using a plan each day instead of trying to use situational management for your staff. It is easier to coach performance and achieve numbers compared to trying to motivate people who don't really know what is expected of them when they come work.

- Knowing the numbers is not enough. You must have a plan that focuses on the how. *How are you going to reach those numbers and what are you going to do in the club today to make money?*

Step Seven — If a Number Isn't Hit Today, then Come Up with Solutions that Will Get You Back on Track Tomorrow

You have two ways to drive the revenue in your club. First of all, *long-term planning* is your core generator. For example, a club might order clothing in August and September for a November arrival. The day after Thanksgiving the club puts all the new stock on the floor taking advantage of the biggest retail day in the country. The owner would have gift boxes ready along with specially priced short-term memberships that could be purchased as gifts for a friends or spouses. The club would also be opened on Christmas Eve to take advantage of the last-minute shoppers. This promotion would be part of a one-year business plan for promoting profit centers in the club and would generate revenue for the entire month.

The other way to drive revenue is when things don't work on a daily basis. For example, a club owner has a daily number targeted at $1,000 per day for the month. On a Monday she expects to do added sales and more profit center income because of heavier traffic, which leads her to an expectation of doing $2,000 that day in non-sales income.

During the afternoon she notices that a heavy rainstorm has cut the daily traffic by about 25 percent, and if she doesn't something she won't hit her

Knowing the numbers is not enough. You must have a plan that focuses on the how. *How are you going to reach those numbers and what are you going to do in the club today to make money?*

numbers for the day. What she does next is what separates the good owners from the ineffective ones.

If there is one secret in the gym business, it's learning to create revenue where none existed before.

If there is one secret in the gym business, it's learning to create revenue where none existed before. In other words, this owner doesn't have the money coming in as planned so she must go out and *make it happen*. This ability is what differentiates a profitable owner from one who merely survives living off the normal flow of the business each month. A proactive owner realizes she can have what she wants. A reactive owner takes what she gets. The secret is learning to generate revenue when you need it.

Every owner can develop a *bag of tricks* she can use when the cash gets slim in the club. This bag of tricks is either full of small ideas that can generate cash when the normal flow in the club stops or slows down, or can include more formal repeatable income busters such as a Monday Mania event, which is a cash generation event developed by the Thomas Plummer Company that can be repeated monthly in the gym.

The hard part of quick-cash generation is to learn how to raise cash, yet not hurt your integrity or your ability to do business in the future. You would not, for example, want to run a discount yearly-membership sale for cash if you were just looking to raise a small amount of money over a day's period of time. In this case you might raise the cash, but you would hurt your business in the long run because of the pissed-off members who paid full price for a membership.

Planning for Cash Throughout the Year

A must-have tool for any club owner is a 12-month promotional plan to drive revenue from members you already have in the system. Your club has a membership base ranging anywhere from several hundred members to 12,000 or more in the large-family clubs. These people have money and will spend it if given the chance.

The members don't, however, just walk by the counter, grab stuff, and then throw money at the staff. As much as you would like this to happen, especially with your cheap-ass old members who are still paying $19 per month for a 1990 step class and who don't ever spend anything in the club and demand everything anyway, it is not something you want to list on your 12-month promo plan as an ongoing source of income.

The club should have something on the schedule at least once a month that can add a surge of income to the club. Twice a month would be preferable, but at least once a month might be the way to get started. For example, Figure 9-9 includes a few sample revenue busters the club might schedule.

January

Reggae Night (A visual- and musical-theme night to promote profit centers that works best on a heavier traffic night such as earlier in the week, and that can also be combined with a *Monday Mania*.)

Monday Mania (A once-a-month profit center driver that can be used to promote education, such as a question-and-answer session about supplements, or a clinic on how to effectively lose that extra weight after your baby, and profit centers including special discount specials and samples.)

February

The Valentine's Day promotion (A two-day gift certificate promotion based on last-minute shopping done by the male population.)

Monday Mania

March

Double-Double Day (A promotion based on a punch-card system to grow frequent buyers in the club's profit centers. A normal purchase is one punch and the punches on *Double-Double Day* lead to extra punches and the chance to earn rewards sooner.)

Spring Break (A Thursday night party in the club featuring a deejay, free alcohol, a club mixer, and of course a sale on featured items in the club.)

Monday Mania

April

Daily Special (The club should have specials every day, but an entire month can be dedicated to pushing product with creative promotions and sales.)

Monday Mania

May

Summer Shape-Up (A two-month promotion based on selling training, weight loss, spa, and other related items that will help people lose those 10 pounds and two dress or pant sizes before swimsuit season.)

Monday Mania

June

Happy Hours (A Thursday or Friday night promotion highlighting the sports bar/juice bar, and features deejays in the club, table service with waiters, and other extras that keep people focused on one of the club's largest and most production profit centers if done correctly.)

Figure 9-9. Revenue busters.

These planned surges should be in conjunction with daily sales using simple techniques to highlight something in club each day. For example:

- 3 bars for $5

- 15% off of a case of your favorite drinks

- Any shake today just $3

- One coffee, $1

- Clothing discounted for one day

- Buy one cooler drink, get a second for half price

The goal is to have something on sale every day that can be promoted in the club. Members hate routine and will stop noticing anything in the club that becomes static.

The goal is to have something on sale every day that can be promoted in the club. Members hate routine and will stop noticing anything in the club that becomes static. A club owner that has a bright, interesting display that changes daily will sell more products and make more money over a month's period of time.

Also note that you want to price anything on sale so that the club nets at least 33 percent. You don't want to get into the habit (where many of your young staff might want to lead you) of putting things on sale just to dump them without a thought to the net. Munchie bars are perfect illustrations of how a simple technique can go wrong if the net is not calculated first (See Figure 9-10).

Munchie bars -- Buy 2 and get the 3rd one free!
    Bar cost to the club $1 each
    Club sells the bars at $2 each
    Buy 2 equals $3 in hard cost versus $4 in income
    $4 revenue
    -$3 hard cost
    ‾‾‾‾‾‾‾‾‾‾‾‾
    $1 net (25% profit margin -- $1 divided by $4 = 25%)

Munchie bars -- 3 bars for $5!
    Bar cost to the club $1 each
    Club sells the bars at $2 each
    Buy 3 for $5 is $3 in hard cost versus $5 in income
    $5 revenue
    -$3 hard cost
    ‾‾‾‾‾‾‾‾‾‾‾‾
    $2 net (40% profit margin -- $2 divided by $5 = 40%)

Figure 9-10.

In Figure 9-10, one slight change generated an additional 15 percent in net, yet the owner was still able to offer something attractive to the members through the 3-for-$5 promotion.

A *loss leader* is an exception to this rule. A loss leader is a promotion that has a planned loss built in, but you do it anyway in hopes of being able to generate more income later on. For example, a club owner adds a new cooler to her drink line featuring a tea-based product. To introduce the product she might sell the first few cases at only $0.50 per bottle. These first drinks might be highlighted in a display on the counter, sticking out of ice in a nice cooler on a hot day, or given in nice plastic glasses as samples during the first week. She will lose money at $0.50 per bottle over the first few cases, but she does it anyway in hopes of developing a taste for the product that will lead to more sales later on.

Remember that the goal for planning a 12-month, internal promotional plan is to add surges of income to the club's revenue stream throughout the year. During weak months, income busters such as the Monday Mania might be repeated twice if the traffic in the club warrants it and the owner and manager can have at least two weeks of solid preparation to pull off a successful event.

Using the Bag of Tricks

The *bag of tricks* is an old ski instructor's term, usually applying to kid's instructors. You might have a class of one student with a bad attitude or a full class of nine-year-olds with different backgrounds and maturity levels. The bag of tricks included learning methods geared for kids, games, songs, secret trails, candy, and almost about anything else the instructor might pull out that would keep the class safe in a learning mode and entertained for the allotted time period. The better instructors always had a bigger bag of tricks they could reach into to keep the kids moving and laughing for a full day, and which would lead to bigger tips if all the kids stayed happy and came home alive.

In the gym business you have to develop a bag of tricks that can be used to get money out of someone's pocket on a slow day. The best owners in the business could be thrown out naked on a street corner in a strange town, and by noon have clothes, a job, and probably a place to live. These are the type of owners who will simply sell themselves into success no matter what the situation.

The term for this ability is *killer instinct* and it means somebody is going to buy something today and they don't even know it yet. Developing a bag of tricks in the gym is just a classier and more functional way to make money when you need it as compared to getting naked on the street looking for work. Think of the bag of tricks as things you can keep in the closet and then pull out one at a time when you need it. Most owners should start with at least five tricks, but over time you should be able to develop an entire month's worth of quickie income busters.

Keep in mind the return is in the details. Putting a sign up in the front of the gym stating, "Introductory training special -- 3 personal training sessions just $99," is not a promotion, it is just a waste of poster board for all the money it will make you.

In the gym business you have to develop a bag of tricks that can be used to get money out of someone's pocket on a slow day. The best owners in the business could be thrown out naked on a street corner in a strange town, and by noon have clothes, a job, and probably a place to live.

Promotion is the key and the money is in the details.

Promotion is the key and the money is in the details. Nice retail quality displays throughout the club that weren't there yesterday will get the member's attention. A table nicely decorated and well staffed during primetimes will enable the members to get involved and interested in learning more about what training can do for them. E-mails to all the members a day before the sale, which cost the club nothing but a little labor, letting them know the club is running an intro to training tomorrow will help drive revenue for that day. All of these things have to be done to get the most revenue from the most members.

You can always develop several easy promotions on short notice if all of the support materials are there to use. The first time you use one of these it may take several weeks or longer to put together decent support material, but after that it's a matter of keeping everything together and pulling out the entire promotion as a kit when needed. The following are some sample tricks for your bag:

- Introductory training special — 3 sessions with a trainer for $99

This special can be run once a month on a slow day to raise quick cash. If you can alert the members a day before with e-mail, it will be more effective and using the trainers at an information desk will add more value and increase the revenues. You can raise additional cash with this promotion if you let the existing training clients buy a limited amount of packages to add to their other sessions they have already purchased.

- Three months of unlimited tanning for $99

This is another once-a-month blowout special that could be used anytime except for your prime tanning months. Modify your pricing on this one depending upon your current tanning model. Make sure you have great visuals for the lobby and the club when you are running this one-day special.

- A spa special

You have a variety of options for this kind of special if your club has a decent day spa. An example might be a makeover and nails for $29. The good thing about the spa specials is that they almost always lead to an additional sale in the next week or so if promoted properly.

- Gold-Card Day

If you have a weight-loss management system in your club and sell supplements, the Gold-Card Day once or twice a month is a natural. On this day the members can purchase any supplements they want at 20% off the normal price. You can have this on a set day every month, similar to the national chain the idea was borrowed from, or you can make it random depending upon the cash flow in the club.

- Sports bar/juice bar

Every club should have a happening sports bar/juice bar as the central social focus in the club featuring shakes and enough televisions to give it a sports-bar feel. Women's-only clubs should definitely have the juice bar concept since it adds socialization and networking areas to the club. Some options for sports bar/juice bar specials could be:

√ Double-Punch Monday.

√ Put $50 on your gym credit and get $10 added free.

√ All add-ons for the shakes (limit 3) free today (develops future add-on business — add-ons are things such as ginseng or soy protein powder that can be added to increase the revenue from a shake).

√ Happy Hours as previously mentioned can be done once or twice a month.

√ Breakfast Club Meeting is a special section of tables set off once a week for the early morning members. They have their own club and get discounts once a week off of shakes and coffee. Give them a special card or recognition.

√ Business After Hours is a networking opportunity for members who have businesses or products to sell. It can be run once a month as a social hour after work, and wine and beer might be appropriate if it fits your audience.

Any of these ideas could be further developed with the proper support material into moneymakers for your club. Think in terms of having a slow day and then reaching into the closet and pulling out a complete kit such as the introduction to personal training promotion.

This concept gives you a lot more options than you currently have today to generate that extra income. Also remember that any of these ideas could be improved if you added things such as e-mails or spend a little more to develop a stronger kit. When you first begin with these ideas, do fewer things but do them better. Instead of spending a little money on many kits, spend more money on fewer kits and make that promotion stronger. A final thought is that if you are not feeling creative, most of these ideas are already available in a kit form through *PromoCoach*, a Thomas Plummer Company support division.

Do fewer things but do them better.

Don't Forget about Membership Sales

If the month is slow you can still work on membership sales. Cleaning up your potential member leads is still a valid way to write some business when times are slow, but you must definitely avoid that *going-out-of-business desperation sale* such as discounting annual memberships for cash.

Cleaning up leads and writing a little business is much easier if the proper groundwork has been laid prior to tossing your entire staff on the phones in a panic mode to reach people. To give yourself the best chance of writing sales from previous leads, you should have done these things already:

- Sent a handwritten thank you note the day the person toured the club, thanking them for inquiring about your club. For example:

  Thank you for inquiring about a membership at Our Club. We realize you have choices when it comes to fitness and we really do appreciate a chance to earn your business. If you have any questions concerning fitness or a membership at our club please feel free to call me personally at 555-1234.

- Sent the person an e-mail thank you, a follow up e-mail reminding them that they can try the club free with no risk or no obligation (trial membership), an e-mail letting them know they can bring a buddy or significant other to share their trial membership, started sending the person the Fitness Tip of the Week e-mail, and your electronic newsletter. Of course, you don't want to send all these emails at the same time, but rather, spread them out over a period of weeks.

- If the person finished the trial but didn't become a member, he should have received a thank you letter from the owner based on this idea:

  Thank you for completing a trial membership at Our Club. I'm sorry we didn't fit your plans at this time but we would like to keep the door open. Bring this letter to the club anytime during the next 12 months and receive $50 off of any membership we offer.

These are basic follow-up points all clubs should begin with when dealing with potential members in the club. As you've noticed, most of these are dependent on e-mails instead of trying to hound someone to death using a phone. Phones are not effective anymore, with most clubs reporting less than a 20-percent contact rate when trying to reach potential members. In the next few years e-mails or other net-based tools will be the major method of reaching out for business.

Phones are not effective anymore, with most clubs reporting less than a 20-percent contact rate when trying to reach potential members.

If you have laid the proper groundwork you should be able to clean up these missed leads during your slow times of the month. Obviously, good clubs are going to try and incorporate this into their normal production schedule every month, but when you start you may just be working on your misses when times are a little slower.

Always remember most people came into a club with serious intentions to join. Many don't because they have been overwhelmed by what they saw, swamped at work, in the middle of family problems, or they are just indecisive people sitting on the fence waiting for someone to push them over to your side.

A final professional contact may be exactly what the person needed to convince him he wants to join your club. In the person's mind, it may be as simple as joining a club that expresses how much they really want his business as compared to another business he may have visited that hands him a price list and walks him to the door. When you are trying to reach missed potential members, try these following steps:

- Use a simple connection point with the person such as, "We would like to give you another opportunity to the join the club and to take advantage of receiving a free gift package if you decide to join Our Club this month."

- Giving away gift packages and other positive incentives, such as the letter previously mentioned that can be used to save $50, are more effective than just dropping the price to get the sale. Offering the person a quality incentive package, such as a nice gym bag, water bottle, and club tee shirt, is often enough to buy the sale. Be aggressive with these packages and don't cheap out here. Spending between $40 and $75 hard cost ($100 or more retail) to buy a full-price membership is still a deal for the club and a strong incentive for the fence sitters.

- E-mails are effective and not nearly as irritating as a phone call. Remember that the person gave you his e-mail address and will most likely read a brief note from your club.

- Letters and handwritten notes are also effective. Getting a hand-addressed note professionally asking for their business is almost a lost art in the business world today and will stand out to the consumer.

- If you use the phone, be polite, too the point, and be prepared to leave a short but concise message since you really don't get to talk to real people too often anymore.

- If you are using e-mail outreach, such as a Fitness Tip of the Week, send a general invitation to those you missed. The missed folks should have been in a separate file anyway and broadcasting one e-mail to everyone in the file should give you results.

- If the person was qualified to begin with, which means they were of a certain minimum age for your club, were local residents with a valid ID, and had a credit card, then consider sending another trial membership to those people several times a year. Besides increasing daily traffic in the club and adding to the profit centers, you may catch someone at the right time in their life. You may have already learned from your experience with trial memberships that some people begin with great intentions, then several days into the trial something goes wrong in their life and they don't get a chance to complete the trial. This doesn't mean you are getting ripped off by extending another trial to them, it simply means that you are reaching out and giving the person another chance to spend money in your club.

- Invite the person to a special event in the club. A Happy Hour, theme night, or party in the club is a neutral way to get someone back in without insulting him or putting on too much pressure.

You have to sell memberships in the club business, but you must learn to sell with style and class. Beating people into submission buys you nothing but memberships that aren't paid, bad word of mouth in your community, and a membership that is not loyal to your club.

> You have to sell memberships in the club business, but you must learn to sell with style and class. Beating people into submission buys you nothing but memberships that aren't paid, bad word of mouth in your community, and a membership that is not loyal to your club.

Professional selling and follow-up will get you the memberships you need. When things are slowing down in your club, reach out to those folks who have shown interest in your business in the past. Many of these people would like to buy but they want someone to pay attention to them first.

A key point here to remember is that no one likes to spend money and then look stupid. Things such as handwritten notes, e-mail follow-ups instead of bothering someone on the phone, and positive incentive packages such as gym bags and workout gear validate the person's decision to buy. Make them look smart by giving them cool stuff for joining your club. Prove to them that they're a genius by letting them know they made the right decision and didn't join your competitor. Developing a professional sales sense will get this done.

Step Eight — Sell Somebody Something Every Day

If you want to stay alive in the fitness business, you have to sell somebody something every day you are open.

Start your day and end your day with one fact: *if you want to stay alive in the fitness business, you have to sell somebody something every day you are open.* You are a production-based business and your goal is to make money. Every employee, every manager, and the owner all have to be grounded in the simple statement that 95 percent of what you do is selling somebody something every day.

As owners you often get out of touch with this part of the business. You get older, burned out on being on the front lines, and just a little tired of putting up with the members and their nonsense. To make money in the fitness business over time you always have to return to this premise: *you have to sell somebody something and you have to do it every day because the bills don't stop even if the income does.* This point cannot be emphasized enough.

This also means that every decision you make has to be attached to this idea. If you add a new sports bar/juice bar it's because it's a vehicle to make money from the members that you didn't previously have in the arsenal. It's good member service, but it's still there to make money. If you put a new rack of medicine balls in the functional area it's because you want to give the trainers new tools to get more people interested in training and because the balls will help member retention.

In other words, the question you always have to ask yourself is, "If I do this, will it give me a better way to sell somebody something?" Are you creating a better delivery system for all types of sales?

Putting It All Together

To make more money over time you must learn to run your business by the numbers using a proactive management approach. This means you target the numbers that are important to production in the business, and then develop a delivery system in the gym that allows you to create revenue on a daily basis.

Most owners can't build this system because they haven't yet identified the numbers that are relevant and because they operate in a reactionary mode. Reactionary management means you wait until business happens to you instead of you happening to the business.

Many owners don't make the money they should because they don't feel they have any control over what happens each day. Understanding the numbers, attacking your targets, and getting your team involved with action plans will enable you to make more money in your business each month.

> **Reactionary management means you wait until business happens to you instead of you happening to the business.**

The Key Points You Should Have Gotten from this Chapter

- Building a business plan that works is based upon understanding the numbers important to your business.

- It is easier to run a business if you have a base number and a target to shoot for each day. In other words, where are you and where do you want to go?

- You are a production-based business. Sell somebody something every day.

- You need to track a handful of key numbers every day. These numbers will have a huge impact on your business.

- Set targets, called expected outcomes, each month for all of your key indicators.

- Visual management is a simple sophisticated tool to grow your business.

- Action plans transfer the expected outcome to the staff. Every dollar you expect to make should be assigned to someone on your staff.

- Proactive management means you react strongly the day your numbers aren't being made. Don't wait until the end of the month and see what happened.

- Plan to make money each month by using revenue busters.

- Develop a bag of tricks you can pull out of the closet for those days that need help.

- 95% of what you do is selling somebody something every day.

10

One Simple Daily Report Can Keep You Focused

The most important thing you should get from this chapter is:

The daily production report ties every key production indicator into one simple report.

Definitions and concepts you will need to know:

- *Daily report:* A report that ties the club's key production indicators into a single report and is current as of the end of yesterday's business day.

- *Revenue projection:* A tool that can take information on key areas of the club, such as sales or daily revenue, and project those numbers through the end of the current month.

- *Cash-position report:* Part of the daily report that gives the owner an idea of how much revenue is in for the month, how much money has been paid out in bills, and how much is needed in additional revenue to meet these needs.

- Owners make bad decisions because they don't always have a true idea of exactly where the business is for the month until it is too late.

- Daily reports should give an owner an exact picture of where they are, and more importantly, where they need to go for the rest of the month.

- Daily reports work better as tools when they are actually done daily instead of being lumped into random time elements and being done whenever the owner can get to them.

The Daily Business Report Ties Everything in the Business Together

Budgets, daily production numbers that keep you thinking about driving revenues, and traffic through the club all are important numbers that keep owners and staff focused on doing the things in the business that will lead to more money over time. Somewhere, however, you have to develop a report that ties all of these numbers together in a simple format the owner or manager can fill out first thing each morning.

This report, usually called the *daily business report,* or *daily production report,* should give you the overall view of the business as of the close of business yesterday. The first thing an owner or manager should do in the morning is complete the report, which then provides a snapshot as to how the business did in the previous business day.

Most owners make bad decisions because they seldom have the right information, or current information on hand. This information can provide an overview on all the important indicators. As mentioned throughout this book, this is a *production-based business.* Owners will make better decisions if they know where the business is today as compared to where it should be and what production goals they have to meet today.

> **Owners will make better decisions if they know where the business is today as compared to where it should be and what production goals they have to meet today.**

All this information may be available in the club, but surprisingly few owners tie it together in a simple three- or four-page form. One report tying all the key numbers together can give an owner or manager the key to solving problems in their business.

What Should a Daily Business Report Provide?

A daily report should first of all provide an overall view as to where the business is through the end of the previous business day. Reporting that is only done once a week, or worse once a month, doesn't allow the owner to get the information fast enough to make necessary changes. This means that to get the most out of this system the report has to be done daily, usually in the morning, and this will bring the numbers up to date through the close of yesterday's work day.

Another important factor is that for the report to be effective, it has to be done every day. This includes the slower days in the fitness business such as Sunday. Don't get in the lazy habit of combining days, because that will cloud the information and make it harder to ascertain just what is happening in your business. For example, you may have two different people working Saturday and Sunday. One might be stronger than the other, but any weakness or non-performance is masked if you combine the days instead of viewing each individually.

Daily reporting can also be used as a tool to compare this year's daily flow through the club against the same month last year. By tracking the business daily instead of lumping work days together, you can better determine the impact of changes in the business such as a different type of marketing, added or subtracted profit centers, or change in personal.

In conjunction with this reporting, at the end of the month you can do a closeout sheet tying everything into an end-of-the-month report. This also gives you an added perspective when comparing historical information against present business.

A minor but still important point is that a daily business report can give you a quick reference as to just what the heck happened last Tuesday. During busy times, the fitness business is at best a blur and trying to make sense of a specific day last week is impossible without some type of daily report. What did happen last Tuesday when you were out of town and how did that compare to other days you were in town?

The most important aspect of a daily business reporting system, however, is that if done properly, it will allow you to project the business forward from the present point in time through the end of the working month. This tool is called an *income projection* and uses averages through the current day and then projected over the remaining days of the month.

For example, during the month of April, a 30-day month, you have collected $4,590 from the profit centers in the club through the 9th. By dividing the $4,590 by the nine days in which it was accumulated, you can reach a daily average. In this case $4,590 divided by nine equals a $510-per-day average.

You can then take this number ($510) and multiply it by the days in the current month (30). This will give you a projection for the month from your profit centers. In this example, $510 multiplied by 30 equals $15,300. This means that on the morning of the 10th day of the month when the manager sits down and brings all the numbers current through the end of the working day on the 9th, she can then project that if the club stays on its current trend it will finish at $15,300 in total deposits from the profit centers.

If the club's management team had projected $12,000 during the last week of March for the coming month of April, then this department is doing fine and the team can focus on other weaknesses in the business. If the projection for April was $20,000, then the owner and other management members have 20 days to get this department back on track and headed toward making the targeted deposits.

This projection system can be used to project any number that is tracked daily in the club including sales revenue, profit center's cash flow, the number of new sales, renewals, the usage rate, and daily number. To review, the basic projection formula looks like this:

Basic revenue and sales projection

- Record the total revenue or sales number through today.
- Divide that number by today's date.

> The most important aspect of a daily business reporting system, however, is that if done properly, it will allow you to project the business forward from the present point in time through the end of the working month.

- Take the new number and multiply it by the number of days in the current month.
- This equals the projected revenue or sales number for the month.

A working example using the previously mentioned numbers

- The club generated $4,590 in multiple profit centers through the first nine days of the month.
- $4,590 divided by 9 (divide by today's date) equals $510.
- $510 x 30 (the example is April, a 30-day month).
- This equals $15,300 in projected revenue from the club's profit centers for the month of April.

Another example using sales

- The club wrote 22 memberships through the first 12 days of the month.
- 22 divided by 12 (divide by today's date) equals 1.83. The club is averaging 1.83 new sales a day through the first 12 days of the month.
- 1.83 x 30 (still using a 30-day month).
- The club is projecting 55 (54.9) sales for the month.

Most owners can get a job done if they know just what they should do. Most owners don't make as much money as they should because they come to work each day without a plan or direction.

Most owners can get a job done if they know just what they should do. Most owners don't make as much money as they should because they come to work each day without a plan or direction. They don't know what they should be doing today to influence the revenues in their business. The production numbers in the previous days traffic, tied into a daily business plan, is a focus tool most owners could greatly benefit from since it forces management to address weaknesses in the business as they occur.

What Should a Daily Business Report Contain?

If you look at a hundred different clubs you will find a hundred different versions of a daily business report. Some owners just use a daily sales report, some call it a production report of some type, and some owners have to refer to two or three different books or papers to answer the questions that should all be available from one source.

Keeping this in mind, you will need to build your own report based on the information outlined in this chapter. Your final version should fit your club and your individual management style, although it should also contain some form of the components listed later on.

The daily report can also reflect the personality of the owner. A few owners even list the weather that day in hopes of finding a relationship between what's happening outside and what's happening inside. Weather by the way is another one of the biggest myths in the business.

For example, you can call a weather-centric owner who firmly states that business is slow today because it is too beautiful outside and no one is coming through the door. Call that same owner a week later and he is crying because it is raining hard and long that day and no one is coming in because the weather is too bad. Wait a minute, is the weather too good or too bad? Unless you can report that your building had been demolished by a tornado, the weather is probably not your problem.

If you want to get the most out of your daily report, then it must contain the following four elements. Figures 10-1 through 10-5 will give you a working model for each of these areas.

- A sales report that accounts for new annual memberships, renewals if you are using a closed-ended renewal system, and other specific new business such as short-term memberships or nutrition programs that may be pertinent to your business.

- Revenue from the individual profit centers in the club.

- The overview numbers of the business such as tracking the daily number and the usage rate both discussed in Chapter 9.

- A cash-position report that gives you an idea of how much revenue is in, how much has been paid out for the month in bills, and how much you need to get in additional revenues before the end of the month.

These management reports can all be adapted to just about any club, or any type of business, quite easily. All the reports should be filled out daily to be effective and as mentioned earlier and don't combine days. Fitness businesses have a certain flow to them that once understood becomes easier to plan for and to manipulate when things go wrong. Daily reporting gives you the tools you need to further understand your business and to be able to make these decisions.

Getting the most out of these reports requires understanding, and understanding usually requires examples. To get the most out of this type of reporting system, work through the following examples as they apply to each type of management report. If you can get an understanding of what the components in each category mean, it may help when you apply these reports to your business.

Fitness businesses have a certain flow to them that once understood becomes easier to plan for and to manipulate when things go wrong.

The Daily Sales Management Report

Information calls only refer to a prospective member calling the club to seek information about a membership. If you could identify one area out of control in most clubs, and most small businesses in general, it's the tracking and handling of information calls from consumers who want to buy something.

Daily sales management report

Today's date_____   Month/Year_____
Location_____   Report filled out by_____

Phone information
Information calls   Today_____   Month-to-date_____
Appointments scheduled   Today_____   Month-to-date _____

1) Prospective members (first time visitors to the club only)
                          Today_____   Month-to-date _____
                          Goal for month_____   Goal-per-day_____

2) Prospective members (reoccurring prospects from trial memberships)
                          Today_____   Month-to-date _____
                          Goal for month_____   Goal-per-day _____

Sales
    3) Annual contracts   Today_____   Month-to-date _____
Goal for month_____   Goal-per-day _____   Today's proj._____
    4) Annual PIF   Today_____   Month-to-date _____
Goal for month_____   Goal-per-day _____   Today's proj._____
    5) Month-to-month   Today_____   Month-to-date _____
Goal for month_____   Goal-per-day _____   Today's proj._____
    6) Short-term   Today_____   Month-to-date _____
Goal for month_____   Goal-per-day _____   Today's proj._____
    7) Renewals
Annual renewals   Today_____   Month-to-date _____
Goal for month_____   Goal-per-day _____   Today's proj._____
Other renewals   Today_____   Month-to-date _____
Goal for month_____   Goal-per-day _____   Today's proj._____

Sales income (membership cash today)
    8) Membership fees   Today_____   Month-to-date _____
    9) PIFs (paid in full)   Today_____   Month-to-date _____
    10) Daily workout fees   Today_____   Month-to-date _____
    11) Short-term   Today_____   Month-to-date _____
    12) Other   Today_____   Month-to-date _____
    13) Other   Today_____   Month-to-date _____
    14) Totals   Today_____   Month-to-date _____

To project sales income (sales $) for the month
    1) Total sales income (sales $) through today's date $_____
    2) Divided by today's date _____
    3) = (Sales $) daily average for the month $_____
    4) (Sales $) daily average $_____ x days in the current month _____
    5) = Projected (sales $) income for the month $_____(sales $)

Figure 10-1. The daily sales management report

Multiple profit center (MPC) management report

1) MPC revenue
2) Apex Weight Loss　　　　　Today_____Month-to-date_____
3) City Blends Juice Bar　　　Today_____ Month-to-date _____
4) Cooler drinks　　　　　　　Today_____ Month-to-date _____
5) Clothing　　　　　Today_____ Month-to-date _____
6) Supplements (Apex)　　　　Today_____ Month-to-date _____
7) Supplements (other)　　　　Today_____ Month-to-date _____
8) Endless Summer Tan Center　Today_____ Month-to-date _____
9) Personal/semiprivate train.　Today_____ Month-to-date _____
10) Munchie bars　　　　　　　Today_____ Month-to-date _____
11) Programming/special events　Today_____ Month-to-date _____
12) Other　　　　　　　　　　Today_____ Month-to-date _____
13) Other　　　　　　　　　　Today_____ Month-to-date _____
14) Other　　　　　　　　　　Today_____ Month-to-date _____
15) Other　　　　　　　　　　Today_____ Month-to-date _____
16) Other　　　　　　　　　　Today_____ Month-to-date _____
17) Totals　　　　　　　　　Today_____ Month-to-date _____

The usage number for today
Total amount collected from all profit centers today_____
Total amount of workouts today_____
Total collected today_____ divided by total workouts today_____
= usage rate for today_____

The usage number running total for the month
Total profit center income through today_____
Total workouts for the month through today_____
Total profit center income through today_____
divided by workouts for the month_____
= running total for the month_____

To project multiple profit center income (MPC $) for the month
1) Total profit center income (MPC $) through today's date $_____
2) Divided by today's date _____
3) = (MPC $) daily average for the month $_____
4) (MPC $) daily average $_____ x days in the current month _____
5) = Projected (MPC $) income for the month $_____(MPC $)

Figure 10-2. The multiple profit center (MPC) management report

Daily number management report

The daily number for the month

1) Target deposit from all sources for the month of_____ is $_____
2) Minus the projected receivable check $_____
3) Equals through the register cash needs for the month $_____
4) Divide this number by the total days in the projected month_____ = $_____
5) This equals daily cash needed through the register $_____(goal)

Goal-per-day $_____

Day-of-the-month deposit	+/-	Monthly total
1) _____	_____	_____
2) _____	_____	_____
3) _____	_____	_____
4) _____	_____	_____
5) _____	_____	_____
6) _____	_____	_____
7) _____	_____	_____
8) _____	_____	_____
9) _____	_____	_____
10) _____	_____	_____
11) _____	_____	_____
12) _____	_____	_____
13) _____	_____	_____
14) _____	_____	_____
15) _____	_____	_____
16) _____	_____	_____
17) _____	_____	_____
18) _____	_____	_____
19) _____	_____	_____
20) _____	_____	_____
21) _____	_____	_____
22) _____	_____	_____
23) _____	_____	_____
24) _____	_____	_____
25) _____	_____	_____
26) _____	_____	_____
27) _____	_____	_____
28) _____	_____	_____
29) _____	_____	_____
30) _____	_____	_____
31) _____	_____	_____

Figure 10-3. The daily number management report.

Cash-flow management report

Projected cash flow from all sources for the month of _____

1) Projected receivable check for the month based upon an average of the last three months of net checks $_____

2) Projected receivable check $_____ divided by total days in the current month _____

3) = Daily receivable check projection for the month $_____(rec $)

4) Daily MPC cash projection for the month $_____(MPC $)

5) Daily sales cash projection for the month $_____(sales $)

6) (Rec $) + (MPC $) + (sales $) = total daily projection from all sources of income in the club (total $)

7) (Total $)_____ x total days in the current month _____

8) = Projected cash flow for the month $_____

Figure 10-4. The cash-flow management report.

Daily cash position management report

Today's date_____

Club_____

1) Total cash in from all sources to date $_____

2) Total amount of bills paid to date $_____

3) Total amount of bills remaining to be paid for the month $_____

4) Cash still needed for the month $_____

5) Cash projected from all sources for the month $_____

6) Anticipated ending cash position for the month $_____

Worksheet

In	Out	Needed
$_____	$_____(paid)	$_____
	$_____(to be paid)	

Projected cash flow for the month $_____

Total projected out for the month $_____

Anticipated ending cash position $ +/-_____

Figure 10-5. The daily cash position management report.

The lifeblood of most small business is the *incoming phone call.* Somewhere a consumer picked up a phone and made a decision to call about your product or service. Business owners need to stop, take a breath, and realize that on the other end of the phone is a person trying to spend money with you. The person has already pre-qualified himself as a buyer by taking the time to research a number and inquire about the product. In the fitness business, that call may represent a $600 to $700 dollar membership, or more, that is just waiting for a properly trained staff person to make happen.

Spend at least four hours a week training everyone on your staff about phone basics, such as answering within three rings, handling information requests, and providing customer service over the phone. It's a basic rule of business: *better phone training equals more money in the club.*

The trial membership gives a tremendous advantage over your competition when it comes to phone inquiries. Due to the non-threatening nature of the trial, at least 80 percent of all inquiry calls should lead to an appointment. Out of that number, approximately 75 percent, or about 60 percent of all phone inquires with the trial attached, will show up in the club.

Sales are tracked by either categorizing them as annual contractual sales or as paid-in-full memberships (PIF). Month-to-month memberships refer to open-ended memberships where the member can quit with a 30-day notice and short-term memberships, which were discussed earlier in the book, refer to memberships with a maximum time of three months. The renewals listed on the daily sales management report refer to closed-ended renewals where the member completes one year and then reenrolls for another year instead of becoming an open-ended, month-to-month member.

Sales income is defined as membership cash today. For example, a member may enroll today in a one-year contract with $69 collected today and 12 future payments of $59. The only thing counted today is the cash received today. In this example, you count the $69. Only count the money you received today paid toward any type of membership even if it is daily workout fee.

However, don't count payments made to the club that should have been sent to the third-party financial-service company. These are not cash flow and this type of payment should be strongly discouraged to the members since they will start to associate attendance with payment. In other words, if they don't attend they don't feel they have an obligation to pay.

The following is an example of projecting sales income (sales $):

- Total sales income (sales $) through today's date = $9678
- Divided by today's date (9th)
- = (Sales $) daily average for the month $1,075.33
- (Sales $) daily average ($1,075.33 = sales $) x days in the current month (30/April)
- = Projected income for the month $32,260

> Spend at least four hours a week training everyone on your staff about phone basics, such as answering within three rings, handling information requests, and providing customer service over the phone. It's a basic rule of business: *better phone training equals more money in the club.*

The Multiple Profit Center (MPC) Management Report

The revenue section on this report refers to income received today from each individualized profit center and then extended for the income from the center for the month-to-date. Do not lump your MPC income into one pile or you will never understand the profit centers that work nor will you find the ones that need to be replaced. For example, it would be easy to throw in cooler drinks and munchie bars under the broad category of juice bar since all of those types of sales occur in somewhat of the same location.

If you lumped them together you might find that the combination of these three profit centers are giving you an across-the-board net of 42 percent. Separating these centers, however, might help you find that the cooler drinks are running 38 percent profitable, but the bars are lagging at 12 percent. The juice bar is carrying the other two, but this owner would never make the needed changes by analyzing the bars and then perhaps changing selection or updating the display area since the overall category is so strong.

Another common problem that leads to confusion occurs when an owner establishes any type of credit system based upon the customer prepaying today against future charges. For example, a member might open a charge account in the club by giving the owner $200 today. The owner then establishes an account and the member can then charge against the $200. The members like this system since they don't have to carry their billfolds or purses every time they work out, and the club owner obviously loves this method since she doesn't ever have to worry about losing money because of the non-payment of an account. The member prepaid, the computer software has a method to track the charges, and the member is warned when his account is getting close to running out of money. If he doesn't have enough money in the account for an item he is denied the charge.

The problem occurs when an owner gives you money today but items are subtracted from inventory weeks in the future. The simplest solution is to stick to a cash-flow system. Count the cash in as it arrives and subtract the inventory and expense as it leaves. Overall this will average out during the month. Even clubs using low-tech credit solutions, such as selling prepaid drink cards have this problem. Keep it simple by thinking *cash in/cash out*.

The Usage Number for the Day

The usage rate has been defined extensively elsewhere in the book. For the sake of example here, remember that usage rate is the relationship between the amounts of revenue generated in the profit centers today compared to the number of workouts the club does today. If a club sold $1,000 in the profit centers today and ran 400 workouts through the door, then that club would have a usage rate for the day of $2.50.

> Do not lump your MPC income into one pile or you will never understand the profit centers that work nor will you find the ones that need to be replaced.

The total amount collected on the management report is simply the total of the categories at the top of the page. Keep in mind that anything related to working out, such as a daily workout fee or payment made at the club, is not counted as a profit center income.

Your computer software should automatically provide the number of workouts for the day. Once you have the number of workouts, simply divided this number into the total amount of revenue collected from the profit centers for the day. This will give you the usage rate for the day.

The Usage-Number Running Total for the Month

This number is simply an extension of the daily-usage number. Instead of using today's number, you should substitute the total amount of profit center income, or the running total for the month, collected through today. You then divide this number by the total number of workouts for the month through today's date. This will give you the overall average usage rate for the month.

The following is an example of projecting multiple profit center income (MPC $) for the month:

- Total profit center income (MPC $) through today's date = $7,444
- Divided by today's date (11th)
- = (MPC $) daily average for the month ($676.72 = MPC $)
- (MPC $) daily average $676.72 x days in current month (30/April)
- = Projected (MPC $) income for the month $20,301.60

The Daily Number Management Report

The daily number has also been extensively discussed elsewhere in the book. Simply put, the daily number is the total amount of income from all sources, adjusted for the club's receivable check that is a constant for most clubs and can be averaged, and that an owner needs to generate each day. Other terms, such as the target deposit, have also been discussed and explained in detail in previous chapters.

> Simply put, the daily number is the total amount of income from all sources, adjusted for the club's receivable check that is a constant for most clubs and can be averaged, and that an owner needs to generate each day.

The following is an example of projecting the daily number for the month:

- Target deposit from all sources for the month of April = $60,000
- Minus the projected receivable check ($33,000)
- = The cash needs for the month ($27,000)
- Divided by the total number of days in the projected month (30/April) = $900
- = Daily cash needed through the register ($900 − goal)

The goal-per-day for this club is set at $900. As was discussed in the section concerning action plans, a club seldom generates exactly the needed daily number, so an owner should adjust to this by dividing production into week-long segments beginning on Monday and ending on Sunday. This necessitates using a weekly production planner that takes into account the club may do $3,000 on a Monday and much less on a Friday and Sunday.

Tracking the deposits daily and weekly with a production planner gives an owner a better idea of how cash actually flows through the business each week. The *+/- signs* are a simple way to track if the deposit is over or under the goal for the day. For example, if the daily goal is $900 and the club deposits $1,100 that day, then it would be plus $200 for the day. The monthly total is the running total for the month as is figured by simply adding each day's new number to the previous total for the month.

The Cash Flow Management Report

The cash flow management report gives an owner an idea of how much revenue she can expect for the month. This is a vital number since this method is very accurate from about the 5th of the month onward.

For example, the owner figures the cash-flow projection on the 5th and finds that she is going to be short by $3,000 for the month if the club stays on the same course for the rest of the month. In a 30-day month she has 25 days to correct her business plan and makes adjustments where needed to compensate for the expected shortfall.

The following is an example of projecting cash flow from all sources for the month of April:

- Projected receivable check for the month based upon an average of the last three months of net checks ($30,000)
- Projected receivable check ($30,000) divided by the totals days in the current month (30/April)
- = Daily receivable check projection for the month ($1,000 = rec $)
- Daily MPC cash projection for the month ($676.72 = MPC $)
- Daily sales cash projection for the month ($1,075.33 = sales $)
- (Rec $/$1,000) + (MPC $/$676.72) + (sales $/$1,075.33) = total daily projection from all sources of income in the club (total $/$2,752.05)
- (Total $/$2,752.05) x total days in the current month (30/April)
- = Projected cash flow for the month $82,561.50

> The cash flow management report gives an owner an idea of how much revenue she can expect for the month. This is a vital number since this method is very accurate from about the 5th of the month onward.

The Daily Cash Management Position

The daily cash management position is an old tool but it is still mentioned often in business magazines and is used as a worksheet by some of the top small business execs in the country. Used correctly and daily, this tool can tell you exactly where you are with total inflows and outflows as of today. To be used most effectively, get in the habit of doing it every single day. For example:

Today's date: April 11

- Total cash in from all sources to date ($24,800)

- Total amount of bills paid to date ($42,000 -- this might reflect rent paid at the first of the month, the first payroll of the month, and assorted other bills usually due and payable early in the month)

- Total amount of bills remaining to be paid for the month ($22,000 -- one payroll left and perhaps a few lease payment scheduled toward the end of the month)

- Cash still needed for the month ($39,200)

- Cash projected from all sources ($82,561.50)

- Anticipated ending cash position (+$18,561.50)

Worksheet

In	Out	Needed cash
$24,800	$42,000 (paid)	$39,200 ($64,000 − $24,800)
	$22,000 (to be paid)	
	$64,000 total	

Projected cash flow for the month = $82,561.50

Total projected out for the month = $64,000

Anticipated ending cash position = $ (+/-) +18,561.50

   In this example, On April 11, the club owner can anticipate needing $39,200 more to pay the bills for the month and a net profit of $18,561.50. This changes of course, but as the month progresses the numbers jell tighter. This example was figured on the 11th of the month, so the club is well on track to hit these numbers and it would take something major to force the club too for off track.

The Key Points You Should Have Gotten from this Chapter

- Daily reporting keeps you focused on the important factors in your business.

- Owners often make bad decisions because they seldom have the right information in front of them.

- Daily reports provide an exact picture of where the business is today and what it needs to do for the rest of the month.

- Daily reporting should contain a sales report, multiple profit center numbers and projections, an overview of the business including the daily number and usage rate, and a cash-position report that tracks the overall cash flow in the business.

- Don't lump days; force yourself to develop the discipline of doing a separate report each day the club is open.

- Use the reporting systems to anticipate making a change of direction in this month's business plan.

Owners often make bad decisions because they seldom have the right information in front of them.

11

Learn to Save Money Before It's Spent

The most important thing you should get from this chapter is:

Budgeting is the art of saving money before it is spent.

Definitions and concepts you will need to know:

- *Budgeting:* Learning to save money, which becomes net, before it is spent.

- Budgeting should be done on a fixed-cost basis and not as a percentage of sales.

- To be effective at saving money, you have to learn to budget before the expenses are incurred. Budgeting after the expenses are incurred is not budgeting, it's bookkeeping.

- *Fixed-cost budgeting:* What does it really cost to keep your facility open and ready for business.

- Three types of expenses you should know are: *fixed*, *variable*, and *accrual*.

- *Accrual expenses:* Money that has to be set aside each month to pay future bills.

- Every item of expense in the club business has a percentage or range it should be in to help keep that expense under control.

Budgeting Is the Neglected Part of Making a Business Profitable

Early expense budgeting in the fitness industry was somewhat of a haphazard art form. It was based more upon production numbers rather than trying to understand just what it should really cost to run a fitness business. This led too many new owners in the industry to a system that sapped the profitability out of a typical business.

Most early budgeting systems, mostly those used in the 1970s and 1980s, were based upon a percentage of sales. Sales were defined as the gross sales or revenues the business produced over a month's period of time. Gross sales, as in, "What's the gross today?" is an outdated term that not only meant gross revenue but could also mean the gross amount of contracts written. Budgeting based on sales meant that every category was somehow applied as a percentage of the current cash flow of the club.

For example, how many people the club hired and how much the payroll would be were determined by a percentage of the gross revenues. If the club was using 30 percent of sales as the base payroll and sales increased, then the payroll and staff in the club could be justifiably increased.

Several problems affected this system of budgeting. The biggest was that no matter how much the gross sales number increased, the expenses were allowed to increase correspondingly, which automatically decreased the net profit for the business.

The club manager could, for example, always add more staff at his discretion, which usually meant more sales people, as long as the gross was going up each month. In this system more staff was supposed to mean more production and an ever-expanding gross. As long as the gross was there, new staff could be added to the mix.

This type of floating percentage also led to the second major problem with this type of system: what happened if the gross went down? It's very hard to run a proactive business using this system since a downturn in the gross might be temporary or the sign of a slight slowing in the business. Either way, the club was stuck with more staff than it probably needed and it carried this excess baggage too long as everyone waited for the gross to return.

This is just one reason many of the old-style clubs failed in the late 1970s and early 1980s. Increased competition, a change in the expectation of what a fitness center should be to the consumer, and other economic factors all combined to leave some of these dinosaur clubs heavily overstaffed and unable to regroup in time to make a difference.

The owners back then also applied this technique to other areas in the business, such as the amount of debt a club could handle, or the number of collectors a club might need to service its membership contracts. Everything

> Increased competition, a change in the expectation of what a fitness center should be to the consumer, and other economic factors all combined to leave some of these dinosaur clubs heavily overstaffed and unable to regroup in time to make a difference.

was dependent on the gross and everything was dependent on driving that number higher no matter how unrealistic that expectation became over time.

Keep in mind that during the early 1970s not many strong third-party financial service companies were in the industry, and most clubs had to service their own agreements unless they just plain sold them out for a discount to a vendor that might specialize in buying contracts. They might have written a two-year membership, and then sold it for a percentage today so they could have the cash instead of waiting for the money to arrive each month through the development of a receivable base.

If you had to collect your own memberships, however, you also had to create a bureaucracy to handle that part of the business, and the associated expenses had to then be tied somehow to the output of the club. Every expense depended on gross sales for the club.

The vicious circle began when the profits weren't there. The club would gross more, the expenses would increase, and the owners would have to somehow drive the gross higher because the net didn't increase as the gross income went up. Once this circle began it was hard to break.

The vicious circle began when the profits weren't there.

The Advent of Fixed-Cost Business

During the late 1980s a few enlightened owners began to realize that a fitness business was indeed a *fixed-cost business*. The more foresighted owners in those days finally figured that there was a certain point in the expense side of the business where a club could service more members without incurring any more major costs.

For example, a 12,000-square-foot club might have expenses of $60,000. This includes payroll, rent or mortgage, and all of the general operating costs including debt service. If the owner worked in the gym as an employee it would also include that salary. If the owner was an absentee owner and just stopped by to scoop out what's left over after the bills were paid, then that amount would not be included.

Another way to think about operating expense is to find the breakeven point in the business, or what would it take to cover all of the club's operational bills. This number is referred to throughout this book as the *base operating expense* (BOE).

The club in this example could service 1,500 members at $60,000, or 2,000 members for just a slightly higher percentage. The only increase after a certain point would be a slight bump in payroll and the hard costs in profit centers as more members make more purchases.

The first owner that figured out expenses should be based upon the fixed costs to run the business, versus the ever upward cost of budgeting against gross sales, had a tremendous advantage in that once he had enough business to cover the BOE, then everything after that point turned into net.

The Basic Premise Behind Effective Budgeting

Besides being the first owner to realize a fitness business should be run on a fixed-cost budget as opposed to a gross sales system, this mythical person was also the first to understand that budgeting should occur before the expenses were incurred, called *zero-based budgeting*, rather than attempting to budget off of the financial statements after the money was already spent. Budgeting off of the statements is budgeting too late because you are working with what *was* spent versus budgeting for what *should have* been spent.

This type of budgeting, referred to as *budgeting out of the checkbook*, is just simply looking at what was spent, dividing this money into categories, and then calling it a budget. The most important thing to remember is that just because the money was spent doesn't mean it is a real expense.

The most common example of this is to look at how most people budget their money in their own lives. A young couple, for example, decides that they are spending too much money each month and want to get control of what they are doing by creating a family budget. They sit at the kitchen table, get out the checkbook and legal pad, and divide everything they spent into categories such as food, utilities, rent, entertainment, and work.

Hours later they have a budget and realize they are spending (not counting future debt on credit cards because that's not real debt yet and the minimum payment is being made) more then they make. At this point the pain begins as they either try to figure out how to make more money to cover their expenses, or one of them has to change their behavior by making cuts somewhere in what they spend personally.

The important thing is this meeting was put off for far too long because of the belief that if you had to write a check for it right then, the expense must be real. In other words, you incur the expenses, then the expenses must be something you have to have in your lives.

Most gyms operate under this same system. The club's expenses run amok for months at a time because if the money is being spent, then it must be a real expense. As the owners say, "Look at our check book; we're not wasting money. We are just paying the bills that come in each month. The problem can't be that we are spending too much; therefore, it must be that we are not making enough money."

But the question really should be, "Are those bills we pay each month really expenses we should be incurring, and is there anything we can do to lower those bills and still run a good gym?" Gym owners and managers must eventually learn one basic rule of business: Money saved by budgeting spends just as well as money made by selling somebody something.

Budgeting done right frees up cash flow, and if this cash flow makes it to the bottom line then you have increased pre-tax profit which makes everyone happy. Your only solution, though, to making more money for most

> Budgeting off of the statements is budgeting too late because you are working with what *was* spent versus budgeting for what *should have* been spent.

of the people who run fitness businesses is to always look to increased production for the net. "If only we could just sell a few more memberships," is the cry heard round the industry when times are lean.

The most effective fitness businesses are representatives of both sides, which are tight budgeting, coupled with solid production skills. These are the businesses that last and the ones that put the highest net in the bank each month.

A Return to Fixed-Cost or Zero-Based Budgeting

Learn to budget before the expenses are incurred and then run the business by that budget. Fixed-cost budgeting is a very simple concept, yet one that few owners ever consider as part of their ongoing business plan.

Learn to budget before the expenses are incurred and then run the business by that budget.

The couple in the previous example represents the common system used by most owners. You spend for a while and then look at what went out and build a budget around those numbers. Remember, if it was spent then it must have been a real expense. They would have less pain and had more money in their lives if they would have created a fixed-cost budget sometime earlier and then made every decision based upon that budget.

A fixed-cost budget is defined as: *What are the basic operating costs necessary to keep this facility open?* The term *zero-based* could also be applied here on a limited basis. Zero-based in this example means that you take an expense all the way back to zero and then build forward until you meet the minimum number you need to have to keep that line item as part of the business.

The term *fixed-cost budgeting* is interchanged throughout this book with zero- based for a little more clarity and accuracy. This basic concept becomes simpler to understand if you apply it to a core element in every fitness business: the telephone. The usual way to budget for most owners would be to go back and look at what they spent on the phone bills for the last 12 months. This is only referring to basic telephone service and not extras such as yellow page ads.

A typical scenario for an owner would be that she sits down in December and starts to put together a budget for the coming year. Even at this stage she is ahead of most other owners who only budget when the bank makes them or when they need a new loan for equipment.

This owner pulls out her financials, notes that she spent $7,632 for telephone service over the last 12 months, divides by 12, and enters $636 as her line-item phone budget for the coming year. She confirms this by pulling out the bills from the year and cross-references them to the statements, and indeed $636 is the average bill for the year.

This is the common way to budget and the most ineffective. Applying zero-based budgeting would have saved her quite a bit of money in this part of her business. Zero-based means she takes the expense back to zero. In this example then, she has no phone and no service. What would it cost her for basic service in this club?

To answer this she again pulls out the bills and looks at the basic service charges for phone service. She finds that although her average bill is $636, her basic service charge is only $400. Beginning at zero means that she should only have a basic bill of $400 to get her phones online in the gym. Where is the other $236 a month being spent?

After carefully reviewing what was spent each month, as compared to just looking at the final total, she finds that the staff is making a few personal long-distance phone calls, money could be saved by switching the long-distance service, vendors are being called on their direct lines rather than on their toll-free numbers, and it appears that a few members might have had access to the phones during the morning hours. Her reaction is to install phone blockers that limit the area codes that can be called from the gym, adds personal code-only long-distance dialing with the codes restricted to the managers and one phone in the office, shop around and find a cheaper long-distance service that takes less than an hour to explore and installs a courtesy phone for the members that also has restricted calling.

A few hours work translates into a new phone bill of $450 per month instead of $636 for a savings of $186 per month. This savings times 12 months equals $2,232 per year in the bank that was being wasted each month in the club.

Budgeting from a zero cost can save money since you get that expense category as low as it will go. Budgeting from the already spent end of the business cost money since this method assumes that the expense is real and already incurred.

When the owner builds a budget for the gym, she should have entered $450 as her phone expense as opposed to the $636 she first came up with in her research. Using this number gives her an advantage each month because as the new bill arrives she can compare it to the fixed cost number, $450, and then take action if the bill rises above that number.

In the other scenario, she is already wasting money and most of the bills coming in will do nothing but further perpetuate the mistake. In other words, she doesn't have a valid reference to use as a control for future expenses.

The most important aspect to budgeting is to build one on a fixed-cost basis tied to a maximum number you are willing to spend each month.

Building a Budget

The most important aspect to budgeting is to build one on a fixed-cost basis tied to a maximum number you are willing to spend each month. One total, that's it, and when that is spent you have no more until next month.

Think of your budget as an old billfold and your budget for the month is $60,000. Assemble your management team, put the $60,000 in the billfold, and hand it to them based on the premise that when you run out you have no more to spend. This is all you get to play with this month, and if you want something you can't live without you can get it if you can find it somewhere else in this month's budget, meaning somewhere else in the $60,000. The expenses pertinent to your business that can be divided into three categories then sort the money in your billfold, again representing your monthly budget:

- *Fixed costs*, which are expense items that don't change each month such as rent, a mortgage payment, or a fixed bank note.

- *Variable costs* are expense items that fluctuate each month and that owners and managers can exert a certain amount of control over throughout the month, such as payroll that typically has a lot of waste. For example, an owner has a day-counter person quit in May. Instead of replacing her right away and carrying an expense that may not be needed since the summers are usually somewhat slower for many clubs, the owner might elect to run short and juggle the staff for enough coverage to get by until September when business picks up again.

- *Accrual expenses* are line items that have to have money set aside for them even though the bill might not have to be paid this month. For example, a licensed club may have its license fee due once a year for $6,000. Clubs that don't plan for this fee take one big hit that disrupts cash flow and the club's stability the month the bill is due. More effective owners would move $500 each month to a separate accrual account and then write the check when it is due from that savings account rather than scrambling for the cash once a year. Other examples of accrual items are repair and maintenance, capital improvements, insurance, staff training, and education.

The variable-cost categories are where the biggest waste and the biggest savings can occur. Other examples in this category are utilities, printing, office and cleaning supplies, and the cost associated with the club's profit centers. These items should be separated in the club's operational budget so the management team can work them harder to keep the expenses lower.

The accrual expenses take the most discipline to work since you are moving money but the expense itself has not been incurred. Effective accrual expense management requires the owner to establish a separate club savings account just for the accruals. Each month the money for all the accruals should be lumped and then moved to the account.

> The accrual expenses take the most discipline to work since you are moving money but the expense itself has not been incurred.

Another example of an accrual expense is repair and maintenance. As discussed later, most clubs should budget $150 per 1,000 square feet of their entire gym toward repair and maintenance. For example, a 10,000-square-foot gym would budget $1,500 (10,000/1,000 = 10 -- 10 x $150 = $1,500).

The club might have a month where it only spends $750 toward repair and maintenance. As every club owner knows who's been in business any length of time, the rest of the bill will come due when you least want it to be there.

Broken mirrors, dying air conditioners, exploding toilets, clogged drains, and fried water heaters all add up to a lot of midnight fun for most owners through the years. Owners who have anticipated these minor disasters, however, by moving money to an accrual account are much more likely to live longer in the gym business.

When to Budget

Budgeting should be done once a year for the coming year, preferably in November. This gives you an overall view of the club's budget and where the big changes might occur. This type of budgeting needs to be adjusted for the seasonal aspect of the business as it applies to your area. The important thing to note is that you are doing a yearly budget broken into monthly segments and further broken down into fixed, variable, and accrual expenses for the business.

The second step for mastering budgeting is to develop an operational budget during the last week of the month for the coming month. This added step adapts the budget to what is happening today in the business, and is then compared to the 12-month budget you did at the end of the last year for the current working year. This operational budget is used by the management team to make decisions on buying and spending for the month and they are forced, and compensated for, working within that budget.

For example, a common mistake is for an owner to use a sliding-scale budget. During the month of April the nutrition department has a special event early in the month and sells $4,000 during of product during one night. The good news is that $4,000 in cash flow came in the door. The bad news is that the club is out of product for the rest of the month.

Your nutrition director comes in and says you need to order $1,500 of stock to get through the rest of the month. An inexperience owner looks at the $4,000, tells the director good job, and says to go ahead and order since the club has the new revenue and the club is out of stock. A budget conscious owner looks at the $4,000, says good job, and then says get together with the manager and see if you can find that $1,500 somewhere else in the budget for this month.

Remember in the example earlier that you only have $60,000 to spend this month. That number doesn't go up just because you made more money. Look in the billfold, send some staff home early, don't replace that evening guy for another week, check the drink stock and see if we can live without that order until the end of the month, but whatever is left in the billfold (monthly budget) is all you are going to have.

Keeping on budget is the issue. A strong tip at this point is to only pay bills twice a month, either on the 5th and the 20th, or on the 10th and the 25th. Get everything on net 30-day terms and get out of the habit of writing checks every day for routine bills or CODs. Also only pay payroll twice a month and never every other week. Pay on the 15th and the last day of the

Budgeting should be done once a year for the coming year, preferably in November.

month to avoid those two months that have a third payroll if you paid every other week.

If you have a larger club include the management team in a weekly bill approval session. Share the bills, ask for suggestions for saving money and cutting expense, and let the team know what is actually being spent in the business. They will do a better job and understand the business better if they get an idea of how the cash flows in and out of the business.

Working Budgets and Percentages

A simple tool that can be adapted to any club is the *expense budget management report* (See Figure 11-1). This low-tech approach is a simple one-page form filled out at the end of the month and then updated each day as the bills arrive. It works well with the *cash flow management report* from Chapter 10 since it ties the bills to the present cash position of the club for the month. Following the expense report will be a section on acceptable expense category percentages for typical clubs, and then some recommended accrual numbers that will help set some guidelines for owners and managers.

What Percentages Should You Look for in these Categories?

The biggest questions for most owners is not what should the percentages be, but what they should be spending overall for a club their size? The application of percentages for each of these line items listed in Figure 11-1 will make much more sense if you first start with an overall broad concept of what a facility should really cost you for its base operating cost (BOE).

The rent factor drives the entire BOE, so begin there when building an overall picture. Keep in mind, however, that some markets, such as Manhattan, Las Vegas, and Southern California, have their own unique rules especially when it comes to rents and membership pricing. The following numbers are basic reference points and can be adapted to your market with a little thought.

The rent factor drives the entire BOE, so begin there when building an overall picture.

Figuring the Overall Expense First

The simple rule for figuring what an overall BOE should be for a new or existing gym is illustrated by following these steps:

- Adjust your rent or mortgage to $12 per square foot if your current rent or mortgage payment is below that number. For example, if you have a 12,000- square-foot building, currently pay $10,000 in total rent including rent and triple-net charges, then use a rent of $12,000 as your reference point. If you pay over $12 per foot for rent then use your actual number. If you have not yet opened your facility and are working on a business plan, find your anticipated rent factor and then you should be able to build a working BOE from that point.

Expense Budget Management Report

Month_____ Club_____ Budget total $_____

Expense	Projected	Actual	+/-
Fixed expenses:			
Rent/mortgage			
Triple-net charges			
Yellow pages			
Accounting			
Loan #1			
Loan #2			
Lease #1			
Lease #2			
Other			
Variable expenses:			
Payroll			
Payroll taxes			
Commissions			
Advertising			
Utilities			
Phone			
Printing			
Office supplies			
Cleaning supplies			
Misc. supplies			
Postage			
Nutrition			
Proshop			
Cooler drinks			
Sports bar/juice bar			
Bars			
Day spa			
Personal/semiprivate training			
Tanning			
Childcare			
Group exercise			
Accrual expenses:			
General liability ins.			
Property ins.			
Workman's comp.			
Repair and maintenance			
Education/training			
License/franchise fees			
Capital improvements			
Legal			
Savings/regular			
Savings/accrual			
Totals:	$_____	$_____	$_____

Figure 11-1. The expense budget management report.

- Multiply your rent times five. Your rent is normally about 20% of your total BOE. For example, a 12,000-square-foot gym should have an approximate operating BOE of $60,000.

    $12,000 adjusted rent x 5 = $60,000

This formula is based upon the following assumptions:

- You have at least four profit centers, and the associated expense, netting 20% or more per month.

- Your short-term debt, referring to leases, car loans, credit cards, and other debt that has a pay-off of three years or less, begins at less than 10% of your total BOE for the first three years you are in business. If your business is over three years old then the short-term debt ratio should be less than 5%. The short-term debt ratio will be discussed more in-depth later in this chapter.

- Your long-term debt, meaning bank loans and long-term leases that are five years or longer, is no more than 10% of your BOE.

This basic formula should give you an overall look at what your business should cost each month to run through the BOE. If you are running your business for substantially less than this, it's usually because you haven't yet installed working profit centers. Another common mistake is that new owners lease just about everything and their short-term debt ratio is too high during their first few years of business.

Expenses and Percentages

Rent—The rent should be 20% of your total BOE.

Short-term debt ratio—A club can only handle so much debt. In the gym business be aware of two types of debt that affect your financial success. First of all is short-term debt, defined as debt that is less than three years in pay-off. This includes short-term leases, credit cards, and car loans, and is characterized by high interest and a rapid payback.

During the first three years of business you should have a maximum of 10% in short-term or garbage debt as it is called. From the end of the second year going forward, the short-term debt should drop to 5% or less of the BOE as the business matures and the owner gains the opportunity to gain long-term debt from banks and leasing companies.

Long-term debt is defined as five years or longer and is desirable because of its lower interest rates. A fitness business can handle 10% or less of the BOE in debt ranging from 5 to 10 years in length.

Combined, your total debt load in the club should be 20% or less during your first two years and then falling to 15% or less from your third year going forward. You will always have debt if you want to stay competitive in the business. Debt is good and the best debt is managed and controlled.

> **During the first three years of business you should have a maximum of 10% in short-term or garbage debt as it is called.**

Payroll, payroll taxes, bonuses, and commissions and other burdens—Your total payroll load should be in the 37% to 43% range. This includes an aggressive group program, but if you have a day spa add 1% to 2%.

Advertising—Advertising is defined as external ads designed to bring in new business (not including yellow page advertising) and should be 8% to 10% of your BOE. More sophisticated business owners understand that advertising brings in new business and it also keeps your competition out of your area playing a defensive role in your business plan. 8% is the minimum number but 10% is the targeted number.

Utilities—Utilities, which includes water, heat, gas, and electric, should be at 4% to 5% of your BOE. It is worth your time and effort to have a utility audit done once a year in your facility. Old lighting, worn thermostats, and bad insulation can add up to a lot of lost money. Many local utility companies offer credits for local businesses willing to upgrade their lights and insulation and will usually provide someone to look at your business and give you ideas as to saving money.

Phones—Phones, including yellow page ads, should be at 1% to 2% of your BOE. A side note is that you should always have a yellow page ad in the main book and line listings in the other books. The ad should be a one-quarter page, black and yellow, and never pay extra for the color. Use a testimonial ad and a try-before-you-buy trial membership offer instead of endless bullet points that don't mean anything to anybody but you. Think about it, do you really have to put a bullet in your ad stating that you're a gym that has free weights? Isn't that like a hotel that runs an ad stating, "Stay with us, we have beds"?

Accounting—Statements that someone can actually read should be done at least once a month. Use your accountant to set up your system and then use Quick Books Pro or some other professional software to generate your own basic statements. Your accountant should then reconcile the statements each month keeping an eye on the end-of-year taxes. Monthly statements are usually $300to $500 per club but that should keep the tax expense to a minimum at the end of the year. This translates to .5% to 1% of the BOE.

> **Never fall in love with your printer. Set a minimum number, such as $250, where anything that exceeds that forces you to get three bids.**

Printing—Never fall in love with your printer. Set a minimum number, such as $250, where anything that exceeds that forces you to get three bids. When you don't shop around, the numbers slowly rise over time. Printing should only be .5% to 1% of the BOE.

Supplies—Supplies, defined as office, cleaning, and miscellaneous, should be bought in bulk and for the true job at hand. For example, using lightweight cleaning supplies purchased at your local grocery store aren't made for cleaning a gym shower. These cleaning agents will take you twice the labor and twice the cost compared to buying supplies made for a commercial environment. This also applies to office supplies that should be bought in bulk from some type of warehouse as opposed to paying full retail at an office supply store.

A side note is that most owners find that local cleaning companies aren't what they used to be years ago. Once you start spending over $1,800 per month for a service, you may be at the point where you want to hire your own full-time cleaning crew.

Total supplies should be 1.5% to 2% of your BOE. If you get your own crew add 1% to 2% to your payroll portion of your BOE.

Postage—Postage is usually .5% of your BOE. Use stamps sparingly and only when you are using internal promotions that need the feel of a personal touch accompanied by a handwritten address. The rest of the time use a postage meter kept under lock and key.

Profit center expenses—These vary widely depending on the type of profit center, number of centers, and the size of the club. A few key points to consider are:

- You must have a point-of-sale system for inventory control and locked closets with manager's keys only for the high-ticket items such as clothing and supplements.

- Get net 30 or use another company.

- Check for savings through placing larger orders where you might get a discount or save on shipping with a higher minimum.

- Labor for personal and semiprivate training and group exercise goes under payroll not profit center expense.

- Childcare is not a profit center. It is a nonprofit profit center for most clubs and you don't have to have it to be successful in most markets.

Insurances—Bid all of your insurances with at least three different companies once a year. Make sure you get an apple-to-apple comparison since some companies will submit a lower bid by cutting your coverage. Insurance will be 2% to 3% of your BOE.

Repair and maintenance—Budget $150 per 1,000 square feet of total space for a typical fitness center per month. This includes locker rooms, workout space, group rooms, and the front areas. If you have a larger facility that includes courts, adjust that space to $75 per 1,000 per month. This is an accrual expense so move the money to your accrual savings account even if the actual expense is not incurred that month.

Education/training—This is easily the most under spent part of the budget, along with marketing, for most gym owners. The classic gym owner statement: "What if I train them and they leave?" The classic answer: "What if you don't train them and they stay?" Budget 3% of your BOE each month for education and staff training.

License/franchise fees—Most of these groups have their own system of collecting your money, but if they don't, you should treat it as an accrual by

> The classic gym owner statement: "What if I train them and they leave?" The classic answer: "What if you don't train them and they stay?"

taking the total amount you anticipate being due and dividing it by 12 payments that are moved to your savings account each month.

Capital improvements—Treat capital improvements as a reinvestment in the business and as an accrual. Budget $150 per 1,000 square feet of your entire space and move the money to your accrual savings account. When you need a down on that next equipment order or to just purchase a few pieces the money will be there waiting for you.

Legal—Legal can be a fixed expense if you are using a retainer system or a variable expense if not. Establish some type of relationship with a lawyer you trust where you can call when you have any questions and not worry about those expensive 15-minute hits. Normal legal bills are usually .5% to 1% of your BOE each month.

Savings—In a perfect world where every gym is doing great, the owner should always have at least one month's BOE in reserve. The tragedy, such as the one that befell this country in September of 2001, is a perfect example of owners suffering due to two to three months of lost business because of something that was beyond their control. A one-month reserve would do a lot to ease the pain until normal business returns. Set up a monthly accrual that allows you to build this reserve over time.

Review the information again from the beginning of this chapter: *you are learning to budget against a fixed number as opposed to developing a budget that is a percentage of revenue for the club.* These percentages are references built upon a fixed-cost budget and would differ from those used in a sliding-scale system.

17 Things You Can Do to Cut Costs in Your Gym

If you are the owner in a single facility, go back to work.

- If you are the owner in a single facility, go back to work. In the gym business 95% of what you do is selling somebody something every day. You are in a production business and if you are in the office spending most of your day doing the 5% of the business you could do at home, in your underwear, in the middle of the night drinking wine, shut your office, fire someone, and go back to selling.

- Only pay your staff twice a month, on the 15th and the last day of the month, and avoid those two months with the extra payroll.

- Consider making the full-time requirement in your club 32 hours. A lot of people would love to work 32 hours a week and still have full-time benefits. This allows you to send people home on those slow afternoons where you fill up the schedule trying to give everyone 40 hours.

- If you require short hours, consider paying higher bonuses and commissions. This should drive a higher production in the hours the person does work and you're still ahead because of the lower base payroll.

- Consider a four-day workweek for employees that would rather work four, eight-hour days.

- Refinance your debt going forward every two years. Once you pay down a note for two years out of an original five- to seven-year note, you can then consider refinancing the note forward for another five years. The first time you do this try and include all of your original short-term debt and get it out of the club.

- Hire older, more productive employees. Cheaper, younger employees may seem like a bargain but they most likely don't get production. One full-time competent person can do the job of three or four tourist part-timers.

- Utilities are one of the biggest wasted expenses in the gym. Lock up those thermostats and if you still have the ones with the little slide to set the temperature get into this century and save a little money. As well as by replacing those, replace those antique fluorescent lights, and especially check out that old water heater that is too small and that has to work at maximum capacity to keep up costing you even more money.

- Post quarterly schedules for your hours and for your group classes. This gives you the opportunity to cut hours in the summer and to drop the dog-group classes that hang on the schedule forever with too few participants to justify the class.

- Switch to a different training model that pays trainers flat rates rather than percentages or splits.

- Pressure your landlord to fight his tax bill every year to lower your percentage of triple-net charges. Also always ask for verification of the money being spent in your name as a tenant.

- Plan your advertising a year in advance that will give you the power to negotiate better long-term rates.

- Consider renting out space in your facility. The vast majority of fitness centers are poorly designed when it comes to space allocation, and even renting a small room to a massage therapist or 800 square feet to a chiropractor will help offset your rent and lower your expenses. Ask at least 50% more that you are paying for your space. For example, if your rent is $10 per square foot, then ask $15 for the space for the chiropractor. You paid less because you took a bigger space and she should pay more for a smaller space that feeds off of your business. Establish a flat rate for single rooms in the $300- $500-per-month range. Charge extra if the person wants to install a separate phone that your staff answers.

- Master an accounting software program that allows you to write checks too. If your accountant helps you set up the right categories for coding the checks, then bookkeeping and accounting expenses should be lower and you will have much more control of your business.

- You have to shop around for insurance once a year and you should look for someone who specializes in the fitness business. Shop with at least three different vendors and understand the coverages you need and don't need.

Hire older, more productive employees. Cheaper, younger employees may seem like a bargain but they most likely don't get production.

- Build it right the first time and you will save money in the long run. Find an architect that can build your facility with materials that will last for the long haul. Many owners use cheap materials when they first open and end up paying again within the first two years to replace flooring and other materials they should have done right the first time. Work with a real architect that can give you real information about gyms. Gyms and fitness facilities are different animals and using a local architect that has only built office space will cost you more money in the long run. You'll pay more for a specialist but you make it back through increased sales and member retention.

Don't cut training costs for the staff. If they are worth training then they are worth overtraining.

- Don't cut training costs for the staff. If they are worth training then they are worth overtraining. You are in a production-based business and your staff has to be trained on selling somebody something. Train them every day they are in the club.

This list can go on and on but these things might trigger other ideas that can lead to lower expenses. Remember that the money you saved from cutting expenses will spend just as well as that money you made from that new membership sale. Effective managers and owners are the ones who understand both parts of the business: *driving production and keeping the backside numbers under control.*

The Key Points You Should Have Gotten from this Chapter

- You are in a fixed-cost business. Once you have covered your basic operating expenses, then the revenue generated after that point would add to the net with only a slight increase in your BOE.

- Budgeting should occur before the money is spent.

- Money saved by budgeting spends just as well as money made from sales.

- Zero-based, or fixed-cost budgeting, means you establish a budget on the necessary operating costs for the business, not on what is spent in waste each month.

- Spend within a budget and don't use a sliding scale that allows you to spend more and more each month just because you happen to make more.

- The largest waste in club expenses is in the variable-expense category and these are also the expenses easiest to control by owners and managers.

- Fitness facilities need an annual budget done once a year and a monthly budget done at the end of the month for the coming month.

- Rent drives the business plan and is usually 20% of your BOE.

- Expenses can be compared to certain industry averages, but always keep the comparison to a fixed-budget as opposed to a percentage-of-sales. Expenses do not proportionately increase as revenues increase.

12

Increasing Return-Per-Member Using Multiple Profit Centers

The most important thing you should get from this chapter is:

Increasing your return-per-member with profit centers will lower your risk as a small business owner.

Definitions and concepts you will need to know:

- *Profit center:* An area in the club where you make money from someone who is already a member.
- Profit center income lowers your dependency on new sales.
- Your goal is to deposit a minimum of 40% of all your revenue from the club's profit centers.
- The future of your business is to learn to make more money from fewer people.
- Profit centers are not effective without a credit system.
- A small percentage of your members will spend the bulk of the money generated in the club's profit centers.

You Really Can Make More Money from Fewer Members

This chapter was written with contributing material from Terry Van Der Mark, a sales, management, and marketing consultant for the Thomas Plummer Company. Terry has over 15 years of experience as a consultant and club owner. He has also developed a software system for tracking profit center statistical data and is currently compiling research data monthly from over 900 clubs nationwide. Terry is also a seminar instructor for the Thomas Plummer Company specializing in increasing revenues in a club's multiple profit centers.

Most owners just don't know any other way to make money than to drive new membership sales through the club.

This industry is *sales-driven*. It started as a sales-driven business 50 years ago. Most owners just don't know any other way to make money than to drive new membership sales through the club.

Sales-driven can be defined as being dependent on new membership sales each month for the club's revenues. In most clubs in the country, over 95 percent of the income generated each month is from new sales cash, such as membership fees, accumulated monthly dues from the club's EFT draft or receivable base, and other short-term cash such as daily fees or shorter-term memberships in the one- to six-month range. In this operating system less than five percent of the club's monthly revenues come from profit centers, meaning someone already in the system bought something.

This type of club has to continually drive new sales each month, because without the cash received from down payments or paid-in-full memberships, the club's total revenues take a dive. This dependency on new sales makes this type of business very vulnerable since the club really only has one source of income. If that particular income stream is damaged or restricted in any way then the business will be hurt within a month or two.

Clubs still have to have new memberships each month, but they also have to find a way to decrease the vulnerability from their dependency on new sales and also develop additional income from other sources. These other sources of income are the club's *multiple profit centers* (MPCs).

This chapter will look at profit centers and the target numbers associated with each individual center, as well overall goals for club owners that add MPCs to their repertoire. Profit center income is defined as making money from members you already have in the system who purchase goods and services not related to working out under the terms of their membership. Keep in mind that if a person pays for a daily fee to work out it is not counted as profit center income.

If the same person bought a sports drink and munchie bar, however, then the money from the sale of those two items would be counted toward the club's profit center income for the day. Another example would be a member who signs up for a yoga class that isn't offered on the club's regular group exercise schedule. In this case, the monthly membership payment is not a profit center but the extra money paid for the yoga class would be since the class is being added as an add-on for members and is not included in the membership.

The club owner's ultimate goal would be to develop profit centers to the point that a minimum of 40 percent of every dollar the club deposits will come from members buying something. This means for instance that if a club deposited $100,000 for the month, a minimum of $40,000 would be revenue generated from other sources than memberships or working out in the club.

Typical industry club average:

95% of income sales related—5% of income MPC related

Target club average:

60% of income sales related—40% of income MPC related

If a club owner wants to reach this goal, she has to move away from general percentages to something more definable that can be controlled on a daily basis. This more accurate way of tracking profit centers is by using the usage rate discussed earlier in the book.

The usage rate in review is the relationship between the number of workouts a club does per day compared to the total amount of income generated from profit centers from the same day. For example, if a club had 400 workouts on a Monday and collected $1,000 in profit center income, then the usage rate for the day would be $2.50 ($1,000/400 = $2.50).

The goal a club owner should target is *$5 per day per member visit*. In other words, every member that comes through the club that day should spend an average of $5 in the club's profit centers. In reality, a smaller percentage of members will spend a larger amount of money.

> In other words, every member that comes through the club that day should spend an average of $5 in the club's profit centers.

For example, a single member may purchase a $500 personal-training package that will change the numbers dramatically for the day. It doesn't matter how the money actually is spent as long as the club owner is still targeting $5 per day per member workout. What is the effect on the business if the owner can hit this number?

Typical industry club average:

$0.50 to $0.75 per day per member visit
400 visits x $0.75 = $300

Target club average:

$5 per day per member visit
400 visits x $5 = $2,000

A typical club in the industry only generates between $0.50 and $0.75 per day per member visit. In the previous example, the club has 400 member visits generating $300 in profit center income for the day.

The club that has profit centers in place and knows how to manage and promote them generates $5 per day per member visit. In this example, the club also has 400 visits but ends up depositing $2,000 for the day in profit center income.

The second club has a $1,700 advantage over the first club every day it is in business if it can continue to hit this target number or higher. It is not unusual for clubs that have truly mastered profit centers to run an average as high as $13 to $15 per day per member visit, which truly switches the emphasis away from being so dependent on new sales.

As mentioned often throughout this book, the goal for an owner for sales generation is to maintain at least *one new annual membership per month*, if the club's prices are at least $39 per month or higher, per $1,000 of base operating expense. For example, if a club has a monthly base operating expense of $80,000, then it has to average a minimum of at least 80 new annual memberships per month during the year. This is the minimum number and includes paid-in-full memberships as well.

The combination of meeting this minimum sales goal for the club, and driving the revenue in the profit centers to $5 per day per member visit, makes a club almost bullet proof in the marketplace since the revenue is spread between new sales income, a strong receivable base check each month, and daily cash flow from current members who are supporting the club's profit centers. This leads to the basic club-operating plan for the coming years of: *The future of the club business is learning to make more money from fewer members.*

> **The future of the club business is learning to make more money from fewer members.**

Increasing per-month pricing per member, combined with income from profit centers, shifts clubs toward a business system that follows this operating statement. This type of club, based on higher sales prices and $5-per-day MPCs, has a tremendous operating advantage over clubs that are dependent on new sales volume alone. The more efficient business plan of combining sales and MPCs leads to a much higher return-per-member through recurring daily internal sales, as opposed to clubs that only have a single source of income and that don't make any money from members beyond their monthly dues once the members are in the system.

Basic Considerations for Profit Centers

The goal of an owner should be to minimize financial risk and vulnerability in the club by decreasing dependence on new membership sales. Risk is decreased if the owner can switch from a single source of income, which is normally membership sales revenue, to multiple sources of income including profit centers and continued membership sales.

Another way to look at this is that membership sales are externally focused. In other words, the club doesn't make any money unless someone comes through the door. The club still has income from membership monthly dues but most clubs are not at a point that expenses can be met through this sole source of revenue. The club still has to generate new monies from new membership sales each month to cover expenses.

Profit centers add an internal focus to the owner's business plan. An owner with profit centers in place can count on generating money each day from members using the club and may have a solid income day even if he doesn't have any new sales. This is especially true for clubs that can hit the $5-per-day-per-member visit average. The following questions reflect what has to be done to cover the basics of installing profit centers in a club:

- How many profit centers are enough?

Owners striving for the $5-per-day number should have at least four profit centers that net a minimum of 20-percent each per month. Four is the minimum but a full configuration might be as many as five to seven individual centers.

- What is the target number for each center?

The minimum is 20 percent but the target for each center is 33- to 40-percent net.

- How do the underperforming centers affect the rest?

To make profit centers a functional part of the club's business plan, you need at least four individual centers all netting a minimum of 20 percent to be effective. If you have underperforming profit centers, such as child care that is almost always at a negative cash flow in the club, then you have to have one center dedicated to canceling out your underperformer plus four more performing centers. For example:

Child care/-$1,500 per month + Cooler drinks/+$1,500 per month
= $0 in total net income

You still need four more profit centers beyond these two to target the $5 number since these two cancel each other out.

- What is the most important thing you can do to guarantee profit center success?

If you want to give yourself a fighting chance to reach $5-per-day-per-member visit, you have to establish some type of credit system for the members. At least 40 percent of a typical club's daily traffic comes dressed and ready to workout. These people don't carry money but they are still hungry and thirsty. Credit systems come in several varieties and the member should have a few options since no one-size-fits-all scenario exists.

√   The first option is a *smart-card system* similar to pre-paid phone cards. The club takes any amount of money, enters that amount in the machine that imprints it in the chip on the card, and the member can then present the card and charge. Each use lowers the balance and this type of card can be reloaded. You should give each new member a card with a minimum amount already added on, such as $5 to $10 so he will start using the club's profit centers.

√ The second option is a *pre-paid account system* set up through the club's software program. This is a standard option and can be found as part of any major software provider's base offerings, such as Aphelion. This option allows the club to take money from the member, open an account in the software, and then the member can charge against that account. Most systems have a warning message reminding the club staff and the member that the account is getting low and needs to be replenished.

√ The third option is low-tech and involves simply getting a credit card number from the member and then opening an account against that card. The member can charge on the account and the charges are run through twice a month with the member signature on file. A word to the club experienced is to never run a card just once a month since some of our younger members will run up charges over their limits. Twice a month is safer and helps the cash flow.

> **Do not create any credit system that requires you to bill a member for charges.**

You should be aware of one unbreakable rule in the gym business: *Do not create any credit system that requires you to bill a member for charges.* The losses will far exceed the profit from your centers in the club. Only allow credit if you have a prepay situation or a credit card backup.

What Are the Basic Profit Centers a Club Owner Should Consider?

Owners should consider quite a number of profit centers for their clubs. Owner's targeting the $5-per-day number should first start with the core centers, which are listed here. Be careful that you don't confuse amenities in the club, such as a climbing wall, that add to the membership as an amenity but seldom add significant numbers to the profit center total.

Each core center will be discussed in brief and the basic target number for each individual center will be listed as well. The basic target number will be given first as a dollar figure per visit and then shown as a total for a 400-member visit day.

Weight-Loss Management

One company of choice over the years for this profit center in the club has been Apex, a health club industry specialist listed at the end of the book in the resource guide. Weight-loss management should be a major part of your profit center business plan over the next few years and will be a club necessity if you are going to reach beyond the national club penetration rate of only 12%.

As of this writing only 12% of the people in this country belong to health clubs or some type of fitness center. That obviously means that 88% do not. According to the IHRSA publication, *Guide to the Health Club Industry for Lenders and Investors*, physical health is the top priority for Americans with 97% of those surveyed stating that it is the most important consideration in their life, second only to having a fulfilling relationship with their family 95%.

Part of attracting a new client base for health clubs and gyms will be appealing to people who are afraid to come into clubs because they are out of shape. It sounds like a contradiction but all gym owners have heard, "I'd love to join your club and I'll be down as soon as I get in shape." Weight loss will be one way to tap this potential in the coming years.

> **"I'd love to join your club and I'll be down as soon as I get in shape."**

Apex Weight-Loss Management target per day per member visit is $0.88 or $352 on a 400-member visit day.

Supplements (Apex)

Supplementation is a natural part of weight loss for most people. Club business plans should be focused on attracting and keeping the top 60 percent of the demographics in their target market, which is traditionally defined as a 15-minute drive time at 5:00 p.m. on a Monday night. This drive time translates into about a three- to five-mile ring for most clubs.

Clubs focusing on the top 60 percent of the people in those rings should find that this population is a natural candidate for weight loss and supplement sales. Supplement sales have long been associated with affluence, and the more affluent the demographic population you seek, the higher the supplement sales should be.

Supplements often become a part of most people's lives when they start to think about getting in shape. Supplements are also very confusing for most people and many end up taking suggestions from magazine articles or friends since they don't really know where to go for expert advice.

Clubs should be able to step in and provide a minimum of guidance for the average member interested in food supplements. Special cases or folks who have unique needs should be obviously passed on to their doctor or other health professional.

The Apex program has its own proprietary supplements that support its weight-loss management system. Clubs using this system can achieve a markup of 125% since the member can't get these core supplements anywhere else except through the club.

Supplements (Apex) target per day per member visit is $0.92 or $368 on a 400-member visit day.

Supplements (Other than Apex)

Apex supplements usually form the core element in the club, but most club owners still feel the pressure to carry some of the trendier powders and supplements. These are also very trendy and change year to year in the business and can range from anywhere from creatine to a hot protein powder. The key is knowing what's hot and how to get the most money from the product. Since these are trendy products, many members will pay full price for the item if you offer it rather than shop.

Supplements (other than Apex) target per day per member visit is $0.23 or $92 on a 400-member visit day.

Clothing and Accessories

Clothing sales in fitness centers have taken a major turn for the worse over the years. General fitness clothing used to be somewhat hard to get and clubs were often the only supplier. Today, almost any department store or specialty sports store can offer clothing at a retail price that is lower than clubs can purchase the same product at a wholesale price due to the store's larger volume.

Clothing is also very trendy. In past years clubs were full of fanny packs and strange workout pants, but today the members have cycled back to just wearing basic tee shirts and shorts. Surveys done several years in a row have shown that 90% of the daily traffic in a health club dresses in basic tee shirts and simple workout shorts. Even most of the women wear tee shirts as an over-shirt with some type of shorts. Crazy pants might come back one day in the fitness business, but the basics sell and will continue to sell in the future.

Clothing and accessories target per day per member visit is $0.56 or $224 on a 400-member visit day.

Cooler Drinks

Cooler drinks, meaning those sold in glass-fronted display cases, are the easiest of all the club's profit centers to install and maintain. Most clubs can benefit from a four-cooler configuration featuring a dedicated bottled water case, a dedicated soft drink case normally based upon the complete line of Coke products, the core case featuring sports drinks, and a fourth case that offers the trendy drinks in the area which usually change every three to six months.

Cooler drinks target per day per member visit is $0.35 or $140 on a 400-member visit day.

Tanning

Tanning is on the rise again in the fitness business with the advent of safer beds, more control systems, and better quality tanning products. Most clubs

> Clothing sales in fitness centers have taken a major turn for the worse over the years.

can benefit from a minimum of two to five beds from a quality manufacturer such as Sun Erogline. Many clubs have moved to having tanning as a separate business within a business, which can also be done with weight loss. Tanning and tanning products are attracting attention again and will fit most clubs' business plans.

Tanning and tanning products target per day per member visit is $0.39 or $156 on a 400-member visit day with two beds.

Sports bars/juice bars

Sports bars/juice bars are the social center of a club and every club, no matter how big or small, should have one. You are in the fitness business and a sports-centered juice bar in a coed club featuring satellite-fed sports programming is a must. The following numbers are based on having a nationally known delivery system for your bar, such as City Blends, rather than a homemade affair with a limited offering and a blender your mama gave you when you got your first apartment.

You should be aware of two basic rules about juice bars in a club. First of all, all your profit centers will do better if you have a juice bar, because if you can stop the person you can sell him just about anything. Juice bars give the member a reason to stop and dawdle for a while which makes it easier to notice other profit centers in the area. The second rule is that you never separate the juice bar from the check-in area. Juice bars are people-watching areas similar to bars in the real world and they need to be situated in the heart of the action in the front-entry areas of the club.

All your profit centers will do better if you have a juice bar, because if you can stop the person you can sell him just about anything.

Sports bars/juice bars target per day per member visit is $1.25 or $500 on a 400-member visit day.

Personal training/semiprivate group training

Training members is one of the most talked about profit centers in the club, and despite years of hype, certifications, and experiments with a myriad of different approaches, it still is one of the last great untapped markets in a club's business plan. Personal training, despite all its effort, has still only shown a limited appeal in health clubs with a penetration rate of only about 3% as a national average.

Members want to be trained and personal training has its place in the club for that type of clientele who appreciates the product. However, some people might want more of a semiprivate approach. They are the ones who want to work out with a coach, but who feel personal training is simply too much for them both financially and in what it has to offer as a product. More efficient clubs have added a semiprivate option for their members, allowing those clubs to achieve a penetration rate as high as 20%, or one out of every five members.

Semiprivate, or small-group training is popular with the members because of the social aspect and because the product can be delivered at a cheaper price per workout than standard personal training. The club owner also benefits because he is getting a higher return per session.

For example, a personal training client might pay $50 for a single session with a trainer. The trainer in that session might get as much as $25 before payroll taxes. In semiprivate training, the clients might pay only $35 per session since they are in essence sharing a trainer. The club is generating $105 for the same hour. The trainer in this example might be paid as much as $40 for the group and is happy while the club owner is netting a much larger percent and is also happy.

Personal training/semiprivate training target per day per member visit is $1.20 or $480 on a 400-member visit day.

Group programming

Group programming is money generated beyond your base group exercise program that is usually offered as part of the club's membership. In this case group programming refers to separate classes and events that members pay extra for in addition to their regular memberships.

For example, a club might offer a floor classes in Pilates but charges for sessions and classes on Pilate's-style equipment. Another example would be the club's group cycling program. The club may offer six to eight classes on its schedule but charge for a two-hour advance class on Saturday mornings.

Most club owners are fearful of charging extra and end up giving virtually everything in the club away for free.

Most club owners are fearful of charging extra and end up giving virtually everything in the club away for free. Members can be satisfied with a strong group offering but will pay extra for unique or special classes, especially if those classes are limited or have finite limits to the amount of people who can take part.

Group programming target per day per member visit is $.11 or $44 on a 400-member visit day.

The total revenue per day for a club that hits all these numbers is $5.89 per member workout, or a $2,356 total deposit for the day from all of the club's profit centers. A club won't hit all these numbers every day and might not even have half of these centers installed at the club at any given time, but these numbers are very achievable with the proper promotion and control systems. If you do not yet have profit centers, start small with just four and add others later on. Make sure you master the ones your club does have first before you add additional profit centers. Many clubs have more profit centers than they can properly take care of leading to reduced revenue and frustration for the owner.

What Is the True Potential for Profit Centers in a Club?

The $5-per-day target number can be projected further to illustrate the overall potential of profit centers in a club. For example, take a look at a 12,000-square-foot club in Figure 12-1 and see what happens if you do indeed hit the target numbers for each individual profit center previously listed. Each individual profit center will be listed with its per-workout dollar target and an equivalent will also be given that may help you translate the number into actual sales in the club.

In the first category the club's weight-loss management program should be generating $0.88 per day per member workout, or in this case 7,035 workouts for the month should yield $6,190. Another way to look at it is a dedicated weight-loss person selling an eight-week program for $329 needs to sell only about 18 programs to make the same revenue for the club.

The Overall Revenue Picture of this Club

What is the true potential for this 12,000-square-foot club with 1,800 members in Figure 12-1? The total of all of these profit centers is $41,432, but that doesn't reflect the overall picture of this club. The true impact is best shown when compared to the total revenue this club is doing.

> The total of all of these profit centers is $41,432, but that doesn't reflect the overall picture of this club.

- 1,800 members x $40 each (not adjusted for losses or cost of collection)

  = $72,000

- The club has a base operating expense (BOE) of $70,000.

- The club averages 70 new annual membership sales per month (1/$1,000 of expense) x $69 membership fee.

  = $4,830

- The club averages 7,035 workouts per month and does $5.89 per day per member visit in profit centers.

  = $41,432

Total expenses for the club	**= $70,000**
Total revenues	**= $118,262**
Net profit	**= $48,262**

This club would actually be profitable without any profit centers at all. The expenses are $70,000 and the check from the member payments is $72,000. Add new sales income of $4,832 ($72,000 + $4,832), which is shown as just member payments and does not reflect any short-term or annual paid-in-full memberships, and the club is netting $6,832 per month.

- 12,000-square-foot coed club

- 1,800 members

- Daily traffic on a typical Monday is 400 workouts and the club averages around 7,035 workouts per month (an average of 1,675 workouts per week x 4.2 weeks per month).

- Weight-loss management (Apex): 7,035 x $.88 = $6,190
  - √   An eight-week program at $329 x 18 programs (normal output for a single Apex specialist) = $5,922

- Supplements (Apex or in-house proprietary): 7,035 x $.92 = $6,472
  - √   Each person on the Apex program is given supplements for the first month of their two-month program. After that point each one should buy $110 in supplements and powders on their first purchase (18 x $110 = $1,980).
  - √   Supplement sales are recurring sales and accumulative sales, meaning each month people already in the program should buy again. Supplements are also impulse items that members not in the program will pick up if they see a quality display. Assuming the club has been in the weight-loss and supplement business for at least 90 days, the $0.92 per head target works.

- Supplements (other than Apex): 7,035 x $0.23 = $1,618
  - √   These are usually impulse sale items for the members who want the hot, can't-live-or-train-without-it supplement. These sales are very short-lived for these products because after the impulse wears off the members realize they can get the products cheaper elsewhere. You probably aren't doing the volume the chain supplement stores do or have the cost savings of buying online.

- Clothing and accessories: 7,035 x $0.56 = $3939
  - √   A relative equivalent for this category is that the club would only have to average about $130 a day in a 30-day month to hit this number from all clothing and accessories, such as gloves or headphones for the Cardio Theater.

- Cooler drinks: 7,035 x $0.35 = $2,462
  - √   Clubs that are good with drink sales will find this number somewhat light since this is only about $60 per day in a 30-day month.

- Tanning: 7,035 x $.39 = $2,743
  - √   Tanning is somewhat seasonal with most clubs making the bulk of their tanning money in March through June. With that in mind, tanning might do big numbers in those months and rather poorly other times of the year. An equivalent target is each bed should average approximately $1,600 to $1,750 per month per bed plus tanning supplies. Another factor that makes tanning hard to predict is that it is also somewhat regional in nature, meaning clubs of equivalent size may do different numbers because of where they are located.

- Sports bar/juice bar: 7,035 x $1.25 = $8,793
  - √   This is less than $300 per day, which is light for this traffic. The key to a solidly performing juice bar is the degree of finish and the delivery system. Most owners try to invent the entire concept themselves and they are usually poor at it. Buy a prepackaged nationally known system and put some money into the finish of your bar and the money will be there.

- Personal training/semiprivate training: 7,035 x $1.20 = $8,442
  - √   If the average training client in either the private format or in semiprivate paid an average of $300 for their package, then this number reflects less than 30 training clients out of 1,800 members.

- Group programming: 7,035 x $.11 = $773
  - √   One six-week advanced yoga class offered at $75 with only 10 students hits this number.

Figure 12-1.

The difference between this moderately successful club and the second version, including profit centers, is over $42,000 a month. Besides the obvious advantage of cash flow, this club would be very hard to hurt in the market since such a large portion of its income comes from members already in the system.

This club has also reached a point where 35 percent of its monthly revenue is from members already in the system. In this example, the profit center manager is having a far greater impact on the club each month than an individual salesperson who might contribute 25 to 30 membership sales for the month. You still have to sell memberships, but efficient clubs will embrace both parts of the equation.

This club has truly moved away from a club driven by sales volume to one that has moderate sales combined with strong profit center revenue. In other words, this club has truly captured a higher return-per-member as compared to a club that is just dependent on new membership sales without profit centers.

The Key Points You Should Have Gotten from this Chapter

- You really can make more money from fewer members.
- The future of the club business is to move away from a totally sales-driven operation system and move toward a business plan that decreases risk by seeking revenue from five to seven different sources. Another way to look at this is a club owner will no longer be dependent on just an external source of income (new membership sales) but will combine external and internal (profit center revenue from members already in the system).
- Your goal is to deposit 40% of the entire month's revenue from the club's profit centers income.
- You need a minimum of at least four profit centers and should work toward having five or more different centers in the club.
- Credit systems enhance profit center income. Profit centers will not reach these numbers without some type of aggressive credit system for the members.
- Your minimum goal is $5 per day per member visit.
- The bulk of your profit center revenue will come from a small percentage of your members. The 80/20 rule does apply in profit centers. In this case, 20% of your members will spend 80% or more of the money taken in from the club's profit centers. This means not everyone will buy and it's okay to have cheap members since the revenue will always come from a smaller percentage.

> The future of the club business is to move away from a totally sales-driven operation system and move toward a business plan that decreases risk by seeking revenue from five to seven different sources.

The Basic Concepts of Business Plans and Strategic Planning

Most fitness businesses are run in the present tense, meaning owners makes decisions that will get them through the end of the month with little regard to the long-term implications of what those decisions might be. Effective owners understand the need for projecting the business into the future and for having tools in place that will help guide them to make the right long-term decisions.

A fitness owner will also at some time in their career need to borrow money or seek investors. A well-written business plan, normally known as a prospectus plan, will greatly reduce the chances for failure when that time arrives. The combination of a well-written business plan and long-term strategic planning can add to any owner's competitive edge in the marketplace

This section covers the basics of writing a prospectus plan for banks and for seeking investor money. A sample plan including a projection is provided. Long-term strategic planning is also discussed including worksheets and exercises that will help an owner write an effective plan.

Chapters 13 and 14 are meant to be read together since each type of plan has a direct bearing on the other. Even if an owner is not looking to borrow money or attract investors at this time, writing a prospectus plan is an excellent exercise and a working model is always nice to have in the desk drawer when needed.

- **Chapter 13: Sooner or Later You Have to Have a Business Plan**
- **Chapter 14: Strategic Planning Moves Your Business into the Future**

13

Sooner or Later You Have to Have a Business Plan

The most important thing you should get from this chapter is:

Sooner or later you will have to present a business plan to borrow money or seek an investor: the prospectus plan is the answer.

Definitions and concepts you will need to know:

- *Prospectus plan:* A type of a business plan to present to investors or lenders usually 15 to 20 pages in length.

- *Development plan:* This type of plan is often confused with a prospectus plan. The development plan is the 150-page conceptualization of a business that is worth the exercise for a new owner but is not a needed tool for an investor or lender.

- *Projections:* Projections are also called *pro forma* and they are tools that predict how money, and how much money, will arrive if a business owner performs according to certain predictions. The most effective projections are done for two years at a time but some banks require five-year plans.

- Updated prospectus plans should be kept on file in case the need arises where an owner may need money or to seek credit, such as a decision to order new treadmills.

A Prospectus Plan Is a Concise Presentation for Borrowing Money

Sometime, somewhere, you will have to write a business plan. It might be for partners, it might be for the SBA when you refinance, or the bank might want to see one when you make major change in your business, such as a divorce, and the loan officer is trying to figure out if the person who ended up with the club can pay off that outstanding loan.

In the fitness industry, you will have to contend with three basic business plans sometime in your career. The first and most often used type is the *prospectus*, which is usually about a 15- to 20-page business plan used primary in conjunction with applying for loans, or for raising money from investors. This is what bankers usually want when they ask for a business plan.

Owners may also use a *development plan*, which is used primarily for start-up owners as a way to define the business before it is actually opened. This type of plan is very detailed and might be anywhere from 75 to 150 pages in length, and includes every minute item such as an advanced breakdown of demographics, staff job descriptions, individual equipment lists, and even information on banking and accounting details such as needed accounts and software.

> **Bankers and loan officers are normally serious people who try their best to loan money to people who are unprepared for banks and business in general.**

This is the plan most new owners confuse with the prospectus plan. Bankers and loan officers are normally serious people who try their best to loan money to people who are unprepared for banks and business in general. According to commercial loan officers, only four out of ten people who come in for money have a business plan. Out of those four, only one can sit down and defend the numbers written in the plan. The other three owners had their accountants write the plan and they have no idea what those little numbers really mean.

If you throw a 150-page business plan (better thought of as a whole lot of paper that means very little to a busy banker) on someone's desk, you won't get the result you hoped for with your presentation. Instead of impressing the banker, you will definitely prove that you have never ever been in business before or you wouldn't have had the time to write such a plan.

New owners should write at least one development plan for their first business, or if they are trying to invent a new concept such as the next big license or franchise concept. The rest of the people who want to borrow money should start with a prospectus.

The third type of plan, called an operating plan, is written to project change for a certain time period in a business's future. Examples are one-year, three-year, and five-year operating plans, which combined form the basis for proactive management in a club by the owner and management team. These plans will be discussed in Chapter 14.

The Prospectus

The prospectus is a brief but intense business plan to give to bankers and investors. It can be read in one sitting, answers all of the important questions, and is normally used in conjunction with a bank's formal application or with a proposal to raise money from a potential investor.

The following prospectus was originally based on the SBA loan application and has since been modified over the years. This particular model has done quite well with banks and investors and is a proven tool for raising money.

The heart of every business plan of this type is the *projection*. The projection is where you tell the loan officer or investor how the business will perform over time. Solid projections can be constructed for a two-year period, but occasionally some lenders want five-year projections, which are at best very weak attempts to project your business environment too far into the future. If you have a choice, limit the projections to two years.

Although you'll find tips included in this chapter for building projections, the formulas and software needed are beyond the concept of this book. The Thomas Plummer Company can develop the entire business plan for you, or a third-party financial-service company like ABC Financial out of Little Rock mentioned in the resource guide at the end of the book, can help you with all or a portion of the plan including how your receivables should develop over time. Your accountant can probably also help you put together this section with a little investigation and reading in this book on loss rates. A two-year example has been included that may help you if you want to experiment on your own. A prospectus should include:

- A cover page
- An overview of the entire project
- A club model
- Estimated costs of the proposed gym
- Proposed financing
- Projections and monthly operating expenses
- Bank and investor considerations
- The operating team for the club
- A summary of the project

> The projection is where you tell the loan officer or investor how the business will perform over time.

The Overview Section

The overview section is a one- to two-page overview of the entire project giving your prospective investors or the loan officer the overall picture of the project. The overview should state what the project is, where will it be, who will run it, why the area was chosen, and how long from concept to completion. Remember the old marketing adage: *Tell me fast, tell me true, or my friend the hell with you.* Writing a prospectus is just like writing a good novel; you have to get the reader's attention early and hold on to it so he will finish the book.

Costing Out the Project

The second section is the projected expense section for the entire project. This section would present an overview of the entire project and then the breakdowns of the individual components. Included in this section are:

- Cost of the entire project
- Land costs (if any)
- Building costs
- Site preparation
- Build out
- Equipment costs
- Reserve capital
- A general category for assorted stuff such as computers, music systems, licenses, etc.
- Marketing costs for the presale and first 90 days
- Architectural fees

Financing Section

The owner should have an initial idea of where she is seeking financing from and should do initial bank investigation before submitting a prospectus plan.

This section should discuss where exactly the money is coming from for the project. The owner should have an initial idea of where she is seeking financing from and should do initial bank investigation before submitting a prospectus plan.

If partners are involved, their participation should be discussed in this section. How will they participate financially, how or if they will participate in the day-to-day operations of the gym, and how they will be repaid should all be discussed.

Projections

Projections are the heart of the prospectus because they demonstrate the ability to repay the lender or the investors. Most projections should be kept to two years since the ability to project beyond that becomes somewhat hypothetical. Be aware of several common flaws with most projections that irritate lenders.

- They're not realistic or too good to be true.

Projections that show no negative cash flow are just too good to be true and the bankers know it. A lender expects a loss in the beginning and is more concerned about your ability to plan for reserve than to expect none at all. Build a best-case projection, a middle-case, and a worst-case. Throw the best case away, give the middle to your banker, and run the club off the worst-case scenario. The worst case is important because it lets you know just how bad it can get and you can still survive.

- You can't defend the numbers.

You're accountant builds the model and then you can't defend or explain the numbers. This scenario makes lenders and investors very nervous.

- You have no personal reserves.

If you have to take money out of the business from the first day to personally survive, the lender knows the plan is weak. Show a personal reserve of at least six months so the gym has a chance to get healthy.

- You show no losses.

Not everyone pays and the banks know it. A rookie mistake is to show members making payments and no one ever drops out. Build in acceptable loss, cancellations, and cost of collection to your numbers.

- They are not adjusted for the seasons.

Straight-line projections are the scariest. Month after month of repetitive sales and income makes everyone nervous. Adjust for the seasons and be realistic about the lean months.

- Use real renewal rates.

Second-year income is often way too high since you show no realistic adjustments for renewals. If you are using the preferred closed- end renewals, figure a 40% retention rate. If you're using open-ended renewals, figure a 5% loss rate per month from the 13th month going forward.

- Build a real working budget.

Build a budget that reflects a realistic cost of doing business. The best projections for owners to use are based on worst-case scenarios. For raising capital, use a mid-case plan. Best-case scenarios are worthless except to entertain yourself.

Projection spreadsheets should be divided into four sections: revenue, MPC, operating expenses, and payroll and related expenses.

Revenue

√   The total members projected are based on a 150-member presale, 150 members during the first month of operation, and 125 members during the second and third months. After that, the club reflects sales that match the demographics and sales history of her first club.

> Build a best-case projection, a middle-case, and a worst-case. Throw the best case away, give the middle to your banker, and run the club off the worst-case scenario.

√ The 90% EFT refers to 90% of the members joining the club are electing some type of monthly EFT or payment plan and are on a contractual obligation.

√ The 6% PIF is the percentage of members who paid in full on an annual membership.

√ The 4% is the percentage of members who took short-term memberships as opposed to an annual membership of some type.

√ The EFT membership is new sales cash paid as downs on the contractual memberships.

√ The PIF membership is the total new sales cash for paid-in-full memberships.

√ Daily-fee membership is the amount of daily drop in cash for the month.

√ Short-term membership is the total amount of cash generated in short-term memberships for the month.

√ Total new revenue is the total of all the income for new sales for the month.

√ EFT base is the monthly draft, or billing check, that reflects all of the member payments collected against the contractual obligation.

√ Total membership sales are the combination of new sales income produced on a daily basis as sales are made and the total of the monthly check received from the outstanding amount of all the member payments.

MPC

√ Clothing and accessories, supplements, drinks, tanning, personal training, group programming, and juice bar reflect the revenue collected for the month from each of the club's profit centers.

√ Total MPC sales are the total of all the revenue from all of the club's profit centers.

√ Net income reflects the combination of the revenue from the profit centers and from the revenue section that comes from club membership sales.

√ Cost of goods sold is the cost of the profit centers to the club.

√ Gross profit is the adjusted net income for the club.

Operating Expenses

√ This section reflects the operating expenses for each of these items in the club.

√ Repairs and maintenance, education, and capital improvements are all based on formulas described elsewhere in the book.

√   Total operating expense reflects the total cost of operating, but not the cost of goods sold or payroll and related expenses.

Payroll and Related Expenses

√   Commission paid is for sales and other bonuses paid to the employees.

√   Salary expense is for all employees and includes the owner's compensation if he is taking a normal manager's salary.

√   Total payroll and related expense is the total payroll and supporting expenses for the club.

√   Total expense is the combined operating and payroll expense for the club.

√   Net income is pretax net for the month (EBIT).

The Bank and Investor Section

This section shows what's in it for the investor as well as the ability to pay back the bank. It is based on the preceding section of projections that should build-in the anticipated bank payment or payments to the investors.

Most investors stay away from a business deal that gives them equity only in a gym business. The numbers are too small and they have too many other options with less risk.

A common method of attracting an investor is to offer a combination of equity and return-on-investment. For example, an investor might put up $250,000 for 25 percent of a gym that will have a million-dollar start-up cost. This investor would be paid back $125,000 over seven years as return-on-investment and the other $125,000 would stay in the business as part of the investor's equity position.

Payment to investors should be included in the projection to demonstrate the ability to repay. Anticipated investor notes should also be discussed to demonstrate that they are built into the club's operating budget and are part of cash-flow needs.

Who Will Own and Operate the Business

This section gives an investor an ideal of who is going to run the club and if they have the experience or expertise to do so. If the owner has been successful before, this is an easy section and is based on a simple resume of the owner's experience and qualifications.

If the owner has never been in the business before, real-life business qualifications are the most important thing, followed by any education or work experience the person might have done to prepare for owning an

> Most investors stay away from a business deal that gives them equity only in a gym business. The numbers are too small and they have too many other options with less risk.

expensive fitness business. A full resume is also needed here. If investors are involved, a simple one- or two-sentence explanation on who they are and what they have done helps an indecisive loan officer see a clearer picture of what kind of guidance and support system the new club owner might have behind her. The key in this section is to show business experience of any kind that can be related to running a health club successfully.

If a co-signer is involved, most banks will want to see a full resume and financial picture of the co-signer. In the business plan, keep the picture simple and clear and let the full picture evolve through the bank-loan package.

The Summary Section

The summary section should tie the entire package together. Often, many loan officers will read the summary first and then start at the beginning to see if the data matches the claims at the end.

Keep the summary brief and to the point. Remember that this is not an old-fashioned business plan built upon endless pages of information. Bank officers get a lot of packages and will only give at most a brief run-through before pursuing the ones that look promising.

> **The inexperience of many small business owners in financial matters often prompts banks to deny loan requests.**

Banks make money by lending money. However, the inexperience of many small business owners in financial matters often prompts banks to deny loan requests. Requesting a loan when you haven't thought through a basic plan sends a signal to your lender that you are a high risk.

To be successful in obtaining a loan, you must be prepared and organized when making your request. You must know exactly how much money you need, why you need it, and how you will pay it back. You must able to convince your lender that you are a good credit risk.

The summary should be used to convey information that gives the lender confidence that you know your numbers and have researched the project. If they like what they read in the short form, they may want you to provide additional information. Make sure you have documentation on all parts of your package and that you can explain and defend all the numbers.

Sample Prospectus

The sample prospectus on the following pages was designed for an actual club with an existing owner who was seeking SBA or conventional financing. This owner already had partners in place since she had an existing gym, had established a banker relationship that could handle conventional financing as well as SBA loans, and had worked with a realtor to get the real numbers on the property. The plan outlined at the end of this chapter is the basis of what she used to present to the bank with her final application.

Prospectus for a New Fitness Facility

Proposed business
The Columbia Workout Company
Highway 9 and Route 3
Columbia, South Carolina

Owned by a newly formed partnership
Operated by Sarah Smith
Owner of the existing Columbia Workout Company

Submitted for review November, 2000

Sarah Smith
230 North Addison
Columbia, SC 33398
321-555-1234

Table of Contents

Project Overview

This project will be a 14,000-square-foot adult-alternative gym located on Highway 9 and Route 3 in Columbia, South Carolina. In this case, adult alternative is defined as a gym built to appeal to the top 60 percent of the area's demographic package. This upscale approach will be reflected in the degree of finish and programming offered in the club as compared to other facilities currently in the area.

The gym will be owned and operated by Sarah Smith, a successful gym owner who currently operates the Columbia Workout Company, located at 2214 South Main in Columbia. Financing for the project will be through the combination of a partnership and either conventional or SBA financing.

The proposed site is currently raw land and comprises 2.7 acres. The property is listed at $900,000, has a 250-foot frontage to Route 3, and would require minimum site preparation.

The projected total cost of the project will be $2,606,000. A partnership group is being formed that will put up the initial cash needed for financing.

This area, referred to as the Highlands, has 67,000 residents meeting our demographic requirements within a five-mile ring from the site. At the current location, 87 percent of the members come from within the five-mile ring of the club. If marketed properly, a club has the ability to attract approximately 3.5 to 4 percent of the population within the five-mile ring. The demographics in the area give more than enough qualified prospective members to operate a successful health club.

Assuming that financing for the project will be done by the first of the year, the new gym will open in December 2001, in time to train the staff and complete the marketing before the New Year. The project was estimated at only nine months but December allows for at least a two-month overrun.

The club and property will be separate partnerships. Sarah Smith is seeking long-term equity partners in the property who will control an 80-percent stake. In the gym, the partners will represent a 40-percent position. The partners will be asked for 20 percent of the total cost of the project as their buy-in dependent on the final type of financing decided upon.

Sarah Smith has already done the groundwork for a 504 SBA loan, although the bankers that have been interviewed up to this point are suggesting conventional financing for 20 years. Again, the total cost for the project will be $2,606,000.

Club Model

An upscale adult club will cater to people in the 25- to 45-year-old range that have household incomes of at least $50,000. This style of club is breaking away from the traditional model offered in this area, reflected by out-of-date equipment, cheap prices, weak programming, poor design, and cheap finish. The area and its residents have no choice when it comes to seeking an upscale facility.

This club will have a very upscale finish, a juice bar that will cater to members as well as a street population, and a sports-activity and conditioning department catering to lifestyle enhancement such as golf improvement and weight management. The club will also offer the Body Training System, a state-of-the-art group exercise system from New Zealand.

The goal for the first 12-months of operation is to achieve an active membership base of a little over 900 members, which is a number adjusted for losses and club cancellations. The club will be built upon a strong receivable base foundation and profit centers that will allow the club to make money from the members it already has in the system. The club pricing will be $90 as a one-time membership fee and monthly dues of $49 per month. The club will also use ABC Financial Services from Little Rock, Arkansas, as its third-party collection-and-service system. ABC is the category leader in the industry for this service and services nine percent of all the clubs in the country.

Currently in the industry, a health club's revenue mix is 95 percent membership workout based and just five percent multiple profit centers based. This means the club is too dependent on generating new memberships every day and has no cash flow from its existing membership base.

This club will be designed to take full advantage of the members it has coming through its doors each day. The goal for the club is $5 per day in income from the members that are working out. This is not related to any monies they might have paid to workout, such as a monthly fee or drop-in payment.

The club will have a City Blends juice license for its juice bar as the central social focus in the club. This will allow for sales to the members as well as developing a traffic flow from the street. The club will also have an Apex Weight Loss Management Program that allows for revenue from nutrition guidance and training support. Other profit centers will be drink coolers, tanning and basic clothing, all proven in a health club environment.

The foundation of the club's image will be its trial membership marketing. The club will allow potential members to try the club before they purchase a membership. This type of marketing puts the emphasis on the clubs operations, not on just salesmanship, allowing the club to get a higher monthly fee from its members compared to other clubs in town.

Estimated Costs of the Proposed Gym

The following costs are based on acquiring the land and building a 14,000-square- foot building on the property. The actual building will have a footprint of 11,000 square feet and a mezzanine of 300 square feet.

Land costs — The land can be acquired for a cost of $900,000 and is 2.7 acres. The lot has a frontage of 250 feet on Highway 3, has high visibility on the front of the property, and slopes toward the rear of the site. The building can be placed on the front of the site for maximum visibility for the business and parking can be situated in the rear. Highway 3 has a daily traffic count of 27,000 cars, considered high for this area.

Building costs — Rudy Fabiano, a noted architect specializing in fitness businesses from New Jersey, has been contracted to design the building. He will work with Joseph Smith, a local architect that will do the site plan in conjunction with Fabiano. The estimated costs for a steel building with a custom front is $40 per square foot, based on an 11,000- square-foot footprint. This will include the shell, HVAC, proper electrical and plumbing for this type of business, and the mezzanine structure. This does not include internal finish or equipment. Total building cost is $440,000.

Site preparation — Initial site preparation for the site was projected at $200,000. This will give the property 140 parking places and allow for the development of a retention pond at the rear of the property.

Build-out costs — This club will be an upscale adult club designed for the top 60 percent of the demographic market. This means that this club will require a slightly higher degree of finish than a typical club in this area. The initial estimate for build-out for this project is $35 per square foot, or $385,000 for the project.

Equipment costs — The equipment costs for this facility will be projected at $332,000. This includes all strength and cardio equipment for the facility, but does not include Cardio Theater, group exercise, or specialty costs.

> (*Please note:* To figure equipment costs use the following formula. For the first 10,000 square feet, use $30,000 per thousand feet. For every thousand after the initial 10,000, use $8,000 per thousand feet. In this example, the club would have an initial cost of $300,000 for the first 10,000 square feet and $32,000 for the other 4,000 square feet.)

Reserve capital — The club is scheduled to open in December 2001, which is the prime month to open a club. Once open, the club will begin to cover its own expenses at approximately nine months from the first of the year, or in September 2002. Based on that time frame, the club will need two months BOE in reserve. BOE is defined as the club's base operating expense. BOE for this club will run $75,000 per month and the club will need $150,000 in reserve capital.

General category — The club will need initial inventory, desks, computers, and other general items to open that are not part of build-out or equipment. Based on a 14,000-square-foot club, the initial budget for general items will be $81,000.

(*Please note:* To figure the cost of general category items use the following formula. For the first 10,000 square feet, use $7,500 per thousand feet. For every thousand after the initial 10,000, use $1,500 per thousand feet. In this example, the club would have an initial cost of $75,000 for the first 10,000 square feet and $6,000 for the other 4,000 square feet.)

Marketing costs — The club will do a 30-day soft sale in December and an aggressive campaign during the first 90 days the club is open. During the presale, the club will spend approximately $8,000 in direct mail marketing, and during the first 90 days the club will budget another $30,000 in marketing dollars. Total marketing costs will be $38,000.

Architectural fees — Architectural fees include design and interior as well as on-site visits by Fabiano. Fees are estimated at $80,000.

Land costs $900,000
Building costs $440,000
Site preparation $200,000
Build-out $385,000
Equipment costs $332,000
Reserve capital $150,000
General category items $81,000
Marketing for presale and first 90 days $38,000
Architectural fees $80,000
Total project cost $2,606,000

Proposed Financing

Two types of financing are being considered for this project: conventional financing with a 20-percent down over 20 years and an SBA 504 with 10-percent down and a 20- year payback. Initial discussions with several banks concerning the project pointed toward conventional financing for the project.

Partners are involved in both scenarios. A partnership is being formed to acquire both the building and the property, which will result in two separate ownership groups. The partners will put up the initial percentage for either type of loan, which will be repaid through the profits of the business. The building partnership will consist of the following people:

Sarah Smith @ 20%
Jim Johnson, a local contractor @ 30%
Randall Washington, a professional athlete @ 30%
Johnny Sindell, an independent investor @ 10%
Susan Vaughn, an independent investor @ 10%

The gym partnership will consist of the following people:

Sarah Smith @ 60%
Jim Johnson, Randall Washington, Johnny Sindell, and Susan Vaughn @ 10% each

The partnership was formed to take part in this project as a long-term real estate investment. Sarah Smith will acquire 20 percent of the building and property as operating partner. The partnership will allow Sarah Smith a larger percentage of the gym business for her role as the on-site operating manager.

The partnership is seeking a loan of $2,020,800 at 10.5 percent over 20 years. This would result in a payment of $20,175, well within the operating parameters of the budget. The total project is planned for $2,606,000 with a down of approximately 22 percent, or $585,200. The down will be cash raised by the partners.

Projections and Monthly Operating Expenses

(See spreadsheets on following two pages)

A One-Month BOE for the Columbia Workout Company

Rent/mortgage payment $20,175
Payroll $28,000
Advertising $5,600
Utilities $2,100
Phone $700
Yellow page ad $700
Accounting $300
Printing $525
Office supplies $350
Cleaning supplies $525
Postage $350
All insurances $700
Apex Fitness $2,500
Basic clothing $1,500
Drinks $1,500
Juice bar $1,500
Tanning $600
Repair and maintenance $1,400
Education and training $1,400
Capital improvement $2,100
Legal $250
Misc. $1400
Total Monthly Base Operating Expense $74,175

Projections Year 1

Revenues	Month 1	Month 2	Month 3	Month 4	Month 5	Month 6	Month 7	Month 8	Month 9	Month 10	Month 11	Month 12	Total
Total New New Members Projected	150	125	125	115	90	75	75	68	90	75	75	63	
Presale: 150 Members													
Total Members	300	398	495	585	674	764	854	944	1033	1123	1213	1283	
90% EFT	135	113	113	104	81	68	68	61	81	68	68	57	
6% PIF	10	8	8	7	6	5	5	4	6	5	5	4	
4% Short Term	7	6	6	5	4	3	3	3	4	5	3	3	
Daily Fees	15	13	13	12	9	8	8	7	9	8	8	6	
EFT Membership $	12,015.00	10,012.50	10,012.50	9,211.50	7,209.00	6,007.50	6,007.50	5,406.75	7,209.00	6,007.50	6,007.50	5,046.30	
PIF Membership $	6,903.00	5,752.50	5,752.50	5,292.30	4,141.80	3,451.50	3,451.50	3,106.35	4,141.80	3,451.50	3,451.50	2,899.26	
Daily-Fee Membership $	225.00	187.50	187.50	172.50	135.00	112.50	112.50	101.25	135.00	112.50	112.50	94.50	
Short-Term Membership $	1,208.25	1,006.88	1,006.88	926.33	724.95	604.13	604.13	543.71	724.95	604.13	604.13	507.47	
Total New Revenue	20,351.25	16,959.38	16,959.38	15,602.63	12,210.75	10,175.63	10,175.63	9,158.06	12,210.75	10,175.63	10,175.63	8,547.53	152,702.21
EFT Base	15,930.00	21,107.25	26,284.50	31,047.57	35,810.64	40,573.71	45,336.78	50,099.85	54,862.92	59,625.99	64,389.06	68,116.68	
Total Membership Sales	36,281.25	38,066.63	43,243.88	46,650.20	48,021.39	50,749.34	55,512.41	59,257.91	67,073.67	69,801.62	74,564.69	76,664.21	665,887.16
MPC Sales													
Clothing and Accessories	783.29	1,037.86	1,292.43	1,526.63	1,760.83	1,995.03	2,229.24	2,463.44	2,697.64	2,931.85	3,166.05	3,349.34	
Supplements	1,174.93	1,556.78	1,938.64	2,289.94	2,641.25	2,992.55	3,343.86	3,695.16	4,046.47	4,397.77	4,749.08	5,024.01	
Drinks	308.57	408.85	509.14	601.40	693.66	785.92	878.18	970.45	1,062.71	1,154.97	1,247.23	1,319.44	
Tanning	249.23	330.23	411.23	485.75	560.26	634.78	709.30	783.82	858.34	932.86	1,007.38	1,065.70	
Personal Training	593.40	786.26	979.11	1,156.54	1,333.96	1,511.39	1,688.82	1,866.24	2,043.67	2,221.10	2,398.52	2,537.38	
Group Programming	249.23	330.23	411.23	485.75	560.26	634.78	709.30	783.82	858.34	932.86	1,007.38	1,065.70	
Juice Bar	1,471.63	1,949.91	2,428.19	2,868.21	3,308.23	3,748.25	4,188.26	4,628.28	5,068.30	5,508.32	5,948.34	6,292.70	
Total MPC Sales	4,830.28	6,400.12	7,969.96	9,414.21	10,858.46	12,302.71	13,746.97	15,191.22	16,635.47	18,079.72	19,523.98	20,654.26	155,607.34
Net Income	41,111.53	44,466.74	51,213.83	56,064.40	58,879.85	63,052.05	69,259.37	74,449.13	83,709.14	87,881.34	94,088.66	97,318.47	821,494.50
Cost of Goods Sold	1,869.21	2,476.70	3,084.20	3,643.09	4,201.98	4,760.88	5,319.77	5,878.67	6,437.56	6,996.45	7,555.35	7,992.74	
Gross Profit	39,242.32	41,990.04	48,129.63	52,421.31	54,677.87	58,291.17	63,939.60	68,570.47	77,271.58	80,884.89	86,533.31	89,325.72	761,277.90
Operating Expenses													
Advertising	5,600.00	5,600.00	5,600.00	5,600.00	5,600.00	5,600.00	5,600.00	5,600.00	5,600.00	5,600.00	5,600.00	5,600.00	
Yellow Pages	700.00	700.00	700.00	700.00	700.00	700.00	700.00	700.00	700.00	700.00	700.00	700.00	
Insurance	700.00	700.00	700.00	700.00	700.00	700.00	700.00	700.00	700.00	700.00	700.00	700.00	
Outside Services-Janitorial	1,200.00	1,200.00	1,200.00	1,200.00	1,200.00	1,200.00	1,200.00	1,200.00	1,200.00	1,200.00	1,200.00	1,200.00	
Accounting/Legal	550.00	550.00	550.00	550.00	550.00	550.00	550.00	550.00	550.00	550.00	550.00	550.00	
Printing	525.00	525.00	525.00	525.00	525.00	525.00	525.00	525.00	525.00	525.00	525.00	525.00	
Rent	20,175.00	20,175.00	20,175.00	20,175.00	20,175.00	20,175.00	20,175.00	20,175.00	20,175.00	20,175.00	20,175.00	20,175.00	
Cleaning Supplies	525.00	525.00	525.00	525.00	525.00	525.00	525.00	525.00	525.00	525.00	525.00	525.00	
Repairs/Maintenance	1,400.00	1,400.00	1,400.00	1,400.00	1,400.00	1,400.00	1,400.00	1,400.00	1,400.00	1,400.00	1,400.00	1,400.00	
Supplies	350.00	350.00	350.00	350.00	350.00	350.00	350.00	350.00	350.00	350.00	350.00	350.00	
Postage	350.00	350.00	350.00	350.00	350.00	350.00	350.00	350.00	350.00	350.00	350.00	350.00	
Sales Taxes	253.59	336.01	418.42	494.25	570.07	645.89	721.72	797.54	873.36	949.19	1,025.01	1,084.35	
Telephone	700.00	700.00	700.00	700.00	700.00	700.00	700.00	700.00	700.00	700.00	700.00	700.00	
Utilities	2,100.00	2,100.00	2,100.00	2,100.00	2,100.00	2,100.00	2,100.00	2,100.00	2,100.00	2,100.00	2,100.00	2,100.00	
Education	1,400.00	1,400.00	1,400.00	1,400.00	1,400.00	1,400.00	1,400.00	1,400.00	1,400.00	1,400.00	1,400.00	1,400.00	
Capital improvements	2,100.00	2,100.00	2,100.00	2,100.00	2,100.00	2,100.00	2,100.00	2,100.00	2,100.00	2,100.00	2,100.00	2,100.00	
Miscellaneous	1,400.00	1,400.00	1,400.00	1,400.00	1,400.00	1,400.00	1,400.00	1,400.00	1,400.00	1,400.00	1,400.00	1,400.00	
Total Operating Expenses	40,028.59	36,611.01	36,693.42	36,769.25	36,845.07	36,920.89	36,996.72	37,072.54	37,148.36	37,224.19	37,300.01	37,359.35	446,969.39
Payroll and Related Expenses													
Commission Paid	3,618.75	3,015.63	3,015.63	2,774.38	2,171.25	1,809.38	1,809.38	1,628.44	2,171.25	1,809.38	1,809.38	1,519.88	26,862.72
Salary Expense	23,400.00	23,400.00	23,400.00	23,400.00	23,400.00	23,400.00	23,400.00	23,400.00	23,400.00	23,400.00	23,400.00	23,400.00	
Total Payroll and Related Exp.	28,218.75	27,615.63	27,615.63	27,374.38	26,771.25	26,409.38	26,409.38	26,228.44	26,771.25	26,409.38	26,409.38	26,119.88	322,352.69
Total Expenses	68,247.34	64,226.63	64,309.05	64,143.62	63,616.32	63,330.27	63,406.09	63,300.98	63,919.61	63,633.56	63,709.38	63,479.22	
Net Income before Taxes	(29,005.02)	(22,236.59)	(16,179.41)	(11,722.31)	(8,938.45)	(5,039.10)	533.51	5,269.49	13,351.97	17,251.32	22,823.93	25,846.50	(8,044.17)

298

Projections Year 2

	Month 1	Month 2	Month 3	Month 4	Month 5	Month 6	Month 7	Month 8	Month 9	Month 10	Month 11	Month 12	Total
Revenues													
Total New Members Projected	104	104	104	115	90	75	75	68	90	75	75	63	
Renewals	83	50	50	46	36	30	30	27	36	30	30	25	
Total Members	1187	1329	1472	1622	1741	1839	1937	2026	2144	2242	2341	2423	
90% EFT	93	93	93	104	81	68	68	61	81	68	68	57	
6% PIF	7	7	7	7	6	5	5	4	6	5	5	4	
4% Short Term	5	5	5	5	4	3	3	3	4	3	3	3	
Daily Fees	10	10	10	12	9	8	8	7	9	8	8	6	
EFT Membership $	8,290.35	8,290.35	8,290.35	9,211.50	7,209.00	6,007.50	6,007.50	5,406.75	7,209.00	6,007.50	6,007.50	5,046.30	
PIF Membership $	4,763.07	4,763.07	4,763.07	5,292.30	4,141.80	3,451.50	3,451.50	3,106.35	4,141.80	3,451.50	3,451.50	2,899.26	
Daily-Fee Membership $	155.25	155.25	155.25	172.50	135.00	112.50	112.50	101.25	135.00	112.50	112.50	94.50	
Short-Term Membership $	833.69	833.69	833.69	926.33	724.95	604.13	604.13	543.71	724.95	604.13	604.13	507.47	
Total New Revenue	14,042.36	14,042.36	14,042.36	15,602.63	12,210.75	10,175.63	10,175.63	9,158.06	12,210.75	10,175.63	10,175.63	8,547.53	140,559.30
EFT Base	63,007.61	70,574.36	78,141.11	86,152.84	92,422.89	97,647.93	102,872.97	107,575.50	113,845.55	119,070.59	124,295.63	128,684.66	
Total Membership Sales	77,049.97	84,616.72	92,183.47	101,755.46	104,633.64	107,823.55	113,048.59	116,733.56	126,056.30	129,246.22	134,471.26	137,232.19	1,324,850.94
MPC Sales													
Clothing and Accessories	3,098.12	3,470.19	3,842.25	4,236.19	4,544.49	4,801.41	5,058.33	5,289.55	5,597.86	5,854.77	6,111.69	6,327.50	
Supplements	4,647.19	5,205.28	5,763.37	6,354.28	6,816.74	7,202.11	7,587.49	7,934.33	8,396.78	8,782.16	9,167.54	9,491.26	
Drinks	1,220.47	1,367.04	1,513.61	1,668.80	1,790.25	1,891.46	1,992.67	2,083.76	2,205.22	2,306.43	2,407.64	2,492.65	
Tanning	985.77	1,104.15	1,222.53	1,347.88	1,445.97	1,527.72	1,609.47	1,683.04	1,781.14	1,862.88	1,944.63	2,013.30	
Personal Training	2,347.06	2,628.93	2,910.79	3,209.23	3,442.80	3,637.43	3,832.07	4,007.24	4,240.80	4,435.44	4,630.07	4,793.56	
Group Programming	985.77	1,104.15	1,222.53	1,347.88	1,445.97	1,527.72	1,609.47	1,683.04	1,781.14	1,862.88	1,944.63	2,013.30	
Juice Bar	5,820.72	6,519.74	7,218.77	7,958.90	8,538.13	9,020.83	9,503.52	9,937.95	10,517.18	10,999.88	11,482.58	11,888.04	
Total MPC Sales	19,105.09	21,398.48	23,693.86	26,123.16	28,024.36	29,608.69	31,193.02	32,618.92	34,520.11	36,104.45	37,688.78	39,019.61	359,099.53
Net Income	96,155.07	106,016.20	115,877.33	127,878.63	132,658.00	137,432.24	144,241.61	149,352.48	160,576.42	165,350.66	172,160.03	176,251.80	1,683,950.46
Cost of Goods Sold	7,393.25	8,281.12	9,169.00	10,109.09	10,844.81	11,457.91	12,071.01	12,622.80	13,358.52	13,971.62	14,584.72	15,099.73	
Gross Profit	88,761.82	97,735.07	106,708.33	117,769.54	121,813.19	125,974.33	132,170.60	136,729.68	147,217.89	151,379.04	157,575.31	161,152.07	1,544,986.89
Operating Expenses													
Advertising	5,600.00	5,600.00	5,600.00	5,600.00	5,600.00	5,600.00	5,600.00	5,600.00	5,600.00	5,600.00	5,600.00	5,600.00	
Yellow Pages	700.00	700.00	700.00	700.00	700.00	700.00	700.00	700.00	700.00	700.00	700.00	700.00	
Insurance	700.00	700.00	700.00	700.00	700.00	700.00	700.00	700.00	700.00	700.00	700.00	700.00	
Outside Services-Janitorial	1,200.00	1,200.00	1,200.00	1,200.00	1,200.00	1,200.00	1,200.00	1,200.00	1,200.00	1,200.00	1,200.00	1,200.00	
Accounting/Legal	550.00	550.00	550.00	550.00	550.00	550.00	550.00	550.00	550.00	550.00	550.00	550.00	
Printing	525.00	525.00	525.00	525.00	525.00	525.00	525.00	525.00	525.00	525.00	525.00	525.00	
Rent	20,175.00	20,175.00	20,175.00	20,175.00	20,175.00	20,175.00	20,175.00	20,175.00	20,175.00	20,175.00	20,175.00	20,175.00	
Cleaning Supplies	525.00	525.00	525.00	525.00	525.00	525.00	525.00	525.00	525.00	525.00	525.00	525.00	
Repairs/Maintenance	1,400.00	1,400.00	1,400.00	1,400.00	1,400.00	1,400.00	1,400.00	1,400.00	1,400.00	1,400.00	1,400.00	1,400.00	
Supplies	350.00	350.00	350.00	350.00	350.00	350.00	350.00	350.00	350.00	350.00	350.00	350.00	
Postage	350.00	350.00	350.00	350.00	350.00	350.00	350.00	350.00	350.00	350.00	350.00	350.00	
Sales Taxes	1,003.02	1,123.47	1,243.93	1,371.47	1,471.28	1,554.46	1,637.63	1,712.49	1,812.31	1,895.48	1,978.66	2,048.53	
Telephone	700.00	700.00	700.00	700.00	700.00	700.00	700.00	700.00	700.00	700.00	700.00	700.00	
Utilities	2,100.00	2,100.00	2,100.00	2,100.00	2,100.00	2,100.00	2,100.00	2,100.00	2,100.00	2,100.00	2,100.00	2,100.00	
Education	1,400.00	1,400.00	1,400.00	1,400.00	1,400.00	1,400.00	1,400.00	1,400.00	1,400.00	1,400.00	1,400.00	1,400.00	
Capital Improvements	2,100.00	2,100.00	2,100.00	2,100.00	2,100.00	2,100.00	2,100.00	2,100.00	2,100.00	2,100.00	2,100.00	2,100.00	
Miscellaneous	1,400.00	1,400.00	1,400.00	1,400.00	1,400.00	1,400.00	1,400.00	1,400.00	1,400.00	1,400.00	1,400.00	1,400.00	
Total Operating Expenses	40,778.02	37,398.47	37,518.93	37,646.47	37,746.28	37,829.46	37,912.63	37,987.49	38,087.31	38,170.48	38,253.66	38,323.53	457,652.73
Payroll and Related Expenses													
Commission Paid	2,496.94	2,496.94	2,496.94	2,774.38	2,171.25	1,809.38	1,809.38	1,628.44	2,171.25	1,809.38	1,809.38	1,519.88	26,682.79
Salary Expense	23,400.00	23,400.00	23,400.00	23,400.00	23,400.00	23,400.00	23,400.00	23,400.00	23,400.00	23,400.00	23,400.00	23,400.00	
Total Payroll and Related Exp.	27,096.94	27,096.94	27,096.94	27,374.38	26,771.25	26,409.38	26,409.38	26,228.44	26,771.25	26,409.38	26,409.38	26,119.88	320,193.50
Total Expenses	67,874.95	64,495.41	64,615.86	65,020.84	64,517.53	64,238.83	64,322.01	64,215.93	64,858.56	64,579.86	64,663.04	64,443.40	767,140.66
Net Income before Taxes	20,886.86	33,239.66	42,092.47	52,748.70	57,295.66	61,735.50	67,848.59	72,513.75	82,359.34	86,799.18	92,912.27	96,708.67	

Bank and Investor Considerations

The total cost of the project is estimated at $2,606,000. The partnership will put up 22 percent, or $585,200 in cash. The projected loan amount will be $2,020,000 at 10.5 percent over 20 years.

Based on these numbers the club will only have a $20,175 payment per month. If the club were renting in the same area, it would be paying $12 per foot plus triple net. At this cost, the projected rent for the same site would be $14,000 per month plus an estimated triple- net number of about $2.50 a foot, or another $2,900 per month for a total of $16,900.

For a difference of only about $3,000 per month, the partners will have a long-term investment, tax benefits, and the ability to refinance in the future to keep the facility current. This long-term investment was what attracted the investors to the project in the first place.

The partners are looking for a long-term investment and will not take anything out of the building partnership. They are in fact looking for the business to carry the note on the property and will not participate in the business except as needed financially in the future.

Only bonuses based on the profitability of the club will be offered investors in the club partnership. No other participation or salaries will be offered. Sarah Smith will be paid a managing partners salary capped at $75,000 per year and will participate in bonuses paid on profits.

The partnership has agreed to invest in another club once this club has shown itself to be at least 20-percent net profitable before taxes on a monthly basis for six consecutive months. The partnership has initially agreed to fund up to five additional clubs if the units meet the minimum profitability needed.

The Operating Team

Sarah Smith has been a successful club operator for three years. She is a graduate of the University of Arkansas in business and has completed several graduate level courses. She has completed two Thomas Plummer and Company weeklong training seminars of advanced club operations and has attended three TPC two-day management seminars.

Her current club has been profitable since its inception and it has been expanded once since it was opened using cash from operations. The club currently has a receivable base held by ABC Financial Services valued at $425,000. Current loans are held by First Federal of Columbia and are current.

The manager of the club will be Thomas Jenkins, who has been assistant manager in the current club for two years and has been training to take over the new facility. Thomas is a graduate of the University of Michigan in sports management. He has graduated from a Thomas Plummer and Company weeklong advanced school and has also completed an advanced sales training seminar by the same company.

Jim Johnson is a local contractor who has been in the community for over 15 years.

Randall Washington is a pro athlete who has played professional basketball for the last six years.

Johnny Sindell is a local investor and member of the current club. He is the owner of several restaurants in the area.

Sarah Vaughn is a local investor and member of the current club.

Summary

This is a proposal for a new upscale health club in Columbia that will open in late 2001. The club fills a need for a quality club and has no competitors in the upper-end of the marketplace. The club will specialize in members in the 25 to 45-year-old ranges.

According to American Sports Data, the more important demographic trend is the growth of members aged 35 to 54, which has skyrocketed 55 percent from 1987 to 1998, while the 18- to 34-year-old group could produce only a 20 percent growth in the same period.

All competitors in the Columbia area are concentrating on younger markets and no one yet has built a club seeking an older and more affluent population. This club will have the finish, programming, and profit centers that cater to a wealthier and older membership. The demographics in the area support the membership needed for a club of this type that includes 67,000 households within five miles that have an average household income of over $50,000.

The project has been estimated at $2,600,000 by one of the premier architects in the health club industry who has build over 100 clubs in his career. The club will seek conventional financing and has built a partnership to contribute 20-percent down. The partners are all successful business people in their own right and are looking for a real estate investment that is passive based on the club business paying the note payment.

A successful businesswoman who has run a profitable fitness business similar to the new project for over three years will operate the club. During that time she has trained a staff and management team to run both projects.

The partnership would like to have all loan packages completed and funding in place by the first of the year allowing for a full 12 months to build and then open the gym. This is allowing for at least a two-month overrun for the build-out and completion of the project.

Demographic data, club plans, and additional financial information are available upon request.

SBA Financing

SBA is the *Small Business Administration* that works with banks to guarantee loans for small businesses. You should know that several types of loans are available through the SBA, such as a 504 designed for an owner who wishes to purchase physical assets including a building, and the 7A loan that is designed for owners who aren't buying property.

If you are seeking money, find a banker who understands both conventional financing through the bank itself and who can also help you with SBA. If you have experience and a track record, most banks will take your loan and your conventional financing, although this may vary bank to bank. You can get further information on the SBA's website at SBA.gov.

Tips for Loan and Investor Seekers

- Interview more than one banker if it is your first project.

Tell them you would like to submit a loan proposal and ask about various loans and what they like to see in a project.

- Show some type of personal participation.

Very seldom can you do an entire project without having some personal money involved. Even investors like to see at least $50,000 on the table. The investors might put up the rest but they also like you to know they are vested in the project.

- Leave your ball cap at the door.

You are there to borrow money and ties or dresses are back and considered proper business attire. You are dealing with very conservative people who like to loan money to other conservative people.

- Contact IHRSA.

You should be a member of IHRSA, mentioned in the resource guide at the end of the book. This group has many publications that can add to your loan package, such as the *IHRSA Guide to the Health Club Industry for Lenders and Investors*.

- Get a job in the business first.

If you are new at this, go get a job in a gym and learn how to sell a membership. If you are not willing to do this then don't get in the gym business. Even if you have a lot of money and have been successful somewhere else, learn to sell somebody something in this business before you invest.

- Be prepared.

As mentioned earlier, very few owners can defend their business plans. Understand how cash flow works and be able to discuss every aspect of the

> **You are there to borrow money and ties or dresses are back and considered proper business attire. You are dealing with very conservative people who like to loan money to other conservative people.**

business. Again, if you have never worked in a gym, this will be a short discussion followed by a *no* from the lender.

• Consider a family partnership for the first club.

Almost everyone started with his family first. It's the rare owner that didn't have some type of family help to get that first gym opened.

• Investors are more interested in the real estate than they are in owning a gym.

Owning your own building often makes more sense to investors, and is better for your long-term future in most cases, than renting and putting all that money in some else's space. It is easier to attract investors if they are gaining a passive investment such as a building with a built-in tenant. It is like buying a great rental house and having a tenant that even paints the place and does his own plumbing. He pays rent while you get appreciation. Investors look at the gym business in the same way. You own the real estate, you make the payments, and it becomes a passive appreciation growing business deal.

• Give up a lot to get your first gym but make sure you can't get kicked out of your own business.

If you have nothing and investors want a large portion of your business to do it then go for it. Give up 60% if you get 40% with little of your own money, but make sure your attorney structures the partnership deal so you can't get kicked out of your own business.

• A loan may be as simple as a co-signer.

You may need less cash but a stronger co-signer to get into your first gym. Ask you lender about what it would take for a co-signer.

• Look for used gyms.

Have a lawyer send a blind letter, meaning his name is on it but not yours, to every gym in the area you are interested in. The letter states that the lawyer represents a qualified buyer wishing to purchase a gym in the area. You may get no responses, or a few outlandish dream deals, but you might also get the real thing. Most used gyms are stupidly overpriced but at least start there and see what's in the market. The valuation section in Chapter 16 may help you get a better idea of what a gym is worth.

• Build smaller than you think.

You could have an excellent gym at 1,300 square feet that would make you a decent salary and get you into the business. Most first gyms are too much for the market since the owners had too long to think about building the perfect gym. Start smaller because you can always expand or build a second unit later. One of the dumbest things heard from even experienced owners is, "I have to build a gym really big. If it's too small it will get too crowded." In other words, you are too successful and the gym is too popular. Tough

Most first gyms are too much for the market since the owners had too long to think about building the perfect gym.

problem easily remedied by another unit or expansion. Remember, because of the increasing start up costs the gym of the future will be a smaller, more intimate delivery system probably in the 5,000- to 20,000-square-foot range.

The Key Points You Should Have Gotten from this Chapter

Borrowing money through a lender or investor is much easier if you are prepared with the right documentation.

- Writing a business plan is a basic skill all owners in the fitness business will someday have to learn.

- The prospectus plan is a simple 15 to 20-page plan used as the primary tool to borrow money or seek investors.

- Borrowing money through a lender or investor is much easier if you are prepared with the right documentation.

- The heart of any business plan is the projection because it shows how money arrives and demonstrates your ability to repay money over time.

- Update your prospectus yearly in case you need it on short notice for leases or for a presentation to your bank.

14

Strategic Planning Moves Your Business into the Future

The most important thing you should get from this chapter is:

A good working strategic plan today is worth much more than a perfect plan you are going to write later.

Definitions and concepts you will need to know:

- *Strategic planning:* projecting your business into the future by writing plans for all the key areas.

- Gym businesses are not perfect businesses and therefore don't need perfect planning.

- Every owner should have written the following nine working plans:
  - √ A prospectus plan
  - √ A one-year operational plan
  - √ A three-year conceptual plan
  - √ A five-year equity and escape plan
  - √ A 12-month staff training and development plan
  - √ A 12-month external marketing plan
  - √ A 12-month internal promotion plan
  - √ A 12-month member-service implementation plan
  - √ A separate 12-month budget

- Planning should be done once a year for the coming year.

- For planning to be effective it has to be in writing.

- Gym people don't plan. Business people plan. You can be both.

Why a Good Plan Today Is Worth More than a Perfect Plan Later

The very nature of the fitness business forces most owners to become month-to-month creatures. After a few years in the business, their entire lives become centered on one-month segments because that's how you run the businesses, count sales, schedule classes, and plan your marketing.

Sooner or later this way of doing business even permeates your personal life. "Yeah honey, I know our anniversary is next month, but just let me close out this month and I'll worry about it then."

The problem with this system is that it makes most owners terribly shortsighted about their businesses. When your world closes down into one-month time periods, you lose your ability to recognize or anticipate problems with your business. Most importantly, you become totally reactive to small things in the market that force you to make mistakes.

For example, an owner that has been open for several years, and is taking a nice salary from his club, recently gets a new competitor moving in about a mile away. This competitor comes in with a lesser gym and pricing $20 per month less than he is charging.

Since the first owner hasn't had much competition, he also hasn't done much marketing, hasn't updated much in the gym beyond basic paint and a few pieces of equipment, and hasn't done much to upgrade programming or club offerings since he opened his doors. The competitor, while a lesser gym, is fresh, new and hungry, and takes a bite out of the first owner's numbers.

The first owner then goes into a total reactionary mode trying to get marketing started, fix up the club, and figure out programming, all the while trying to stop the numbers from bleeding. The chances he'll make a mistake are huge since he is operating from a scrambling position.

The preferred scenario is the same situation, but with an owner who does strategic planning for his business every year. Once a year, usually in November, he takes a few days away from the club and writes a one-year, three-year, and five-year operating plan for his business. Strategic planning for your purposes is writing a business plan, or combination of plans, that establishes an overall focus and course for your business over the one- to five-year time span.

The one-year plan, for example, includes planning for immediate improvements in the club in the coming year, maintaining key components such as the 12-month marketing plan, staff development, internal profit center promotion, and planning customer service. The three-year plan looks

The competitor, while a lesser gym, is fresh, new and hungry, and takes a bite out of the first owner's numbers.

306

at broader concepts such as refinancing and replacing major groups of equipment, while building a long-term view of the owner's career and retirement are integral segments in the five-year plan.

Because of these plans the second owner who planned strategically is not taken by surprise with his new competitor. He is already protecting his market with a 12-month external and internal marketing plan, has budgeted for the entire year for steady improvements in the physical plant and equipment, and is focused on the top 60 percent of his market, a group the competitor will not get because of his gym and marketing.

He may lose a few members during the first year, but he knows that if he is patient and follows the plan, he will get most of them back when they realize what type of service and gym they will get for that cheaper price in the long run. Because he had a plan he didn't panic and was able to maintain his business and his lifestyle.

Gyms are not perfect businesses and never will be. A fitness business, due to vast amount of influences affecting it each day from members, market conditions, staff problems, owner attitudes, and even the weather, has to be constantly adjusted as you stay within guidelines you establish to keep you at least on the right path.

Gyms are not perfect businesses and never will be.

Think of your business as a giant ball. Too many owners want the ball painted beautifully, hand polished, perfectly balanced, and absolutely brilliant in every way before they will even consider sending it down the hill into the marketplace.

Effective owners understand that it will never be perfect, and in effect perfect doesn't really make you more money anyway, so they just push the sucker down the hill, run along side as fast as their overly developed legs will carry them, and fix it on the fly adjusting to the market but never, ever losing sight of the overall plan they created to keep the ball rolling down the right part of the hill.

Developing plans for your club will help keep the ball on the right part of the hill and keep you as an owner or manager in a proactive mode looking forward past the one-month mental blocks. No planning, coupled with the month-at-a-time mental trap, keeps you forever locked into a reactive phase and constantly worrying about what the competitor is doing instead of worrying about your own business.

Owners don't plan because they want to write the perfect plan. Any first attempt is better than no plan. A plan you wrote over lunch that has sandwich stains on it is better than no plan at all. A plan you wrote in your underwear with your laptop drinking cheap beer in the middle of the night is still better than an owner who doesn't start at all because of his need to create the perfect time and space to write the perfect business plan.

A plan you wrote over lunch that has sandwich stains on it is better than no plan at all.

What Plans Do You Really Need that Will Add to Your Business?

You have nine plans to work with that will make a difference in your business if you take the time to create them. One of the plans, the prospectus, was detailed in Chapter 13. The other eight are explained in this chapter.

Even if you can't use a computer, just the act of writing each one on a legal pad will help you get a focused start.

It should only take a few days to sit and get a working draft of these plans. Even if you can't use a computer, just the act of writing each one on a legal pad will help you get a focused start. Each year after your initial attempt you can add to your worksheets and improve your working plans over time. The nine working plans you should work on are:

A prospectus plan that is updated every year (see Chapter 13).

A one-year operational plan—This is a very detailed plan about the things you want to get done in your facility during the next year, such as adding certain equipment by a set date, launching programming in a certain month, or painting the club. This plan would contain an exact layout for each month including anticipated costs.

A three-year conceptual plan—This plan is more conceptual in nature and looks at the business with a broader view. Will there be key staff that you might lose and need to replace, can you refinance your business and lower overhead or eliminate debt, or is your lease coming up and you need to explore moving, staying, or perhaps getting your own building?

The five-year equity and/or escape plan—The primary purpose of this plan is to set a course for your long-range financial options and should include an escape plan. One constant in business planning that cannot be ignored is that nothing lasts forever. You have to prepare a five-year plan that always allows you to get out of your business if the need arises. Where will you be financially in five years, what can you do today to influence that outcome, how many units do you want if you stay in the business, and what, if any, real estate do you want to own? All of these issues need to be reviewed in a plan because the decisions you make today influence where you will be five years from today.

A 12-month staff training and development plan—The biggest breakthrough you will ever have in the business will be when you learn to manage a staff instead of a business. All long-term successful owners have eventually mastered staff leadership, training, and management. Without these skills, you are destined to run a couple of units, never take a vacation, and be held hostage by your own businesses for the rest of your career. More importantly, you will never maximize your revenue potential for the work that you do every day.

This plan should address how you are going to train and develop yourself as well as your staff. Who are your key people today and can they grow in the future? What key people are you missing that would help your business surge? Where and how will you train the people you have today on your staff? All of these questions should be answered in this plan.

A 12-month external marketing plan—Marketing should not be such a hit-and- miss affair. The biggest mistakes owners make in marketing is the lack of consistency. They simply start and stop too often to develop any real marketing brand of momentum. Marketing is accumulative, meaning you should get increasingly better results over time if you stay the course and maintain a presence. This plan should detail your marketing and associated expense for the next 12 months. Where, how much, how many leads will it take me to get how many sales, and when should I load up with an extra presence all need to be answered in this plan.

> **The biggest mistakes owners make in marketing is the lack of consistency.**

A 12-month internal promotion plan—Never forget that 95% of what you do is selling somebody something every day. Profit centers should be a big part of your business plan, but you need to have an exact layout as to how you are going to promote each center for the year. Daily sales, theme nights, special events, guest parties, month-long featured parts of the business, and the introduction of new profit centers should all be considered in this plan.

A 12-month member-service implementation plan—Customer service seldom just happens. Most owners define customer service as a little training and a lot of smiling, and the nature of the employees that are hired give the club whatever customer-service image it has. If you want to be known for customer service you have to have a 12-month implementation plan. Service has to be planned and implemented just like adding a new nutrition program or group exercise change.

A separate 12-month budget reflecting monthly deviances—This plan gives you an overview of how the money will arrive and be spent for the coming year. As discussed in Chapter 11, this annual budget should then be compared to a monthly budget written at the end of each month for the coming month.

The Components of a Plan

Every plan should have certain components that make it more effective and more likely that it will be carried out. Keep the following ideas in mind as you attempt your first planning session.

Work With an Expected Outcome

Most new plan writers build their plan from the wrong end. It seems so logical to start writing and see where you end up. Effective plans are based on expected outcome. This means you start at the end and then work backward. Start with where you want to be and then create the steps forward that will get you to that point.

For example, take something simple such as ordering equipment for your club in the next 12 months. Ineffective planning would center on just ordering the equipment while you are at a trade show and happen to be in front of a very good salesperson. Yes, you may need equipment and today is as good as time as any to order, but does getting the equipment today really help your business and did you budget for the down being spent today?

Effective planning would consider your busiest time of year, an analysis of equipment usage in the club, the replacement of equipment that is getting little use, and the age and demographics of your members. Based upon these factors, you might anticipate being slammed in February in the cardio area. The end solution would be the addition of six treadmills. Using this expected outcome, you write a plan that considers breaking the down payment into money that needs to be saved over four months, the equipment that needs to be ordered in December for a January 15th delivery date. Therefore, you would have to write a plan that includes money being moved to the accrual account in September and every month through December, contacting the equipment rep in November, and scheduling wiring needs in mid-December.

Having an expected outcome allows you to start at the end and work backward. It helps you to budget your money more efficiently and make better decisions that will lead to more money in your business.

If It Ain't In Writing, Then It Ain't Real

If it ain't in writing, then it ain't real. Putting plans into writing gives you a much higher probability of getting the plan done.

If you can ignore the poor grammar, then you'll see an important message: *putting plans into writing gives you a much higher probability of getting the plan done.* Putting it in writing is one of the cornerstones of all goal-setting courses. The theory expressed consistently in all of these courses is that the simple act of putting your thoughts into print is 90% of accomplishing the goal.

In other words, if it's in print, then your unconscious mind works toward that goal because it instinctively wants to move toward the path you have laid out with your writing. The same concept can hold true for business planning.

You have a lot of power with a plan because you'll come to work every day focused on moving the business forward as opposed to spending the day being reactionary to things you can't control. Owners working without a plan are the ones that take the biggest beating in their businesses every day. Unfortunately, without a plan, it's too easy to work an entire day and feel that you got nothing done that made you any money.

Written strategic plans, combined with action plans mentioned in Chapter 10, can give an owner and the staff a sense of accomplishment each day because they have a better standard of performance to compare themselves against. Owners and managers especially thrive on plans because they can get the feeling they've accomplished things that will ultimately make the business more money.

Include Your Management Team in the Project

Some of the plans previously mentioned will have to be done by the owner with consultation from accountants and even the banker. The five-year plan, for example, is an extension of what you want financially in your life and how you will someday walk away from your gym. Most of the planning, however, can be done as a team effort using your management team.

Plans are best written away from the gym. It's well worth the cost of putting a few of your part timers in for a few days, or relatives, and focus on getting a working draft of these plans together. Your team can help, especially on seeing the big picture of what needs to be done in the coming year and what needs fixed or improved in the gym.

> **Plans are best written away from the gym. It's well worth the cost of putting a few of your part timers in for a few days, or relatives, and focus on getting a working draft of these plans together.**

Strategic Planning Works Better When It Is Defined in Specifics

Each item in the plan should be broken down into these four points:

- What exactly do you want or what exactly should happen?
- When is this going to happen?
- How much will it cost and where is the money coming from to do it?
- How much lead-time will this project require?

If you don't include these four points, then it is not a plan; it is a wishful dream. If you can't quantify it into exact terms, then it comes off the plan and moves to those funny thoughts and kinky dreams you have the last five minutes before you fall asleep at night.

For example, imagine a 15,000-square-foot club that needs a remodel in its men's locker room. The steps for this project, and the entry in the one-year plan written in November for the coming year, should look like this:

- Set a target date when you want the project to be finished (target outcome). In this example, the club is in a northern city and the owner has slow summers so he wants the locker room to be closed and rebuilt during the slowest months if possible. Keeping this in mind, he targets September 1 as the opening date for the finished room.
- He contacts the architect who built the club in January and asks her to come and look at the new project. The architect visits the club and comes back within two weeks with these facts:
  - √ The projected cost for the project is $50,000 due to having to move and improve the plumbing.
  - √ Plans will take 30 days to create.
  - √ The project should take three weeks for the construction.

- Based upon this information, he then writes these steps and timeline in the one-year plan:

  √ Order plans from architect on April 1.

  √ Bid project during May.

  √ Start construction mid-July because of the 20/20 Plummer rule: it always takes 20% longer than promised and it will always cost 20% more than you budgeted.

  √ Starting in January, move $3,000 a month to the accrual account with a target of having saved $25,000 against the project by August 1.

  √ Approach the bank in May to borrow the rest.

  √ Set the first bank payment up in July when the small equipment lease on four treadmills is paid off.

  √ Send letters and e-mails to all members June 1, followed by a second e-mail on July 1, letting them know that the locker room will be closed for remodeling during the month of August. Give them whatever alternatives the club can offer. Add a special letter and details of the project to the club's e-newsletter in June and July with a progress report in August.

  √ Post a large artist rendition of the finished locker room July 1 in the lobby of the club. Order this sketch as part of the architect's package with the plans.

The owner has a plan that will take a lot of the last-minute pressure off of doing this project. Each day when he comes to work he can concentrate on moving this project and others in the plan ahead.

He also should be keeping control of the club through action plans and through running his business by the numbers. In this case, he is learning to manage by the numbers and to work on the business, not in the business.

Do Fewer Things But Do Them All Better

This is an old adage but one most owners should print on their foreheads so they see it in the mirror at least a few times a day. If you learn one thing in the fitness business, it's this: *The money is in the details.*

Somebody, somewhere, created a misleading rule that every new owner coming into the business secretly agrees to before he gets his first lease: only finish everything to about 80% completion and then move on to something else and only half-finish that, too. Get everything sort of done and then move on to something else.

In the gym business, the money is in the last 10% of the details. Don't just build a juice bar; build a legendary sports bar/juice bar that people come into the club just to see it. Don't just do a group program; commit to a group program that gets you on the Oprah show.

If you learn one thing in the fitness business, it's this: *The money is in the details.*

When you do something in the club, finish it to a higher standard than you are used to applying. Raise your standards by looking at businesses outside the gym business. Restaurants, sports bars, great retail businesses can all give you an idea of what a finished project looks like and feels like. Do fewer things but do them better than anyone else in the business and you'll find the money in the details.

Creating Your First Plans

Your first plans will be easier if you have a few trigger questions to get you started. The one-year plan is the most detailed of the three and should be the one done first. The rest of the plans may only be several pages and can be used to give you a sense of direction you want the business to go during the next year and beyond.

The one-year operational plan, again meaning how you are going to direct all aspects of your operation during the coming year, is usually written in conjunction with the other 12-month based plans such as the 12-month marketing plan and the 12-month member- service plan. In this example you are going to write all of the 12-month plans together.

All the components of the plan are listed here as well as questions you should use to get your thought process started. Keep in mind that these are just general trigger questions and you may have issues in your club that aren't covered here.

The One-Year Operational Plan

The one-year operational plan is just that: a plan the drives the operation during the coming calendar year. For an operational plan to be effective, it should include these components:

- 12-month budget adjusted for monthly deviances
- Physical plant plan
- Equipment replacement or addition plan
- Sales plan based on adjusted net sales goals
- Member-retention goals and implementation plan
- 12-month external marketing plan
- 12-month detailed revenue projection plan adjusted for monthly deviances
- 12-month staff-development plan
- 12-month member-service implementation plan
- 12-month internal promotion plan

The one-year operational plan is just that: a plan the drives the operation during the coming calendar year.

A one-year operational plan should answer and address the following questions and issues:

- Who in the club's infrastructure will be responsible for the implementation of these plans? Are you working too much in the business and can't work on the business? Maybe you need to hire a strong production person that can free you to grow your business?

- What profit centers need to be replaced? What profit centers need to be added? When? Are you hitting $5 per day in member visit? How much are you hitting today and what is preventing you from hitting the bigger numbers?

- What increases are you seeking in the core elements? What sales increase over last year? How will you drive this increase? How will it affect your marketing budget? How will you improve your closing percentages?

- How much will you take out personally this year? What are you going to do with this money? Have you established your retirement plan? Are you feeding this plan?

- How deep is your staff? Can you take a major hit by losing one or two key people in less than 30 days? Where is your biggest weakness in staff? Are you the problem because you are a control freak that can't let go?

- If you are going to open another club next year, can you walk away from your existing club and expect the same revenue stream? Is the next manager already on your team and being trained in your system, or are you still doing everything and aren't really prepared to grow?

- What are you going to do over the next 12 months to develop your own personal business skills? How many seminars? Where? What do you need to learn to get better? What are your weaknesses that need to be improved?

- What is your educational budget for staff training for the next 12 months and how will it be spent?

- What are the major weaknesses in your physical plant? What is the plan to correct this? How old is your design and is it more dated than you admit? Could you make more money with a total redesign? Are you better than your businesses or are your businesses better than you? Is your physical plant getting in the way of production in your company? Are people not buying memberships because of the way your gym looks and feels? Most importantly, if you finished a few key details in your business, could you make more money?

- Can you take a three-week vacation and not go out of business? If not, start with your staff structure.

- What five things could you add to your member-service presentation that would make the biggest difference to your business? What things could you add that would truly set you apart from your competitors?

- Do you have more competition than last year? Do you need to reposition

If you are going to open another club next year, can you walk away from your existing club and expect the same revenue stream?

your club against this competition? Have you outgrown your concept personally? Have you outgrown your name?

- Are you burned out on the business because you are still doing $7–per-hour work? Start with your staff and infrastructure and don't forget you might be the problem.

- Do you know what your businesses are currently worth? If not, how could you respond to an offer?

- Is there future trauma in your life such as a divorce? Have you positioned the clubs to take the hit? Do you really know all of your options, or are you working off false assumptions?

- Have your trained a strong number two that can lead your businesses if you were ill or out for an extended period of time? Start with your infrastructure.

- Do you have a person to implement a 12-month promotional plan? If not, start with your infrastructure.

Another tool you can use to build a plan and keep you focused on the important issues in the business is a one-year operational plan score sheet. This focus tool is primarily based upon the financial foundation of the business and is where every owner should start when they seek change that will lead to more revenues in the shortest period of time. All of the following numbers listed are explained elsewhere in this book. Keep in mind that scoring the sheet is easy. The more yeses you get, the more stable and productive your business will be over time.

The Three-Year Operational/Conceptual Plan

This plan should be updated once a year for three years in advance. The purpose of this plan is to give the owner a broader vision of her club, where she wants it to be in three years, and adds focus to the big concerns, such as refinancing or restructuring the business. The questions that need to answered and the issues that need to be addressed in a three-year operational/conceptual plan:

- The club owner should consider refinancing and combining debt every two years. When will you refinance your existing debt? Do you have too much debt or too little debt? Is it worth buying out partners or adding partners that will allow you to grow?

- If you are going to be open a second club, allow between 12 and 18 months for the project unless you are acquiring existing clubs. Who will run it, how will you finance it, where will it be, and what systems will you have to upgrade in your existing unit to allow you to run additional units?

- Do you have systems or a strong personality? Most clubs run off of a strong leadership/ownership personality base and don't have true systems. What are your weakest systems and how can you improve them over the next three years?

Do you have too much debt or too little debt? Is it worth buying out partners or adding partners that will allow you to grow?

315

The One-year Operational-Plan Score Sheet

1) Do you have at least one month BOE per club in reserve?

2) Do you have at least 70% of your BOE covered each month by your net billing check (draft)?

3) Out of every 100 members, do more than 10 prepay their entire membership in some form?

4) Do you have at least four profit centers in your club that net 20% or more each month?

5) Have you netted at least 20% per club for six consecutive months?

6) Is your receivable base per club at least 5 times greater than your BOE?

7) Is your yield payment at least 60% to 75% of your current price?

8) Do you have a 12-month budget in place?

9) Do you have a 12-month external marketing plan in place?

10) Do you have a 12-month member-service plan in place?

11) Do you have a 12-month internal promotional plan in place?

12) Do you have a 12-month staff-development plan in place geared toward overall staff development and individual staff enhancement?

13) Do you use staff performance contracts and action plans to drive daily production?

14) Do you use visual management with your managers and senior staff to keep them focused?

15) Would a third-party financial-service system add more stability to your business?

16) Do you use trial memberships?

17) Do you use closed-ended renewals?

18) Are you averaging $5 per day per member workouts in your profit centers?

Figure 14-1. The one-year operational-plan score sheet.

> **Very few staff will continue to grow over the years. It's best to plan their end and build in replacements today instead of becoming too dependent on key staff people.**

- What key staff should be moved on in the next few years? Very few staff will continue to grow over the years. It's best to plan their end and build in replacements today instead of becoming too dependent on key staff people. Are you people driven or systems driven? If losing a key person would dramatically affect your business, then you are personality driven and need to switch to a systems-based business over the next three years.

- Every club needs to be reinvented from the ground up every three or four years. Concepts wear out, members age, owners especially age, and the competition usually increases at a more sophisticated rate. What will have to change in your concept to keep you competitive in the next three years? What will have to change in your physical plant to keep your members in the club in the next three years? If you didn't have a club, what type would you open today? Can you get your existing club to that level in the next three years?

- Where do you want to be financially in the next three years? You have to learn to take money out of the club and pay yourself first. Nothing lasts forever including your clubs. Do you have an escape plan? How far can you go with a plan if you start today and work on it for the next three years in your business?

Concepts wear out, members age, owners especially age, and the competition usually increases at a more sophisticated rate.

The Five-Year Conceptual Plan

This plan should be updated once a year for five years in advance. The expected outcome of a five-year plan is to develop an escape plan for the owner, review equity options, and do long-range planning for additional units. This plan should also be heavily focused on retirement planning. The questions that need to be answered and the issues that need to be addressed in a five-year conceptual plan:

- If market conditions changed dramatically, do you have a financial escape plan from your clubs? Have you done all the things necessary to sell the clubs at the maximum dollar if the time came? Can you take enough money out of your units during the next five years to either start again or to get into another business? Have you protected yourself legally to walk away from the clubs and still get out financially solvent if everything went wrong at once? Do you know what your clubs are worth?

- All leases should be negotiated with the option to buy the building or plaza. Can you acquire your buildings during the next five years? Have you trained the next buyers of your clubs, meaning your existing managers? Is it worth moving an existing unit into a building you can buy? Is the next remodel serious enough to justify a new building anyway?

- Where do you want to be personally in the next five years in the fitness industry? Do you want to teach at national trade shows? Do you want to be more involved in your national license group? What are you doing to keep the business fresh and exciting?

- Can partners be bought out in the next five years giving you an advantage of then selling the business for maximum dollars and taking an additional profit on the buyout? Have you outgrown the need for partners and can you rely on the banks for growth?

- Do you have too little debt? Can you refinance the clubs, take out the cash, and build an overnight portfolio that is serviced by the clubs and becomes part of the monthly operating expense? Do all of your units need to be refinanced during the next five years anyway to reinvent your concept and move the clubs to another level of play?

- How many units in how many years? Do you have a growth plan dictated by owning your market and strategically placing units against your competitors? Have you done the demographic research for your next units? Do you have weak competitors in your area actually worth buying that could speed your growth?

- Have you contacted a lawyer and explored trusts for your kids, tax shelters for your money, and other advanced ways of looking at your money?

The 12-Month Staff-Training Plan

As mentioned earlier, the biggest breakthrough you will ever have in the business will be when you learn to manage a staff trained in production instead of running a business. Staffing and effective management are skills any owner can learn and master, and in fact has to if she wants to have a life at all outside the business. Flat revenues and high turnover are all signs you have a poor infrastructure in your business and things will not change until you deal with staff development and training for them and yourself.

The questions that need to be answered and the issues that need to be addressed in a 12-month staff-training plan:

- All staff training should be planned for the year but all of the key elements should be repeated each quarter. For example, basic accounting procedures for the senior management team should be repeated at least four times a year and core training such as handling the phones should be offered weekly.

- All procedures in the gym should be broken down into repeatable formats. For example, how to make a shake at the juice bar should be a one-hour course that is repeated monthly.

- All training should result in a certificate. An accumulation of certificates should result in a pay increase. The basic one-hour training sessions, such as how to make a shake, basic front-counter computer skills, or how to fill out a contract, should be repeated monthly. These might only be worth one credit with a certificate. More advanced topics, such as closing out the register at the end of the day, might warrant more than one hour and might be worth two credits. Management and leadership training, such as a four-hour leadership seminar on how to manage junior employees, might be worth four to five credits. Ten credits might be worth a $1-per-hour raise with a maximum of 30 credits possible in a year's period of time.

- The senior managers should have their own training monthly with more in-depth one or two day training done quarterly.

- The second-level and third-level managers in each club should have their own training monthly and more in-depth training done quarterly.

> **All procedures in the gym should be broken down into repeatable formats. For example, how to make a shake at the juice bar should be a one-hour course that is repeated monthly.**

- The entire senior management team should be trained together quarterly for at least two days at a time. Remember, a major breakthrough for most owners is when they learn to manage a staff instead of running their business every day. The work you put into training will come back to you in increased revenues.

- If you are not comfortable training your staff then train yourself first. More effective owners dedicate at least one day a week to personal development in seminars offered in their areas. Bring this information back to work and teach it to your team.

- If you don't have anyone to train, build an infrastructure first and then start your training program. Your BOE will increase slightly but your revenues will increase even more if you build the proper staff model. Your first addition should be someone that can help you with daily production in sales and selling profit centers.

- The entire staff should get at least four hours of training per week from their managers and from you. Train with a plan and repeat the basics so the new people will have a chance to earn their certificates. Individual training should be done by the managers as needed and can even be done in small, five- minute increments.

- The entire staff, including the janitors and group instructors, should receive basic salesmanship training every other month. If you do not have a sales training manual, write one as soon as possible, or hire on outside trainer who will leave you with a manual you can use in the future.

- Send your senior managers on the road often. Education is considered a perk by staff and is a motivational tool. IHRSA shows, Thomas Plummer Company events, and other non-industry events are all places to start when you build a training schedule.

- Set up a reading program for the management team. Pick about five books that you believe will benefit them, set up small essay exams to make sure they read the books, and then give them small bonuses for reading them.

- Weekly staff meetings for all full-timers are mandatory. The best time to have a staff meeting is Tuesday, Wednesday, or Thursday mornings around 7:30 for an hour and a half. Keep it functional, educational, and include at least one if not two 15-minute training blocks in the meeting. Remember that you always praise in public and chew ass in private. Don't use these meetings as complaint sessions. And yes, you should pay those not on the clock a minimum training wage of about $6 per hour.

- Build a solid number-two person you can count on in your system. If you had to step out of your business for a month could it survive? If not, then start building a backup immediately and let this person take part in the training. And don't forget to train a backup for your backup.

If you are not comfortable training your staff then train yourself first.

319

- Use action plans as the core to driving your performance. Remember from Chapter 10 that action plans are daily performance sheets that give the employee direction and the tools they need to do their job each day. The managers then manage performance by coaching from the plans.

This means that you train employees to follow set steps outlined in procedures manuals, and not decision making based on the situation at hand.

- Practice linear training progressions. This means that you train employees to follow set steps outlined in procedures manuals, and not decision making based on the situation at hand. Having set procedures will get an employee ramped up and ready to produce faster than having to teach decision making dependent upon the situation at hand. Set procedures for common occurrences in the club also give the staff confidence that they can then handle the situation without your help.

The 12-Month Customer Service Plan

Service is not a random act of kindness. The best businesses plan their customer service around the premise that they truly want to exceed the member's expectations. Delivering customer service is a learned skill just like learning to give someone a workout, teaching a group exercise class, or learning to sell a membership. It takes a coach, a standard of what's acceptable and what's not, and a lot of training and practice over time. Customer service will lead to higher member retention and should be just as important to your business plan as selling memberships.

The questions that need to be answered and the issues that need to be addressed in a 12-month customer-service plan:

- Objectively determine where you are at today for customer service and then build an expected outcome of where you want to be in 12 months

- Survey the members heavily and start to learn a new definition of what customer service is really like. What the members want and what the club offers is seldom the same.

- Study one really good role model at a time and then add key components you see being practiced in that business. Unfortunately, you won't find many good role models in this industry, but when you do, make them your mentors.

- What 12 things, implemented at the rate of one per month, would set you apart from your competitors and meet the high standards you found in your role model?

- Who in your club will take responsibility for customer-service training on an ongoing basis? If you don't have anyone that can take the responsibility, start with your infrastructure.

- How often do you survey your members about service? What are you looking for when you do survey? Are you actually sitting with the members and asking or leaving it up to junior staff and questionnaires? Surveys and more information on customer service can be found in depth in the first Thomas Plummer book listed in the resource guide.

- In the next few years it will all come down to who has the best service. The competition can buy the same equipment and build the same physical plant you can. The only thing that will separate you is your customer service and the training you give your people. Do you have a 12-month customer-service plan and a 12-month customer-service staff-training plan in place?

The 12-Month External Marketing Plan

Clubs prosper if the owners can stabilize a steady stream of leads through the club. Times have changed in the industry and it is no longer possible or cost effective to have salespeople responsible for having to drive traffic through the door.

Effective long-term marketing, coupled with using trial memberships, will drive sufficient potential memberships through the door each month. The key to making this happen is to create a consistent marketing approach for the club.

The issues that need to be addressed for creating a 12-month external marketing plan:

Effective long-term marketing, coupled with using trial memberships, will drive sufficient potential memberships through the door each month.

- Build the plan around cost effective core elements such as direct mail and flyer inserts. Most clubs should start by sending at least 2,500 direct mail pieces out per week all year long.

- Create an electronic immediate response system where you can get seven to eight pages of information into someone's hands within minutes. This can be done with e-mail and should be something every salesperson has available as a tool. This is also a step done before you would point someone to the club's website.

- The trial membership, as detailed heavily in the first Thomas Plummer book, is your core marketing tool and should be part of every piece you send out.

- Testimonials are far more effective than semi-naked model ads and less offensive to your potential members.

- Seek deals with your vendors if you commit to a 12-month marketing plan.

- Focus your all of your marketing within a 15-minute drive time from your club. At least 80% to 85% of your membership base will come from that ring.

The 12-Month Internal Promotion Plan

Your goal is to generate at least $5 per day per member visit from the profit centers in the club. Doing this requires an effective promotion plan that keeps what you have to sell in the member's faces. Members like to buy but only if they are teased, tantalized, taunted, and tempted to purchase what you have on sale. Your 12-month plan should focus on building awareness and selling more product to members you already have in the gym and who already have taken the first step by buying a membership.

The issues that need to be addressed for a 12-month internal promotion plan:

Start with a limited number of profit centers, usually no more than four or five, and master these before you move forward with any more.

- Start with a limited number of profit centers, usually no more than four or five, and master these before you move forward with any more.

- Add new profit centers slowly, no more than one every three months and master that center before adding other.

- Consider taking retail classes during the coming year as part of your plan.

- Something needs to be on sale every day in the club. Create a 12-month plan that has one major event a month, such as a theme night, in conjunction with other minor events such as a Monday Madness party.

- Plan all of your events and sales for the year in advance. The number one reason events and promotions fail in clubs is that the owner and her team started too late. Most successful events need at least 90 to 120 days to be promoted properly and pulled off; don't try and do one within two weeks. Hanging handwritten signs on a wall two weeks before an event isn't going to get you the success you might anticipate.

- Divide your internal promotions into two categories: those focused on moving profit centers and those focused on creating new sales through guest events and parties.

- Other companies, such as PromoCoach, are listed in the resource guide at the end of the book. These companies specialize in helping clubs manage their 12-month promotions. If you aren't confident you can create and manage your own program, you might consider using one of these companies.

The Prospectus Plan and the 12-Month Budget

Both of these plans are detailed in other parts of the book, but you should also consider the following key points in regards to overall strategic planning.

- The prospectus should be updated once a year just in case you have to make a bank presentation or need a major equipment lease. The basics can be kept current and the details can be added as the situation arises.

- Write a 12-month overall budget at the end of the year as part of your one-year planning session. Use this big-picture view to compare your monthly budgets with your managers. The 12-month budget can also be added to any bank package since it is an obvious tool a banker would love to see and very few businesses create as part of their normal package.

Summary on Plans and Planning

Gym people don't plan. Business people plan. In the last five years, a whole new breed of owner has entered the gym business. In the past, the same types of people who started restaurants started gyms. These people were seldom business people but they were folks very passionate and emotional about what they did.

Restaurants have traditionally had a very high failure rate because of the owners they attract. These people dream of having a little Mom-and-Pop place where they work the tables, host the bar, and serve carefully prepared food from family or favorite recipes. They lay awake at night dreaming about building the perfect place to eat because they know they will be different and customers will love to hang out with them.

Two weeks after they are opened reality sets in. Restaurants are 100-hour-per- week nightmares with high turnover, high theft, and work at a pace that will leave the soft and the weak in the dust crying for their mothers.

The fitness business still attracts these dreamers who believe if you build it they will come. They too lay awake at night building the perfect gym room by room and can't wait to open so they can show everyone else how it is done. They don't need business skills because they are great trainers or group people who can do it better than anyone else and no place they have ever worked has really let them show their skills.

It doesn't even take two weeks after opening to realize you are in someone else's nightmare. Employees, broken toilets, marketing, advertising, accountants, taxes, and ill-mannered, bad tempered, poorly dressed fat-for-life members can all kill the passion in a very short time.

The new owners coming into the arena are business people who also happen to like the fitness industry. These owners understand the great financial potential in the business but they also understand foremost that it is a business and has all the rules and obligations that govern all good successful businesses.

If you want to be in same game as these people and also live your dream, you need to become a businessperson, and business people plan beyond the month they are living in today. Remember:

Business people plan their businesses one to five years in the future and run them proactively.

Gym people don't plan and run their businesses one month at a time.

This contest isn't fair and will result in a severe financial beating for the gym people unless they change the rules by planning.

Business people plan their businesses one to five years in the future and run them proactively.

The Key Points You Should Have Gotten from this Chapter

A good plan today is worth much more than a perfect plan later (or never).

- You have to break the month-to-month mindset held by most owners.

- A good plan today is worth much more than a perfect plan later (or never).

- You should utilize nine separate plans that add focus and direction to your business.

- Plan backward by starting with the expected outcome.

- Plans must be written or they are nothing more than dreams.

- Include your team in the writing of your plans.

- Plans need to be specific in detail.

- Do fewer things but finish them. The money is in the details.

- Ideal planning is done in November for the following year.

- Not writing a plan is planning -- planning to fail.

- Gym types don't write plans. Business people write plans. You can be both.

Accountants and Business Valuations Are Two Areas Neglected by Most Owners

Most owners get into the fitness business because of their passion for some aspect of the fitness lifestyle. These owners are seldom prepared for the business world they are entering and often give up too much control of their businesses to other business professionals, such as accountants. If an owner is going to become successful at being a small businessperson, he needs to understand how to approach and guide accounting professionals through the nuances of the fitness business.

Another issue neglected by most owners is that they don't know what their most valuable asset is worth, which is the business itself. *Business valuation* is a science and an art and every owner should understand at least the basic concepts of small business valuation.

This section covers two of the more neglected areas of small business: how to work with an accountant without giving up total control of your business and how to value a small business. Business valuation is a very complex subject, but Chapter 16 should give any owner a basic guide in valuing their business.

These final two chapters may seem like they don't belong, but a typical owner will rely on accountant to the extent that he will let the accountant make decisions in the business. One of these decisions that is so important is how to value a business if a sale should ever occur. Learning to work with an accountant is the first step toward adding a team of business professionals to your business support group.

- **Chapter 15: Working with an Accountant**
- **Chapter 16: Building a Business that Will Sell for Top Dollars**

15

Working with an Accountant

The most important thing you should get from this chapter is:

Getting the most out of the accountant/gym owner relationship begins with understanding what you really want from your accountant.

Definitions and concepts you will need to know:

- *Accounting:* The language of business that very few small business owners can understand or speak.

- Standard accounting practices were not designed for small businesses.

- Accounting is a system of recording your past numbers, but not projecting your future numbers.

- Accountants know accounting. Accountants know tax. Accountants don't always know business.

- To get the most out of your accountant/owner relationship, you have to learn to give direction as to what you want and need to see.

- Accountants for small businesses should not be just black or white in their belief system. Good accountants operate in the gray, aggressively seeking the maximum legal breaks you can get.

Learning to Get the Most Out of the Owner/Accountant Relationship

This chapter was written with contributing material from Steve Parker, a partner in Hopkins, Parker and Company, PLC, in Scottsdale, Arizona. Steve is the Director of Marketing and Financial Planning for the firm. He is a Certified Public Accountant, a Certified Financial Planner, and holds a Master Degree in Taxation from Golden Gate University in San Francisco. Steve helps successful entrepreneurs with advanced tax strategies, creditor protection, and business continuation planning.

The relationship always starts out with wine and roses, but it isn't long before most business owners end up with an adversarial relationship with their accountants.

The relationship always starts out with wine and roses, but it isn't long before most business owners end up with an adversarial relationship with their accountants. Signs that this marriage may be failing are statements no one bothers to read that get tossed in a drawer, calls to the accountant only when the bank wants something for a loan, resentment because of the seemingly petty charges for phone calls and simple requests, and the overall feel that this relationship just isn't working.

This owner may want to change accountants, but he has been there before and knows that another accountant will soon just turn out to be the same thing again. The problem is most likely not with the accountant but with the approach the owner takes in working with his most important business support partner.

Accounting is often the language of business, a romantic take on an otherwise straightforward and boring profession, at least to those in the fitness business who get to wear fun clothes and jump up and down with semi-naked people all day long. Unfortunately, it is a language, similar to ancient Sanskrit or medieval German, which very few small business owners can speak or understand. When an accountant talks extensively on a subject to a club owner sitting in a plain claustrophobic office with white walls and degrees from colleges only geeks who can't do fitness go to, it is similar to a person talking to his dog. Blah, blah, blah, blah, Lucky, blah, blah, blah. The owner only hears his name and little else translates or gets through the protective shield of glaze over the eyes.

If an owner is to be truly successful he must learn to communicate in this language and to be able to direct an accountant in the direction the club owner wants to go. Left alone, accountants have to make judgment calls trying to guess what best fits the needs of this particular client.

Why accounting is a difficult language to learn for most small business owners has very clear reasons. Understanding why it is difficult is the first step in understanding how you can better use accounting information, and your accountant, to better manage and understand the dynamics of the small business world you function in every day.

- *Reason Number One: Accounting standards, the basic rules, practices, and procedures shared by all accountants are designed to provide information for very large and usually publicly traded companies.*

The end user of this information is often other accountants or other types of financially sophisticated readers such as financial analysts and investors. This style of accounting is often referred to as the investor model and is designed, according to most accounting texts to "present fairly the financial position and financial results of a company on a consistent and comparable basis."

As a gym owner it's easy to laugh at and make fun of the two accountants involved in a discussion of deep accounting issues at the table next to you at lunch. Stories of geeks or nerds in ties come to mind and other comments about glasses and pocket protectors. But the language and culture of the fitness business is probably just as strange to them as their language is to us.

The bigger problem is that as small business owners you never had a chance in the first place. Besides being an incomprehensible language, you also find that basic accounting standards were never written for you. The language of accounting was written for financial professionals as a tool of comparison and evaluation for investors and other financial professionals who are seeking a consistent comparative format to compare a diverse assortment of businesses.

Nowhere in this model are separate standards, or an easier language, dedicated to providing management information useful for the control and management of a small business with less than 50 employees. Fifty full-time employees don't seem like a lot, but it is a real definer of just what a small business is and how it is managed.

Another way to look at this is that the goals of a small business and a large business are the same, but at the same time different. Both hope to show a profit and give a return-on-investment to the owners. The difference is that the big businesses have accounting departments that generate reports to aid in the management of the company, but more importantly provides a means of evaluation for potential investors since the other companies that an investor is considering provides the same general reporting and uses the same general accounting.

Your goal as owner of a small business is totally different. You need to make a decision today and you need viable financial information today that can help you make that management decision effectively.

You need your accounting to provide information to help you run your business better. The large companies need information that paints the best picture possible so investors will continue to invest. It is hard to tweak a system that was never designed for the guy that wants to use it.

You need to make a decision today and you need viable financial information today that can help you make that management decision effectively.

- *Reason Number Two: Accounting is based on a historical cost system, meaning the only information you will ever get on your statements is based upon the past.*

Running a business off of financial statements is sort of like driving a car that has a rear view mirror, but where the windshield should be is just solid metal with no way to look out. You might know where you have been but you have absolutely no way of knowing where you are going.

Big businesses are like monstrous oil tankers. They lumber along and if they want to change direction it might take them three miles just to do that. Change of direction is slow and something done over time.

Small business is like a jet boat running down a wild river canyon. Decision-making has to be immediate and based upon the conditions that might present themselves today.

Small business is like a jet boat running down a wild river canyon. Decision-making has to be immediate and based upon the conditions that might present themselves today.

The historical nature of accounting is designed for the lumbering tankers of the world because they have the time and room to move. Accounting and the information gotten from most standard issue financial statements were never designed for someone driving a speedboat and hanging on for dear life.

- *Reason Number Three: Accounting is a cost-based system requiring most financial information from your business to be stated as a cost without respect to what the true value might be.*

The most obvious representation of this weakness in the normal practice of accounting for small business is the purchase of your first building. Your true financial situation is that you just purchased the biggest asset of your life that most likely will appreciate over time and be a big part of your retirement.

Accounting standards, however, require the building to be carried on the balance sheet at the actual purchase price of the building. These rules of accounting then allow for an annual expense charge (depreciation) for a fraction of this original cost.

On paper you are losing value on your main asset. In reality, you are increasing the value of your business and building by gaining appreciation in your asset. You have no provision in accounting standards that allows you to record this increase in value.

- *Reason Number Four: Financial reporting is a static system in that it generally presents financial information as a fixed point in time or period whether it is a month, a quarter, or a year.*

The analogy at this point is a picture of jet fighter plane hanging on your office wall. By just looking at the picture it is almost impossible to tell just what the jet is doing at the time. Is it at an air show? Is it on maneuvers somewhere in a war zone? Was the picture just taken to hang on a wall? For the picture to make sense, you would have to see a series of these pictures, taken over a period of time, to give you a sense of direction and mission.

Standardized financial information is a fixed picture in time of your business and tells very little as to the direction of your business. Even adjustments to standardized statements that show the entire historical picture of the business year-to-year doesn't give enough information to project your business into the future.

In other words, as a small business owner, if you keep doing what you're doing, where will this lead you into the future? Financial reporting is a picture of where you are at a fixed period in time, and shows where you have been, but is a poor projector of where you and your business are going.

- *Reason Number Five: Accountants, meaning Certified Public Accountants (CPAs), are by training and licensing supposed to act as true independents providing a high level of integrity to the public.*

Accountants have to follow the rules that guide their profession and that are the core elements in the licensing and training that allows them to practice. Rules are rules and by following these guidelines they assume an independent stance in their profession.

For example, you need to borrow money from the bank but last year's statements were flat. This year, however, you have turned the business around and are back on track financially in your business.

When you present your statements to the bank, the banker has a certain level of trust in these statements because they were prepared by an independent CPA whose job is not working for you the client, but as a fair and independent representative of the accounting profession.

You would not want to have a CPA that would fabricate statements, but as a small business owner fighting for a loan you don't need an independent accountant who in essence is working for the bank, or worse the IRS.

Because of this independent position, accountants are presenting your numbers in a standardized form that will assist the banker or auditor more than they will help you. What you really need at this point is an advocate who will present your case in the best light and help you secure money.

Because you are in small business, you normally don't have the resources to hire a sophisticated internal accountant that will be an advocate for you and your business. This leaves you working with an independent that is far more concerned about maintaining that status than growing your business.

Where does all of this leave the average small business owner? You are working with someone who speaks another language that takes a great deal of practice and training to understand, who is using a set series of practical standards designed for businesses that gross in the hundreds of millions compared to your $3,000,000 or less per unit, and uses a system that records nothing but history.

You would not want to have a CPA that would fabricate statements, but as a small business owner fighting for a loan you don't need an independent accountant who in essence is working for the bank, or worse the IRS.

This same system is also incapable of representing the true assets of the business and uses a static viewpoint that fixes a business at an exact point in time without any indication of what future performance might be. And don't forget that despite what you pay your accountant, he is truly an independent following rules designed to assist your bankers and the IRS far more than they assist you. And after all of this you still can't live without them, flawed or not.

Thousands of CPAs all over the country devote their lives to helping small businesses survive. In most cases, it is not the accountant that is the problem; it is the system they follow. But most importantly, it is the small business owner, due to the difficulty of learning the new language and who is unwilling to master that part of their business, who is the true problem.

Leadership will fill a void and small business owners are notorious for abdicating all control to their accountant. Accountants, left with little or no guidance, and not being an expert in our business, will do the best they can to provide the service the client needs. To get the most out of the small business owner/accountant relationship, start with these points in mind:

Accountants know accounting and taxation, but that does not make them business experts in the management and development of a fitness business, or any other business for that matter.

- Accountants know accounting and taxation, but that does not make them business experts in the management and development of a fitness business, or any other business for that matter. Their job is to record your decisions, not to make your decisions for you. In other words, you make the decision and several months from then they will tell you if it was a good one. Then they will figure out the tax implications.

- Accountants are capable and business-orientated people who can give you the information you need for your business if you know what you are asking for and why, while you're giving them the direction they need to do a good job for you.

- Accountants have totally different personalities, just as gym owners do. You need to find one that matches you and the way you do business. If you are ultra-conservative you should find an ultra-conservative accountant. If you are more on the edgy side you will still end up with a conservative accountant, but he might wear wild ties just to make you happy. Edgy owners still need an anchor and often it is your accountant. Keep in mind they are accountants with limits as to how wild they can be.

- Educate your accountant about the fitness business and if possible, get them to a trade show or seminar. They will do a better job for you if they have a wider view of the industry.

- All accountants hate last-minute people. If you are going to develop systems that will enable you to make better decisions in your business, you need to get your information to the accountant in a timely fashion. It's your fault if you're last minute and then expect it to be done tomorrow. If your accountant is a last-minute person after you have done your part in a timely manner, get a new accountant.

What Do You Need and Want from Your Accountant?

You will get the most from your accountant if you provide guidance on what you need, when you need it, and what it will do for your company. If accountants have that information they can usually tweak it to provide any type of report you want. The following are a few of the things you'll need from your financial professional.

Management Information

In Chapters 9 and 10 the numbers you need to track in your business that will help you transform from being reactive to proactive were discussed. These numbers are unique to your business and represent information that an accountant is not trained to get for you since he is not familiar with the intricate operations of a fitness business.

Your accountant can, however, take these numbers and turn them into *functional reports* that can be used as a *management tool*. For example, when you submit your normal data to be prepared for statements you can also submit your sale information as well.

The accountant can then add the sales information, such as the total amount of leads for the month, total number of annual sales, and the closing rates for the team and individual salespeople, to your financial statements as an addendum. The accountant can then tie the new information to your historical sales data and generate year-to-year comparisons and trend lines that will help you manage more effectively. This will also help you with bank loans since you are presenting knowledge of your business few other owners have.

Yes, you could do this yourself, but a compiled statement with all the information in one report instead of 13 random piles is far more likely to help you get an idea of where your business is today.

You will also find numbers that are pertinent to your own management style that would be powerful to add to your compiled reporting. Keep a list of the numbers you look for each day and then sit down with your accountant and build a report that can be added to your financial package.

Cash-Flow Information

Cash flow is the lifeblood of any small business since most owners don't have the financial resources to float major deficits if they occur. In Chapter 10, you were presented with a daily cash-flow position report that can be used as a tool to track your daily position in relationship to your incoming and outgoing cash, and how much you need to make by the end of the month to pay your bills. Your accountant can use this basic management tool

Cash flow is the lifeblood of any small business since most owners don't have the financial resources to float major deficits if they occur.

designed for owners and turn it into a part of your monthly statements that gives you a bigger picture of your cash position for the month. For example, the form would look something like Figure 15-1.

Beginning cash position at the beginning of the month
Checking-account balances at the start of the month
Payroll accounts
Money-market accounts
Savings accounts
Other cash-holding accounts

Cash inflows
Gross revenues for the last month
Other club revenue such as rents

Cash outflows (only actual cash taken out of the business – not depreciation or amortization or any other non-cash expense)
Payables for the last month
Other club expenses beyond normal payables last month
Anticipated payables for this month

Ending cash balances at the end of the month
Checking account balances at the end of the month
Payroll accounts
Money-market accounts
Savings accounts
Other cash-holding accounts
Loan balances including interest and principle – just the payment and the outstanding balance

---

Figure 15-1.

Your goal with Figure 15-1 is to remove all accrual or non-cash related items, therefore giving you a more accurate cash position for the business at the start of the month. This would be a very valuable tool if you could get it during the first five days of the month.

Dynamic Information about Your Business

You can relate this information to the concept of *base and trend line*. Where is the business today and what are the trends at this point in time? For example, you know that it cost you more to run your business today because the monthly total on the statements, and the pain of writing the checks, reflect that you are spending more than you used to in the past. But that is all the statement tells you.

Review the fighter-plane analogy from earlier in this chapter. That single picture represents a month's financial statement for your business. Both are

Where is the business today and what are the trends at this point in time?

static and give an image of that point in time, but unless you are a really trained financial statement expert, or pilot, it's hard to ascertain more from that snapshot. For example, if you are a pilot, you might notice something about the approximate altitude of the plane, where the flaps are, wheel status, or something else only a trained pilot would see.

An accountant with experience could dissect your statements and give a better story that goes beyond the single point in time. You on the other hand, being a small business owner and not a trained financial professional that has dedicated years to learning the nuances of statement analysis, are limited in your vision.

One of the expectations you should have for your accountant is that he take the static reports you already have and uses them as a base to create dynamic information that shows trend lines and comparisons. This is very basic report and any accountant will do it if you ask. What you are asking for is a report that shows comparisons between certain time periods including a percentage of change either up or down over time.

For example, you might look at expenses laid out on the same page for the last three years, including the percentage of overall expense for each category and the change in percentage of each expense over the three-year period compared to today. Going back to the fighter-plane analogy again, this is similar to adding more pictures of the plane over the next hour of its flight. If you had a picture every five minutes you could get an idea of its movement and position and also get a much better idea of where it is going by the trend of movement in the pictures. The key points to remember are:

- Compare each month to the same month last year.

- Each quarter compare the overall performance of that quarter against the same quarter last year.

- At the end of the year, or more often, compare the total year against the last five years you have been in business, although three years may be sufficient if you have made major changes somewhere in that time period and the earlier information would not be relevant.

- Comparing the expenses and the percentage of each category to the overall expense of the business is the most important part of this since it is also what most owners let slip. If the revenues are up, the expenses rise behind them. Your goal is to keep the revenues and the expenses as far apart as possible so make sure an expense comparison is part of your monthly financial package

> **Comparing the expenses and the percentage of each category to the overall expense of the business is the most important part of this since it is also what most owners let slip.**

Timeliness with Your Financial Package

Timeliness may be the hardest issue of any financial relationship. Even in a perfect world, by the time you get your statements back from the bank and your check stubs off to the accountant, and assuming he turns those statements around immediately, you still won't have any information until at least the middle of the month.

In a more accurate description, you probably won't get your statements back until the end of the month or even at the end of the quarter. The information by that time is stale and way beyond use to help in any type of decision-making process in your business. That is why the majority of statements just get tossed in a drawer when they arrive; by the time you get them, and if you could read them, they are too late to help you with decisions you had to make a month ago.

An area your accountant should be able to help you in, although some of the old-school guys still haven't embraced computers in their accounting practices, is with the installation and use of a professional accounting software system for your club such as QuickBooks. This type of system should allow you to generate working statements any day of the month you need them and then the electronic file is sent to your accountant at the end of the month for reconciliation.

If you use this type of system get your accountant to help you establish account codes so your taxes and end-of-year work will be easier. Also make sure that your accountant sets up statements that are cash flow in nature. You don't need to know your depreciation mid-month, but it would be nice to know what your statement looks like that specific day in relation to cash in and cash out. Once you establish this type of system you can then expect statements from the accountant by the 10th of the month reconciled and including your other requested financial information.

Tax Planning Has to be a Proactive Process that Begins with You

Proactive tax planning is not something usually found in a typical accountant's repertoire. Accountants know the deadlines for taxes being filed, gather your information as it comes in, and then once numbers are put in the right little boxes they inform you that you are going to have some serious tax problems this year. They gave you the right information, but they gave it to you far too late to do anything about it.

One of the most important things you want from your accountant is ongoing tax guidance available at least monthly. You and your accountant discuss where you are, what is happening in your business, and then apply that information to your expected tax liability while you still have time to make changes that might affect the final outcome.

You should then go proactive at least 60 days prior to the end of your tax year and work with the accountant to get an anticipated year-end idea of the expected damage. This far out also gives you enough time to make changes and take actions that can reduce your tax liability.

It is your responsibility, and not your accountant's, to actively inquire

> One of the most important things you want from your accountant is ongoing tax guidance available at least monthly.

monthly and to seek opinions about anything that happens in your business that might change your tax position at the end of the year. For example, if you buy equipment, call your accountant. If you have noticed your profits are up for three months in a row over last year, call your accountant. If you have extra money and want to reduce your debt, call your accountant first and find out what your overall tax responsibility is going to be if you take that action.

Financing and Bank Relations

This is about the only place that traditional CPA-prepared financial statements, accompanied by all the necessary disclaimers, really come in handy. Almost all financing today works with a banker applying a series of preset ratios to your numbers, such as debt to equity. If the ratios are right you get the money, and if not you get a chance to explain and perhaps try again or you are turned down.

Any of these statements can be enhanced, however, with the specialty reports you asked your accountant to generate. Bankers want to be comfortable when they loan money and nothing makes them happier than to give money to somebody who knows what the heck is happening in their business.

For example, look at the process of presenting a business plan to get a loan. As mentioned elsewhere in this book, according to bankers who do commercial loans for a living only 4 out of 10 people who apply for a loan have a business plan, and then only one out of four can defend the plan. This means their accountant did the plan for them and that three out of four owners don't understand what they just presented.

Finding an Accountant You Can Work with in Your Business

Every phone book in every town is filled with accountants and tax professionals. Unfortunately, this is much like choosing a surgeon; you really don't know how good he is until you wake up after the surgery.

A common mistake many owners make is that they want an accountant to be in an office somewhere next to the club. With the advent of e-mail, modems, and faxes, your accountant doesn't have to be that close to be effective. The important thing is that you find someone who can become an effective part of your management support system for your business. Consider the following points when choosing a financial professional:

Rapport—You have many choices in the accounting field, so don't settle for someone you don't enjoy working with as part of your management team. Look for someone who will take an interest in your business, who has worked with a number of other small businesses, and someone who might match your personality and style of business. Another point to this is that it

Every phone book in every town is filled with accountants and tax professionals. Unfortunately, this is much like choosing a surgeon; you really don't know how good he is until you wake up after the surgery.

helps to find someone that actually belongs to a gym and is a member somewhere. This person will at least understand some part of what goes on in a fitness business.

Technical competence—If you want to find an accountant who can make a difference in your business, you are going to have to interview more than one. Technical competence is one of the things you are looking for, yet it is also one of the hardest things to judge directly unless you too are a financial expert. Ask for an appointment and let the person know up front that you are going to interview several accountants for your business. Tell them a little about your business but also ask them about themselves, their hobbies, and other outside interests. After you get a feel for their interests and how they communicate, give them a copy of your latest tax return and statements and ask them if they have any ideas that might improve your tax and financial situation. If you talk to several different people it won't take long to find one who has ideas and suggestions that will help you.

Some owners have more fear of being audited than they do of dying in a flaming car wreck. Others want their accountants to be a Star Trek captain and go where no accountant has gone before, giving them extremely aggressive advice on their tax matters.

Risk tolerance—Some owners have more fear of being audited than they do of dying in a flaming car wreck. Others want their accountants to be a Star Trek captain and go where no accountant has gone before, giving them extremely aggressive advice on their tax matters. It is important to find a tax professional who shares your risk tolerance for audits.

The recommendation for a fitness-business owner is to find an accountant who will push hard for any legal deduction that can be defended in an audit. Aggressive but defensible deductions are the only way to maximize your tax savings over the years. Many accountants are too conservative and fear an audit more than the business owner does. The fear of being audited, however, is not a reason to avoid taking a clearly legal but aggressive deduction, since the worst that can happen is you were right but wrong. Yes, that is a legal deduction, but no, you can't use it for your business. You tax situation may change at that point but your are fighting a fair and legal fight to save the most money you can.

The Supreme Court has stated, "There is nothing wrong in structuring ones business in a manner which avoids tax." If your accountant frequently points out that if you take this deduction you may get audited, then always counter with the questions, "Is this deduction legal?" If yes, then take the deduction because it is poor business to pay extra tax because you are afraid to get audited.

Another way to look at this is that some accountants work only in the black-and-white areas. A deduction to them is either right or wrong. A more aggressive accountant can work in the gray areas. This type of accountant would say this deduction might work but you are pushing it a little. This is the type of accountant a small business owner needs; one who can venture into the gray areas because he has no fear of defending his decision.

Fees—Like anything else in the world, including a health club membership, you get what you pay for when it comes to paying professional fees. In the accounting field, it is seldom the lowest bidder who has the greatest ideas and tax strategies, both which can save you thousands of dollars per year. Avoid first year guys, your brother-in-law who just got out of school, and other family friends you will live to regret unless they truly are qualified professionals. Focus more on finding someone you can work with and who can give you the information you need to grow your business and pay the least amount of taxes possible.

Fees should be discussed up front and you need to know how much, how you will be billed, and when your bill will arrive with the proper documentation to support the bill. You are the client and you have the right to understand what you are paying for and why and the accountant has an obligation to verify how the bill was determined. Owners are not good at this and usually don't question how a bill was arrived at. Understand how and why you were billed and challenge the bills that don't make sense.

How to Work with an Accountant

Once you have chosen an accountant, you should begin to *manage the relationship*. This is not the time to take a passive approach and let your accountant decide how you will work together. Before the actual accounting work begins, meet in person or have a conference over the phone to establish expectations from both sides.

Discuss what you can expect from his firm as far as service, his personal availability for help, timeliness issues, and his willingness to develop a financial product that fits your needs and your business. Most of this should have been done during the interview process, but this is the perfect time to go over all of these items again to make sure you have total communication before you begin.

It is vitally important that you reach an understanding that can separate professional business advice from basic functions of an accounting firm. It is hard to get both of these functions from one person, especially in a one- or two-person small accounting practice.

If you picked right, the accountant you chose should be strong on professional advice. Examples of professional advice would be questions such as, "What is the best way to structure my business?" or "What type of retirement plan should I consider at my age and this stage of my career?" These types of questions should lead to answers your accountant's professional knowledge and expertise in areas that can save you large amounts of money over time. This type of advice is by far the most important product you are buying from your accountant.

On the other hand, many accounting firms specialize in more functional assistance such as recording transactions, reconciling accounts, preparing payroll and payroll taxes, and tax returns. This type of functional service is much different from working with someone who can give you professional advice to improve your business, and is much less valuable.

> **Fees should be discussed up front and you need to know how much, how you will be billed, and when your bill will arrive with the proper documentation to support the bill.**

Your accountant of choice then should be someone who can perform as a professional advisor. Think of that person as a team leader. This person should have others on the team who can handle the functional aspects needed for your business or set you up with someone who can. Your accountant should then help you to manage the others on the team and help you find the best value available from each of the other professionals.

The Key Points You Should Have Gotten from this Chapter

Accounting is something most owners shy away from in their businesses because they don't understand the language.

- Accounting is something most owners shy away from in their businesses because they don't understand the language.

- Standardized accounting was designed for large public companies and does not give the small business owner the information he needs.

- Accounting is based upon a historical cost system that records what happened in your business in the past.

- Accounting is cost-based, meaning it considers what things cost but not the true current value.

- Accounting is a static system that views your business as one small snapshot at a fixed point in time.

- It is up to you as a business owner to give your accountant the guidance to provide information that will help you make better, and more current, decisions.

- Accounting, if used correctly, can help you get a dynamic picture of your business showing trends and comparisons in all aspects of your business.

- The key to timely and efficient accounting is to use a professional software program, under the guidance of your accountant, to obtain information on a daily basis if needed.

- Accountants should be part of your professional management support team for your business. Find one you can relate to and that takes an interest in your business.

- Accounting should not be black and white. The best accountants for small businesses are the ones that operate in the gray areas of accounting and seek aggressive, but legal deductions for your business.

16

Building a Business
That Will Sell
for Top Dollars

The most important thing you should get from this chapter is:

Nothing lasts forever – sooner or later you will sell your business.

Definitions and concepts you will need to know:

- The biggest killer of a fitness business is moderate success.

- *Two important rules:* You will sell your business at sometime in the future and every single decision you make should lead to an increase in value for your business.

- *Cash flow:* The total amount of revenue flowing in an out of a business each month.

- *Three types of cash flow you should know: new sales cash, multiple profit center revenue, and the revenue from the club's receivable base.*

- *EBITDA: Earnings* before *income tax, depreciation, and amortization.*

- *Depreciation:* A real expense in the fitness business since an owner has to constantly replace and upgrade a facility and equipment to stay competitive.

- *Amortization:* Intellectual property, patents, membership lists, or possibly your initial franchise fee.

- Your lease is important in the sale of the business since the right to perpetuate the business adds value.

- Most fitness businesses sell at 3.5 to 4 times their adjusted earnings.

Every Decision You Make in Your Business Should Be Made to Increase the Future Sales Value of that Business

The goal of every gym owner should be to build a business that can be sold at any time for *maximum value*. To ensure this will happen, each decision you make should enhance the future sales value of your business.

At this time you may not be thinking of selling your business. In fact, you may never plan to sell your business at all. But one constant in the gym business, as well as the universe in general, that can humble even the most passionate owner is: nothing lasts forever.

You may not be planning on selling today. You may have turned down offers for your business already that just weren't right. But one thing you always have to remember is that sooner or later you, or your business, will be gone.

One of the most arrogant and self-defeating attitudes you can have as a business owner is that you can totally control your exit from the business world. If you have an escape plan at all, and most fitness business owners don't, it is usually vague and centered on selling out somewhere in the distant future for really big bucks to some mega gym company that will vastly overpay for your life's work. The arrogance comes into play when you *think* you can control all of the factors that will actually lead to a sale and that you can channel all of these factors into a specific time you set.

First of all, the factors that force a sale are seldom if ever in your control. Divorce is something very few people actually anticipate and plan for in their lives. Death is also one of those things you only quietly whisper about to insurance people and attorneys, and then only when you are forced to sell by family or bankers who want guarantees there will be money left when you are gone.

Either of those factors, as well as a host of other personal problems, can take a person from a happy ownership of a successful business to selling his assets cheaply to a low-ball bidder in a very short period of time. Life has a way of humbling even the most successful owners and anyone can hit rock bottom.

Competition is also something that can force a sale and is completely beyond your control. Good owners that understand the business and are running solid systems- dependent gyms can usually last against virtually any competitor, and in truth may benefit from having competitors in the area.

A new fitness business spending a lot of money in advertising can raise awareness about fitness in the area and can lead to increased sales for all competitors in the same market. For example, you may be a vegetarian

At this time you may not be thinking of selling your business. In fact, you may never plan to sell your business at all. But one constant in the gym business, as well as the universe in general, that can humble even the most passionate owner is: nothing lasts forever.

driving down the road and hear an advertisement for a hamburger fast-food place. You may never eat in that type of restaurant but all of a sudden you are hungry. Efficient owners can benefit from competition if they are ready and able to take advantage of the changes in the market.

The reason most owners don't benefit from competition, and are not ready to sell their businesses for top money if they had an offer or were forced to sell, is that it's almost impossible for most owners to maintain the killer instinct that makes someone successful. The passionate edge that gets an owner into the gym early and eager, and then finds herself still there selling memberships at 8:00 p.m. that night, lasts for only a year or two. They are forced to back down a level or two because they finally consider themselves successful, or because of other factors such as family or the need to actually enjoy life for a change. This backing away from the edge, or losing your killer instinct for business, is a major contributor to perhaps the biggest killer of small business anywhere: being moderately successful.

> The passionate edge that gets an owner into the gym early and eager, and then finds herself still there selling memberships at 8:00 p.m. that night, lasts for only a year or two.

An owner pays herself $100,000 a year and the club still nets $10,000 to $15,000 per month. After a year or two, the killer instinct fades and autopilot switches on. The excitement and the feel of living on the edge is replaced by an owner who is backing away from the energy and drive that made her business successful in the first place.

At this point, she is relaxed and operating in a maintenance mode instead of running off of the manic energy that enabled her to grow and invent the business. In this case, her own complacency is doing what her competitors couldn't do; force her away from aggressively trying to capture market share and continually setting the standard for other businesses to follow.

Very few businesses are sold during the two-year killer-instinct stage. Who wants to sell when you are living your dream? If businesses were sold at this stage more owners would get more money for their businesses and for the work they put into them because their numbers are usually at their peak during this time.

Most businesses are sold when the numbers are flat and in the maintenance stage and the owners are burnt out and tired of the game. The owner isn't prepared to sell or to get on with her life if the business was indeed taken away from her, but she sells because she often doesn't know what else to do. If you are in any type of small business, be aware of two basic personal rules you must live by and apply to whatever you own, every day you own it.

Rule Number One: You will sell your business at some point in time.

Rule Number Two: Every decision you make every day you are in business should lead to an increased value of your business.

Your goal then is to build a business that can be sold at any time, in any situation, for the top money you can possibly get. If you run your business by this philosophy, you will make more money today while you own it and you will make much more money later when you do sell it.

Selling a Fitness Business

Remember that the value and the price of the business are interchangeable terms but the ultimate worth of the business is determined by what someone is willing to pay for it. The value is also determined by a combination of the preparation and mental state of the owner and the sophistication and emotion of the buyer. A sophisticated buyer and an emotionally wrecked owner/seller going through a divorce are going to reach a totally different price for the business, as compared to a prepared and stable seller and an emotional and not as sophisticated buyer.

Owners will come across five basic types of sales situations in the gym business. An owner in each situation has a different motivation, and if the same business was sold under that particular situation, it would probably sell for five different prices. The following are the five types of situational business sales you will find in the fitness industry:

Opportunistic

This type of sale is signified by a prepared and emotionally stable owner selling to a competitor or buyer that was not anticipated nor expected. This would be a positive sale since the owner was prepared to sell at any time and there was no trauma in her life forcing the sale. An example here would be a big chain coming into town and her gym is in a prime location. The chain might want the location for a presale working gym until their new building is in operation and she was sophisticated enough as a businessperson to hold out for real money.

Motivated Sales

This type of sale is signified by traumatic or personal issues such as divorce, a death in the family, drug problems, lawsuits such as sexual harassment, or legal issues such as an arrest that makes the newspapers and destroys the business. This is obviously a negative sale and the price usually reflects this since the business is dumped for a low bid or the owner in question is forced to sell to a partner for little or no money.

Conceptualization Sales

This type of sale usually happens during the third to fifth year of business and is a forced sale. These sales are due to the fact the business was never properly conceptualized in the beginning. Most owners don't fail during the

> A sophisticated buyer and an emotionally wrecked owner/seller going through a divorce are going to reach a totally different price for the business.

first year but later during those crucial years 3-5. Owners usually have enough energy and cash flow to keep even a really badly conceptualized businesses going for several years, but eventually the cracks show.

Conceptualization problems include being undercapitalized, flat businesses where the owner never planned for reinvestment, gyms that opened poorly finished and are then hurt by better capitalized competitors, overbuilt clubs that were simply too much for the area or market, and clubs built in a market they didn't fit into such as a hardcore bodybuilding gym in a small town with a limited target population. These problems also include certain types of owners who have to have everything in a fitness business and spend themselves out of business. These owners are constantly looking for the next toy that will give them a big breakthrough in membership and solve their clubs' money problems. These sales are also negative sales since the owners are very frustrated by the time they sell and often feel they never had a fair chance because they never had enough money.

Never-had-a-chance Sale

Sometimes you see people who should have never been in the gym business in the first place, or any other business for that matter. This type of sale is signified by the wrong people in the wrong business. Usually this type of person is a type of born-again fitness person who is going to change the world by telling and living their story.

This is the classic case of a person who loses a hundred pounds with a trainer, changes his life, has money, and then gets into the gym business. This person is the money person and the trainer will be the gym person. This scenario is far more common than you might think and usually ends in failure. Few people want to hear the story and few trainers thrust into the management of a full fitness trainer right off the training floor are prepared to run a business. These are also the hardest people to give business advice to since their passion far outweighs any business sense they might have ever had elsewhere in their life. These are also negative sales since by the time the person gets to the point where they realize their business concept doesn't work, the trainer is long gone, lots of money is lost, and the sale usually involves a mere liquidation of the assets of the company.

The Planned Sale

This sale is signified by an owner who had an escape plan and carried it out when the time was right. Every decision she made during her years was made to enhance the ultimate value of her business. Over time she built a strong receivable base, strong financial statements with moderate or low debt, signed a long-term lease through the use of options that would let someone after her perpetuate the business, and developed operating systems that were documented and could be followed by a future owner who wanted the business but who may not yet have the business experience.

> **Usually this type of person is a type of born-again fitness person who is going to change the world by telling and living their story.**

This owner might have also targeted a possible buyer before the sale, such as a long-term manager or key member, who she knew could be cultivated to someday buy the club when she was ready to sell. This sale is positive since the club would be sold for top money and since the owner had probably put enough money away over the years to allow her not to be dependent on the money from the sale of the club.

As you can see from these five situations, the key to get the highest price possible for your business from a sale is to properly conceptualize the business and then make every decision from that point forward to enhance the final sales value. An efficient owner should actually plan for the later sale of the business before it is built.

For example, an owner would sign a five-year lease that included three five-year options with fixed CPI increases and a cap. Then, at the end of her first lease period, she would go to the landlord and add another option in the future giving her and any future buyers the right to perpetuate the business.

> **You will someday sell and the decisions you make should enhance the future value of what you own.**

Every owner in each one of these selling situations could benefit from remembering the two key rules listed earlier: *You will someday sell and the decisions you make should enhance the future value of what you own.* Even the owner who was terribly undercapitalized could have probably gotten options in his lease that might have increased the value of his business if at some point he was forced to sell. The point to be learned from all these situations is that you *control* the ultimate value of your business and the decisions you make *determine* the ultimate price you receive.

Factors that Increase the Value of a Fitness Business

A number of factors can increase the value of a fitness business. Most are controllable by the owner and can be enhanced through the decision-making process. A few factors affecting the value are not controllable and they can either enhance or lower the perceived value of a business. Each factor will be listed and then discussed in-depth. The decisions an owner can make to build value associated with each factor will also be considered.

Controllable Factors

- The receivable base and club cash flow
- Investment quality equipment
- The acquisition of a long-term lease that allows the business to be perpetuated into the future
- A name that is not stupid (brand image and perception)
- Development of systems that can be transferred and sold as part of the sale of the gym

Factors You Can't Control that Affect Your Business Value

- An improving or declining area in income level and demographics

- New roads or increased access can enhance a business while the rerouting of traffic away from your location can negatively affect your business plan

- Increased competition, especially if you are unprepared, can have a down affect on your business, or a major competitor fails or stumbles and you benefit from his current free membership

The Buying and Selling of any Business Begins with the Cash Flow

Most fitness business sales are centered on the sale of your membership and the cash flow the membership generates monthly through the club's receivable base. *Cash flow* is defined as the total amount of money flowing in and out of the business each month. Net cash flow, or the pretax net, is defined as what's left over after expenses each month, or on an annual basis, but before the owner pays income tax.

As mentioned throughout this book, the only real asset a club owns in the eyes of a banker or sophisticated buyer is the total outstanding receivable base, which is composed of all the club's members paying monthly membership payments. This receivable base is not static. Static means the receivable base would only be defined in a one-month or some other fixed time frame and would produce the same income in each time period. Static also refers to something that is consistent and ongoing in nature and that is hard to change.

A receivable base and the cash flow it generates are anything but a static part of a business. Owners are better off thinking of their receivable base and the income generated each month to the club as *dynamic* in nature. Dynamic is defined as something that can change suddenly and is different each time you work with it.

The cash flow from the receivable base is something that is bought and sold in the sale of a club business. Receivable bases are dynamic in that a new owner of a club, lacking experience or business skill, can lose a large portion of this asset due to mismanagement in a very short period of time. For example, a new owner may do something dramatic to the business too soon without understanding the members or the club culture. The members retaliate by canceling their memberships in a large number, therefore, decreasing the outstanding receivable base and future club income.

Dynamic can also mean something positive in the business. Changes in the financial structure of a poorly run club or a needed increase in pricing can

Cash flow is defined as the total amount of money flowing in and out of the business each month.

both have a large effect on the receivable base and cash flow in just a few months, and this new income for the business can then be projected into the future.

The members comprising a receivable base must have some type of obligation to the club, such as signing a 12-month contractual membership, or you have no receivable base. Because of that contractual obligation, the income from all your members combined can be projected beyond the current month, which means you can then project cash flow that will arrive at some point in the future.

If you are buying or selling a club, the strength and validity of this receivable base, and the individual members it represents, becomes the most important part of the transaction. Put another way, the buyer is not just buying income from this month, but is buying income that can be projected after she takes over the business. The stronger the receivable base, the more the business will sell for, since a buyer is buying present and future income.

The cash flow from the receivable base is usually segmented in the month it arrives and a normal buyer question is always, "How much is your monthly EFT (or draft or billing check depending on the region of the country)?" Everyone starts with this question because the net amount of the total payments is such a large part of a typical club's income stream. For example, in a club without profit centers the net-receivable check might be as high as 80 to 90 percent of the club's total monthly deposit each month and annually.

Clubs that have profit centers and are effectively promoting them to the members may have as much as 50 percent of their total deposit coming from these centers. Profit centers usually add to bottom line since most clubs net between 35 to 40 percent each month from their centers. A sophisticated buyer looking at a gym project is trying to establish how much cash flow is in the business, where it comes from, and how much of that cash flow is actually net cash flow.

Cash Flow and EBITDA

The fitness industry is a true catch all for *buzzwords*. Between the mad scientists in the industry, meaning a few trainers who are so in love with their own product that everything is reduced to a technical term concerning some body part or function, new business people coming into the club market, owners who read their first business books, and lecturers at trades shows trying to impress with an extensive and often overused vocabulary, words catch on and end up being worked into every possible conversation and magazine article for a year or two.

For example, the term *branding* is a core concept in the real business world and is the beginning of any real conversation concerning marketing, market share, and product development for a business. In the fitness

> **If you are buying or selling a club, the strength and validity of this receivable base, and the individual members it represents, becomes the most important part of the transaction.**

business you can go from zero use of the word branding to 60 seminars at a tradeshow, magazine articles, workshops, and the appearance or recycling of old consultants who have become brand developers for clubs, in 90 days or less. The word is the buzz and it's a very small industry.

One of these terms that popped up as a new buzzword, *EBITDA*, actually is a real business word and does apply to the buying and selling of a business. You may be late to the dance as an industry, but adapting and implementing common, real world business practices to small fitness businesses can be very beneficial if what is being applied actually can be used in a small-business landscape.

It is very important to note that most of the fitness industry is comprised of small independently owned gyms and fitness businesses. These businesses usually represent one to an owner with very few owners owning 10 units or more in their portfolio.

The national chains get all the press, but as of this writing the three biggest chains in the country still comprise less than a 1,000 clubs out of the almost 18,000 clubs listed as doing business in 2002. Even if you take out the nonprofit fitness businesses such as the Y's you still have at least 15,000 mainstream independently owned fitness businesses.

License and franchising groups control at least 3,000 clubs, but each of these units is still independently owned by a single owner or small partnership. These numbers are changing every day and new clubs are still opening every day.

Problems occur in this business because 90 percent of all the clubs gross less than $3,000,000 a year per individual unit. Small chains look better by combining units but individual clubs seldom break the $3,000,000 mark.

You are all most likely small businesses, but most of the rules of business were written and applied to businesses much larger than you produce in your industry. In fact, you can find very little written anywhere that directly adapts big- business techniques and business practices to a small Mom-and-Pop independently owned fitness business.

EBITDA is a term that is normally applied to very large or public companies and confusion reigns when this term is directly applied to a small business. For example, during the hot market years in 1999 and 2000, many businesses were selling for an average of seven to eight times EBITDA.

When these same investment groups that were buying and selling in those heady days moved into throwing money into the fitness industry, they brought their method of valuation with them. When you are buying a national license/franchise chain with 500 units, big-world business rules are easily applied. When you buy a single unit applying a one-size-fits-all formula doesn't always match.

EBITDA is a term that is normally applied to very large or public companies and confusion reigns when this term is directly applied to a small business.

EBITDA is a standard way in the business world to evaluate the performance of a business and compare it against another similar business or industry standard. EBITDA provides a common language that should be able to give a fair evaluation of a business without the emotion usually associated with the sale of a small family owned business. However, this method does have certain flaws when applied to these smaller units.

EBITDA has two definitions and business authors and even textbooks can't seem to agree on how to actually define it. Chad Simmons, in a book titled *Business Valuation Bluebook: How Successful Entrepreneurs Price, Sell, and Trade Businesses* defines EBITDA as:

Earnings before Income Taxes, Depreciation, and Amortization.

Simmons primarily writes about small businesses with less than 50 employees. This is an excellent book with an easy-to-read introduction to the basics of business valuation. The debate comes, however, in that other authors and most business books define EBITDA differently. The other, more widely used definition is:

Earnings before Interest, Taxes, Depreciation, and Amortization.

The obvious difference is that one definition refers to earnings before income taxes and the other states earnings before interest and taxes. The important thing to note is that vast majority of the books written that discuss the buying and selling of a business are usually discussing businesses with gross annual revenues over $5,000,000.

Most health clubs and fitness centers are below that number and many of the formulas and discussions applied to small businesses seem like overkill when applied to a small business doing $3,000,000 or less in annual gross income. Interest expense when figured as part of EBITDA, for example, is important for larger businesses since much of the debt may be acquired as part of the purchase price.

When comparing two similar companies with gross revenues of $10,000,000 or more, a heavily leveraged company might be worth substantially less than its competitor that is showing less debt on the balance sheet. Interest as a valuation factor then becomes more important since it may affect the final selling price by a larger sum than most fitness businesses actually do in annual gross revenue in the real world.

> The large majority of gym sales are based upon a buyer bringing her own financing to the table.

The large majority of gym sales are based upon a buyer bringing her own financing to the table. This means she is not assuming the debt service of the current owner. In most cases, the current owner is bought out and he then pays off his debt out of an escrow account at the time of sale.

The new owner would then recapture the interest being paid out of cash flow by the current owner as part of her new cash flow in the business. For example, an owner might have $36,000 annually in interest expense. This interest is being paid out of the normal cash flow of the club therefore reducing the actual net.

When he goes away he pays off his debt at the time of sale. The new owner coming in would then have $36,000 of newly free cash flow in the business, before adding back any of her own interest expense, since the old debt has been retired.

The intent of this chapter is to give you a simple place to start when figuring your business value, to help you to make decisions that will ultimately enhance the value of your business, and to give you as a buyer or seller basic information that will help you get the most from your business.

As always when learning new material, use of this material is at your own risk and is offered merely as a reference point to help you better understand the buying and selling process. If you are actually buying and selling a business, seek out a qualified business professional or professionals who understand taxes, accounting, and the legal aspects of business sales.

To keep it simple and to keep a consistent common language, you will be using the following definitions throughout the remainder of this section. All these terms will be directly applied later in the business-pricing section.

- *EBIT* is defined as: *Earnings before Income Taxes.*
- *EBITDA* is defined as: *Earnings before Income Taxes, Depreciation, and Amortization.*
- *Depreciation* is defined as: *Funds a business owner would have to reinvest each year to maintain the same level of current production.*

Specific assets purchased by an owner that are used in the business for production can be deducted from the gross revenues (expensed). Depreciation is the government's way of allowing a business owner to recapture the costs of the physical assets purchased by the business over time.

For example, you might buy equipment for the gym valued at $25,000. This equipment might have an assumed depreciable accounting life of five years. This also means that this equipment is losing $5,000 of its value per year (depreciates by $5,000). An interesting side note is that in the fitness business, depreciation is a real expense meaning that you have to reinvest an equivalent amount or more each year to stay competitive in the market place and to retain members.

Depreciation is important if you are buying or selling because it is a non-cash expense applied against the club's gross revenues. In other words, it lowers the net, but if you buy the club the net or working cash flow is actually larger because depreciation expense is shown.

Depreciation is important if you are buying or selling because it is a non-cash expense applied against the club's gross revenues.

For example, an owner may have statements that show $60,000 of depreciation for one year. If you were buying the business, you would add $60,000 back to the net since the owner didn't really spend the cash. It is merely a paper entry for tax purposes and you would actually have $60,000 of cash flow to work with beyond the actual net.

- *Amortization* is defined as: *The depreciation of an intangible asset.*

Normally this is some type of intellectual property such as a patent or copyright, although it might also include start-up costs, the amortization of the purchase of your name if you are a license or franchise, or the purchase of a customer list from a competitor that sells you his members and then closes his club. In the fitness business you don't usually have big entries in this category.

> **Owner's compensation is defined as: The total compensation an owner or partners take from a business each year including salary, bonuses, car expense, cell phones, credit cards ran through the business, and anything else the owners wrote off as a business expense.**

- *Owner's compensation is defined as: The total compensation an owner or partners take from a business each year including salary, bonuses, car expense, cell phones, credit cards ran through the business, and anything else the owners wrote off as a business expense.*

You also add this back to EBITDA when valuing a club since the new owner wouldn't have the same expense. Another way to look at this is that these are expenses a current owner might have because he ran everything through the business. Say for example that the owner's total compensation package for a small club is $150,000, which includes salary, a car payment, personal credit cards being run through the business and a cell phone. If you buy this club you may only pay yourself a total of $75,000 in total compensation freeing up an additional $75,000 that is added to the net as free working cash flow.

What Is EBIT?

EBIT, or earnings before income taxes, is your pretax earnings at the end of the year. For example, look at the numbers from this small club:

> Gross revenues for the year (defined as the total deposits into the bank for the club from all sources of revenue) = $600,000
>
> Total operating expenses for the year (defined as all operating expenses including debt service and depreciation) = $500,000

$$\begin{array}{r} \textbf{\$600,000} \\ \textbf{-\$500,000} \\ \hline \textbf{\$100,000} \end{array}$$

This club has a pretax net (before any income taxes are paid) of $100,000. This also means the club has earnings of $100,000 in operating profits, or in other words, has an EBIT of $100,000.

The receivable base is normally the club's biggest source of cash flow. In this example, $400,000 to $500,000 of the club's total gross sales might come from cash flow from the receivable base assuming that the club hasn't done much with its profit centers. Obviously, the most important asset the club owner has to increase the overall earnings of her business is to increase the size and stability of her receivable base.

If you are a buyer, you are looking at a business that has an EBIT of $100,000, or $100,000 in cash flow without any other adjustments such as depreciation or owner's compensation, both of which will be further discussed in the section on how to figure what a business is actually worth.

What Is EBITDA?

As defined earlier, EBITDA is earnings before income taxes, depreciation, and amortization. But what does this mean and how do you use it as a buyer or seller? For example, a club might have financial statements that show the following:

> EBIT (earnings before income taxes/pretax net/pretax cash flow) of $100,000
>
> Depreciation (D) of $40,000
>
> Amortization (A) is $6000
>
> In this case the club has an EBITDA of $146,000

This club has a pretax free cash flow of $146,000. The owner has a verifiable asset to sell in the form of a business that is netting $100,000 before taxes and has another $46,000 in cash flow that would be available to a buyer in the form of non-cash expenses. This number is not adjusted for owner's compensation, which would add more cash flow to a buyer.

As will be discussed later, clubs are bought and sold using the EBITDA as the base number and then applying a multiplier to that number. If you are a seller you want to show the maximum EBITDA you can since a larger number will result in a higher sale price. If you are a buyer you want to know what cash flow will be available if you buy the business, and how the situation will differ when you own the business compared to the owner who is selling you the business.

Decisions the Seller Can Make to Enhance the Receivable Base and Cash Flow

As you can see from this section one of the most important decisions you will make as an owner is how to build a viable receivable base that will provide long-term stability in your business. Review Chapter 6 dedicated to receivable bases as well as the suggestions made here.

You have a number of things you can do to enhance your receivable base. The financial foundation of the club, defined as how an owner charges and collects from the members, is the single most important decision you

> The most important asset the club owner has to increase the overall earnings of her business is to increase the size and stability of her receivable base.

will make in your business. If the foundation is right, you can make a lot of mistakes and still stay in business. If the foundation is wrong, over time your business will fail since your club is very inefficient at collecting money from the members it does acquire.

Trial Memberships

Club owners who still insist on closing too strongly during the first visit of potential members will find the losses to their receivable base to be very high over time. In other words, the harder the pressure, the larger the losses through first payment defaults or defaults during the first six months of the member's agreement.

High-pressure sales tactics also keep prices artificially low for memberships. Most clubs that still slam or pressure at point-of-sale seldom if ever get their average monthly membership price over $34 to $39 per month. This $34 range is where most potential members draw the line as far as risk factor.

At least 70% of your guests to the club will need at least two or more visits before they are comfortable buying a membership. Some people will buy on their first visit and actually walked in the door ready to hand over a credit card. Other people will buy on their first visit and regret the decision that then leads to nonpayment somewhere down the line. Most of your potential members, however, need more than one visit to the club before they commit, especially if you ever hope to get your price over $34 per month per member.

Trial memberships with incentives are the only way to maximize on new sales during the first visit, and later sales from the people who really do need a second visit and a discussion at home before they will buy. Trial memberships are marketing tools that let someone try before they buy a membership. Trials were discussed extensively in *Making Money in the Fitness Business*, but for clarity need to be reviewed in this context.

The normal trial membership is 14 days. This means the potential member may use the club up to 14 times in a 14-day period. The potential member has no risk or any obligation and he can truly experience the club before he buys a membership.

You still have to sell memberships in the club business, however, and most clubs use some type of positive incentive offered during the first seven of the 14 days to aid in the sales process. For example, a club might offer a package of goods and services valued at retail price of $250 if the person becomes a member during this time period. This package might include a water bottle, tee shirt and gym bag, 30-day gift certificate for a friend or relative, and other small items such as free tanning packages, munchie bars, or sports drinks. This package might also include an extra 30 days on the membership effectively giving the person 13 months for the price of 12.

Most clubs that still slam or pressure at point-of-sale seldom if ever get their average monthly membership price over $34 to $39 per month.

This same club might offer an additional incentive package such as Club Bucks that can be spent in the gym and another free month for people who are ready to sign during their first visit. A minimum of 30 percent of the people who buy memberships will buy during their first visit. Experienced salespeople might do better than this but too high of a first- visit close rate normally means too much pressure is being applied.

Trial memberships lower the loss rates on memberships since the person had a chance to experience the club before purchasing a contract. The person also gained an incentive package that validated the sales process for the buyer, something that doesn't happen in a typical club sale, sending the person to their automobile with a pink copy of a contract and an aerobic schedule.

People need to feel they made the right buying decision, and incentive packages coupled with trial memberships allow this to happen. If you don't validate their decision, losses in the form of nonpayment are eventually higher as buyer's regret sets in on the member who questions what they bought and why they bought it.

The Length of the Contract

The length of the contract or membership tool is also a decision an owner makes that can enhance or weaken the club's receivable base. In a short form, the longer the membership contract usually means the higher the loss rate and the more expensive the sales process is to the club.

Most clubs have moved away from 24-month and longer memberships because the losses are just too high and mostly occurring during the first year of the person's membership. Unfortunately, the fascination remains for many owners with longer memberships because the total outstanding receivable base is so large. This is a false sense of security for the owner since the losses are so large with this type of membership tool, usually in the 36- to 48-percent range, and the cost of selling this type of membership is so large in commissions. Loss rates and other problems with long-term memberships are discussed in-depth earlier in Chapter 6.

Most clubs have moved away from 24-month and longer memberships because the losses are just too high and mostly occurring during the first year of the person's membership.

The tool of choice for building a solid performing receivable base is the 12-month contract. Losses for this tool are 10 percent or less per year and it is much easier and less costly to sell at point-of-sale.

A trend in the industry in early 2000 and beyond was the recycling of the open-ended membership. This is a no-obligation, month-to-month tool that a member can walk away from at any time with a written notice while being current with his last payment. The losses for this tool are usually in the 36- to 48-percent range and can be even higher in a declining club or with the introduction of a sophisticated competitor in the area. Because of the excessive loss rates and ease-of-member loss, this tool does not enhance the receivable base or the long-term value of the club since the club's most important asset, its membership base, can walk out at any time without a great deal of notice.

Buyers of clubs that use open-ended memberships are buying cash flow but not long-term stability. The buyer's ability to project income from the club into the future is also in question since no one has any sort of obligation to the club.

Many clubs, including some of the large chains, use open-ended memberships as their exclusive membership tool. This exclusion doesn't make sense, however, and is unnecessary. This type of club could offer an open-ended membership and a slightly discounted 12-month membership and let the member decide without forcing the buying decision.

For example, a club might have a 12-month contract priced at $49 per month and an open-ended membership at $59. In this type of system at least 80 percent of the buyers will take the 12-month option adding to the club's receivable base and enhancing the ultimate sales price of the business.

Third-Party Financial-Service Companies

Strong third-party financial-service companies that specialize in servicing club memberships can add a lot of value to the receivable base.

Strong third-party financial-service companies that specialize in servicing club memberships can add a lot of value to the receivable base. Due to economy of scale, a third-party service company should be able to collect the most money from the most members over time.

A third-party also has the advantage of having leverage against the members who are late or problem payers. Third-party companies service the memberships from a power position the club can't match since the club really has nothing to threaten the late payer with when they experience a problem.

Third-party companies also make the verification and transfer of the club's largest and most valuable asset easier to a new buyer. Someone buying a business from an owner who is servicing her own memberships has to also master the collection system as well as learning to run a new business. Verification is an issue when buying a club because you are in actuality buying a paying membership base.

This issue becomes cloudy when a seller is representing future business from paid-in-full memberships and renewal income based on the names in the club's database. Often these are misrepresented and are seldom viewed as income in the future. Third-party companies solve this problem because they maintain the database for the club and it is much more definable and verifiable to a potential buyer of the business.

Closed-Ended Renewals Versus Auto Renewals

What happens during the thirteenth month of a person's membership should be a big issue for a club buyer. A common system in place throughout the country features a person buying an initial 12-month membership, and then from the thirteenth month onward becomes an open-ended member without a contractual obligation to the club.

This is called an auto renewal because the person doesn't have to make a buying decision. He is simply kept on the books and money is drafted from their account until they complain. This is a stronger system compared to pure open-ended membership clubs, but still does little to enhance a receivable base since except for first year members, the rest of the club's membership becomes open-ended and has the same problems and restrictions as a pure open-ended membership previously mentioned.

The recommendation is to use a closed-ended renewal that locks the member into another year contractually. Loss rates with closed-ended memberships are only about three percent annually as opposed to open-ended losses that can run from five to nine percent monthly, or compounded annually at 60 to 108 percent. Closed-ended renewals greatly enhance your long-term receivable base because everyone has some type of obligation to the club. To a buyer, cash flow and obligation is worth far more than just cash flow.

Enhancing Your Club Through Investment Quality Equipment

It's the rare owner who buys equipment for his club with the thoughts of selling it later. Equipment is an immediate purchase for most owners, meaning that they buy it today because they identify a need in the club for the members.

It's the rare owner who buys equipment for his club with the thoughts of selling it later.

You might find other owners who simply buy because they can't live without a particular piece of equipment, which adds again to an already overcrowded club. These owners are an equipment salesperson's dream but they too seldom buy with the thought that someday someone else might own all their equipment.

To enhance the ultimate sale price of the club only buy investment quality, name brand equipment from vendors that have strong enough financials to ensure you can get parts for your purchases years down the line. Buying cardio from an internationally recognized company such as Star Trac for example, as opposed to buying treadmills from that *just-sold-for-the-fourth-time-in-five-years* cardio/strength/flooring/file cabinet company, will add curb appeal and emotional value to a buyer who recognizes your investment.

It seems like a small point, but rubber plates are a must for every club since they protect the curb appeal of your business. Steel plates and painted equipment is a match made in equipment hell and as an owner you realize this a few days after you open your gym and every piece of equipment becomes scratched and looks months old.

Another side note is that if your club is under around 25,000 square feet, buy about 80 to 90 percent of your equipment from one manufacturer. Besides the matching showroom factor of having equipment from the same company, you will also make it easier to buy and stock replacement parts. For example, buy all of your treads from one company and then you only have to stock replacement parts for one line as opposed to three or four.

Owners used to mix equipment with the thought that the members get bored and want variety. In the case of equipment, the members want quality equipment and enough that it is never broke or they never have to stand in line to use it. Your father was right; buy once and buy right and you won't have to buy again. *As far as selling a gym goes, buy once and buy right and sell for bigger bucks.*

> **As far as selling a gym goes, buy once and buy right and sell for bigger bucks.**

You Have to Establish the Right to Perpetuate the Business

If you don't own your building then you are obviously leasing space. Your lease can either enhance the ultimate sale of your business or can be a major detriment to a potential buyer.

A negative example is an owner who has a business for sale but only has three years left on her current lease term. Her current lease is $12 per square foot on an annual basis that includes all triple-net charges. At the end of her current lease, she has the option to renew for another five years at *fair market value*. Fair market means that her rent may not increase if the commercial real estate market is down, may increase slightly in the form of a cost of living increase, or may take a sharp rise if commercial property is hot and her space is in demand.

Most fair market leases don't have any set provision to determine an increase. In this case, the landlord may own several plazas and may decide that he can seek full retail for his space, especially if he wasn't full when he first rented it to the club owner and today wants to make up for lost ground. Fair market leases are usually dependent on an arbitrary decision by a landlord to how far he can push an owner.

The landlord may also have a hidden agenda. The owner's competitors might have approached the landlord and offered to pay more for the space if it ever became available and the landlord, having a backup renter, has nothing to lose by aggressively raising the rent during the option.

The point is that she doesn't know and her potential buyer doesn't either. For example, a buyer might be interested in the gym because the rent factor is low for the area and he can run his new business with a competitive edge over the competitors. In three years, however, he may lose this edge and in fact may then be operating at a disadvantage compared to the competitors.

Bankers are also leery of this type of leasing situation. The new owner would have trouble borrowing money since most banks hesitate to loan money beyond the initial lease term. In this case, he may have his borrowing power restricted to just three years, which is what's remaining on the current lease period.

To enhance a sale of a business, an owner should always think in terms of *perpetuating* the business into the future. Part of any sale to any sophisticated buyer is the ability to project the business forward and to be able to borrow money over an extended period of time. Leases that are too short or have unknowns that could disrupt the business plan could easily end a potential sale or lower the value of the business.

Option periods should be five years each and an owner should always have the right to perpetuate the business at least through her current term plus 10 more years. In a perfect world, the right to do business through the current term and 15 years would be ideal.

The most important aspect is that these options are tied to some type of set or formulated increase that can be built into a new owner's business plan. The normal method of setting rent in option periods is through the use of the *Consumer Price Index* (CPI), which is a government provided service that compares the buying power of money today against a reference year in the past. For example, the CPI might be 1.5 percent for the year, which means that it takes 1.5 percent more this year to buy the same product than it did during the base reference year.

Most CPI option clauses have caps of three percent that limits the maximum a landlord can raise an owner's rent to three percent. On the other hand, smaller markets often use fixed-option raises defined to set numbers such as 2.5 percent per year. Both of these methods are good for an owner and good for a potential buyer because both parties will know what it will cost to project the business in the future.

Club owners should also make it a must to have a decent assignment clause in their leases. This clause gives you the right to sell your business without undo hassle from the landlord. Standard assignment clauses in most leases are weak in this point and the landlord will use the potential sale as a way to increase the rent, or he will deny permission for you to sell your business. Before signing any lease make sure your attorney has given you the right to sell it to a qualified buyer.

It is also standard practice to leave the original owner on the lease unless your new buyer has serious financial statements. Most landlords play it safe and move the current owner to a number-two position with the new buyer in the number-one. This protects the landlord and isn't necessarily bad for the current owner if she sells the club on terms and might need to step back in if the buyer would default.

> **To enhance a sale of a business, an owner should always think in terms of *perpetuating* the business into the future. Part of any sale to any sophisticated buyer is the ability to project the business forward.**

A side note at this point is that most buyers will bring their own financing to the closing table. If the current owner doesn't carry the note, then the buyer will have to seek bank financing. Most banks will not give this type of loan for less than a five-year period of time. If less time than that is in the current lease period, the buyer and owner may have to go to the landlord together and get landlord permission for the buyer to resign for a five-year initial lease period that would replace whatever current lease is in place.

These type of resigns need to be done carefully since landlords consider this a prime opportunity to raise rents or add additional burdens to the lease, and nothing should be signed by any of the parties until closing of the transaction between the seller and buyer of the club. When negotiating a resign, get a letter of intent explicitly spelling out the new terms and the ability for a new lease to be put into effect from the landlord, but don't sign any actual documents until the club transaction takes place.

There Can Be a Lot of Value in a Name, Or None at All

As a seller of a business, have you established a *brand?* This sounds like a simple question but it is actually more complicated than it looks. A brand means you have established a recognizable identity in the marketplace that makes your business worth more to a buyer than just the cash flow and assets.

For example, if you want to open a hamburger restaurant, would you be better to open your own or to buy a national franchise? In the fast-food world, a national name seems to be a mandatory concern.

In the fitness business, it is not that simple. The largest part of your business, usually 80 to 90 percent of your members, will come from a 12- to 15-minute driving distance from the club. This restricted marketplace will sometimes negate the need for a nationally known name since the members come simply because it is the closet place to their home.

> You may buy a national franchise and ruin the name because you are a lousy owner, or you may start a company with your own concept and become the fitness source in your community.

Names in the gym business are really what you do to enhance them. You may buy a national franchise and ruin the name because you are a lousy owner, or you may start a company with your own concept and become the fitness source in your community. Keeping all of this in mind, the following are a few key points to consider about your business name and whether it can enhance the future sale of your business, or if you are a buyer, whether it adds to what you are wanting to buy:

• Does the name clearly identify the business?

For example, *Powerhouse Gym Westin* clearly tells the potential member what it is and where it is, mandatory points for businesses that draw upon such narrowly defined marketplaces as fitness clubs. On the other hand, *New Age Wellness* clearly doesn't identify nor does it lend itself easily to building a brand since it is hard to conceptualize just what this company sells as a product. Is it a wellness center for working out, or is it a group of holistic doctors banded together to provide medical services?

• Is the name current?

Club names can easily become dated in a short period of time and often reflect popular sayings or words in the current culture. For example, *living on the edge* or *cutting edge* were popular and trendy mainstream sayings in the mid-1990s and led to a large number of clubs using some form of *the edge*. This saying also went away very quickly and clubs using any form of *the edge* in their name began to appear somewhat dated since those terms have that *been-there-done-that* feel.

Another pitfall in names is tying yourself to a name that loses its impact. An example would be the term, *athletic club*. This was a very trendy name last century that lost its impact as the word *gym* came back into style. Several clubs were successful in tweaking their name and still keeping their identity. For example, a club named *Five Points Athletic Club* could easily be renamed the *Five Points Fitness Center*. This club doesn't lose anything from the change and may gain market share by appearing more able to provide a current product.

Initials are also a negative in name recognition. Most brand developers shy away from trying to build market recognition on any form of initials since that type of name can easily be diffused by a similar competitor. The classic example is the industry rage in the late 1980s and early 1990s to initialize every big gym. The club wasn't just the *Middletown Athletic Club* — it was the *MAC*. Fortunately this trend is about dead.

> **The club wasn't just the *Middletown Athletic Club* — it was the *MAC*. Fortunately this trend is about dead.**

Licensing and franchising may add to your sale price or add value to your purchase, but the real key is what the seller has done with the name. If he has taken a solid nationally known name and then sold $19-per-month presale prices, today he has ended up with a gym full of the lowest bidders as members and the name does not add value. If he has, on the other hand, developed two nice clubs with a national franchised or licensed name that caters to the top 60 percent of the area demographics and has market impact through being part of the community, then the name does enhance the sale for both parties. Most franchise and licensed gyms still operate as individuals and the owners may not always reflect on the quality of their national organizations.

• Does the name have a negative reputation?

Club sales in smaller markets are usually done between people who live in the same community. The buyer may realize that the name on the club has a negative image in the community due to being too low rent or due to personal image problems with the current owner. Buying this club should include a name change immediately and is usually an easier task than most buyers realize. Budget for this in your purchase and allow at least $25,000 to $40,000 to change a name including signs and forms. It is almost impossible, though, to get the seller to compensate for this since he probably thinks the name is great and won't be happy hearing you are changing the name the day he sells the business because his personal reputation in the community is so bad.

The Better the Business Systems in Place, the Higher the Sale Price of the Club

Buyers want *systems* in place because they then have the ability to duplicate what you have been doing in the club. Without verifiable systems, a buyer gets all the problems but has none of the answers, since she cannot find the information she needs anywhere to solve the issue at hand.

Having a system means you have *manuals and procedures* for all aspects of your business. For example, you may be successful at sales but most of the sales training is done old Indian style. In those days, you set around a campfire and the chief would tell the braves what they would need to know to run the tribe when the chief passed on to the spirit world.

Gyms aren't really much different. An owner hires a new salesperson and spends a few hours training her on the club forms and computer. She then works with other salespeople in the club who teach her their procedures and sales concepts. Eventually she becomes a reasonable salesperson that can follow the club system, which is really mimicking the club sales culture since nothing in writing exists defining a system.

Problems arise when the club is sold and the new owner wants to hire a new salesperson. If the owner has experience he will bring his campfire stories and culture to the gym and repeat the process. But if the owner doesn't have experience in club sales, then how do you train your new staff?

The club owner should have had a detailed training manual that fully explains the club's sales procedures, how to fill out all necessary forms, and everything a new person would need to learn to have a reasonable chance to do a membership sale. The new owner who wants to train can go to the sales manual and can then duplicate the former owner's sales success because club sales is defined in a system that can be replicated.

Can you imagine buying any major national franchise, such as a Subway sandwich shop, and not having set procedure manuals detailing every phase of the operation?

Can you imagine buying any major national franchise, such as a Subway sandwich shop, and not having set procedure manuals detailing every phase of the operation? Those businesses thrive because any person with reasonable intelligence can be taught to run the system from the manuals.

Besides sales, do you have a manual and system for personal training? How about for your back shop and computer systems? Have you detailed your juice bar? Could a new buyer walk into your club and find out how to run and promote your profit centers through a detailed training manual?

Most owners can't answer yes to very many of these questions. If you want to increase the value of your club then build systems that can be followed by the next owner. If you do not have systems then it will take at least a year to build them, so anticipate that if you want to sell your business in the future. If you are buying a club you either have to have experience or you have to have systems to follow. If you don't have the experience in the club business and the club owner doesn't have the systems in place so you can duplicate the business, then it is probably not the business for you to buy.

The Sales of any Business Involves Two Different View Points

If you understand going into any buying or selling situation that the buyer and seller look at the same transaction from two different viewpoints, then your chances of success and avoiding frustration will be much higher.

The seller's viewpoint is always one of history and the recreation of glory years or numbers. Sellers want to sell you the past and place extra value on numbers that may have happened years ago but have not been duplicated in recent times.

The seller says, "Three years ago was a great year and although we haven't had one of those since then, and in fact never had one prior either, the business should be priced on the true potential, which we demonstrated during that one great year when everything went perfect." History can predict the future but does not guarantee any performance either good or bad.

The buyer's viewpoint is always in the future. Everything he thinks about is how to take the seller's business and make even bigger numbers at some later date. The buyer doesn't always care about past performance since he most likely is going to use a different approach and business plan.

Somewhere in the middle is the true value of the asset. All businesses have a value: *getting to the reality is the issue and everyone involved in the deal colors this reality.*

The viewpoints of the buyer and seller collide because business valuation is not an exact science and because very few businesses are ever sold that involve only two people. Each side has a team and all the players in the game bring their viewpoint to the process. For example, look at this short list of players and their predisposed viewpoints:

The banker for the seller—He wants the valuation as low as possible so he doesn't have to loan as much money, therefore decreasing his risk and the risk to the bank.

Ex-spouses—This depends which side they are on at the time. The ex-spouse of the seller wants big bucks for the sale because he will benefit from more

> "Three years ago was a great year and although we haven't had one of those since then, and in fact never had one prior either, the business should be priced on the true potential, which we demonstrated during that one great year when everything went perfect."

money. The buyer's spouses may be holding out and restricting the purchase because they haven't been paid or their income stream may be disrupted. Both sides also have issues because you might never know who actually owns the club. For example, a sale of a club in upstate New York was on the table, and then the buyer found out at the last minute that the ex-spouse of the seller was in the picture and still listed as a partner. She had never worked in the club and had no idea what it was really worth. The deal fell through because she felt that it was worth more money although she didn't really know why it was worth more money. After splitting the sale money by two and with tax implications, it probably didn't appear to be all that much money although the club was properly priced.

The seller—This is simple. Give the seller the most money. Sellers without experience usually price their clubs by the I-need-it method. This method is usually based on these issues:

- I need so much to pay off my folks.
- I need so much to pay off the loans.
- I need a new car.
- I need a little to hold me until I get a job.
- I need to pay off the house.
- Therefore, my asking price for the business is the combination of all of these *I- need-its.*

The buyer—Cheap, cheap, cheap -- their system of valuation is based on the *this-is-all-I-have-so-that's-the-offer* method.

Accountants—Most accountants value businesses based on formulas from textbooks that pertain to very large businesses. Buying and selling small businesses is truly an art and a science, and unless your accountant or attorney has had experience selling and buying many businesses, she might not be the right one for you.

Business brokers—The question at this point is who does the broker work for in the sale? If the broker represents the seller and is getting paid a percentage of what the sale price is, then the broker's business valuation may need work. If you are using a broker that is declaring neutral ground but is still charging someone a percentage, then you may still have a problem with optimistic pricing. Business brokers should get a flat fee for the sale that keeps them working in the right direction.

> Buying and selling small businesses is truly an art and a science, and unless your accountant or attorney has had experience selling and buying many businesses, she might not be the right one for you.

A Standard Business Valuation Guideline

Many different versions and methods of valuing a business have been discussed throughout this section. Most of the models used in the textbooks and by most business professionals are based upon buying and selling big businesses with revenues that far exceed independently owned fitness businesses.

Pricing and valuation in the fitness business have also changed dramatically over the years as newer business-based players have come into the industry. As the numbers get bigger in the clubs, outside investors today want to play, and that also changes how you buy and sell health clubs.

Valuation of a business is very situational and may change in a short period of time or from another perspective. In the fitness business, a valuation may only last a few months if action is not taken on the sale of the club. For example, a club may have a flat fall season, have a competitor close and dump his members in the club, and then have an outstanding January through May. In just those few months the value of that business might change substantially because of the increased revenues.

Fitness Businesses Are Fixed-Cost Businesses

One of the most appealing aspects of a fitness business is that after your basic expenses are met, an owner can increase the revenue in the business dramatically without increasing cost in proportion. Think of the business as a ski mountain. After a certain number of skiers, the mountain can add literally thousands of more skiers without adding that greatly to the expenses. In other words, after a breakeven number of skiers, say 5,000 for example, the mountain can take up to capacity, which might be 12,000, without adding much expense. After a certain point it all becomes profit.

> One of the most appealing aspects of a fitness business is that after your basic expenses are met, an owner can increase the revenue in the business dramatically without increasing cost in proportion.

This means that valuations can change quickly in the business because a few good months can mean quite a difference in the cash flow and the business. Valuations then have to be timely or they are of little value to the buyer or seller. The seller may, however, rely on an older valuation if business has changed for the negative.

EBITDA as Your First Method of Valuation

As mentioned earlier, EBITDA is *earnings before income taxes, depreciation, and amortization*. This definition differs from the one using interest because businesses in the fitness industry usually have gross revenues of less than $3,000,000 per unit, and for the fact that a buyer usually brings his own financing to the table and is not assuming major bank loans or other debt. Even if the seller finances the business for the buyer, the debt structure becomes a hybrid and should be considered separately because it will change from the current structure. Figure 16-1 will further define EBITDA and how it applies to a club valuation.

Additions to EBITDA

Once you establish EBITDA you then have to adjust it for other factors. In Figure 16-1, go back and add the owner's compensation to the EBITDA. Owner's compensation is cash flow the new owner will have as free cash flow to run the business or to make change, or the amount can again be taken out all or a portion of as salary.

The Club
- 12,000 square feet
- Co-ed free standing building
- One owner taking $100,000 in total compensation from the club including salary, a car, credit cards, and personal phone
- Annual gross revenues of $1,000,000
- Operating expenses including cost-of-goods and debt service of $850,000
- Leased space not owned by the owner -- three years remaining on the initial lease and three five-year options in place at CPI

Calculating EBITDA
- Gross revenues for the club $1,000,000
- Expenses   -$850,000
- EBIT $150,000
- Depreciation $40,000
- Amortization $7,000
- **EBITDA**   **$197,000**

Important point
- This club has pretax cash flow of $197,000, or another way to look at it is that a buyer will have almost $200,000 of cash flow available when she buys the club.

EBITDA	$197,000
Owner's compensation	$100,000
Adjusted earnings	**$297,000**

Figure 16-1.

Using Multipliers to Determine an Actual Valuation

Once you have established the real adjusted earnings or cash flow in the business, you must then take this cash flow and translate it somehow into a value for the business. This translation is based upon a *multiplier* that is used to multiply the adjusted income a certain amount of times to ascertain the value of the business.

But where does this multiplier come from in the first place? Most business classes and books on valuation always return to the same base assumption: *the value of any business is the present value of the future cash flow accruing to the owner.*

What this phrase is really asking is why would you buy a business and take risk when you could put your money elsewhere without the risk? And if you are absolutely sure you want to risk your money, how much return would you have to see to make it worth that amount of risk?

> This translation is based upon a *multiplier* that is used to multiply the adjusted income a certain amount of times to ascertain the value of the business.

If you put your money into a CD you might make a two- to three-percent return at the time of this writing, but the risk is zero. If you stepped it up a notch in your tolerance for pain, then you might put the money you were going to use for the club into the stock market, which historically has shown a steady return of 10 to 11 percent over the years.

So if you wanted to risk the family fortune on a gym, it seems that you would at least want to get a return higher than these numbers to make it worth your time. For most investors willing to live with a higher risk level, the expected return would have to be a minimum of 20 percent.

The technical term for multipliers is *capitalization rate* or *cap rate*. Simply put in relation to a buyer's perspective, what would the money invested in this business be worth to you over time compared to safely investing today for a lower interest rate at little or no risk?

As previously mentioned, during the glory market days in 1999 and 2000, businesses were selling for seven to eight times EBITDA. These were very large companies beyond the scope of what most of you do in the fitness business, but the numbers are still a good illustration.

When a company sells for seven to eight times EBITDA, it means the buyers are willing to live with a return of 12.5 to 14.2 percent on their money. Looking back this seems like a low return for the risk considering how many of those companies from that era failed. What these buyers are betting is that they can change the EBITDA over time as the companies move out of their start-up phase and into profitability, and that they can increase total gross sales as the companies capture more market share. At some point in the future you should theoretically be able to roll the company over to the next buyers and walk away with profit, or better yet go public and let the investors of the world enjoy the success of your company while making you rich.

Fitness facilities can generate a lot of cash flow, often in the 20- to 40-percent range, which is quite substantial compared to other retail and service businesses. This also means that more non-traditional fitness center owners will be entering the industry in the coming years.

Although the money can be good, the perceived risk is considered high for many investors because of the capital investment needed to enter the market with a competitive facility. While it's true a new owner can sneak into the business for less than $300,000 and open a gym, this type of player will be seen less and less in the near future because those facilities are usually not competitive in the marketplace.

Using a 10,000-square-foot club in rented space with moderate finish at only $35 per square foot and standard equipment, and you're at least looking at an ante of $750,000 to $1,500,000 to get into the game. The cash flow and return may be high but you can get into a decent franchise for far less than those numbers with less risk.

So if you wanted to risk the family fortune on a gym, it seems that you would at least want to get a return higher than these numbers to make it worth your time.

Based on the nature of the market and the associated risk, the vast majority of club sales include using a multiplier in the three to five range, or an expected return of 20 to 33 percent. If you are not familiar with cap rates or multipliers, think of it this way: *the higher price you pay for the gym the lower the rate of return, or the less you pay the higher the return for your investment assuming you are starting with the same adjusted earnings.* For example, go ahead and apply multipliers to the club discussed in Figure 16-1:

Adjusted earnings of $297,000
$297,000 x 3 = $891,000
Rate of return is 33%

Adjusted earnings of $297,000
$297,000 x 5 = $1,485,000
Rate of return is 20%

If the club sold for the higher price then the expected return would be lower. If the buyer got it for a lower price the return would be higher. In this example, the return spread is 20 to 33 percent and this club would sell for somewhere in the $891,000 to $1,485,000 range. These prices assume the seller is paying off the debt at the time of sale.

Determining the correct multiplier is where the science of valuation ends and the art form takes over.

What determines such a spread? Determining the correct multiplier is where the science of valuation ends and the art form takes over. Put another way, this is where the person who is valuing the business has to look at other factors that might be subjective to make a proper determination. Some of these were mentioned earlier in this chapter, but the following are some of the factors that determine the correct multiplier:

• The seller is going to use the higher number

• The buyer is going to use the lower number

• The age and condition of the club

• The equipment needs in the club

• The lease and right to perpetuate the business

• The quality of the staff that will stay with the buyer

• If systems are in place that will help the buyer

• The name and brand power of the business

• Cash flow is either growing or declining

• Competition

• Market potential

All of these factors influence the final sale price. For example, if a club has flat cash flow, needs equipment and a remodel, and has a young staff that the buyer doesn't want to keep, the multiplier would be closer to three.

On the other hand, if the club has shown steady growth, has equipment that is competitive, and has a management team in place that is worthy and will stay, the multiplier will be in the four to five range. All of these prices again assume the owner is paying off the debt and this is a leased property.

Applying all of these factors to all club sales in the independent club market in this country and you will ultimately come to this: *The typical club sells for 3.5 to 4 times adjusted earnings.* Using the club example in Figure 16-1, this business would sell in the range of *$1,039,500 to $1,188,000, or 3.5 to 4 times adjusted earnings.*

Clubs during the early 2000s sold for as much as eight times EBITDA, but these were rare. This sale usually involved something beyond the physical acquisition of a business. For example, an investment company buys a small chain of 10 clubs for $180,000,000. Did the EBITDA warrant that or did the investors see something beyond the clubs?

Many outside investors are looking for the next big chain concept or franchise possibility and will pay more for a concept than the actual clubs are worth. For example, you may have 10 clubs that have developed a unique nationally recognized brand identity, have received a lot of national press, and have the possibility and uniqueness to be franchised or built into a national chain that could obtain a high market share against the current operating chains.

> Many outside investors are looking for the next big chain concept or franchise possibility and will pay more for a concept than the actual clubs are worth.

Your 10 clubs are worth more than what they would sell for as individual units, or as a group to someone who merely wanted to be in the club business. In this example, you aren't buying the clubs, you are buying a concept that can be made into something bigger and that is worth a much higher multiplier.

However, the average club still sells in the 3.5 to 4 range. Few clubs in the market are worth five times adjusted earnings and even fewer clubs are so bad they trade for only three times.

Other Valuation Issues that Need to be Discussed

The following are other issues that may affect the sale of a club that should be discussed and that may affect the final value of the asset.

The Interest Issue

The most often asked question about this method of valuation is, "Why isn't interest used as part of the EBITDA formula as it is everywhere else?" The answer is simple: *fitness businesses are too small and it doesn't change things that much anyway.* For example, take a look at the same numbers from the club in Figure 16-1 adjusted for interest in Figure 16-2.

Gross revenues for the club	$1,000,000
Expenses	-$850,000
EBIT	$150,000
Adjustments:	
Interest	-$30,000
Depreciation	$40,000
Amortization	$7,000
EBITDA	**$167,000**
EBITDA	$167,000
Owner's compensation	$100,000
Adjusted earnings	**$267,000**

Figure 16-2.

This would obviously change the sale price of this club dramatically if you stopped here. For example:

$267,000 times 3.5 = $934,500

This sale number is $105,000 less than the sale price in Figure 16-2 using $297,000 as the adjusted earnings number, which is a substantial number to a buyer of a small business. But in the majority of small business transactions, the seller retires the debt freeing up the interest he has been paying as cash flow for the buyer. In that case you have to make this adjustment in Figure 16-3.

EBITDA	**$167,000**
Owner's compensation	$100,000
Cash flow from recaptured interest expense	$30,000
Adjusted earnings	**$297,000**

Figure 16-3.

In Figure 16-3, you are back to where you started from using EBITDA as earnings before income tax, depreciation, and amortization. If you have a business with gross revenues of less than $3,000,000, use this version. If you are buying or selling a unit producing numbers higher than this, or working with multiple units that will sell with the debt in place, you should consult your business professional for what's right for your current business situation.

The Real Estate Issue

All the previous examples have discussed the sale or purchase of a business in a rented property. If you are buying or selling a fitness business that includes the *real estate*, you have to separate the two. As a buyer, never buy

If you are buying or selling a fitness business that includes the *real estate*, you have to separate the two.

a combined business. Treat the sale of the business and the sale of the property as two separate issues.

The real estate should be purchased as a standard property deal with appraisals and will most likely end up in a separate partnership anyway. The gym is the gym and should stand alone in the buying process. If they are combined it is easy to overpay since you have no clear lines of where one begins and the other ends.

If you are selling, you will have a much easier sale if the two assets are separated even if the gym business has little value. For example, many of the old racquet facilities built in the 1970s and 1980s were developed as long-term real estate deals. Those owners are today selling for the increased appreciation in their real estate and almost throwing in the businesses for free.

Remember that many of these original investors are sitting on properties that are paid for and can run a really bad fitness facility for very little money a month. When it's time to sell it is a real estate deal for them and the business adds little value to the deal.

Owner Financing

Small businesses selling locally to someone already in the gym or to local investors usually require some type of seller financing. If you are considering owner financing these points may help make it somewhat painless:

- Never consider financing the buyer unless she can put at least 20% down and has additional reserve capital equal to two months operating expense.

- Reserve the right to recapture the business at 40 days delinquent. For example, the payment is due to the seller on March 1st and is not paid. Another payment is due on April 1st and again is not paid. On the 10th of April the seller should have the right to step in and take the business back before it is to late to save it.

- All major bills should be paid through an escrow company or an agreed upon accountant attorney for the first year so the seller will have immediate verification if the bills are getting paid on time.

- There may be major tax advantages of financing a business to a buyer versus taking the hit all at once. Check with your accountant about this.

- Financing should be for five years so the buyer will have at least a chance to make it. Accelerating the payoff too quickly can force the buyer out of business.

- Don't forget to get personal guarantees from the buyer.

- If you are using a third-party financial-service company, don't turn complete control of the account over to the buyer until at least one year. Have the money dispersed from the third-party to the escrow company and then to the club.

Never consider financing the buyer unless she can put at least 20% down and has additional reserve capital equal to two months operating expense.

- The seller should not be removed from the lease until the final buyout in case the seller would have to step in and take the business back in case of default.

- Depending on the type of corporation the seller has set up for the club, it may be wise to take 40% of the agreed upon price as a consulting fee rather than the purchase of the business so the seller can take the income personally.

- If the seller agrees to stay on for any time after the sale, put it in writing and spell out the expectations for that time period.

Looking Back Further for Income

Some sellers present a partial year's worth of income projected for 12 months as the basis for the selling price.

Some sellers present a partial year's worth of income projected for 12 months as the basis for the selling price. This is usually done when a seller has just come off of a flat year and finally has a few good months going. If he based his price on last year's numbers the business would be worth less, so he ignores that time period and uses the good months as a basis for an annual projection.

Income weighting is the solution to this problem. With income weighting you go back one or two years and then weight the income coming up with an average that can be used for the basis of determining cash flow and EBITDA. For example, a club uses a partial year as its basis:

- The club does $516,000 in gross revenue in January through June of 2003 for an average of $86,000 per month.

- Based upon the $86,000 average for the first six months of the year, the owner projects annual gross revenues of $1,032,000.

- The club's expenses for the first six months are $432,000 or an average of $72,000 per month.

- Based upon the $72,000 average for the first six months of the year, the owner projects an annual expense of $864,000.

- The projected EBIT is $168,000.

The buyer should not, however, base a bid for the club on these numbers alone since no one can determine if these numbers can be sustained. To refigure the EBIT, the buyer should consider what happened during the last two years of the business and then weight these numbers. For example:

Projected EBIT for 2003 is	$168,000
Actual EBIT for 2002 was	$138,000
Actual EBIT for 2001 was	$122,000

The trend is up but will it hold? And how does the trend relate to past performance? Weighting means you give recent numbers more importance and older numbers are counted but should have less impact. For example, apply a *3/2/1 weighting* to these numbers:

Projected for 2003 is $168,000 ($168,000 x 3 = $504,000)
Actual for 2002 was $138,000 ($138,000 x 2 = $276,000)
Actual for 2001 was $122,000 ($122,000 x 1 = $122,000)

$504,000 + $276,000 + $122,000 = $902,000

$902,000/6 (3 + 2 + 1 = 6) =$150,333

The weighted average for this club sale for EBIT would be $150,333, a truer reflection of what the club can actually do over time.

Protect Your Information

The last issue to discuss is in some ways one of the most important ones. Finding a qualified buyer for any business normally takes a great deal of time. You may have to deal with many people who just want to waste your time because they don't have the resources to buy, or another type of waste in the form of competitors who just want to discover inside information about your business.

The first type of individual is the easiest to weed out of the mix. Serious buyers should be willing to present financial statements and proof of funds before they enter a serious negotiation. If they aren't willing to show any proof of being substantial enough to play, then don't waste your time.

The second type, the competitor seeking information, is not new but the intensity and lack of ethics this new breed of person is bringing into the industry has risen substantially over the last several years. Much of the damage being done by these folks can be traced back to some of the bigger chains.

As the chains moved into new markets they were attempting to employ terror tactics on local owners. For example, a large chain was moving into the Orlando market and had issued press releases and notices but had not yet announced a date. A person representing himself as in charge of club development for this chain called an owner and asked if the owner knew of the building site being developed directly across the street from the club. The chain rep then proceeded to state that the new club was going to open in a year in that location, they were looking for an existing club to do presales in until their new building was complete, and since the chain would run the local guy out of business anyway, why not just sell the membership and walk away from the business before it was too late.

This type of tactic will create panic in a young owner, which is the intent of the chain. More importantly, the chain promises to buy the membership for some big numbers that entices the local owner to consider selling. The

> Serious buyers should be willing to present financial statements and proof of funds before they enter a serious negotiation.

local owner panics but is also allured by the hint of money in the air. If the local guy calls the chain rep back serious numbers are discussed, but the chain rep stalls the deal by saying he needs more information and more time to consider the local club since the chain is buying clubs everywhere at the same time.

An unsophisticated owner will turn over his membership information to the chain and then wait for the check. The chain is looking for a cheap deal and to take the owner's focus away from his business until the chain opens. The chain rep will promise big numbers, stall for a longer period of time and continually ask for more information. If the rep is good he can stall the owner for months at a time, giving the chain a chance to keep their project moving closer toward completion.

> **The chain is looking for a cheap deal and to take the owner's focus away from his business until the chain opens.**

Somewhere down the line the chain rep throws an offer on the table that is far less than the owner was counting on getting. The chain wants the club membership, but only at a major discount. By this time it is too late to react to the new club coming into town. Instead of focusing on improving his business for the year, he has wasted a big part of that chasing a number that was never going to happen. The chain either picks up a cheap deal or walks leaving the owner unprepared to do business when the new club opens. The following are things to be learned from this lesson:

- Serious buyers seldom call out of the blue to throw an offer on the table. This is done to create a panic mode and to see who will roll over and die. If a buyer is serious he will call in person, or have a representative call on the owner and start a more serious discussion.

- The owner made a serious mistake by giving away too much information without a nondisclosure agreement. This agreement prevents the potential buyer from using the information against your business for a set period of time, usually one year. In this case, the chain rep would never have signed one of these agreements since the core of these agreements is that if you don't buy you can't open in a prescribed distance from the club for one year.

- Never ever give out any information that can't be obtained through a normal club tour to anyone without a nondisclosure agreement. This includes membership lists, receivable balances, cash flow information, or lease information.

- Your attorney or accountant should be able to provide you with a strong nondisclosure agreement.

Other Assorted Tips for Buying or Selling a Business

- CPAs may know accounting and taxes, but this doesn't mean they know business. Lawyers may know what is legal and how to protect you, but that doesn't mean they know business. Only work with people who have bought and sold small businesses.

- *If it ain't in writing, it ain't real.* Bad English but true words — if what you agreed to isn't in writing, then it isn't real. Never assume anything will happen if you didn't write it down and both parties sign it.

- All gyms are the same but all are uniquely different. When you buy a gym look at the basics but also look for the quirks that might make this gym work when others don't.

- An old truism in small business: *don't start a business that might fail when you can buy one that hasn't.* The problem with this in the gym business is that young owners who want to start their own dream won't find any glamour in buying a previously owned business.

- Most businesses are overpriced because the owner has emotional attachments and uses the concept of sweat equity.

- The buyer's viewpoint should always be: *can you defend your price, do you offer terms, and can you verify the club's cash flow?*

> **Don't start a business that might fail when you can buy one that hasn't.**

Buying and selling a business is something unique in the business world that is hard to prepare for without a lot of thought and study. Out of all the things that can kill a deal, the one that is the most painful is getting too emotional about it. You want more than the business is worth because you created it, watched it grow, and you know how much hard work you put into it.

The buyer is going after a dream, and first time buyers are the worst because they will really overpay if they let their emotions run away with them. Buyers and sellers need to be able to walk away at any time if they are too emotional and are making decisions based on anything but the real numbers the business generates.

The Key Points You Should Have Gotten from this Chapter

- Every decision you make as a business owner should add value to the future sale of the business.

- You will sell your business at some point in time.

- The major factors that control value in a business are controllable by the owner.

- Cash flow is the prime determiner of a small business selling price.

- EBITDA is defined as earnings before income taxes, depreciation, and amortization for small businesses.

- Systems and staff increase the sale price of a business.

- A fitness business has a higher perceived risk than other businesses because of the cost of starting one.

- Clubs normally sell for 3.5 to 4 times adjusted earnings.

The Thomas Plummer Resource Guide to the Fitness Industry

The Thomas Plummer Resource Guide to the Fitness Industry

Suggesting a vendor or support company for a fitness business owner to use always comes with a certain amount of risk. If the person who took the suggestion should have a bad experience, no one is happy and the relationship is strained.

In the fitness business, category leaders who come and go are usually determined by mergers, the shelve life of any particular product, the loss or rise of key players, or just pure mismanagement. During my career, several great companies have practically become extinct due to the failure to innovate their products, or living by the rule that greatness is a right and will last no matter what the company does or sells.

For example, in the 1980s a gym owner couldn't live without a stair-climbing machine and companies specializing in those machines had a great run. A few years later the members were done with those machines and had moved on to something else, such as embracing tread mills and elliptical machines. If your business reflects an out of date product that the members aren't using, it is only a matter of time until you start to decline. Going from *category killer* to *being killed* is only a few years difference in the gym business.

Despite this problem, everyone needs a starting place of help and support for buying fitness products , especially those who are not familiar with what's out there in the market. The following list of vendors is not all-inclusive but merely reflects the companies I personally believe in and who have a sense of longevity and history. These companies have proven themselves over time with the people they work with and sell to in their business. Again, keep in mind that these are my opinions and come from years of working in the industry.

But before I present the list, I would like to go over a few tips for anyone dealing with a vendor or any type of support company. These tips come after years of experience and represent what my clients and I have learned throughout the years:

- *Never buy first-generation anything:* If it is new, being sold too hard, and isn't in production yet, don't under any circumstance buy it. Wait a year for someone else to work the bugs out and for the second generation to hit the market before you invest.

- *Never buy one of anything:* Don't just put one different treadmill or one sun bed in your business. The members will feel you aren't sure yourself, and if the piece is any good then all you create is frustration because only one person can get to it at a time.

- *Price should never be the final decision:* What separates a good company from a great company is what happens after the sale. The lowest priced product seldom comes from the best company. Will that rep be around after the sale? Will the rep set the equipment up and train your staff, or does your order just get dropped in your parking lot? Is the price low because the company is in trouble and going out of business? Buy off of a relationship and not just price.

- *It's not what you want that will make you money, it's giving the members what they want:* Most owners let their personal tastes dictate the gym and the entire thing is built for them. The market changes often and most owners are years out of date in giving their members what they really want.

- *Buy at least 80% of your equipment from one vendor:* You will get a better price and the members don't really care that you have five leg extension machines from five different companies.

- *Keep the cardio consistent:* When you buy treads, buy all the treads from the same maker. When you buy 80% of your equipment from one vendor you will get a better price, the gym will look better, and most importantly you will be able to stock replacement parts. The same goes for all of your cardio. The members don't want the variety of four different treads; they want equipment that works when they get to the club for their workout. To the member, variety means a choice of different types of cardio, not a variety in the pieces themselves.

- *Equipment doesn't bring them in but it does keep them staying and paying longer:* The brand name on any equipment seldom brings a new member to a gym, but the quality of a well made piece of equipment will keep members happy for a long time.

- *Pick your support companies carefully:* Your financial-service company, national organization, consultants, and other support people should be carefully chosen through research and reference checks. Never believe that any product sold by any company will allow you to make carts of money without working in your business. If it is too good to be true, it is too good to be true.

- *Above all else protect your credit:* Your ability to grow your business is based on an ability to borrow money in the future. Understand how credit works and keep yours intact.

My selections will be listed as *my favorites, other companies worth looking at*, or other categories specific to the particular category.

- *My favorites:* These are my favorite companies to deal with and the ones that get the rave reviews from my seminar participants and clients. Many of these companies have also traveled on the seminar tour with us at one time or another.

- *Other companies worth looking at:* These are companies that are solid and shouldn't be left out, but I haven't worked with them much personally over the years. A few of the companies in this category I haven't worked with at all but their reputation warrants a listing.

The Equipment Companies

My Favorites

Star Trac/Unisen: A cardio-specific company with strong leadership and solid financial backing. They've been a quiet leader in cardio for a number of years with perhaps some of the best sales reps in the business.

> Star Trac by Unisen
> 14410 Myford Road
> Irvine, CA 92606
> 800-228-6635
> www.startrac.com

Free Motion Fitness: Anything designed by Roy Simonson is worth having but it always comes with a warning that the equipment is probably ahead of its time. A legendary designer, strong financial support, an expanded line, and an experienced sales staff are what you're buying here, and the equipment is truly unique in the market.

> Free Motion Fitness
> 1096 Elkton Drive
> Suite 600
> Colorado Springs, CO 80907
> 719-955-1100
> 877-363-8449
> www.freemotionfitness.com

Icarian/Fitness Products International: Icarian is the lead brand here and it provides solid, well-built equipment, an aesthetically pleasing and design-friendly look, a solid financial history, and a small yet elite sales team. The service is unusually good for an industry not known for follow-through.

> Fitness Products International
> 12660 Branford Street
> Sun Valley, CA 91352
> 800-883-2421
> http://www.fpifit.com/

Other Companies Worth Looking At

Life Fitness International: An amazingly big company with a consistent front-line presence with their staff. They have been solid and consistent for a number of years.

> Life Fitness International
> 10601 West Belmont Ave.
> Franklin Park, IL 60131
> 800-634-8637
> www.lifefitness.com

Body Masters Sports: A strength-only company that recently reinvented itself with a stronger product line and good service. They are a long-term survivor in the gym wars that have delivered a consistent product for years.

> Body Masters Sports
> 700 East Texas Avenue
> Rayne, LA 70578
> 800-325-8964
> www.body-masters.com

Flex: They have been solid year after year with a small but extremely knowledgeable and professional sales team.

> Flex Equipment
> 41180 Raintree Court
> Murrieta, CA 92562
> 800-966-3539
> www.flexfitness.com

A Unique Company

MedX 96: They have a unique product line with a heritage from Arthur Jones, with great players and a niche market, solid financially, and a well-proven sales team.

> MedX 96
> 1401 NE 77th Street
> Ocala, FL 34479
> 800-876-6339
> www.MedXonline.com

Financial Services and Data Management Companies

This category is evolving. These used to be called third-party financial-service companies, but they have become full-support data-management companies during the last several years. You don't have many options in this category so you should spend extra time with this decision since this a major strategic part of any fitness business. If you understand how to charge and how to collect from your members the first time, you can still make a lot of mistakes and stay in business.

My Favorite

ABC Financial Services: This company has been the category killer for a number of years. The company has embraced a moderate tech-heavy customer service approach that has worked well for them over the years. They have great ownership with a history in the business and a service-driven management team.

> ABC Financial Services
> PO Box 6800
> North Little Rock, AR 72116
> 800-622-6290
> www.abcfinancial.com

Another Company Worth Looking At

ASF International: A solid and honest company with a long track record. They put a heavy emphasis on the tech side that can work well with clubs of all sizes.

> ASF International
> 640 Plaza Drive
> Suite 300
> Highlands Ranch, CO 80129
> 800-227-3859
> www.asfinternational.com

Computer Services and Data Support

This has been a come-and-go business for years with one specialist emerging from the pack. This is a tough field due to the variety of fitness businesses and their needs. Knowing what you are trying to accomplish and solve in your business makes working with a computer-service company much easier. Other companies such as ABC that was previously mentioned provide software and support for their clients, but this category is for the specialist and is the category leader for a stand-alone system.

My Favorite

Aphelion: A bunch of rocket scientists with a software touch and an understanding of the fitness business. They have full computer software for any fitness business that even I can use and understand.

Aphelion
1100 NASA Road 1
Suite 606
Houston, TX 77058
800-324-9800
www.aphelion.net

In-Club Entertainment Systems

This is also an evolving part of the industry. We are in the entertainment business and part of your presentation and brand should be based on your ability to entertain and control the energy of the club. The two companies that were emerging as the category killers merged to form one entertainment solution.

My Favorite

Cardio Theater/Club Com: Entertainment in the club is usually separated into two parts: the cardio area and the rest of the club. This company covers the cardio with its theater division and also provides a personal television network that can be incorporated into the rest of the club including the cardio area.

Cardio Theater/Club Com
For Cardio Theater
21420-D NW
Nicholas Court
Suite 12
Hillsboro, OR 97124
800-CARDIO-1
www.cardiotheater.com

Club Com
Six Penn Center West
Suite 200
Pittsburgh, PA 15276
888-588-7717
www.clubcom.com

Web Site Design and Support

This is a unique category that has seen many players in the game, but few survivors. A web page is a must for every gym, but a good page should be more of a marketing and sales tool that can drive a potential member into a gym as well as support member retention and e-commerce.

My Favorite

Fitness Venture Group: It's unique to find tech people who can actually understand the fitness industry. This company has great market penetration, solid leadership, cool design people on the backside, and a cost-effective product that works.

> Fitness Venture Group
> 3038 East Cactus Road
> Phoenix, AZ 85032
> 800-787-3955
> www.fitnessventuregroup.com

Nutritional Support and Weight-Loss Management

Weight-loss management will be the biggest profit center for gyms in the coming years. People want guidance and they are willing to pay for it as well as buying supplementation. This is also a major strategic decision for most clubs since this area can have such a major impact on the club's revenue stream.

My Favorite

Apex: The Apex Fitness Group was founded by one of the true innovators in the fitness business, Neal Spruce. The company is on the cutting edge in weight-loss management and supplements, and backs it up with a full educational-support division.

> The Apex Fitness Group
> 100 Camino Ruiz
> Camarillo, CA 93012
> 800-656-2739
> www.apexfitness.com

Sports Bars/Juice Bars

Sports bars/juice bars are the central social focus in any club driving daily cash flow, enhancing the club's other profit centers, and aiding member retention. Homemade versions seldom work since the money is indeed in the delivery system.

My Favorite

City Blends: An innovative company with a deep penetration into the market. Edgy artwork, creative menus, and a frontline delivery system put this company in the category killer department.

City Blends
31255 Cedar Valley Dr. #207
Westlake Village, CA 91362
877-525-3637
www.cityblends.com

Club Support

This is a lumped category of companies that provide a variety of services to clubs. Each company listed here has a specialty niche within the business and has provided solid and dependable service over time. All of these would be considered my favorites.

Club Support for Profit Centers

Lone Star Distribution: A total support company handling just about everything a club could need in its profit center areas, from bags and bars to nutritional supplements.

> Lone Star Distribution
> 9669 Wendell Road
> Dallas, TX 75243
> 800-503-4933
> www.lonestardistribution.com

Club Support for Collections

First Credit Services: A company that specializes in collecting from the hard-to-collect-from member. This company would be used in conjunction with your third-party financial-service company to handle non-payers and member accounts that your primary company cannot collect.

> First Credit Services
> One Woodbridge Center
> Suite 410
> Woodbridge, NJ 07095
> 800-606-7066
> www.firstcreditonline.com

Back-Shop Support for Your Locker Rooms

Am-Finn Sauna: A specialty company with great service and support that handles saunas, steam rooms, and other amenities for your club.

> Am-Finn Sauna
> PO Box 29406
> Greensboro, NC 27249
> 800-237-2862
> www.am-finnsauna.com

Phone Support

TAC On Hold: A small thing but often neglected by owners: what do people hear when they are on hold as they call in to the club?

> TAC On Hold
> PO Box 311024
> New Braunfels, TX 78131
> 800-613-3197
> www.taconhold.com

Insurance for Your Club

Owners neglect insurance and risk management because most won't take the time to truly understand how the process works. Proper coverage and risk management can be the difference between surviving and failing due to neglect. Understand what you buy, and also understand you are better off with a specialist in the business and not your local insurance guy who doesn't understand how strange the health club business really is to insure.

My Favorite

Sports and Fitness: A solid firm with all of the right credentials including A-rated coverage and a recommendation from IHRSA. They've been in business since 1985 and only work in the fitness industry.

> Sports and Fitness
> 19809-B North Cove Road PMB 140
> Cornelius, NC 28031
> 888-276-8392
> www.sportsfitness.com
> E-mail at: jkurmston@aol.com

Another Company Worth Looking At

Association Insurance Group: A company with a track record and consistent service with strong ownership and fitness owner support.

> Association Insurance Group
> 274 Union Boulevard
> Suite 340
> Lakewood, CO 80228
> 800-985-2021
> www.clubinsurance.com

Club Design and Architecture

It is much more difficult to design a fitness center that works than almost any local architect thinks. Gyms that look like office space, have too many offices, flat colors, and no energy were designed by local people who build anything presented to them. Your building, inside and out, is a major part of your success and should be handled by a specialist who has built a lot of clubs.

My Favorite

Fabiano Design: Rudy Fabiano is the premiere club architect working in the industry and has been for a number of years. His contribution to design through color, space allocation, and how the member reacts to the gym has had a major impact on the fitness business.

Fabiano Designs International
6 South Fullerton Avenue
Montclair, NJ 07042
973-746-5100
www.fabianodesigns.com

Direct Mail Specialists and Promotional Support for Clubs

Direct mail specialists can enhance a club's image, bring in potential members, and build a target-specific ad campaign that can get your message into the hands of a target member in your demographic area. Direct mail is a core marketing item for any club and is the right place to start for new clubs.

My Favorite

Getmembers.com: Getmembers is the category killer in direct mail due to its depth of product and consistent delivery system. Great reps and strong financials keep the company growing and current in the field.

Getmembers.com
750 Hammond Drive
Building 6, Suite 300
Atlanta, GA 30328
800-827-0133
www.getmembers.com

Other Companies Worth Looking At

Peak Performance: Owned and managed by James Smith, creator of the Peak Performance Newsletter and nationally known speaker and consultant.

Peak Performance
2285 116th Ave. NE
Suite 101
Bellevue, WA 98004
800-574-4400
www.healthclubpros.com

Sun Beds and Support

My Favorite

Sun beds are back, safer, and the members want them. Tanning is a desirable profit center or even a stand-alone business for an owner who has the business skill.

Sun Ergoline: This company has been in business since 1979 and is the true category killer in tanning beds. It is an international company with strong domestic leadership, an innovative product line, and major customer support and service.

> Sun Ergoline
> 2049 Industrial Drive
> Jonesboro, AR 72402
> 800-643-0086 ext. 2288
> www.sunergoline.com

Equipment Leasing

Sooner or later you are going to need to lease some equipment. This part of the industry has dramatically changed over the years with terms and rates that are extremely competitive.

My Favorite

Macrolease International: The reps in this company have a lot of years of placing equipment into a gym. If any body can find a way to get a lease done it would be this company.

> Macrolease International
> 1 East Ames Court
> Plainview, NY 11803
> 800-645-3535
> http://www.macrolease.com

Professional Associations

You can choose from several companies that can enhance your education, serve as a resource for your employees and new ideas, provide legal guidance, and otherwise make your life much easier than just going it alone. Every owner should be a part of the following two groups:

IHRSA (International Health, Racquet & Sportsclub Association): IHRSA is a not-for-profit trade association that has membership worldwide. It is a membership organization providing the biggest trade show in the industry, a national publication, and a host of membership services for owners and managers.

IHRSA
263 Summer Street
Boston, MA 02210
800-228-4772
www.ihrsa.org

ACE (American Council on Exercise): ACE is another nonprofit organization specializing in education and certification for any type of fitness instructor working in a typical fitness facility. The company also serves as a resource for employees and can provide in-house training materials club owners can use for staff development.

American Council on Exercise
4851 Paramount Drive
San Diego, CA 92123
800-825-3636
www.acefitness.org

NASM (National Academy of Sports Medicine): The research leader in all aspects of sports training and fitness development offering a variety of certifications and staff development opportunities.

NASM
26632 Agoura Road
Calabasas, CA 91302
800-460-6276
www.nasm.org

License and Franchise Groups

Becoming a license or franchise is a major issue for many new owners getting into the business. You'll find a number of groups out there but only a select few that have longevity and leadership. License and franchise groups have changed over the years and the good ones are attracting well-capitalized businesspeople looking for a brand name to enhance their businesses.

Powerhouse Gyms: This group was founded in 1973 and has evolved into a mainstream fitness brand with a strong heritage and solid leadership. The company was founded by the Dabish family and still reflects a family nature even with the size of its organization.

Powerhouse Gyms (PWRfitness LLC)
2546 3rd Street Suite
Suite 6
San Francisco, CA. 94107
www.powerhousegym.com

World Gyms International: Founded by Joe Gold with a great history and longevity.

> World Gym International
> 3223 Washington Blvd.
> Marina del Ray, CA 90292
> 310-827-7705
> www.worldgym.com

Accountants and Tax Specialists Who Understand the Gym Business

Advanced ownership in the fitness business brings with it some advanced tax issues and concerns. Most local accountants who specialize in the fitness business, or at least have an understanding of it, will be able to give the leadership and guidance you might need.

My Favorite

Hopkins Parker and Company: Steve Parker has been working with fitness-industry clients since 1980. He is a tax specialist who has an understanding of owners' concerns , including those who own multiple units or are working at an advanced level in his business.

> Steven Parker, CPA, CFP
> Hopkins Parker & Company, PLC
> 7575 East Redfield Road
> Suite 201
> Scottsdale, AZ 85260
> 800-525-2826
> www.arizcpa.com
> E-mail at: steve@arizcpa.com

Group Exercise Programming Training and Education

Group exercise is back! It's in demand everywhere and is a strategic part of any fitness business in the coming years. Old style aerobics, however, are dead and are not coming back. Owners who want to get into group exercise can't simply resurrect old aerobics queens and dust off the leg warmers. The industry has changed and to be successful you need a newer model.

Body Training Systems: The absolute leader in the field providing programming, management training, instructor certification, and a new model that makes group financially successful in a club. This company has very innovative leadership, is based in New Zealand and has programming going on in over 50 countries.

Body Training Systems
1395 South Marietta Parkway
Building 200
Suite 222
Marietta, GA 30067
800-729-7837
www.bodytrainingsystems.com

Other People and Companies Worth Looking At

A number of other people and companies are also worth looking at in the industry. I don't work with any of these personally, but they all have great reputations and do great work for their clients.

Consultants/Speakers Worth Seeing If You Have a Chance

(All of these people have great reputations as either speakers or consultants.)

Michael Scott Scudder
Mike Chaet
Joe Cirulli
Jim Smith
Casey Conrad
Karen Woodard
Blake Collins
Rick Caro
Cathy Spencer
Rod Stewart
Neal Spruce
The guys from Sales Makers
John Heagle

Names You Should Know

These are the names of people who have truly made a difference in the fitness business and are worth knowing and seeing if you have the chance.

Augie Nieto: A pioneer in the industry who doesn't get the recognition he should. He made cardio equipment mainstream at a time when the typical club had manual treadmills.

Bill Pearl: The father of modern training and a true gentleman.

John McCarthy: The most passionate man in the industry and the leader of IHRSA.

Jim Bottin: The founder of ABC Financial Services, a company that handles more clubs than any of the bulk of their competitors combined.

Norm Cates: Publisher of the Club Insider, a founder of IHRSA, and still making change in the industry.

Rick Caro: A founding father of IHRSA and a financial wizard on the business side of the club industry.

Rich Boggs: Without Rich and the Step, we would still be going back and forth instead of up and down and modern group wouldn't be the same.

Mike Katz: A pioneer in bodybuilding and a breakaway gym owner who was ahead of his time.

Johnny Johnson: An Oregon pioneer who laid a foundation of successful fitness centers in the mid-1940s.

Dave Draper: Made training in the 1960s hip and cool and is still a force in the fitness business.

Joe Gold: His legacy is in his name and through the founding of two of the major franchise groups.

Dick Reed: He created the first mainstream billing-and-collection company for karate schools and health clubs in the early 1970s.

Will and Norm Dabish: The founders of Powerhouse Gyms who have probably gotten more young owners started in the business than any other guys.

Mike Uretz: Quietly built the World Gym name into an industry power one gym at a time.

Wally Boyko: Created a funky magazine and trade show to go with it.

Arthur Jones: He simply created a legend -- the first Nautilus machines.

Roy Simonson: The modern Arthur Jones who rides a snowboard and still creates the most innovative equipment ever developed.

Derek Barton: The man behind the brand for Gold's.

Tony de Leede: He understood personal branding before anyone ever talked about it in a major magazine and still had time to create Australian Body Works and Cardio Theater.

The list could go on and on and I've probably left off over a hundred people who have also made an impact on the industry.

A Company for the Owner Who Wants More from their Business

The TPC Education Group
The Source of Financial Success for Your Business

Thomas Plummer founded the company in 1991 with the sole purpose of helping fitness business owners be more successful by providing education and support materials not available anywhere else in the industry. The TPC team, comprised of 12 teaching and support professionals, teaches over 4,000 seminar participants a year the applications of good business principles and the Plummer System. The Plummer System was developed through 26 years of research and the application of the system to clubs throughout the country. The company also offers PromoCoach, a promotion company providing turnkey internal and external promotions designed to help clubs drive revenues and sales on a year around basis.

TPC Education Group
Lloyd Collins, president
800-726-3506
www.thomasplummer.com

About the Author

Thomas Plummer has over 20 years experience in the fitness industry. He is the founder of the Thomas Plummer Company, which currently has eight full-time employees and does approximately 22 major seminars per year. Thomas Plummer is in front of over 4,000 people a year, including acting as MC for special events such as the national Powerhouse convention, writes numerous articles, and does independent consulting around the country. He has recently been featured on the cover of the IHRSA magazine and *Club Insider*.

In 1980, Thomas became the Vice-President of Operations for ATA Fitness Centers located in San Francisco. This chain had 90 commercial fitness centers and 150 commercial martial arts schools. He was also a club manager and martial arts instructor in San Diego from 1980 to 1998.

From 1985 to 1989, he became the Vice President of Marketing for American Service Finance, the largest third-party financial-service provider in the industry. Soon afterwards, he became the Executive Director of the National Health Club Association from 1989 to 1990, which was founded by the owner of American Service Finance to capture the independent market.

He created Thomas Plummer and Associates in 1991 and started a limited tour with industry sponsorship. In 1999, he reformed the company as the Thomas Plummer Company and added Lloyd Collins as president and partner and moving the offices to Los Angeles.

Thomas attended Western Illinois University and then attended graduate school at the University of Arkansas. He started working in the martial arts (taekwondo) in 1976. He worked as a ski instructor in Colorado for 10 years, raced bicycles in the 1970s, reached a 3rd-degree black belt in the 1980s, loves hiking, music, and books. He lives in Indialantic Florida and Cape Cod, travels extensively, and is currently working on his next book project.